Law and Power in the Middel Ages

Per Andersen, Mia Münster-Swendsen
and Helle Voght (eds.)

Law and Power in the Middel Ages

Proceedings of the Fourth Carlsberg Academy Conference on Medieval Legal History

2. edition

DJØF Publishing
Copenhagen 2012

Law and Power in the Middel Ages
Proceedings of the Fourth Carlsberg Academy
Conference on Medieval Legal History
2. edition

© 2012 by DJØF Publishing
Jurist- og Økonomforbundets Forlag

All rights reserved.
No part of this publication may be reproduced, stored in a retrieval system, or transmitted in any form or by any means – electronic, mechanical, photocopying, recording or otherwise – without the prior written permission of the Publisher.

Cover: Bo Helsted
Print: Toptryk Grafisk, Gråsten

Printed in Denmark 2012
ISBN 978-87-574-2686-1

Sold and distributed in Scandinavia by:
DJØF Publishing
Copenhagen, Denmark
Email: forlag@djoef.dk
www.djoef-forlag.dk

Sold and distributed in North America by:
International Specialized Book Services (ISBS)
Portland, USA
Email: orders@isbs.com
www.isbs.com

Sold in all other countries by:
The Oxford Publicity Partnership Ltd
Towcester, UK
Email: djof@oppuk.co.uk
www.oppuk.co.uk

Distributed in all other countries by:
Marston Book Services
Abingdon, Oxon, UK
Email: trade.orders@marston.co.uk
www.marston.co.uk

CONTENTS

INTRODUCTION

Per Andersen, Mia Münster-Swendsen and Helle Vogt

The articles in this volume are the second edition of *Law and Power in the Middle Ages* of which the first edition was published in 2008. The articles are based on papers given at the conference ”Law and Power in the Middle Ages” which was held at the Carlsberg Academy in May 2007 in the line of conferences known as *The Carlsberg Academy Conferences on Medieval Legal History*.

In the second edition the articles by Eldbjørg Haug, Hans Jacob Orning, John Gillingham and Helle Vogt have been edited. The rest are the same versions as were published in the 2008 edition.

This volume of proceedings is the fourth in an interdisciplinary series that aims at discussing new approaches to the study of medieval law and legal practice. In May 2007 scholars from Belgium, Denmark, England, Finland, Germany, Iceland, Norway, Scotland, Sweden and the United States gathered in Copenhagen to discuss the interconnection between law and political and social power in Western European societies. The conference was part of a planned series of annual international conferences on medieval legal history organized by an interdisciplinary committee connected to the Legal History Research Unit at the Faculty of Law, University of Copenhagen and headed by Professor Ditlev Tamm.

The first conference in the series examined the question of how ‘Nordic’ the medieval Scandinavian law codes actually were. The outset was the prevalent notion of a recent paradigm shift in the study of medieval laws, in which focus has been moving away from insularity towards a perspective in which regional laws are seen in a wider context as part of general European developments. The second conference covered a broad range of aspects concerning the development of medieval learned law and for the third conference we invited a number of distinguished scholars to present their views on aspects of law and jurisprudence – secular as well as ecclesiastical – in the period before the twelfth-century systematization of law heralded by the emergence of Gratian's *Decretum.* The fourth installment of the series focuses on the nexus of law and power and follows the now established interdisciplinary tradition of the Carlsberg Academy Conferences on Medieval Legal History in combining approaches from legal, political, social, ecclesiastical and intellectual history.

Hence this collection of essays covers themes such as royal legislative power and its limits, the power-struggles between political elites, the social impact of theological and legal concepts and debates, and the role of legislation in cases of treason and rebellion, while offering the reader a variety of regional case-studies showing law as an instrument of political power together with more wide ranging discussions of the long-term application of legal principles and practices and the development of socio-political structures within medieval European societies.

The conference and the publication of this volume of proceedings were made possible through generous grants from *Carlsbergfondet* (The Carlsberg Foundation), *The National Research Council for the Social Sciences* and the *Ernst Andersen og Hustru Tove Dobel Andersens Fond.* Equally, as organizers we would like to express our gratitude to The Carlsberg Academy for providing us with the splendid setting of the Academy buildings in Valby which provides the conference with its special ambience of convivial serenity. Our thanks go especially to the manager of the estates, Svend Rasmussen, for his patience and helpfulness.

The King's Power to Legislate in Twelfth and Thirteenth Century Denmark

Helle Vogt

1. Introduction

In the preamble to the Law of Jutland from 1241 it is stated that: 'The law that the king gives and the province accepts …' It appears from this statement that clear guidelines existed for the making of new legislation. The king had the right to promote new legislation, but it was up to the various provincial assemblies[1] to accept or reject it. However, the text of most of the preamble should not be taken as a literal description of the conditions in Denmark in 1241 because great parts of the preamble are either a paraphrase of or are directly copied from Isidor of Seville's *Etymologiae,* probably via Gratian's *Decretum.* But the last part of the preamble, from which the above quote is taken, does not come from canon law but was written specifically for the preamble. Does this mean that the quoted passage gives a realistic picture of the legislation process, and thus about the king's power to legislate? Taking a starting point in the words of the preamble, in the following I will try to map the king's power to legislate in twelfth and thirteenth century Denmark. But before doing so it is

1. The Danish medieval word for an assembly was *ting* (Latin *placitum*). *Ting* meant both a court and an assembly, and should be understood in its broader, medieval meaning of a public assembly which discussed any matter of public concern in addition to settling legal disputes. The adoption of legislation and the election of kings also took place at the provincial assemblies. Michael H. Gelting, 'Circumstantial Evidence: Danish Charters of the Thirteenth Century', in Paul Barnwell and Marco Mastert (eds.), *Medieval Legal Process; Physical, Spoken and Written Performance in the Middle Ages,* note 26 (forthcoming).

necessary to give a short introduction to the political and legal landscape in Denmark in that period.

The kingdom of Denmark consisted of three provinces (*lande*) – in modern Danish meaning country – but in the Middle Ages signifying a separate nation. Each province had its own legislation (*provincial law*) and provincial assembly. The provincial laws were written down in the period between 1170 and the 1240s,[2] the Law of Jutland dating from 1241 as mentioned. According to the preamble, the Law was given by King Valdemar II 'the Victorious' with the concurrence of the bishops and the nobility and was subsequently accepted by the provincial assembly. As for the laws for the two other provinces, Zealand and Scania, hardly anything is known about their appearance and their datings are merely best estimates. The Law of Scania can be roughly dated to between 1202 and 1220.[3] Two laws are known from the province of Zealand, both named after kings, but the sources do not tell us whether this is because the laws were promulgated by the kings in question or whether their names were added at a later date. 'King Valdemar's Law for Zealand' is known in two versions, an older from the early 1220s and a newer one from around 1240. In the 1240s a supplement, 'King Eric's Law for Zealand', was added to the Law.

The provincial laws are the finest examples of legislation in Denmark from the Middle Ages, and they are the main written sources for understanding Danish society in the first half of the thirteenth century. Quite few charters and other written sources from the period have been preserved, due to wear and tear and especially due to a royal passion for fireworks made of parchment in the renaissance period and the many fires in the eighteenth century. The surviving charters are they almost exclusively related to an ecclesiastical institution.

The status and the power of the king underwent great changes in the twelfth century. Until absolutism was introduced in 1660, Denmark was not officially a kingdom that was automatically inherited by the king's oldest male descendant, thus any male relative of a king could seek election by the provincial assemblies. In some periods the system worked quite well, but when King Eric IV retired to a convent in 1146, without leaving a son or other strong candidate to the throne, civil war broke out between two, and

---

2. King Eric's Law for Zealand and the Law of Jutland were added to in the second part of the thirteenth century, but these additions will not be discussed here. See Per Andersen, *Lærd ret og verdslig lovgivning. Om retlig kommunikation og udvikling i det 13. århundrede.* (Copenhagen 2006), 152-164, 220-226.
3. For a discussion on their dating see Michael H. Gelting: 'Skånske Lov og Jyske Lov. Danmarks første kommissionsbetænkning og Danmarks første retsplejelov', in H. Dam et al. (eds.), *Jura & Historie. Festskrift til Inger Dübeck som forsker.* (Copenhagen 2003), 73-74; Helle Vogt: *The Function of Kinship in Medieval Nordic Legislation.* (Brill 2010), 63-73; and Andersen, *Lærd ret og verdslig lovgivning*, op. cit. 94-101.

later three, pretenders to the throne. The civil war ended with the victory of Valdemar the Great in 1157. Under his reign and that of his sons, Cnut VI (1182-1202) and Valdemar II (1202-1241), the kingdom prospered both domestically and abroad. Estonia and some parts of the pagan north-east Germany were conquered, and many reforms, both legal, ecclesiastical and economic, were implemented through the close cooperation of royal and ecclesiastical powers. The period between 1157 and 1241 is often called 'the Era of the Valdemars', and it is seen as a golden age in Danish medieval history. However, these stable domestic conditions broke down after Valdemar II's death, and bloody fighting for the succession began again. It was not before 1319 that a Danish king again died peacefully in his bed. Two or three[4] were murdered, one by his own brother, and the last one, Abel, died in battle.

2. The oldest Danish legislation

The first known written law from Denmark is from 1170. It is uncertain whether there had been previous laws in the modern sense of the word. In both Saxo Grammaticus's *Gesta Danorum*[5] and the *Chronicle of Roskilde,* the latest part of which is probably from the 1170s,[6] there is mention of earlier legislation from the legendary King Frode the Peacemaker (who according to Saxo ruled at the same time as Augustus and created a Nordic counterpart to Augustus's *Pax Romana*) to more recent kings such as Svein Forkbeard, Cnut the Great and Harald III. Whether these laws really existed and what form they may have had, the sources do not allow us to know. Nevertheless there is no doubt that there was some kind of legal system before 1170. The oldest source mentioning some kind of legal system is the monk Ælnoth's *vita* of King Cnut the Saint, who was martyred in 1086. The *vita* is from the beginning of the twelfth century, and Ælnoth describes the provincial assembly at Viborg in Jutland as follows: 'Often a large crowd gathered here from all parts of Jutland, both to negotiate common matters and to discuss whether the laws were just, whether they continued to be valid, and to ensure their enforcement. And whatever is decided by the public assembly will not be allowed to be suspended with impunity in any

4. It is uncertain weather Christopher II, who died suddenly in 1259, was poisoned or not; see Niels Skyum-Nielsen, *Kirkekampen i Danmark 1241-1290. Jakob Erlandsen, samtid og eftertid.* (Copenhagen 1963), 146-148.
5. Saxo Grammaticus, *Gesta Danorum*, ed. Karsten Friis-Jensen. (Copenhagen 2005), vol. 1-2.
6. *Roskildekrøniken.* Translated and commented by Michael H. Gelting. (Copenhagen 2002).

part of Jutland'[7] Even though Ælnoth's description does not tell us much about the nature of the legislation that was decided at the provincial assembly, we are informed about the importance of the assembly. Royal influence on the assembly's decisions is not mentioned, but we know that the king acted as a legislator because of some of the complaints about Cnut's interference in the ancient legal system, both in strengthening the church and the canon law and in gaining power over all uncultivated land, such as forests and foreshores.[8]

Between Cnut's death in 1086 and 1170 very little is known about royal legislative initiatives,[9] but the annals of the Cistercian abbey at Ryd from 1170 states that: *Leges Danorum edite sunt*[10] – 'the laws of the Danes were promulgated'. This is interesting because it suggests that in this early period the legislators promulgated laws for the entire kingdom. It is difficult to understand the word *Danorum* in any other way, since one would expect that, if the legislation was for a single province, the writer of the annals would have written 'the laws of the Jutes were promulgated', for example. Most legal historians agree that the law referred to could be 'The Book of Inheritance and Felony'[11] (*Arvebog og Orbodemål*)[12] even thought the sources not allow us to be sure. Whether or not laws were promulgated in this period for the entire kingdom has been much discussed recently by legal historians[13] who see a major distinction between provincial laws and laws for the entire kingdom; but was there necessarily such a great difference between a law for the entire kingdom and provincial laws that were on the

---

7. 'Ubi ex totis Jutiæ partibus quam sæpius non minima multitudo, tam de causis communibus tractatura, quam & de legum veritate, sive sirmitate, discutienda simul & stabilienda, comvenit: &, quod ibi communi consilio aggregatæ multitudinis stabilitum fuerit, non im pune uspiam in Jutiæ partibus irritum sieri valebit.' Ælnothus Monachus Cantuariensis, *De Vita, & Passione S. Canuti*, 1631.
8. Aksel E. Christensen, *Kongemagt og Aristokrati – Epoker i middelalderlig dansk statsopfattelse indtil Unionstiden*, (Copenhagen 1968), 25.
9. The Danish legal historian Ludvig Holberg gathered together the few sources that might indicate royal legislation in this period, Ludvig Holberg, *Dansk og fremmed Ret. Retshistoriske Afhandlinger,* (Copenhagen 1891), 193-194.
10. *Danmarks middelalderlige annaler*, published by Erik Kroman, (Copenhagen 1980), 166.
11. This was first suggested by the Danish legal historian Ole Fenger in 1991. O. Fenger, 'Jydske Lov og de øvrige danske landskabslove' in O. Fenger et al. (eds.), *Jydske Lov 750 år,* (Viborg 1991), 43 and 47, and has been taken up by, for instance, Per Andersen, *Lærd ret og verdslig lovgivning*, 80-85 and M. H. Gelting, 'Skånske Lov og Jyske Lov', who however believe that it only was The Book of Inheritance, which is from 1170.
12. *Orbodemål* – cases that could not be settled with fines - were breaches of one of the central peace resolutions of the church. If such a breach was committed the whole of society was offended, and therefore outlawry, total exclusion from the community, was the only acceptable punishment.
13. See note 11.

whole identical, perhaps because they were all written by the royal chancellery?[14]

The choice of the year 1170 for the legislation was hardly a coincidence. This was the year in which King Valdemar I achieved his triumph when Archbishop Eskil of Lund placed on the high altar of the abbey church of Ringsted a reliquary containing the bones of his father Saint Cnut Lavard, who had been killed in 1131. Valdemar's six year old son, Cnut, was also present at the same celebration and was crowned as his father's co-ruler. There is no doubt that the 'Church feast in Ringsted' was of the highest importance for King Valdemar, since it both marked the fact that his dynasty was descended from a saint, and that his bloodline had a future right to the throne.

Apart from what is known from 1170, there is no further information about legislation during the reign of Valdemar I. For the rest of the twelfth century all we have is a short notice in *Gesta Danorum*, where Saxo tells that in 1184 King Cnut VI and the best men of the kingdom, both secular and clerical, gathered on the island of Samsø to settle some disputes and 'to improve the civil laws'.[15] Which laws Saxo refers to has been debated. It has been suggested that it was the *Lex castrensis*[16] but this is not likely since *Lex castrensis* was – as recently showed by Mia Münster-Swendsen – a learned treaty and not an actual law.[17] It is more likely that Saxo was referring to a new edition of the Law of Inheritance and Felony, as that had by then been in force for sufficiently long for deficiencies in it to have been identified.[18] It is also possible that the practice in the various provinces differed, which was why different solutions were suggested. This could be

14. Poul Johannes Jørgensen, *Dansk Retshistorie. Retskilderne og Forfatningsrettens Historie indtil sidste halvdel af det 17. Aarhundrede*, (Copenhagen 1947), 46. Helle Vogt, *Slægtens funktion i nordisk højmiddelalderret – Kanonisk retsideologi og fredskabende lovgivning,*(Copenhagen 2005) 87-88.
15. Saxo Grammaticus, *Gesta Danorum*, ed. Karsten Friis-Jensen, (Copenhagen 2005), vol. 2, 16:4:2, 520.
16. P. J. Jørgensen, *Dansk Retshistorie,* 59-60.
17. Mia Münster-Swendsen, 'The Making of the Danish Court Nobility. The *Lex castrensis sive curiae* of Sven Aggesen reconsidered' in *Statsutvikling i de nordiske rikene i mellomalderen* eds. Sverre Bagge, Michael H. Gelting, Thomas Lindkvist and Bjørn Poulsen. (Oslo, forthcoming: expected late 2011) and Mia Münster-Swendsen, 'Saxos skygge. Sven, Saxo og meningen med *Lex castrensis*' in *Saxo og hans samtid,* eds. Per Andersen and Thomas Heebøll-Holm (Aarhus, forthcoming: expected late 2011).
18. Michael H. Gelting has suggested that the 1184 law was the Book of Felony and that the two laws were first united in one law at the beginning of the thirteenth century. Michael H. Gelting, 'Pope Alexander III and Danish Laws of Inheritance' in D. Tamm and H. Vogt (eds.), *How Nordic are the Nordic Medieval Laws?* 2. eds. (Copenhagen 2011), 85-114. Gelting does not explain how that corresponds with the fact that, at this time, each province had its own law.

an explanation for why the provincial laws did not develop in the same way in all details.

The few surviving traces of legislation from the twelfth century give hardly any information about the procedure which was followed or the role of the king and the provincial assemblies. However, Saxo lets us sense that there was legislative activity when the king and the best men of the kingdom were gathered.

3. Legislation in thirteenth century Denmark

In 1200, according to his own statement, the king stepped onto the stage as legislator. King Cnut VI issued the Ordinance on Homicide (*Knud VI's Manddrabsforordning*) for the province of Scania. According to the preamble: 'We [the king] decide by virtue of our royal power to publish this law' (*legem hanc auctoritate regia decernimus promulgare*), and later in the postscript he continued: 'it is in the king's power to give and change laws' (*leges condere vel mutere*).[19] If these statements are taken literally, it was accepted that the king, on his own initiative and purely on the basis of his royal power, had the right to legislate. However, a closer look on the text shows that it is not as simple as that. The preamble tells that the motivation for the law was that more than any of the other provinces, Scania was tormented by homicides and many of the inhabitants, both high and low, had complained to the king who felt obliged to legislate. In the postscript it was stated that it was not actually a new law, but an old law which had been forgotten over time, and was now restated and put into force again.[20] In the postscript it was also stated that the law was promulgated in the town of Lund after it had been negotiated with of the Archbishop of Lund, the king's official and many of the noblemen from the province.[21] How could the king simultaneously have the power to issue and change laws and have to negotiate his legislation with the best men of the province? The simple answer is that he did not have absolute power to legislate, but he might very well have the right to initiate new legislation.

The confirmation of the legislation by the provincial assembly is not mentioned. Why not? Is the reference to the best men of the province an implicit way of saying that it had been accepted by the assembly? Or maybe royal decrees did not need to be negotiated at the assembly. The sources do

19. *Diplomatarium Danicum,* 1. ser., vol. 4, 1200-1210 (Copenhagen 1958), No 24, 45.
20. Of course, this was not the case, but a stylistic feature which was commonly used in the Middle Ages to give the law legitimacy. Fritz Kern, *Recht und Verfassung im Mittelalter*, Historische Zeitschrift 120 (1919), 1-79.
21. See Aksel E. Christensen, *Ret og magt i dansk middelalder* (Copenhagen 1978), 31-32.

not say. The difference between the provincial laws written in Danish, and royal decrees written in Latin will be discussed below.

If the king did not have the power to legislate on his own, why does the Ordinance say that he had? Like the preamble to the Law of Jutland, the Ordinance is strongly influenced by canon law, especially Gratian's *Decretum* and the ideal image of the king as legislator and through that as peacemaker, defender of the church and the weak (*persona miserable*) and of justice.[22] This was an ideal that dated back to the time of Augustine, and was developed further by the theologians and panegyrists of the eleventh and twelfth centuries.[23]

From the first decades of the thirteenth century we have a couple of examples of 'royal legislation' on the abolition of trial by ordeal and the paying of wergeld. Valdemar II's 'Ordinance of Ordeal by Hot Iron' probably from the years after 1215, says in the prologue "The pope has forbidden all Christians ordeal by red-hot iron. And since it is the case, do we [the King] not, and can we not avoid this general command", why the king with the advise of the best men in the kingdom had changed the procedural law.[24] The problem with the Ordinance is that it not had survived in its original, probably Latin text, but only in a later Danish version, but it gives the same impression as the Ordinance of Homicide, that the King had the power to legislate. As mentioned at the beginning, the preamble to the Law of Jutland stated that the king gave the law and the provincial assembly accepted it. But that is not all. As with the Ordinance from 1200, that law has also a postscript stating: 'King Valdemar II let this book be written and gave this law … with the consent of his sons, all the bishops and, moreover, with the consent of all the best men who reside in his kingdom'.[25] Compared to the Ordinance from Scania it refers not just to the best men of the province but of the kingdom. Why is that? It has been suggested, though not convincingly, that the law was intended to be for the entire kingdom, but the death of the king before the law was accepted at all the provincial assemblies put an end to the plan.[26] Whether or not the Law of Jutland was intended to be for the entire kingdom is not so relevant in this context. We know from Saxo that the best men of the kingdom met in 1184 to improve

22. On the connection to canon law and the Gregorian reform see A.E. Christensen, *Kongemagt og Aristokrati*, 47-49..

23. See for instance J. van Engen, 'Sacred Sanctions for Lordship' in T. Bisson (ed.), *Cultures of Power. Lordship, Status, and Process in Twelfth-Century Europe* (Philadelphia 1995); and G. Tellenbach, *Church, State and Christian Society at the time of the Investiture Contest*, Studies in Medieval History III (Oxford 1966).

24. *Danmarks gamle Landskabslove med Kirkelovene*, (eds.) Johs. Brøndum-Nielsen and Poul Johs. Jørgensen, Det Danske Sprog- og Litteraturselskab, (Copenhagen 1933), Vol.I, 2, pp. 781-782.

25. *Diplomatorium Danicum,* 1. ser., 4. vol. No 24, 47.

26. For the arguments for and against see Per Andersen, *Rex imperator in regno suo – Dansk kongemagt og rigslovgivning i 1200-tallets Europa* (Odense 2005), 59-69.

the laws, and during the thirteenth century it became more and more common for the kings to gather the best men of the kingdom once a year to discuss national matters such as warfare, domestic policy, taxes and legislation. So the postscript probably refers to such a meeting.

In the decades following Valdemar II's death the kingdom was not only riven by fighting between his sons, but also by the struggles between the Church and the King. In spite of, or maybe because of, these unstable conditions the King gained power, as is illustrated most clearly in the Ordinance of Abel (or Christopher). The Ordinance's genesis is uncertain, but it seems likely that the legislation was initiated by Abel and finished by Christopher after Abel's death in 1252. In the Ordinance the number of *crimen læsæ majestatis* was greatly expanded, and the king's men were allowed to imprison on the basis of suspicion alone. [27] Very little is known about how important the Ordinance was, but it is evident that the king tried to expand his power on behalf of the Church, and some of the nobility were opposed to the king's policy.

The king's ability to legislate on his own was greatly reduced under the reign of Christopher's son Eric VI. In 1282 he was forced to sign a charter, also known as 'the Danish Magna Carta', in which it was stated that he should gather the best men of the kingdom once a year to discuss the matters of the kingdom, that no one should be imprisoned without trial, and that 'We [the king] also ordain and promise strongly to obtain and to respect the laws of King Valdemar of illustrious memory, as they are written in his law books by revoking completely all abuses of and deviations from the laws'.[28] The concept of King Valdemar's Laws as an expression of the good, just law survived until the seventeenth century. The charter did not mean that all legislation from between 1241 and 1282 was repealed (King Eric's Law of Zealand and the later versions of the Law of Jutland were still in force), it merely meant that the ordinances of royal privileges from kings Abel, Christopher and Eric VI were annulled. Even though the signing of the charter was probably a humiliation for the king, it seems that the cooperation between the king and the best men went very well, because in the following years a lot of new legislation saw the light of day, and a lot of more or less identical ordinances were given to each of the provinces, all with the 'consent and advice of the best men of the kingdom', a pattern for legislation that was followed throughout the Middle Ages.

---

27. Kai Hørby, *Velstands krise og tusind baghold. 1250-1400*. Gyldendal og Politikens Danmarkshistorie, ed. Olaf Olsen, (Copenhagen 1989), 40-41.
28. 'Ordinamus insuper et firmiter promittimus leges regis Waldemari clare memorie, prout in suis libris legalibus continentur, inuiolabiliter obseruare, omnes abusiones et dissuetudines contra leges introductas penitus in irritum reuocantes expresse.' *Diplomatarium Danicum* 2. ser., 3. vol. No 45, 40.

4. Provincial laws, ordinances and the king's power to legislate

Understanding the distinction between ordinances and provincial laws may be the key to understanding how legislation functioned in medieval Denmark. After the formative period in the late twelfth and thirteenth century, no changes or only very small changes were made to the provincial laws; instead changes to the laws were made by ordinances that supplemented or changed the rules in the provincial laws. The Swedish historian Gabriela Bjarne Larsson has studied the differences between the provincial laws and ordinances, and her conclusion is that in their early stage ordinances were a means by which the king could grant a privilege to an institution or a defined group of people. To remain valid an ordinance had to be renewed by the next king. Quite soon this procedure lost its importance, and ordinances became supplements to the provincial laws. The alternative to this practice with the ordinances was a slow and cumbersome procedure to change the provincial laws. For this it was necessary not only to get the consent of the provincial assembly, but the laws also had to be rewritten, and this was a process that got more and more difficult as the number of copies of the laws increased.[29]

The state of law in Denmark was described in 1198 in a letter from Pope Innocent III to Archbishop Absalon of Lund. The pope wrote that he understood from a letter from Absalon that 'in matters of secular law, the kingdom of Denmark is completely ruled by its customs and the instructions of its kings'.[30] Since, according to the learned definition, customs also could be written[31] it is quite possible that in his letter Absalon had described the state of the law in Denmark as consisting of provincial laws and royal ordinances.

This distinction between ordinances and provincial laws is important because it made it possible to legislate without changing the understanding of the close connection between the provincial laws and the provincial assemblies. It helped to maintain the illusion that the provincial assemblies were autonomous in relation to the king,[32] while their importance was slowly eroded by the ordinances. It is possible that one of the reasons why

29. Gabriela Bjarne Larsson, *Stadgelagstiftning i senmiddeltidens Sverige.* (Lund 1994), pp. 1-21.
30. 'Manifeste quod regnum Datie [sic] quantum ad ea que ius fori contingunt consuetudinibus suis et institutionibu. regum suorum omnino regatur.' *Diplomatarium Danorum* 1. ser., 3. vol. No 238, 378.
31. *Corpus Iuris Canonici* published and edited by Friedberg, (Leipzig 1879) Decretum Magistri Gratiani, prima pars. Dist. I, causa V, § 2, p. 2.
32. Which can be seen e.g. in a couple of places in the Law of Scania and in Anders Sunesen's Latin Paraphrase, where it is mentioned that the king's opinion of the matter differed from that of the assembly *Danmarks gamle Landskabslove med Kirkelovene*, Vol. I, 1, The Law of Scania, Text 1, Chapter 125, and Vol. I, 2, the Paraphrase, chapter 24.

the ordinances were written in Latin was so that they then had to be translated into Danish before they could be read aloud at the assemblies,[33] and the difference between them and the provincial laws was thereby underlined. Theoretically the assemblies had the power to accept or reject ordinances, but in reality the provincial assemblies had lost their importance in matters of legislation and public matters by the end of the thirteenth century, and their acceptance of new legislation was a mere formality.

In the written sources the kings often appear as legislators both in respect of their present time and in respect of their past. This can be taken as an indication of the existence of a consciousness that legislation was linked to the king. This article has shown that this was the ideal. It was important for the king to appear as the legislator, but on a more practical level most of the legislation came from the royal chancellery. However, before it could be issued it had to have the acceptance of the both the clerical and secular elite, and if the king tried to get round this, the legislation would be short lived.

33. P. J. Jørgensen: *Dansk Retshistorie,* 53-54.

NOBILITY IN COURT

Gerd Althoff

1. Introduction

Growing up, as they do in a modern state, medieval historians necessarily internalise the functions of this state. They are habituated to a clearly defined legal sphere in which precisely fixed procedures, based on written norms, regulate problems in all fields of life. Law and legal procedures in the Middle Ages were, of course, different.[1] In the Middle Ages it is, for example, impossible to identify a legal sphere separate from the political, social or religious spheres. Thus the rituals of a king's election, crowning and anointing are simultaneously legal, political and religious. There is little to support the view, common among German medievalists of former generations, that legal norms possess a higher validity than norms in the sphere of politics or social life. [2] Exactly what the term 'law' meant in the Middle Ages is still debated. Did it mean merely everything that happened in the courts of justice, as has recently been proposed by a German historian of medieval law?[3] Such a definition would assign to the extra-legal sphere

---

1. See Jürgen Weitzel, *Dinggenossenschaft und Recht. Untersuchungen zum Rechtsverständnis im fränkisch-deutschen Mittelalter*, Quellen und Forschungen zur höchsten Gerichtsbarkeit im alten Reich 15, 2 vols. (Cologne/Vienna; 1983); Dietmar Willoweit (ed.), *Die Begründung des Rechts als historisches Problem*, Schriften des Historischen Kollegs: Kolloquien 45 (Munich: 2000); Albrecht Cordes and Bernd Kannowski (eds.), *Rechtsbegriffe im Mittelalter*, Rechtshistorische Reihe 262 (Frankfurt am Main: 2002) esp. 1–27.
2. See Gerd Althoff, 'Recht nach Ansehen der Person. Zum Verhältnis rechtlicher und außerrechtlicher Verfahren der Konfliktbeilegung im Mittelalter' in Cordes/Kannowski, *Rechtsbegriffe*, 9–92.
3. See Jürgen Weitzel, 'Der Grund des Rechts in Gewohnheit und Herkommen' in Dietmar Willoweit, *Die Begründung des Rechts*, 137–152; Idem, '„Relatives Recht" und „unvollkommene Rechtsgeltung" im westlichen Mittelalter. Versuch

many activities aimed at establishing order and peace. This is really not very satisfactory.

I shall try to elucidate the problem by means of a case study investigating the ways in which the king's courts worked when kings, from the Carolingians to the Staufer, came into conflict with members of the high nobility. I shall show that the weight given to court judgements was often disputed and certainly varied over time. Various factors came into play here, in particular the political influence enjoyed by nobles close to the king. This sometimes resulted in other forms of settlement partly or totally replacing judicial procedures. Members of the ruling classes regarded it as incompatible with their honour and rank to be brought before a court. They demanded other means of conflict resolution, even when the king was their opponent. For a while, as in effect partners of the king, they were successful in achieving this. Since mediators were mentioned more often than law courts, the institution of the mediator will play a special role in my discussion here.[4] It will also be necessary to talk about rituals, which both brought about and symbolised the end of conflicts.[5] Hence I include events which are traditionally characterised as extra-judicial, partly even as extra-legal. But let us first look a bit closer at the ways in which, from the 9th to the 12th century, conflicts between kings and members of the high nobility were settled.

2. Conflicts in the Carolingian period

In conflicts during the Carolingian period the law court played a dominant role in many respects. Recorded are spectacular lawsuits, in which high nobles and relatives of the ruling dynasty lost their lives, status, eyesight or freedom, because they had opposed and rebelled against the ruler. The fact of the *crimen laesae maiestatis* was generally acknowledged and the law court reacted correspondingly rough. Resistance towards the king, which was manifested in *conspiratio* and *coniuratio* and aimed at armed conflicts, was not accepted as a right of the nobility. *De coniurationibus et conspirationibus, ne fiant; et ubi sunt inventae, destruantur* is a quote from Carolingian capitularies![6]

---

einer vergleichenden Synthese zum „mittelalterlichen Rechtsbegriff" in Cordes/Kannowski, *Rechtsbegriffe*, 43–62.

4. On this aspect see Hermann Kamp, *Friedensstifter und Vermittler im Mittelalter*. Symbolische Kommunikation in der Vormoderne (Darmstadt: 2001).

5. See esp. Gerd Althoff, 'Das Privileg der *deditio*. Formen gütlicher Konfliktbeendigung in der mittelalterlichen Adelsgesellschaft', in Idem, *Spielregeln der Politik im Mittelalter. Kommunikation in Frieden und Fehde* (Darmstadt: 1997), 99–125.

6. MGH *Capit.* 1, no. 28, ed. by Alfred Boretius (Hannover: 1890), 77.

The meetings of the *populus Francorum* functioned as law courts. Warriors passed the sentence, which the ruler only had to execute, but which he as a Christian king occasionally also mitigated – in this way, for example, he modified the death penalty into blinding or sending someone into a monastery or both!

The spectacular beginning of a long series of examples is the lawsuit against the Bavarian Duke Tassilo, who in 788 was finally shut up in a monastery. The sentence of the *populus* was death. Charles, who conceived himself as a mild king, finally mitigated the capital punishment into a shutting-up in a monastery; a judgement passed not only on Tassilo but also on his family.[7]

In the next generation, the Carolingian Bernhard did not fare much better when he, together with his followers, entered into a *coniuratio* against Louis the Pious, because he felt he had been passed over in the *Ordinatio imperii*. Also here the lawsuit of the Frankish army imposed a death penalty, which Emperor Louis mitigated into blinding. Bernhard, however, died as a result of this procedure.[8]

There are bloody examples throughout the history of the Carolingian Empire, which tell of executions and blinding even of members of the dynasty, of relatives and other high nobles, which were executed on the basis of sentences, even when the judicial proceedings are usually not described in details. As a typical example it is quoted in the Fulda Annals of 885: 'Hugo, king Lothar's son, ... was accused before the Emperor (Charles III), that he supported Geoffrey's conspiracy against the reign of the Emperor, and after he had been proven guilty, he was – together with his uncle – blinded and shut up in the monastery of Saint Boniface of Fulda.'[9] As the reader may have noticed, it is not directly mentioned how and in which lawsuit the guilt of the Carolingian was brought forth and whether the blinding had been ordered and legitimized by a sentence. But it is possible, that the author took this for granted.

---

7. *Annales regni Francorum*, for the year 788, ed. by Friedrich Kurze, MGH SS rer. Germ. 6, (Hannover: 1895), 80–82; *Annales Nazariani*, ed. by Georg H. Pertz, MGH SS 1 (Hannover: 1826), 23–30, 40–44, for the year 788, 43–44. See e. g. Matthias Becher, 'Zwischen Macht und Recht: Der Sturz Tassilos III. von Bayern 788', in Lothar Kolmer and Christian Rohr (eds.), *Tassilo III. von Bayern. Großmacht und Ohnmacht im 8. Jahrhundert* (Regensburg: 2005), 39–55.
8. Thegan, *Gesta Hludowici imperatoris*, ed. by Ernst Tremp, MGH SS rer. Germ. 64 (Hannover: 1995), 168–277, and chapters 22 and 23, 212.
9. *Annales Fuldenses sive annales regni francorum orientalis*, for the year 885, ed. by Friedrich Kurze, MGH SS rer. Germ. 7 (Hannover: 1891), 103: 'Hugo Hlotharii regis filius… insimulatus est apud imperatorem, quod eiusdem conspirationis Gotafridi contra regnum imperatoris fautor existeret. Quamobrem ad imperatorem vocatus et noxa convictus lumine oculorum una cum avinculo suo privatus est et in monasterium sancti Bonifatii apud Fuldam…'.

Even in 906, during King Louis IV's minority, the ruling group of counsellors executed a death penalty of the *populus* against the Babenberg Count Adalbert. Bishops, in all probability, had been responsible for this. The fanciful stories of slyness, fraud and betrayal, which circulated and were partly considerably late additions to the historiography, show, perhaps, how problematic such a procedure had become.[10] et even in 917, King Conrad I allowed or arranged for his brothers-in-law, Erchanger and Berthold, to be beheaded, although the year before, a synod in Hohenaltheim had sentenced these Swabian counts because of their crimes only to a lifelong penance in monasteries.[11] Also here the echo of this proceeding resounded for a while. But we don't know, who was responsible for the final decision, whether it was based on a judicial sentence or the king's arbitrariness.

Additionally during the crises of the Carolingian Empire, other forms of ending conflicts had been successfully practised, which were not based on sentences: They were first and foremost the result of conflicts between fathers and legitimate sons of the ruling family, and they facilitated a demonstrative, public subjection of the sons to the fathers, which was followed up by the father forgiving his sons. This is recorded for the first time in the conflict between Louis the Pious and his son Lothar,[12] then in conflicts between Louis the German and his sons.[13]

The model for the new forms of dispute settlement was the penitential ritual that included a prostration and the petition for forgiveness, which was then granted. This practice was transferred to the field of solving conflicts within the secular, political sphere. The son who openly submitted to his father and obtained from him the forgiveness of his deed got off unharmed – in the true sense of the word. But this end had been previously arranged and

---

10. *Reginonis abbatis Prumiensis Chronicon*, ed. by Friedrich Kurze, MGH SS rer. Germ. 50 (Hannover: 1890), 1–153, for the year 906, 151–152; *Widukindi monachi Corbeiensis rerum gestarum Saxonicarum libri tres*, II 22, ed. by Paul Hirsch and Hans-Eberhard Lohmann, MGH SS rer. Germ. 60 (Hannover: 1935), 31–34. For further stories see Gerd Althoff, 'Verformungen durch mündliche Tradition. Geschichten über Erzbischof Hatto von Mainz' in Hagen Keller and Nikolaus Staubach (eds.), *Iconologia sacra. Mythos, Bildkunst und Dichtung in der Religions- und Sozialgeschichte Alteuropas. Festschrift für Karl Hauck zum 75. Geburtstag* (Berlin: 1997), 438–450.
11. MGH *Conc* 6/1, no. 1, c. 21, ed. by Ernst-Dieter Hehl (Hannover: 1987), 28–29; *Ekkehardi IV Casus Sancti Galli*, c. 20, ed. by Hans F. Haefele, FSGA 1 (Darmstadt: 1980), 52.
12. Thegan,*Gesta Hludowici imperatoris,* chap. 55, 250; *Nithardi Historiarum libri IIII*, I.,ed. by Ernst Müller, MGH SS rer. Germ. 44, (Hannover/Leipzig: 1907), 10–11. See Althoff, 'Das Privileg der *deditio*', 116–119.
13. *Annales Fuldenses*, the year 862, 55, and the year 871, 74; *Annales Xantenses*, ed. by Bernhard von Simson, MGH SS rer. Germ. 12 (Hannover/Leipzig: 1909), 1–39, the year 873, 31–32. See Winfried Hartmann, *Ludwig der Deutsche*, Gestalten des Mittelalters und der Renaissance (Darmstadt: 2002), 68, 71–73.

the persons involved knew of these arrangements. Here the peacemakers and mediators found their field of activities, which occurred in a completely confidential sphere, whose results, however, were presented through public rituals. This new form became very successful.

3. A new form of peacemaking

Conflicts between the Ottonian kings and their relatives as well as other high nobles, on the other hand, were no longer decided by judicial sentences, but in a way that had been developed within the Carolingian family: by negotiations between the parties with the help of third persons, with the results performed in public rituals. That was the new form of establishing order whose legal character may, perhaps, be difficult to recognise by modern people. Nevertheless, it was equipped with a high claim to recognition and it is my contention that we ought to concede these procedures a legal quality too.

Nowhere is this easier to see than in the numerous conflicts, which Otto the Great during the first decades of his reign fought with virtually all his relatives and with many high nobles. Despite the fact that these conflicts were handled with considerable intensity and toughness, there is no attempt recorded to influence or to end them by a judicial sentence. In the case of armed resistance the king called together his loyal followers (*familiares*) and fought with arms against the conspirators. In addition, there were direct negotiations or contacts through third persons who were intended to set up conditions for an amicable settlement of the conflict. The end of a conflict usually meant that the enemies of the king had to give him satisfaction by surrender: but then they were granted his *clementia* and sooner or later regained their former status. But this is only recorded in connection with high nobles; their helpers and vassals could be executed, if they were caught.

Duke Eberhard of Franconia, the king's brother Henry, and his son Liudolf gave satisfaction by public prostration in front of the ruler and then regained their former or acquired new seignorial rights.[14] Earlier too, in the reign of Otto's father Henry, several dukes had kept their office after conflicts with the king, having previously publicly surrendered.[15] Counts, as well as royal relatives and dukes, received the king's mercy in this way.

During personal negotiations with the leading rebels even Otto the Great is said to have in principle granted in a public speech the right of his

14. Widukind,*Rerum gestarum Saxonicarum*, II: 13, 78 (Eberhard), III 40, p. 122 (Liudolf); Adalberti Continuatio Regionis, ed. by Friedrich Kurze (MGH SS rer. Germ. 50), Hannover 1890, pp. 154–179, a. 942, p. 162 (Henry).
15. Widukind, *Rerum gestarum Saxonicarum*, I: 26, 39, 27, and 39–40.

enemies to resistance: 'I could bear it' argued the king according to Widukind, 'if the rage of my son and the other conspirators had tormented only me and had not upset the whole people of Christendom. It would have been bearable if they had attacked my castles like robbers and deprived me of much of my dominion, if they had not also satiated themselves with the blood of my relatives and my dearest companions ... And even this might have been bearable, had not the enemies of God and men[16] been dragged into these quarrels.'[17] A Carolingian king would not have argued in this way.

In the same conflict Otto's brother Brun saw himself as mediator authorized even to give fixed guarantees to the rebellious son of the king, Liudolf, that his father would forgive him, if he agreed to surrender: 'Being convinced that thereby he [Brun] could best serve the Empire and the king, he met Liudolf ... soothed his uneasiness with words sweeter than honey and promised that he would regain his former rank.'[18]

These two examples stand for many which prove that in the early Ottonian Empire the armed feud against the ruler was accepted – contrary to the situation in the Carolingian Empire. It follows therefore that such conflicts were no longer decided by judicial sentences and death penalties; on the contrary, mediators negotiated with both sides for an amicable end to the conflicts and ensured that both sides could save face. In order to re-establish the king's honour, damaged by the rebellion, his enemies had to approach him barefoot and prostrate themselves before him. In return for this *satisfactio* they gained his mercy and emerged without real damage from the conflict. I ask again: is this a legal or an extra-legal procedure?

The social logic behind this procedure can be illustrated by another example, recounted by Thietmar of Merseburg about his own grandfather. The grandfather was one of the conspirators who, in 941, allegedly wanted to murder Otto the Great, whereupon Otto had some of the persons of lower rank killed: 'He would also have preferred to see the execution of my grandfather Liuthar, who was involved in the conspiracy. But by the council (*consilium*) of his *familiares* he was persuaded to send him into custody with Count Berthold. All his property was confiscated and widely

---

16. I.e. the Hungarians.
17. Widukind, *Rerum gestarum Saxonicarum*, III: 32, 118–119: '"Paterer", inquit, "si indignatio filii mei caeterorumque insidias tendentium me solum torqueret et non totum Christiani nominis populum perturbaret. Parum esset urbes meas more latronum invasisse regionesque a mea potestate rapuisse, nisi propinquorum meorum ac carissimorum comitum sanguine satiarentur. ... Tolerabile hoc utcumque foret, si non Dei hominumque inimici his causis introducerentur".'
18. *Ruotgeri vita Brunonis archiepiscopi Coloniensis*, c. 36, ed. by Irene Ott, MGH SS rer. Germ. N. S. 10 (Weimar: 1951), 37: '...arbitratus sic se regno consulere votisque imperatoris sic amplius deservire, Liudolfum... convenit, egrum eius animum blandiciis melle dulcioribus delinivit, statum pristinum... repromisit.'

distributed. After a year he regained the king's favour and all his property.'[19]

The king, as this example, among others, shows, was no longer free to sentence high nobles, for they were protected by their network of relatives and friends, who intervened in their favour, in this way restricting or even totally denying the king's capacity to punish.

This procedure of deciding a conflict without lawsuit can be observed also in the later Ottonian period. Though here we encounter once again procedures in which mercy was replaced by punishment. So Otto II let his cousin Henry the Quarrelsome and his helpers, who rebelled for the second time, be excommunicated by a synod and then sent Henry into custody, from which he was not released until the death of the ruler.[20] King Henry II demonstrated his firmness when dealing with enemies so spectacularly, that Brun of Querfurt fundamentally reproached the king for trying to achieve everything with harshness and rigor and nothing with mercy.[21] During the reign of Henry II we again find legal sentences, as in the case of a noble called Ernest who was sentenced to death. Only because of urgent requests of Archbishop Willigis did the king amend the death penalty into a fine.[22]

The case of the Margrave Gunzelin, who in 1009 aroused Henry II's anger due to various reasons, illustrates the new pace of this ruler towards high nobles. The king got the opportunity to intervene as mediator in a conflict between Gunzelin and his relative, Count Herman, and Thietmar of Merseburg describes Henry's activities as follows: 'To all these complaints and to the defence of Gunzelin and his vassals the ruler asked for a common advice (*consilium*) of the princes, who after a long, secret discussion responded: "Obviously he does not totally stand in front of you unjustified. Thus, we believe that he should commit himself without any reservation to your grace. But the merciful God let you not act according to his behaviour but to your immense mercy – as an example for everyone who returns to you." The king agreed to their advice (*consultus*), received him graciously and entrusted him to Bishop Arnulf's safe custody.'[23]

---

19. *Thietmari Merseburgensis episcopi Chronicon*, II: 21, ed. by Robert Holtzmann, MGH SS rer. Germ. N. S. 9 (Berlin: 1955), 62: 'Avum autem meum nomine Liutharium, eiusdem consilii participem, libenter perdere voluit; sed sibi familiarium devictus consilio principum, captum hunc misit... ad comitem Bertoldum, comprehensis sibi omnibus suimet rebus ac late distributis, usque in annum integrum; tuncque gratiam regis et sua omnia... acquisivit.'
20. MGH *LL* 3, ed. by Johannes Merkel (Hannover 1863), 485; Thietmar, *Chronicon*, III: 7, 104 and IV: 26, 130.
21. Bruno Querfurtensis, *Epistola Brunonis ad Henricum regem*, ed. by Jadwiga Karwasińska, MPH Series Nova 4/3 (Warsaw: 1973), 97–106, and 102.
22. Thietmar, *Chronicon*, V: 34, 260.
23. Thietmar, *Chronicon,* VI: 54, 342: 'Inter tot lamentationes et eiusdem suorumque excusationes principum communiter consilium a rege quaeritur, et ab hiis diu hoc secrete volventibus taliter respondetur: ‚Scimus hunc erga vos inexcusabilem non

The advice of the princes to the king to show mercy towards the margrave – an advice which significantly is called *consilium* and not *iudicium* – brought, however, the margrave into custody, which according to Thietmar of Merseburg ended only eight years later. And this only, according to the source, because the margrave had miraculously lost the chains that bound him at night.[24] Henry – the case can hardly be interpreted in a different way – had brutally taken advantage of his position as mediator in order to withdraw an embarrassing vassal from circulation for a long time; and this evidently against the advice of the princes.

4. True or false allegations

These types of behaviour already point at a change, which can be more directly observed in the behaviour of the Salian kings. Simply said, there are many trials involving the kings trying to free themselves from the ideological ties of the much too mild and always merciful king and to strengthen the authority of the monarchy through the means of penal power. Here, apart from other means, legal sentences were again definitely used. Although the obligation to show mercy was not forgotten, it was now partly connected with commands, which show that here a new spirit reigned. The change was often the result of extrajudicial negotiations. Legal procedures were next to, but not above these negotiations.

One example is the behaviour of King Conrad II towards his stepson, the Swabian Duke Ernest. After several *coniurationes* and *rebelliones* Conrad promised him once more that he could regain his Swabian ducal rank, but the king attached a condition to his offer which could hardly be met: namely that Ernest had to hunt down his former fellows and friends and fight against them. It meant a glorious, lasting fame to the Swabian Duke Ernest, that he refused this unreasonable demand. Only after having this expressed during the negotiations he was sentenced (*diiudicatus*) as an enemy of the emperor and lost his duchy.[25] Wipo's description seems to be a clear hint regarding the fact that now legal sentences begin to play again a bigger role in the conflicts between kings and nobles. Yet that they were rarely accepted as the last means to decide conflicts is shown by the information that the mother of Duke Ernest, Empress Gisela, who was

---

esse et, ut vestrae pietati se omni reluctatione remota tradat, nobis bonum videtur. Ammoneat vos misericors Deus, ut non qualitate suimet meriti, sed pro quantitate ineffabilis clementiae vestrimet, ad exemplum omnibus ad vos conversis in eo faciatis. Horum consultu rex asspirans, suscepit eundem et Arnulfo antistiti firmiter custodiendum tradidit…'

24. Thietmar, *Chronicon,*VII: 66, 480.
25. Wipo, *Gesta Chuonradi II. imperatoris*, c. 25, ed. by Harry Bresslau, MGH SS rer. Germ. 61 (Hannover/Leipzig: 1915), 1–62, 43.

Conrad's II wife, publicly proclaimed after the sentence, that she would take revenge upon nobody, who would now act against her son.[26] Despite the sentence against Ernest this statement was obviously necessary.

The direction in which the Salian kings changed their behaviour in conflicts with the high nobility shows this case as well as in the behaviour of Henry II discussed above. Enemies of the kings were arrested without sentences. The times of boundlessly granted mercy seem to be over. Yet legal sentences were only slowly secured again a place in the complex procedures of dispute settlement. They did not dominate such procedures in any way.

The next step of new royal behaviour is marked by the order of a duel by which the enemies of the king were forced to show whether the allegations against them were true or false. With such orders a judicial practice is used as means to end conflicts. In the Salian Empire, this order is encountered several times in connection with the reproach that a nobleman had planned the perfidious murder of the king. For the first time, in 1048, Emperor Henry III used this means against a member of the Saxon ducal family, Count Thietmar. This count had been accused by his own vassal of planning to murder the ruler. The Count accepted the duel and was killed by his vassal. Thereupon the relatives of the deceased count seized the winner, hung him by his legs between two dogs and brought him to death in this way.[27] This vile punishment illustrates what that procedure meant to them, which had obviously never been used against a nobleman before.

Nevertheless, in 1070, Henry IV tried to use the same order when Duke Otto of Northeim was suddenly accused by a street robber of bad reputation, but of noble birth, of having wanted to hire him as an assassin to murder the king. As proof the accuser showed the sword which Duke Otto had given him for this purpose. In vain, Duke Otto tried by negotiations to get the king to concede that the princes should decide which procedure should be used to end this case. Obviously he saw his chance in entrusting the responsibility of the procedure to the princes, so to speak, which probably would have meant using a mediator. When Henry refused this, Duke Otto refused the duel and initiated a feud against the king and the royal properties.[28] Later this conflict was indeed solved amicably by the interference of mediators.

---

26. Wipo, *Gesta Chuonradi,* c. 25, 44.
27. *Magistri Adam Bremensis gesta Hammaburgensis ecclesiae pontificum*, III: 8, ed. by Bernhard Schmeidler, MGH SS rer. Germ. 2 (Hannover/Leipzig: 1917), 149.
28. *Lamperti monachi Hersfeldensis Annales*, ed. by Oswald Holder-Egger, MGH SS rer. Germ. 38 (Hannover/Leipzig: 1894), 3–304, for the year 1070, 113–115; *Brunos Buch vom Sachsenkrieg*, c. 19, ed. by Hans-Eberhard Lohmann, MGH Dt. MA 2 (Leipzig: 1937), 25; *Annales Altahenses maiores*, for the year 1070, ed. by Edmund von Oeferle, MGH SS rer. Germ. 4 (Hannover: 1892), 79. See e. g. Gerd Althoff, *Heinrich IV*. Gestalten des Mittelalters und der Renaissance (Darmstadt: 2006), 76–80.

The duke publicly surrendered to Henry IV, was taken into custody for some time, but soon he regained his freedom and his properties – but not his duchy.[29] For ages it had become practice that even amicable solutions in favour of the enemies of the king could bring about punishments and losses.

What both cases have in common is that judgements were not passed by the royal law court, but that the king wanted to speed up the trial by using duels as means of evidence – and in one case he succeeded. This shows that the means how to end conflicts had undergone a process of change. The mediating interventions of other magnates, which in the tenth century had provided the king with the satisfaction that the enemies surrendered, but had also obliged him to show mercy and forgiveness, were now replaced by acts by the kings, which by means of orders and duties considerably increased the risk of a conflict between the king and his opponents. Even without judicial judgments the imprisonment of high nobles now became an option for the kings. Obviously they enforced such more or less long imprisonments in confidential negotiations as means of achieving satisfaction, which was necessary to regain the king's grace. And the procedure of the duel was also an option, which for the persons concerned involved a considerable risk. It seems to be symptomatic that this risk was created with the reproach of a special malice, which the opponent had allegedly planned.

It is therefore hardly surprising that also King Henry IV himself was soon confronted with the indictment that he had wanted to induce a ministeral to malicious murder of dukes. This ministerial called Reginger also declared himself prepared to confront the accusation in a duel with the king or a proxy of the king. And, indeed, a duel with a proxy of the king was considered and a certain date fixed. But this duel did not take place, because this ministerial suddenly became possessed by a demon and died. Previous research has considered whether in this case the use of poison should be assumed.[30]

The procedure by which the Saxon wars 1075 were brought to an end shows that even during the critical times of Henry's IV reign the old rules of how to end a conflict had not been forgotten. Indeed, in this case, the sentence of a law court was not needed for the procedure of peacemaking. In negotiations with both parties imperial princes acted as mediators and arranged conditions of surrender, which stipulated that after their surrender nothing should happen to the Saxons' life, freedom, honour and property. Since the Saxons feared that Henry IV would not keep such agreements, the princes allegedly made sure that they got the explicit confirmation from the king that he also agreed to these conditions. Under these assumptions the Saxons surrendered in Spier in 1075; they performed the ritual of *deditio*

29. Lampert, *Annales*, for the year 1072, 127, 137.
30. Lampert, *Annales*, for the year 1073, 166–168, 170, 174.

face to face with the royal army. After the surrender, to which nearly all clerical and secular magnates of Saxony had submitted, Henry IV, however, broke the quoted agreements and had the Saxon magnates imprisoned.[31] But the further development plainly demonstrates that such arbitrary acts of the king were not accepted.

In the late Salian period there are other cases which additionally demonstrate that in conflicts between the kings and the high nobility more and more sanctions pushed the mercy and the forgiveness into the background, although they were more often threatened than actually carried out. More and more frequently we now hear of official sentences of the royal law court by which not only fiefs and offices were withdrawn but also death penalties imposed. Yet the death penalty seems never to have been executed. The case of the Saxon Count Wiprecht of Groitsch is an example of such procedure. The count had been condemned to death and Henry V changed this judgment into a mere three year's of imprisonment after the count's son had transferred all his father's properties to the ruler.[32] Those were the new 'rules of the Game' between king and nobility.

Let's finally look at the 12th century. In this century and the Staufen Empire too it is a fact that judicial sentences against high nobles were only one way to end a conflict. We likewise observe cases in which, after a surrender, the enemies of the kings found the total forgiveness and regained their status and offices. Thus King Lothar of Süpplingenburg after long fights made his peace with the Staufen brothers Frederick and Conrad. After the mediation of his wife Richenza both brothers publicly surrendered to Lothar, gained the forgiveness they had asked for, and maintained their ranks, although they had for one decade succesfully opposed the king.[33] But we also find cases in which negotiations for an amicable agreement and legal sentences coexisted side by side. This, for example, is recorded in the case of the conflicts which King Conrad III had with Duke Henry the Proud, who also refused the new king his allegiance – just as the Hohenstaufen brothers had done against Lothar. First there were negotiations with the help of *internuntii* in order to come to an amicable agreement. When this did not succeed, Conrad III let a meeting of princes pass a sentence against the duke that deprived him of his duchies Bavaria and Saxony.[34] Only Conrad's closest advisor, the learned abbot Wibald of Stablo and Corvey, blamed the

31. Lampert, *Annales*, for the year 1075, 238–239.
32. *Annales Pegavienses*, ed. by Georg H. Pertz, MGH SS 16 (Hannover: 1859), 232–257, for the year 1114, 251.
33. *Annales Magdeburgenses*, ed. by Georg H. Pertz, MGH SS 16 (Hannover: 1859), 105–196, for the year 1135, 185.
34. *Historia Welforum*, c. 24, ed. by Erich König, Schwäbische Chroniken der Stauferzeit 1 (Stuttgart/Berlin: 1938), 46–48. See Gerd Althoff, 'Konfliktverhalten und Rechtsbewußtsein. Die Welfen im 12. Jahrhundert' in Idem, *Spielregeln*, 57–84, 73–77.

ruler in a letter for this procedure: He should not confide in the effect of sentences of which nobody takes any notice. Instead, a military campaign *cum splendore* against the opponent would promise much greater effect because everbody talked about it.[35] Conrad followed this advice, but his campaign ended ingloriously and without any *splendor* because the duke's loyal followers had not let themselves be impressed by the sentence.

Even for the most famous conflict of the twelfth century, the one between Henry the Lion and Frederick I Barbarossa in the late 1170s which has often been analysed in a legal perspective, judicial and extrajudicial steps to end the conflict stood side by side. So after the sentences of the royal law court, which deprived the Duke Henry of his duchies because of his failure to show up at the court (*contumacia*), Frederick confidentially met the Lion and offered him his mediation for an amicable settlement of the conflict. But such an agreement was not made, because Barbarossa claimed 5000 marks in silver for his mediation, what Henry the Lion thought to be much too expensive.[36] But when the situation of the Lion had become hopeless from a military perspctive, the conflict ended in a very traditional way: In Erfurt Henry surrendered to Frederick in public by a prostration and then promised to go voluntarily into exile.[37]

5. Conclusion

Here I finish my survey of practices and proceedings of how to end a conflict between Frankish and German kings and nobles throughout the period in which law and politics were inseparably weaved together. The many descriptions of the developments of sensational conflicts show that two procedures were in competition with each other and carried different weight in different times. The one accentuated the judicial decision, the other the amicable settlement of the conflict on the basis of negotiated claims of satisfaction. However, in many cases a mixture of both was also characteristic. In the chronological succession the weigth of the two procedures is distributed as follows: In the early Carolingian Empire the legal trial and sentence are totally dominating. Negotiations on amicable agreements with 'conspirators' among the relatives of the Carolingians or the nobility seem not to be conducted, at least they had no chance to be recorded, and this means that they were not an option accepted by the kings by which to decide conflicts. But this changed during the reign of Louis the

35. *Wibaldi epistolae*, ed. by Philipp Jaffé, Bibliotheca rerum Germanicarum I. Monumenta Corbeiensia (Berlin: 1864), 76–616, no. 234, 354.
36. *Arnoldi Chronica Slavorum*, II: 10, ed. by Johannes M. Lappenberg, MGH SS rer. Germ. 14 (Hannover: 1868), 48. See Althoff, 'Konfliktverhalten und Rechtsbewußtsein', 77–80.
37. Arnold, *Chronica Slavorum*, II: 22, 67.

Pious when the dissent split the innermost core of the ruling family. Here for the first time negotiations are recorded, which led to the end of conflicts because both sides contributed to the compromise by doing without maximum demands.

In the tenth century, this model of doing without punishment against plain claims of satisfaction by surrender became the standard and considerably replaced the use of judicial sentences. This unmistakably reminds of the behaviour of the repentant sinner, whom forgiveness and remission was granted for sure, and, thus documents the development how the secular politics were influenced by Christian doctrine as can be seen since the Carolingian Empire.

This model was used exclusively – and this is important emphasize – in regard to the highest social ranks. Consequently the leaders of the rebellions against the kings repeatedly got off rather lightly, while the followers lost their lives. But the withdrawal of royal penal authority had contributed to intensify the readiness to end a conflict and to make the conflicts more controllable. Negotiations to end a conflict usually happened already during the first phases of the conflict and were often successful before the use of violence. The fact that after acts of satisfaction enough was done and that the result of regaining the former position was no vague hope, but guaranteed by mediators, and therefore a secure outlook – a *spes firma* – has surely increased the willingness of the nobility to opt for a peace treaty. On the other side of the conflict, the obligation to *clementia* on the example of Christ was so urgently pointed out to the kings that they usually obeyed. The churchmen have done much work in this direction!

Still, the development is characterized by the fact that since the late tenth century, punishment and sentence regain firm ground. Mercy and justice now compete with each other and the procedures to decide conflicts in court occur parallel to the trials of amicable solution, but in none of the cases did the judicial sentence alone dominate the field.

We can recognize an increasing hardening of the fronts – this becomes especially apparent in the construction of particularly serious allegations. Thus we repeatedly meet the claim that the resistance to the king aimed at his perfidious assassination. Equally, increased accusations of breaking agreements and the threatening gesture of strict royal penal authority were employed. All this marks a change since the eleventh century. Hence, at the moment of his coronation Frederick Barbarossa himself did not forgive a ministerial begging by prostration, but left him to lie on the floor unheard. Otto of Freising enthusiastically praised this *rigor iustitiae*, by which – as the bishop wrote – Frederick had replaced the *vitium remissionis*, the vice to forgive.[38]

38. *Ottonis et Rahewini gesta Friderici I. imperatoris*, II 3, ed. by Georg Waitz, MGH SS rer. Germ. 46, (Hannover/Leipzig: 1912), 104–105.

Yet still in the early thirteenth century, Arnold of Lübeck was astonished that Frederick Barbarossa had not reinstalled Henry the Lion in office after his prostration and he therefore denied that the emperor had real clemency and mercy. If he were a *vere miseratus*, he argued, he would have given Henry his duchies back at once.[39] His argument witnesses that the old ideas of amicable conflict solution were not forgotten.

39. Arnold, *Chronica Slavorum*, II: 22, 67.

The Interplay between Law, Sin and Honour in Conflicts between Magnates and Kings in Thirteenth Century Norway

Hans Jacob Orning

1. The anthropological turn

In *Feudal Society* Marc Bloch described the phase between the Carolingian collapse in the 9th century and the establishment of a more stable Capetian kingship in the 12th century as a period of social disorder. In this period, public power was usurped by castellans who used it for their own private and violent ends.[1] Subsequent French historians have hotly debated at what time public order had disappeared, with Georges Duby arguing for a later date than Bloch.[2] However, the very notion of breakdown of order was hardly touched upon. 'The feudal anarchy' lived on and was reinforced by historians like Pierre Bonnassie, Jean-Pierre Poly, Eric Bournazel and Guy Bois.[3]

In 1970, Fredric Cheyette argued in a short article that prior to the 13th century southern French society was characterised by the establishment of another type of order: that of compromise and settlement. Violence was not

1. Marc Bloch, *Feudal Society I-II*, (London, 1975 and 1978) (orig. 1940).
2. Georges Duby, *La société aux XIe et XIIe siècles dans la région Mâconnaise*, (Paris, 1988) (orig. 1953).
3. Pierre Bonnassie, *From Slavery to Feudalism in South-Western Europe* (Cambridge, 1991); Jean-Pierre Poly, Eric Bournazel,: *The Feudal Transformation 900-1200* (New York, 1991); Guy Bois, *The Transformation of the Year One Thousand. The Village of Lournand from Antiquity to Feudalism* (Manchester, 1992).

uncontrolled or unmotivated, but was governed by a rough sense of balance between parties organised collectively, and normally solved by compromise.[4] In the 1980's and onwards Cheyette was followed by several historians, most of them American, who developed and revised his basic notions about conflict resolution through settlement and compromise, as well as opening up new fields of enquiry, such as religious practices, economic transactions, social bonds and networks, and emotions.[5]

A basic inspiration came from legal anthropology, formulated among others by Roberts and Comaroff in an African context. They argued for another conception of law than that prevalent in legal studies, which they claimed was biased by Western conceptions of law as an autonomous sphere enforced by a coercive power. In contrast, Roberts and Comaroff proposed a concept of law enmeshed in the social fabric, in which sanctions were not primarily exercised by a central body, but were part of the informal norms of society. Moreover, they reacted against the structural tendency towards giving priority to order on behalf of process.[6]

In the mid-1990's a debate in *Past and Present* on 'the feudal revolution' brought the opposing views of the *Annales*-school and the legal anthropological tradition into a lively dialogue, which revealed basic differences in the conception of the feudal society. Interestingly, the positions intersected the national camps, as the 'French' view about the feudal anarchy was defended by the American Thomas Bisson, and the

4. Fredric L. Cheyette,'"Suum Cuique Tribuere" (Giving Each His Due)' in *French Historical Studies* 6, 1969-70; reprinted in L.K. Little and B.H. Rosenwein (ed.), *Debating the Middle Ages: Issues and Readings*, (Oxford, 1998), 171-79.

5. Important works include Stephen D. White, *Custom, Kinship and Gifts to Saints. The Laudatio Parentum in Western France, 1050-1150* (London, 1988); Stephen D. White, 'Pactum... Legem Vincit et Amor Judicium: The Settlement of Disputes by Compromise in Eleventh-Century Western France', *American Journal of Legal History* 22, 1978, 281-308; Stephen D. White, 'Proposing the Ordeal and Avoiding It: Strategy and Power in Western French Litigation, 1050-1100', in T.N. Bisson (ed.), *Cultures of Power. Lordship, Status, and Process in Twelfth-Century Europe* (Philadelphia, 1995) 89-123; Patrick J. Geary, 'Humiliation of Saints', in S. Wilson (ed.), *Saints and their Cults* (Cambridge, 1983), 123-40; Lester Little, *Benedictine Maledictions. Liturgical Cursing in Romanesque France* (Ithaca and London, 1993); Barbara H. Rosenwein, *To Be the Neighbor of Saint Peter. The Social Meaning of Cluny's Property, 909-1049* (Ithaca and London, 1989); Barbara H. Rosenwein, *Emotional Communities in the Early Middle Ages* (Ithaca and London, 2006). Good introductions in Scandinavian languages are given in Kim Esmark, 'Feudalisme og antropologi. Nye perspektiver på magt, orden og konfliktregulering i højmiddelalderen', *Svensk Historisk Tidskrift* 1 2006, 3-22, and in the introductory article in Hans Jacob Orning, Kim Esmark and Lars Hermanson (eds), *Gaver, ritualer, konflikter. Et rettsantropologisk perspektiv på nordisk middelalderhistorie* (Oslo, 2010).

6. Simon Roberts and John L. Comaroff, *Rules and Processes. The Cultural Logic of Dispute in an African Context* (Chicago and London, 1981), 1-21; Simon Roberts, *Order and Dispute: An Introduction to Legal Anthropology* (New York, 1979).

'American' view by, among others, the French historian Dominique Barthélemy.[7] However, it would be too simplistic to label the legal anthropological tradition as a school. It should rather be viewed as a perspective influenced by ideas from legal anthropology about how law and conflicts function in decentralized societies. In this broad sense, this perspective can be found also among British scholars such as Janet Nelson, Wendy Davies, Paul Fouracre, and partly Susan Reynolds,[8] and historians on German history as Gerd Althoff, Karl Leyser and Timothy Reuter.[9] The Icelandic society prior to 1262 has been a particularly active area of this type of research.[10]

Even though historians inspired by legal anthropology have produced studies of a remarkable wideness of scope, they have mostly focused on the the period prior to the 13th century. Some have continued beyond this, but to my knowledge Paul Hyams is the only one who has covered the whole

---

7. Thomas N. Bisson, 'The "Feudal Revolution"', in *Past and Present* 142, 1994, 6-42. Replies by Dominique Barthélemy and Stephen D. White in *Past and Present* 152, 1996, 196-223, and by Timothy Reuter and Chris Wickham, with a reply by Thomas Bisson, in *Past and Present* 155 1997, 177-225.
8 . Janet Nelson has written many influential articles on ritual, some of the earlier of them presented in *Politics and Ritual in Early Modern Europe* (London and Ronceverte 1986). Wendy Davies and Paul Fouracre have edited the two important anthologies *Settlement of disputes in Early Medieval Europe* (Cambridge, 1986), and *Property and power in the early Middle Ages* (Cambridge, 1995). Susan Reynolds' *Fiefs and Vassals. The Medieval Evidence Reinterpreted* (Oxford, 1996) represented a severe critique on traditional views on feudal society, but not all concurrent with a legal anthropological view, cf. Fredric Cheyette's critical review of *Fiefs and Vassals* in *Speculum* 71, 1996, 998-1006. Among British historians Chris Wickham's studies on Italian history should also be mentioned; *Courts and conflict in twelfth-century Tuscany* (Oxford, 2003).
9. Gerd Althoff, *Verwandte, Freunde und Getreue: Zum politischen Stellenwert der Gruppenbindungen im früheren Mittelalter*, (Darmstadt 1990) (transl. C. Carroll) *Family, friends and followers: political and social bonds in Medieval Europe* (Cambridge, 1994); Gerd Althoff, *Spielregeln der Politik im Mittelalter: Kommunikation in Frieden und Fehde* (Darmstadt 1997). Apart from Althoff, research inspired by legal anthropology has mainly been conducted by historians partly situated in UK, namely Karl Leyser, *Rule and conflict in an early medieval society: Ottonian Saxony* (Oxford, 1979); and Timothy Reuter, *Germany in the Early Middle Ages, c. 800-1056* (London and New York, 1991); Timothy Reuter, *Medieval Politics and Modern Mentalities* (Cambridge, 2006).
10. Jesse L. Byock, *Medieval Iceland* (Berkeley, 1988); William Ian Miller, *Blood-Taking and Peace-Making* (Chicago, 1990); E. Paul Dürrenberger, *The Dynamics of Medieval Iceland* (Iowa, 1992); Sverre Bagge, *Society and Politics in Snorri Sturluson's Heimskringla* (Berkeley, 1991); Preben Meulengracht Sørensen, *Fortælling og ære. Studier i islændingasagaerne* (Oslo, 1995) (orig. Århus, 1993); Jón Viðar Sigurðsson, *Chieftains and Power in the Icelandic Commonwealth* (Odense, 1999).

Middle Ages in his *Rancor and Reconciliation in Medieval England.*[11] Why this preference for the period before c. 1200? For one thing, this was a period marked by the weakness of central power, thus well suited for analysing an alternative type of social order not based on coercive power from a central body.[12] But this focus may also stem from a propensity towards functionalism in studying society as a quite static system. This tendency has perhaps been most marked in the Icelandic studies, in which a 'saga society' became isolated as an object of study. Scant attention was directed towards social change, a tendency made even more problematic by the fact that the sagas were written several hundred years after the incidents they reported had taken place.[13]

Thus, the character of the transition towards a stronger state formation in the high Middle Ages is still far from being fully investigated and understood within this legal anthropological tradition of medieval studies. There is no return to Joseph Strayer's explanation of the state formation by 'the agreement on the need for an authority which can give final judgments, and acceptance of the idea that this authority should receive the basic loyalty of its subjects.'[14] As Fredric Cheyette has pointed out, 'There is no reason to believe that individuals (any more than collectives called "nations") prefer objective neutrality to partiality in their own favour.'[15] But if the change was 'neither smooth nor rapid,'[16] how did it come about at all?

2. The conflicts

In my doctoral thesis I tried to analyse conflicts in high medieval Norway using the insights and methods from the legal anthropological tradition.[17] In

11. Paul R. Hyams, *Rancor and Reconciliation in Medieval England* (Ithaca and London, 2003). Another exception is Daniel Lord Smail, who focuses mainly on the later Middle Ages in *The consumption of justice. Emotions, publicity, and legal culture in Marseille, 1264-1423* (Ithaca, 2003).
12. W.C. Brown og P. Gorecki, 'Where conflict leads: On the present and future of medieval conflict studies in the United States', in W.C. Brown og P. Gorecki, *Conflict in Medieval Europe: Changing Perspectives om Society and Culture* (Aldershot, 2003), 265-86.
13. Arnved Nedkvitne, 'Beyond Historical Anthropology in the Study of Medieval Mentalities', in *Scandinavian Journal of History* 25, 2000, 27-51; Jón Viðar Sigurðsson 1999; Preben Meulengracht Sørensen, 'Ære, politik og litteratur', in S. Hansson and M. Malm (eds.), *Gudar på jorden: Festskrift til Lars Lönnroth* (Stockholm, 2000), 117, 121.
14. Joseph R. Strayer, *On the Medieval Origins of the Modern State* (London, 1972), 10.
15. Cheyette 1970, 172.
16. Ibid, 176.
17. Hans Jacob Orning, *Unpredictability and Presence. Norwegian Kingship in the High Middle Ages* (Leiden, 2008).

Norway the sources are much sparser than in the core regions of Europe. There are hardly any charters before the 14th century. The main sources are sagas written about Norwegian kings from the late 12th century onwards and regional laws, which in the late 13th century were replaced by national laws.

As in the rest of Scandinavia and most peripheries of Europe, Christianisation around the millennium was accompanied by state formation processes. This resulted in a comparatively strong state in the 13th century, characterised by peaceful internal relations, an ambitious foreign policy, and the early promulgation of national laws. But what about the structure of society and its political culture – did these change dramatically following the peace and growth in state power in the high Middle Ages? The usual version says partly yes – state formation had serious repercussions in society, but partly it says nothing – as the social implications of state formation have not been very much investigated.[18] In line with the legal anthropological tradition I maintained a focus on conflicts in my thesis. Due to the character of the kings' sagas, that meant largely conflicts which involved the kings. This, however, proved to be a fruitful area of research as the sagas are above all stories about conflicts.

3. The legal and religious dimension

My initial answers were disappointing viewed from my anthropological viewpoint. The conflicts recounted in the sagas did not look like informal encounters between equals resolved by compromise. On the contrary, they showed clear signs of being both autonomous and hierarchical. Normally, the king would accuse a magnate for breach of the law. Often a trial followed, terminated by a verdict, where king acted as the defender and enforcer of the law.[19]

However, the discourse prevalent in these conflicts was not exclusively legal. In accordance with the *rex iustus*-ideology it contained a distinct religious dimension. Here Geoffrey Koziol's analysis of supplication rituals from medieval French sources provided inspiration and new insights.[20] Though Norwegian cases are seldom described in as much detail as French ones in the sources, they reveal much the same pattern: The king accused the magnate not so much of violations against the law as of having sinned against himself, and sometimes also explicitly against God. The issue was not so much a legal one as it was a moral one. Rather than being compulsory, loyalty ought to be the norm, as the opposite would remove the

---

18. Orning 2008, 28-34.
19. Orning 2008, 165-74.
20. Geoffrey Koziol, *Begging Pardon and Mercy. Ritual and Political Order in Early Medieval France* (Ithaca and London, 1992).

subject from royal justice, and leave him open to the ruler's 'ira et malevolentia', to paraphrase Jolliffe.[21] The royal accusations contained a strong affective component, most clearly demonstrated in the king's anger or wrath. In this, the king followed Biblical precedents, as has been shown in the anthology *Anger's Past*, edited by Barbara Rosenwein. *Ira regis* was no sin, as ordinary wrath was, but a necessary reaction to correct wrongs – insofar that it was just.[22] The royal anger most often succeeded in bringing the adversary back in line. Normally it made the culprit admit and regret his fault and beg the king to forgive him. The king in his turn would normally forgive the sinner, granting him mercy. In this, the king acted as a *rex iustus* following God's example.[23]

4. The dimension of honour

However, this was not how the king's adversaries interpreted the conflicts, and in practice hardly the kings themselves. There is very little we can know about this with certainty, since a double grid prevents us from analysing their views: the king being the main focus of the conflicts, and the saga writer's partial and preconceived ways of retelling and framing these stories of conflicts. Nevertheless, it is possible to retrieve another perspective on these conflicts from these biased sources, for two main reasons: Sagas presuppose an external reality with some traces of historicity; and the occurrence of conflicts presupposes alternative views on kingship. There is no general method to reconstruct this perspective. Rather it is necessary in each situation to try to analyse the probable actions of the participants by sorting out what may be seen to be explicitly ideological loaded statements and acts.[24]

When turning to practice, it becomes impossible to analyse the king as an actor situated above the rest of society and conflicts as taking place within a separate legal sphere. The conflicts were exchanges of honour between men of roughly equal standing. This is not to deny royal pre-eminence in the 12th or 13th centuries, but there is a crucial difference between being the most powerful player in the game on one hand, and on the other, being situated above the game altogether, as in the *rex iustus*-ideology. If the king was operating within and not above society, what implications does this carry for the analysis of the conflicts between kings and magnates?

21. J.E.A. Jolliffe, *Angevin Kingship* (London, 1955), 97.
22. See the articles in Barbara H. Rosenwein (ed.), *Anger's Past. The Social Uses of an Emotion in the Middle Ages* (Ithaca and London, 1998).
23. Orning 2008, 174-92.
24. Orning 2008, 34-40.

Firstly, conflicts were less autonomous than suggested earlier, when operating within the legal and religious idiom. When dealing with the conflicts from the perspective of practice, they are virtually impossible to isolate from a wider political context of strategy and manoeuvring. They are embedded in the social and political culture. This does not imply that law did not exist as a separate field of knowledge and of legitimising power, but it means that in practice law could not be sharply separated from other ways of legitimising behaviour. Thus, in a situation of conflict it was not possible to predict in advance whether the king would conduct a law-suit, use his dominant force to force others to comply, act in a reconciliatory manner, or rather ignore the matter altogether.

Secondly, conflicts in the sagas were characterised by compromise. This may seem a paradox, as they normally ended with the king showing mercy. The royal ideology explained mercy as a voluntary act, because in this he acted as a vicar of God. But the royal clemency can also be interpreted as a less voluntary act, and also as a less unilateral one. If the king wished to secure the future support of an adversary, he often had few other options than to behave leniently. Behind the play for the gallery, a more pragmatic give-and-take manoeuvring took place. A magnate had to bow to the king to obtain his good-will. But if he did, he could be fairly certain that he would regain his former position with no serious disadvantages.

5. The society

Until now I have focused on the conflicts, and discussed their contextuality and character of compromise. However, the analysis of these conflicts can also say something about the society in which they occurred. We have seen that the conflicts in which the king was involved could be interpreted as a form of supplication ritual. Normally it contained the elements of royal accusation and anger, the adversary's submission, and finally the king's granting of mercy. *Ritual* has been a key word in many medieval studies in recent years, though the definitions have varied, and strong objections have been raised against perceiving ritual as a window to the past.[25] I consider

25. Ritual is a key concept in the works of Gerd Althoff and Geoffrey Koziol. Historians have been heavily influenced by Clifford Geertz, *The interpretation of cultures: selected essays* (New York, 1973). For a more critical stance towards ritual, see Philippe Buc, *The dangers of ritual: between early medieval texts and social scientific theory* (Princeton, 2001); and among anthropologists, see Maurice Bloch, 'The past and the present in the present', in *Man* 12 1976, 278-92. Good discussions of rituals can be found in Catherine Bell, *Ritual: Perspectives and Dimensions* (New York and Oxford 1997); and Kim Esmark, *De hellige døde og*

ritual a fertile concept because it brings attention to the public character of medieval politics,[26] and because it offers a good opportunity to discuss in what way this society was 'ordered' and 'disordered'. Let us look at the two aspects in turn.

6. Ritual and order: the importance of royal presence

We have seen that the primary goal of the king in these confrontations was to obtain the submission of the adversary. Normally he achieved this, even though he sometimes had to revert to threats to obtain it. This again paved the road for his mercy, which he normally granted those who were willing to submit.

But the highly hierarchical relation created by the adversary's submission and the king's mercy did not last. For one thing, the king most often granted a settlement which was much more reciprocal than the unilateral submission implied. Secondly, kings hardly made any attempt to continue a hierarchical relation in future dealings with adversaries, and they did not refer to the submission on subsequent occasions as a model for the relation between the two. Historians have often interpreted the leniency of kings towards their adversaries as a result of a Christian attitude – forgiveness of sinners being the main motive for this practice. But in practice there can be little doubt that such leniency was dictated by political urgencies. It was rarely possible to be both stern and popular. To gain and maintain support it was necessary to behave leniently. This brings attention to a double set of complementarities of royal power.

Firstly, there is the complementarity between centre and periphery. The king was not equally eager to have support from everyone. Somewhere he had to obtain his resources, and he had to be careful not to put too much strain on his supporters in core areas. This implied that it was easier to collect resources from those whom he did not count as his supporters. Thus, one can distinguish between the centre of the realm, where royal leniency was most prominent, and the periphery, where the king behaved more ruthlessly.[27] However, it would be misleading to consider the border

---

den sociale orden. Relikviekult, ritualisering og symbolsk magt, Anjou 10.-12. århundrede, PhD-dissertation, Roskilde University 2002, 49-66.

26. On the importance of an atmosphere of maximum visibility, see G. Althoff, J. Fried and P.J. Geary (eds.), *Medieval Concepts of the Past. Ritual, Memory, Historiography* (Washington and Cambridge, 2002), 136ff; Michel Foucault, *Discipline and punish: the birth of the prison* (London, 1977).

27. On centre versus periphery see Thomas Lindkvist, *Plundring, skattar och den feodala statens framväxt. Organisatoriska tendenser i Sverige under övergången från vikingatid til tidlig medeltid* (Uppsala, 1988).

between centre and periphery as a fixed one, as there were large overlapping areas.

The second form of complementary relates to the form of royal authority: In the royal presence his authority was confirmed in the most lavish manner, whereas in his absence relations were much more reciprocal, and the king had to pay more heed to the wishes and ambitions of others. Thus, there was a marked contrast in royal authority when he was present as compared to when he was absent. This may be seen as a shortcoming in royal authority, especially in the light of the Weberian concept of legal authority. The king was far from having the obedience of all the inhabitants of his realm. However, this complementarity should not solely be interpreted as a sign of royal weakness. The king probably never *intended* to generalise obedience from the submission he received in the confrontations. The acts of submission were not interpreted primarily as expressions of a universal obedience, but rather as specific manifestations of royal supremacy on a symbolic level.

Instead of a bureaucratic authority based on constancy, the king to a large degree based his authority on the contrast between the submission he received while present viz. when absent and his travelling around at meetings with the magnates and populations formed the nexus between his ideal and real authority. Clifford Geertz has put it this way:

> When kings journey around the countryside, making appearances, attending fetes, conferring honors, exchanging gifts, or defying rivals, they mark it, like some wolf or tiger spreading his scent through his territory, as almost physically part of them.[28]

In one of his articles, with explicit reference to Clifford Geertz, Timothy Reuter lamented 'the absence of any attempt to show how the elaborate structures of logistics, ritual and consciousness impinged on the great bulk of the population.'[29] He insisted that the focus had to be drawn towards the meetings between king and population: 'In a world largely lacking transpersonal permanence, an ongoing public sphere and adequate communications, virtually everything had to be settled face-to-face.'[30]

---

28. Clifford Geertz, 'Centers, kings, and charisma: Reflections on the symbolics of power', in J. Ben-David and T. Nichols Clark (ed.), *Culture and Its Creators. Essays in Honor of Edward Shils* (Chicago and London, 1977), 153. Cf. Stephen P. Blake, 'The Patrimonial-Bureaucratic Empire of the Mughals', in H. Kulke (ed.), *The State in India 1000-1700* (Oxford, 1997), 278-303.
29. Timothy Reuter, '*Regemque, quem in Francia pene perdidit, in patria magnifice recepit*; Ottonian ruler representationin synchronic and diachronic comparison', in Reuter 2006, 145.
30. Timothy Reuter, 'Assembly politics in western Europe from the eigth century to the twelfth', in Reuter 2006, 209.

In my opinion, this complementary and ritual aspect of medieval kingship has not been sufficiently highlighted in previous research. When dealing with medieval kingship were are certainly dealing with a weaker royal power than later on, but more important and interesting is the radical difference of medieval kingship compared to that of later states, even if a development towards a more 'modern' authority was about to take place.

Until now we have focused on the aspect of 'order' in medieval society by studying conflicts as rituals. However, we have stressed the uncertainty of the outcome of ritual. This brings attention to the other side of the coin: the strategy of the individual actors.

7. Ritual and strategy: the importance of royal unpredictability

One of the main aims of legal anthropology was to challenge the supposition that obedience to rules form the foundation of society. Societies do have rules in the form of norms stipulating what behaviour is considered good and bad, but such rules are seldom or never all-encompassing or compelling. This means that conflicts cannot properly be considered as deviations or crises in the system, but rather as part of it.[31] Historians in the legal anthropological tradition have criticised the proponents of the history of mentalities for similar issues. The history of mentalities has done much to widen the scope of historical enquiry, but the concept of mentality has tended to become a strait-jacket, reducing human intentionality and choice to a mere epi-phenomenon of rule-governed, unconsciously motivated behaviour.[32]

In the social sciences, a similar criticism has been levelled against the tendency towards determinism in the structuralist paradigm. Pierre Bourdieu has formulated it this way:

> Even in cases in which [...] the interlocking of actions and reactions is totally predictable *from outside*, uncertainty remains as to the outcome of the interaction as long as the sequence has not been completed.[33]

---

31. Comaroff and Roberts 1981, 1-21; Patrick J. Geary, 'Living with Conflicts in Stateless France: A Typology of Conflict Management Mechanisms, 1050-1200', in *Living with the Dead in the Middle Ages* (Ithaca and London, 1994), 61.
32. Christian Kvium, 'Anderledeshed og historie', *Studier i historisk metode* 19, 1987; Erling Sandmo, *Slagsbrødre. En studie av vold i to norske regioner i tiden fram mot eneveldet* (Oslo, 1997), 41-58; Roger Chartier, 'Intellectual History and the History of *Mentalités*', *Cultural History* (Cambridge, 1988), 19–52; Peter Burke, *Varieties of Cultural History* (Cambridge, 1997), 162–82.
33. Pierre Bourdieu, *Outline of a theory of practice* (Cambridge, 1977), 9.

This uncertainty is not a mere detail which can be neglected in studying the normal workings of society, because it constitutes the very precondition for social change: 'This uncertainty [...] is sufficient to modify not only the experience of practice, [...] but practice itself.'[34] Bourdieu illustrates this by example of Marcel Mauss' famous analysis of gift exchange. Even though the overall pattern of gift-giving and reciprocation is clear, in every single instance of gift-giving, the actors are confronted with a multiplicity of choices. The gift as seen from outside brings the system to the fore, whereas analysis of the gift as experienced highlights the strategy and element of choice involved. This is highly relevant to the study of rituals, which can be considered fairly regulated patterns of behaviour. On the other hand rituals could fail, as they do not constitute a 'mechanical interlocking of preregulated actions.'[35] It is only in retrospect that it is possible to judge whether a course of action do conform to the normal pattern of a ritual or not. In line with this, Philippe Buc has drawn attention to the 'bad' rituals, rituals that went wrong, and Gerd Althoff has underlined the variability of ritual in that they built on a common stock of elements, which could be combined in different ways.[36]

The danger or possibility that a ritual could turn 'wrong' is very central to my case. Above I demonstrated that conflicts between king and magnates cannot be interpreted solely as legal or religious conflicts, but also contain strong elements of honour. Unlike law and religion, honour did not operate within a fixed system of norms. The contextual quality of honour has been underlined by many scholars, such as Preben Meulengracht Sørensen, who maintains that honour cannot be meaningfully defined unless in concrete situations.[37] The main reason is that honour not only relates to norms, but also to success, a fact that Sverre Bagge has underlined in analysing Snorri Sturluson's *Heimskringla*. [38] A failed undertaking seldom brought honour, whereas a successful one was prone to do so, even if it implied breaking some norms.

---

34. Bourdieu 1977, 9: 'the passage from the highest probability to absolute certainty is a qualitative leap which is not proportionate to the numerical gap'.
35. Bourdieu 1977, 8.
36. Buc 2001, Althoff 2002. However, in Althoff's opinion the German Emperors took part in rituals of submission and supremacy which were all arranged beforehand. The reason was that medieval society was acutely aware about dissent, and had few mechanisms for handling disagreements in a public context without giving rise to serious troubles. Therefore, eventual disagreements had to be dealt with in advance, so that the ritual became a veritable spectacle meant to create harmony in the eyes of the crowd (Althoff 1997 and 1994). Considering the Norwegian conflicts, my impression is that the supplication ritual was not fully pre-arranged, for reasons that will be explained further below.
37. Sørensen 1995.
38. Bagge 1991.

This concept of honour recovers the importance of individual strategy. The scope of strategy was certainly not unlimited, as the culture sets limits to the scope of action, and norms facilitate and restrict different courses of action in varying degrees. But within this system, people normally had several options in a situation. Some of them were more likely to be realised than others, but that did not close the situation to the point that prediction of the outcome is possible. In accordance with this, William Miller distinguishes between 'the predictability of the disputing process' on one hand, and on the other that 'the model had little predictive power'.[39] Thus rituals could evolve in different directions than intended or expected, and this could not be predicted in advance, because it hinged on the evaluations and actions carried out by the participants in the context. Accordingly, uncertainty played a major role at every moment during a confrontation. Would the king accuse the adversary of disloyalty? Would the magnate submit to the king? Would the king grant mercy to the opponent? In most instances the answers to these questions were affirmative. But in some instances they were negative.

In some situations the king did not forward accusations against magnates who had in some way or another transgressed against norms (whether legal, religious, or related to honour). This probably happened far more often than the sagas recount, as they focus primarily on conflicts. Sometimes the adversary refused to submit. This happened at least twice to king Håkon Håkonsson. Such a response transformed the situation completely. We would expect that the king would be even harsher to the recalcitrant magnate, but that was not always or unequivocally the case. Such protests had to be taken seriously, because they also could imply that the king had misjudged the situation, and had to admit the adversary more favourable conditions. Lastly, sometimes the solution would not be so reciprocal as the granting of mercy implied. Earl Harald Maddadsson of the Orkneys received king Sverre's pardon in 1195, and Sverre promised good terms for the agreement. But when he later pronounced his sentence, it turned out to be much harder than expected. Was this because he considered his power to be so secure that he could enforce strict conditions? Or was it a strategy well known from the peripheries, in which the king preferred to raise resources at the expense of support?

The purpose of these analyses has been to highlight the importance of strategy and manoeuvring in the situations. This can be summed up in the word unpredictability. The magnate Erling Skakke once said to his young and inexperienced son king Magnus, who had been implored to show mercy towards an enemy: 'you will not long rule your kingdom if you behave only

39. Miller 1990, 185.

with mildness.'[40] This is in line with the anger displayed by Angevin kings in England according to Jolliffe: 'For us it has a strangely indeterminate character; but that, for those who use it, is its proper virtue.'[41] Unpredictability was indispensable to a medieval ruler who wished to keep his adversaries at bay.

Three points seem important to note in concluding this section. Firstly, unpredictability is not co-terminous with arbitrariness or haphazardness. Unpredictable behaviour was not meted out irrespective of the strategic peculiarities of the situation. It was, and had to be, intelligible, even though it was unexpected. Secondly, the importance of unpredictability does not imply that it was very widespread statistically. On the contrary, the very effect of unpredictable behaviour resided in its exceptional character. If unpredictability became common, it stopped being precisely that, and became a new ritual. A ritual normally went right, but its dynamic and attraction consisted in the possibility that it could turn wrong. Thirdly, the importance of unpredictability in the Middle Ages contains both universal and culturally specific elements. Politics contain an element of unpredictability also in modern societies. At the moment I write this text, it is uncertain if George W. Bush will use his veto to stop withdrawal from Iraq one more time, and if Sarkozy will continue his battle against the 'scum' of the Parisian suburbs, or rather behave in a more pragmatic manner now that he is in power. The strategic political struggle on the top level may not have changed much over the centuries, but in medieval society unpredictability went all way through the system. There hardly existed any bureaucracy or legal apparatus independently of the political power struggles. The medieval king did not have sufficient resources to reward all who were faithful to him or to punish all who disappointed him. One option was to distribute his scarce resources in a thin layer among all supporters according to their merits, but that would hardly leave many people content. A more effective way of governing was to reward a few lavishly, so that everyone could live in the hope of being among the favoured ones. Similarly, instead of suing all who opposed the king, a few could be punished in a demonstrative manner, so that the rest would learn their lesson from the example. As Walter Map remarked on the Angevin court:

> The court is a pleasing place only for those who obtain its favour, and this favour comes regardless of reason, establishes itself regardless of merit, arrives obscurely from unknown causes.[42]

---

40. *The saga of Magnus Erlingsson*, ch. 35 (*Snorre Sturlasson Kongesoger III,* transl. S. Schøtt, Oslo, 1965)
41. Jolliffe 1955, 95: 'the ruler's personal hates and fears were released as efficient forces to play about the political world' and 'they should be as ambiguous as they were intolerable' (106).
42. Walter Map, *De Nugis Curialium*, 2-4 (New York, 1989).

8. Conclusion

In 1202, the so-called civil wars in Norway were brought to a (temporary) end by a reconciliation between king and church. In the treaty, the contemporary condition of war and strife was described as follows: 'Now neither clerical nor common people fear God or good men. Rather everyone lives as he wishes under lawless conditions.' Several Norwegian historians have cited this passage, not as one (of several possible) statements about society, but as a reliable description of it.[43] They are certainly right in that this became an important and powerful interpretation of the past. In the laws of the second half of the 13th century the civil wars were routinely described as 'a fog of confusion' from which they had fortunately recovered by means of a strong monarchy.

However, if we are to take the insights and methods of legal anthropology seriously, we have to be suspicious about such statements. The medieval king did not overthrow a society prone to disorder and chaos, but interacted with a society marked by a *different* type of order than that of a state society. This implies that the state did not have such an easy way to success, but that it met with resistance from many people who had little or no interest in it, and who mainly wanted to preserve a society characterised by a relatively open game of political influence and honour. This does not mean that no state formation occurred during the high Middle Ages. It is beyond doubt that the king had a much firmer grip on society in the late 13th century than in the century earlier, much due to the development of a more formal and hierarchical apparatus of royal administration. This is a large topic which I have not included in this article,[44] but as a conclusion I would like to add some very brief and preliminary remarks about this development.

The laws of the late 13th century show that a bureaucratic rule was in the making, as they defined what areas royal officials had responsibility for as well as their internal hierarchy. But to what degree were the stipulations laid down in law followed in practice? Unfortunately, sources which tell about how legal principles were enforced are not abundant. Sagas, which constitute the main sources to political behaviour in the 12th and 13th centuries, are as good as non-existent after 1263, but in the 14th century charters become more common. In addition, laws and privileges can throw light on practice. It is probably no coincidence that the areas where we have more sources than normally also are the areas where we can discover most deviations from the legal system. The question is how to evaluate such rare

43. Fredrik Paasche, *Kong Sverre*, (Oslo, 1966, orig. 1920), 109-10; Knut Helle, *Under kirke og kongemakt* (Oslo, 1995); Arne Odd Johnsen: *Fra ættesamfunn til statssamfunn* (Oslo, 1948).

44. In this paper I have not dealt with the material basis of kingship, cf. the discussion on this between Hans Jacob Orning and Knut Dørum in (Norwegian) *Historisk tidsskrift* 3 2005, 1 2006 and 4 2006.

glimpses of practice: Are they to be interpreted as deviations from a bureaucratic norm, or are they typical of an administration in which patrimonial procedures looms large?[45] To answer this question, it is crucial to analyse the sources carefully. However, it is equally important what theoretical and comparative framework one operates within. Thus, in addition to scrutiny of the available sources, I would advocate a comparative outlook – both synchronic to medieval Europe and diachronic to anthropological analyses – in order to gain further insights into the nature of high medieval states and societies.

45. On bureaucratic and patrimonial procedures, see Max Weber, *Economy and Society*, vol. I (Berkeley, LA., London, 1968), 229 ff.

Social Ordering and the Doctrine of Free Choice

The Case of Abjuration *sub pena nubendi*

Charlotte Christensen-Nugues

1. Introduction

One of the most important aspects of the marriage legislation in medieval canon law is the doctrine of free choice. According to this doctrine, established by Pope Alexander III in the second half of the twelfth century, the validity of a marriage depended solely on the freely given consent of the parties. A valid marriage could be formed in two ways. Either by consent expressed in the present form, *verba de presenti*, by which an immediate binding union was created. Words of the future form, *verba de futuro*, were in themselves only an engagement for the future, which could be terminated by agreement of both parties or by a subsequent marriage by *verba de presenti*. If, however, the *verba de futuro* was followed by sexual intercourse it was automatically transformed into a valid marriage.

The church did not only regulate marriage but also all kinds of sexual behaviour. According to canon law all sexual relations outside of marriage were illegal. This did not only apply to casual sexual relations but also to longstanding, stable relationships. The most common penalty for illicit sexual relations was fines. In the case of stable relationships it was also quite common that the couple was forced to abjure one another under a sum of money. The couple could, however, also be requested to abjure one another *sub pena nubendi*. Abjuration *sub pena nubendi* meant that any future intercourse, or even its suspicion, would leave a couple as man and wife.

2. Abjuration *sub pena nubendi*

Abjuration *sub pena nubendi* began to develop on the local level from the beginning of the thirteenth century. It is mentioned in synodal statutes from Germany, France and England.[1] However there seems to be no support for, and no traces of this practise in the centrally established law. I have found no trace of it in the basic canonical texts or in the writings of the canonists. Such eminent scholars as Adhémar Esmein, Richard H. Helmholz and Michael M. Sheehan have apparently not been more successful in finding canonical references to this practice.[2]

Abjuration *sub pena nubendi* developed as a means to stop illicit sexual relationships by transforming them into legal marriages. This practise was contrary to one of the most fundamental principles of the marriage legislation in medieval canon law, the doctrine of free choice. How could the church use marriage as a penal sanction against fornicators, in much the same way as pledges of money, if marriage, according to the laws established by the church itself, depended only on the free consent of the parties? This objection to abjuration *sub pena nubendi* was raised even at the time when it was practised. A gloss to one of the synodal statutes (Exeter II, 1287) said concerning abjuration *sub pena nubendi*: 'Note that this constitution is against right and natural equity, because *de iure* marriages and espousals ought to be free'.[3] Objections against abjuration *sub pena nubendi* were also raised in practise. Helmholz notes several cases where defendants claimed that marriages consequent upon abjuration *sub pena nubendi* were invalid because they had been coerced.[4]

---

1. The first known mention of abjuration *sub pena nubendi* is to be found in the statutes of Roger Niger, bishop of London 1229-1241. *Councils and Synods with other documents relating to the English Church*, ed. F. M. Powicke and C. R. Cheney (Oxford: 1964), vol. 1, 631.
2. A. Esmein, *Le mariage en droit canonique* (Paris: 1891), vol. 1, 158; R. H. Helmholz, *Marriage litigation in Medieval England* (Cambridge: 1974), 173; M. M. Sheehan, 'The formation and stability of marriage in fourteenth century England', *Medieval Studies* 33 (1971), 245 -55.
3. 'Nota quod hec constitutio est contra iure et naturalem equitatem, quia de iure libera debent esse matrimonia et sponsalia', *Councils and Synods.,* vol. II, 999.
4. In one of these cases the defendant claimed that the marriage was invalid because contracted 'by a fear which can affect a constant man and by a penalty condemned by the law ('per metum qui cadere potest in constantem ac sub pena legibus reprobata'), R. H. Helmholz, *Marriage litigation*, 178. The claimant referred to the rule saying that a coerced consent could be declared invalid: 'coactus enim consensus, qui nec consensus appelari debet, conjugium non facit', Peter Lombard, *Sententiae* 4 D. 29, PL 192: 916. See also X 4.1.6. and 14. If the couple lived together and/or had non coerced sexual relations afterwards, the consent was however considered ratified: 'matrimonium per vim contractum, cohabitatione spontanea convalescit' (X 4.1.21.) Thus invalidity because of force and fear could not really be applied in cases of abjuration *sub pena nubendi*.

The practice of abjuration *sub pena nubendi* represents a conflict between a fundamental doctrine of the church, i.e. free choice as the sole foundation of marriage, and one of the most important tasks of the Church courts, i.e. the repression of extramarital sexual relationships. Abjuration *sub pena nubendi* was probably from a social point of view the most practical and appropriate way of dealing with stable sexual relationships outside of marriage. At the same time it was contrary to the principle that marriage depended solely on the freely given consent of the parties.

It is significant that abjuration *sub pena nubendi* developed locally. It was in the local courts that the church was confronted with the problem of extramarital sex. Fornication, whether it was a matter of casual sex or stable relationships, made up the greatest part of *ex officio* business in the local courts. In the canonical texts, however, very little is said about how the problem of fornication should be treated in practice. The canonists contended themselves with forbidding it. The doctrine of free choice, on the contrary, was discussed at length in a number of canonical and theological texts. This doctrine was normally well respected in the local courts, as records of marriage litigation shows.

How then, shall the practise of abjuration *sub pena nubendi* be explained and understood? To try to answer these questions I have studied the *ex officio* actions brought against people engaged in extramarital sexual relations recorded in the register of the official's court in Cerisy-la-Forêt between 1314 and 1346.[5]

5. The manuscript of this register was unfortunately destroyed in 1944, therefore I use the edition of Gustave Dupont from 1880: *Curie officialis cerasiensis*, M. G. Dupont, *Mémoires de la Société des Antiquaires de Normandie*, vol. 30 (Caen: 1880) (in the following *RD*). The edition of Dupont concerns the years 1314-1346, 1369-1380, 1391-1414 and 1451-1457. A smaller fragment concerning the years 1474 -1480 and 1485 have been edited by P. Le Cacheux 'Un fragment de registre de l'officialité de Cerisy', *Bulletin de la Société des Antiquaires de Normandie*, 43, (1935). The evidence relating to sexual morality offences has appeared in an article by J-L Dufresne, 'Les comportements amoureux d'après les registres de l'officialité de Cerisy, xive-xve siècles', *Bulletin philologique et historique du Comité des travaux historiques et scientifiques* (Caen: 1976) and several studies of A. J. Finch, 'The disciplining of laity in late Medieval Normandy', *French history*, vol. 10, no. 2 (1996), 163-181; 'Sexual relations and marriage in later medieval Normandy' *The journal of ecclesiastical history*, 47 (1996) and 'Parental authority and the problem of clandestine marriage in the later Middle Ages', *Law and History review*, vol 8, no. 2 (1990), 189-204. In the present article I will focus specifically on the cases of abjuration *sub pena nubendi*, and how and in what circumstances this institution was used.

3. The case of Cerisy-la-Forêt

Cerisy-la-Fôret was a peculiar jurisdiction within the diocese of Bayeux. The area of the officiality was a largely rural one, with some industry associated with the fulling of cloth. A very rough estimate gives the figure of 6.300 inhabitants.[6] The greatest part of the *ex officio* business was provided by the visitations in the villages of Cerisy, Littry and Deux Jumeaux (approximately 212, 160 and 50 hearts). The process of visitation was based on an enquiry into the behaviour of clergy and laymen through a number of jurors (*jurati*). By far the greatest number of presentments was for offences against sexual morality, especially fornication and adultery. Only 10 out of a total of 315 defamations for lay fornication were purged or dismissed outright. The evidence concerning the imposition of penalties is however incomplete since the initial presentation at visitation and any subsequent action was often recorded separately. Those cases, where both presentment and the penalty survive show, that fornication was most commonly punished with fines ranging between 5 and 50 sous. The penalties could however climb higher if there were some aggravating circumstances. In some cases the court imposed public penance instead of fines, especially if those concerned were too poor to pay.[7]

Fornicators could also, on top of fines or alone, be forced to abjure one another under a sum of money. The pledges were normally ten to twenty times superior to the fines, ranging from 10 to 50 livres. Those concerned could also be requested to, or chose to abjure one another *sub pena nubendi*.

	Fines	Public penance	Pledges	*Sub pena nubendi*	No penalty recorded	Total
Simple fornication	32	4	3	1	70	110
Pregnancy or children	13	1	1		31	46
Longstanding relationships	12		5	2	12	31
Longstanding relationships with children	6		2	2	4	14
Total	63	5	11	5	117	201

6. A. J. Finch, 'Sexual relations', 242.
7. *Contra mulierem : egit penitentiam, quia unde solvere non habebat* (RD no. 4b). See also nos. 130b and c, 138d and 139.

I have listed all the presentments for lay fornication in the register of Cerisy where an abjuration *sub pena nubendi* was possible. I have thus excludes the cases involving an impeachment to marriage, such as when one of the parties, or both were married, when the man was in holy orders, or the parties were related within the forbidden degrees. I have classified the cases according to two variables; the apparent stability and longevity of the relation, and the question of whether the couple had children together or not. There were probably more longstanding relationships than those I have classified as such. I have only noted those where the situation is clear, either because the same couple had been defamed on several occasions or because it is clearly stated in the presentment that the couple had been together a long time. In the cases where the woman was pregnant or had a child I have only noted as 'longstanding relationships with children' those where the father was clearly designated.

The first thing to be noted is that abjuration *sub pena nubendi* was used only in a very small number of cases (5 out of a total of 84 where the penalty was recorded). Abjuration *sub pena nubendi* was, as one could have expected, more readily used in the cases of longstanding relationships (4 out of 29) and especially when the couple had children together (2 out of 10). There is however no indication that abjuration *sub pena nubendi* was systematically used in some specific situations, like for example when the couple had been defamed on several occasions, had been living together a long time, or had children together. There are five cases of abjuration *sub pena nubendi* during the period 1314-1346, and there is no common denominator that explains why the court used abjuration *sub pena nubendi* in these cases and not in others.

Germain le Forestier and the widow of Michel Riquent admitted that they had had sexual relations during the last two weeks. The court ordered Germain to stop seeing Michel Riquent's widow in a 'suspicious' way and the couple abjured one another under a sum of 10 livres and *sub pena nubendi*.[8] In another case the couple had apparently been living together in the same house and rumour told that they had sexual relations. The couple admitted the rumour but denied the facts. They abjured each other under the condition that if they in the future lived together so that one could suspect sexual relations, they should consent to each other as husband and wife.[9]

8. 'Anno Domini MMCCCXXII die veneris ante Judica me [March 11, 1323] in judico coram nobis fuerunt presentes Germanus le Forestier, clericus, et relicta Michaelis Riquent, et confessi fuerunt carnaliter copulasse post XV dies elapsos ; quam fornicationem emendarunt. Injunximus eidem Germano ne de cetero cum dicta relicta suspecte frequentat quod possit probari per famam aut per duos testes fide dignos, et hoc ad penam X librarum et ad penam conjugii faciendi inte ipsos ; quibus premissis ipsi acquieverunt.' (RD no. 113)

9. 'Sanson Vautier diffamatur de Johanna filia Henrici Stephani. Confitentur famam. Negant factum. Indicimus ei purgationem ad diem mercurii [March 12 1315], et

Another couple had been living together for a year and a half, but denied sexual relations. However, they admitted the rumour, and also that they had touched each other. The abjured each other under the same conditions as the aforementioned couple.[10]

In the two remaining cases of abjuration *sub pena nubendi* the couples clearly had a longstanding sexual relationship, and also children together. Thorud Bigal and Pétronille La Rouissole had been living together for three years and had two children together. They abjured each other under the condition that if they continued to live together, they would consider themselves as husband and wife.[11] In the case of Henri le Portier and Thomassie, the daughter of Richard le Guilcour, it seems that the couple themselves chose abjuration *sub pena nubendi*. Henri and Thomassie had been defamed for fornication and had two children together. Thomassie claimed that they had already abjured each other *sub pena nubendi*, which Henri denied. Nevertheless, they then expressed of their own free will (*voluerint spontanei*), as it is recorded in the register, that they would consider themselves married if they had any further sexual relations.[12]

---

ipsi sese abjuraverunt, et injunximus ut seorsum habitent ad penam scale. Mulier reversa ; vir contumax. Abjuraverunt se sub illa condicione quod de cetero simul habitarent in eadem domo solus cum sola in loco de quo posset haberi suspictio de carnali copula, quod ex nunc se consentiunt unus in alium matrimonialiter in virum et uxorem.' (RD no. 26c)

10. 'Anno Domini MCCCXVIII die jovis post Annunciationem beate Marie, videlicet post Judica me [March 29, 1319], Guillotus Evrart diffamatus de Coleta la Flamengue, pro quo ipsa gagiavit emendam, et ambo confitentur famam et factum negat simpliciter, fatentur tamen se se temptasse et per annum cum dimidio simul stetisse ; et finaliter sese abjuraverunt, ita quod si contingat de cetero ipsos invicem habitare solum cum sola in eadem domo aut alias loco suspecto, ex nunc se consentiunt invicem in virum et uxorem et ex nunc volunt [...]. Taxavimus contra quemlibet III (?) libras [...]' (RD no. 65b)

11. 'Anno Domini MCCCXIX, die lune post festum Omnium Sanctoru, [November 5, 1319], se Tourodus Bigal confessus fuit se carnaliter copulasse cum Petronilla La Rouissole per triennium et in ea genuisse duos pueros, et se invicem a modo abjurarunt, ita tamen quod si ipsos contigerit esse solus cum sola aut ipsos invicem habitare in loco suspecto aut alias, ex nunc se consentiunt invicem in virum et uxorem, et ex nunc volunt matrimonium esse contractum, et emendarunt fornicationem quam reservamus.' (RD no. 70)

12. 'Ceraseyum – Anno predicto, die martis ante festum beati Dyonysii [October 8, 1314], coram nobis citati Henricus le Portier et Thomassia filia Ricardi le Guilcour, quia de incontinentia diffamati, hoc confessi fuerunt et quod ipsa conceverat duos pueros de ipso Henrico ; tamen ipsa proposuit quod ipse eam alias abjuraverat sub ille conditione quod si ex tunc eam carnaliter cognosceret quod ex tunc haberet eam pro uxore, et ipsa eum similiter vice versa, et quod postmodum eam pluries carnaliter cognoverat ; ipse negavit abjurationem, sed carnalem copulam confessus est ; et nichilominus voluerunt spontanei quod si a modo ipsam carnaliter cognoverit, quod habebunt se invicem pro marito et uxore ; quod eisdem injunximus observandum, injungentes eis ne de cetero invicem cohabitaret. De tempore preterito pro emenda voluntatem facere promisserunt.' (RD no. 11a). This

The cases where the court used abjuration *sub pena nubendi* were by no means examples if extremely longstanding extramarital relations. Neither was it unusual to have several children together outside of marriage. At the same occasion as Henri and Thomassie another couple was presented before the court. Jehan de Mare and Nicole, the widow of Herbert Jupin, had been living together for more than eight years and had six children together. They were requested by the court to abjure each other under a sum of ten livres.[13] There is no mention of a possible abjuration *sub pena nubendi*. The reason could be that the man seemed to be violently opposed to marriage, as it appears when his partner on a later occasion suggested it.[14] There are several similar cases where the court did not use abjuration *sub pena nubendi*.[15]

Neither does the fact that a couple had been defamed for fornication on many occasions, seem to have influenced the courts practise of abjuration *sub pena nubendi* in a decisive way. There are several cases in the register where the same couple was defamed, and sometimes fined, regularly year after year without the court taking any steps to transform their relationship

---

case ended in marriage on March 3, 1315 when Thomassie and Henri admitted before the court that they had had sexual relations after the abjuration. 'Henricus le Portier, clericus, diffamatus de Thomassie filia Ricardi le Guilcour. Quia confessi sunt postquam sese abjurarunt sub conditione, si carnalis copula inter eos interveniret, quod ex tunc matrimonium contrahebant, et sese matrimonialiter consenserunt, ipse eam carnaliter cognoverit pluries, etiam citra tres septimanas, ipsos adjudicamus in maritum et uxorem. Die lune post Letare Jerusalem' [March 3, 1315]

13. 'Eadem die [October 8, 1314], apud Ceraseyum, Johannes de Mara, clericus, et Nicolaa, relicta Herberti Jupin confessi sunt fuisse incontinentes et invicem cohabitasse per octo annos et amplius, adeo quod ipsa concepit et peperit sex pueros de ipso Johanne, et propter hoc gagiavit emendam ad voluntatem nostram ; et injunximus eisdem, ad penam decem librarum turonensium nobis ab eorum quolibet si contra fecerint solvendarum, ne de cetero suspecte cohabitarent in eadem domo, aut sequatur carnalis copula inter eos, nisi hoc fuerit lege matrimonii ; cui inhibitioni acquieverunt ; sed mulier proposuit coventiones matrimonii quas negavit Johannes.' (RD no 11b)
14. This case finally ended in marriage, on Nicoles insistence. Jehans opposition was however so violent that Nicole during the proceedings feared for her life. *[...] ipsa Nicolaa juravit quod dubitabat ne ipse sibi violentiam faceret et ne eam occideret vel malfeceret [...]* (RD no. 17a) For this case see also nos. 16b, 18a and 25b.
15. I third couple was present before the court the same day as Henri and Thomassie, and Jehan and Nicole. Richard le Prevost and Emmelie de Vasteigneio lived together and had two children. The court ordered them to stop living together under a sum of ten livres, and they were fined 25 sous (11c). The daugther of Robert Morice and Jehan de Thaone were defamed for fornication four times between 1330 and 1341 and had three children together (138d, 184b, 206c, 213b). See also nos. 12, 17b, 25d, 70, 75a and 96d.

into marriage by the use of abjuration *sub pena nubendi*.[16] In one case a man was said to have a 'certain wife' whom he ought to take as his lawfully wedded wife.[17] The court, however, did not request an abjuration *sub pena nubendi*.

Thus it is impossible from the register of Cerisy to discern any specific situations where the court systematically used abjuration *sub pena nubendi*. The social facts do not completely explain why the court used it in some cases and not in others. The explanation could of course be that it was used completely at random. Another – and to my view more plausible explanation – is that the court was reluctant to use it against people clearly opposed to marriage. The case of Jehan and Nicole, for example, seems to suggest that the court had that kind of considerations.

The constitution of abjuration *sub pena nubendi* developed as a means to fight the widespread concubinage by transforming it into marriage. It was, as a general principle, not compatible with the doctrine of free choice. This does not mean that the courts, in the actual practise of abjuration *sub pena nubendi*, were indifferent to the doctrine of free choice, which they at other occasions respected. I think that the seemingly hazardous use of abjuration *sub pena nubendi*, that several scholars have commented upon,[18] could at least to some extent be explained by the fact that the courts only used it when the defendants more or less agreed. The actual practise of abjuration *sub pena nubendi* could thus be described as a pragmatic compromise between the wish to transform concubinage into marriage, and the doctrine of free choice.

---

16. Richard Foin and the widow Moquet were defamed seven times between 1325 and 1339 (126c, 130b. 138c, 152c, 184b, 199b and 206b). The court calls them *quasi uxorati*. Colin le Heriz and Guillemette de Bayeux were defamed four times between 1331 and 1339 (143b, 152b, 199b and 206a), they are also called *quasi uxorati*. Thomas Beuslin and a woman called Pulchra Femina (or Bella femina or Belefame) were defamed eight times between 1322 and 1333 (110d, 126d, 130c, 133b, 138e, 143b, 152c and 168c). Several other relationships, that did not result in an abjuration *sub pena nebendi*, can be traced between 1314 and 1346.
17. *Johannes le Moys habuit quendam uxorem vocatam Pujein quam debet accipere in uxorem* (RD 137c).
18. R. H. Helmholz, *Marriage litigation,* 173-174; M. M. Sheehan, 'The formation', 253-254.

TWELFTH CENTURY VIEWS OF POWER IN PETER THE VENERABLE'S *CONTRA PETROBRUSIANOS* AND IN CANON LAW

Dominique Bauer

1. Main points of interest and general outline

Around 1140, Peter the Venerable, abbot of Cluny, wrote a polemic work against the Petrobrusian heresy, *Contra petrobrusianos hereticos*. This work is interesting for various reasons. The work is the major account of the heresy of Peter of Bruis and his followers and takes as such an important place among the sources dealt with in studies on the subject of the eleventh and twelfth century heresies. Furthermore however, and from a somewhat different angle, *Contra petrobrusianos hereticos* also expresses significant ideas and concepts of power, order and justice. More precisely, it is an important source for better understanding Cluniac political thinking and for the way in which this thinking contrasted with new views that came up during the Gregorian reform.

This contribution aims at explaining two things. First, what ideas of power, order and justice come forward in the *Contra Petrobrusianos heriticos* and how do they relate to the specific position of Cluny, to its political convictions, its liturgy and its political choices? In order to explain this, reference will be made to other sources that differ in similar ways from the Gregorian programme such as Ivo of Chartres and Gerhoch of Reichersberg.

Second, how does this position contrast with Gregorian political ideas? In order to answer this question, Cluniac political thought will be compared to the concepts of power that come forward in one of the main representative sources of the Gregorian reform, Anselm of Lucca's *Collectio Canonum,* and in the *Decretum Gratiani.*

2. Spiritual versus institutional views of the Church

In order to understand the positions taken by Peter the Venerable and Gregorian party, a few necessary words need to be said on the 'heretical' preachers and apostolic groups that appeared on the scene from the eleventh century onwards, among them the Petrobrusians. One of the typical features of these groups was that they all had a non-structural character and strived for salvation off the official beaten track of the Church. In this sense, the mediating role of the sacramental Church between God and the faithful disappeared. The fact that these groups did not care for the sacraments and for the external features of religion, and their aim to form small social islands bear testimony to this disappearance. The emergence of the personal, radically spiritual and intentionalist dimension of religion and the simultaneous expansion of various kinds of communities, such as fraternities, guilds, new villages and parishes, 'textual communities' et cetera[1] were in this sense the two sides of the same coin. Equally the fact that chiliastic expectations and socio-economical upheaval went side by side[2] expresses the same coherence of the twofold alienation of sacramental and social organisation.

Prior to the Gregorian reform, these apostolic communities were not actively rejecting or attacking a world that was alien to their aspirations. Things changed however with the Gregorian reform. The reforming papacy tried to use this religious and social potential as an instrument to overthrow ecclesiastical structures, attitudes and customs that had come to form a constitutive part of the Carolingian, Ottonian and Salian makeup of a world in which ecclesiastical and secular authorities on their various levels had formed an organic unity. The great vice of simony that was labelled by the Gregorians as a 'heresy',[3] was a vital aspect of the *Reichskirchenwesen*, as

---

1. As part of the independent religious life that came up in the eleventh centuries, 'textual communities' consisted of people reading and preaching texts. See B. Stock, *The Implications of Literacy: written Language Models of Interpretation in the Eleventh and Twelfth Centuries* (Princeton: 1983), 90.
2. Regarding this aspect, see Michel Molat's classic work on poverty in the Middle Ages, in which he states that the poverty movements and the socio-economic rebellious groups, in their fierce attempts to accomplish the Gregorian programme of the *libertas ecclesiae* attacked both local lords and simonist clergy, were opposed to the ecclesiastical hierarchy and the administration of the sacraments and replaced them by personal piety and good intentions, at times from an eschatological view of reality. M. Mollat, *Les pauvres au Môyen Age* (Brussels: 1984), 104.
3. Vices, abuses and immoral behaviour of the clergy attacked by the reforming party and their supporters were commonly indicated as being heretical. J. Leclerq, 'Simoniaca heresis', *Studia Monastica* 31 (1989), 267-278 and U.-R. Blumenthal, *Gregor VII: Papst zwischen Canossa und Kirchenreform* (Darmstadt: 2001), 123-124.

were the possession of *regalia* by bishops and the widespread Nicolaitism. The apostolic groups were no part of this traditional structure.[4] If they did not overtly attack the 'official' social order, they at least did not consider it to be relevant. Their sense of purity and their ambition to return to the uncontaminated ideal of the New Testament principles made them look for means of salvation that their contemporary socio-ecclesiastical context could not provide.

However, the alliance between the papacy and these apostolic groups involved great risks and would moreover, at various instances and in an ever growing intensity, prove to be a recipe for disaster. Although the twelfth century context and the Gregorian reform displayed the integration of some of the core aspects of these movements into the official structure of society to a great extent[5] and in that in that sense drew them from the margin into its centre, fundamental incompatibilities continued to exist. In the early reform, spiritual elements were clearly present. To a great extent, the reform incorporated the strong demand of personal moral rigidity and the strong sense of distinction between the material and the *saeculum* on the one hand and the spiritual realm of transcendence on the other hand. This manifested itself in two things: the attempt to disentangle the Church from worldly bonds and temporal power and the questioning of the validity of the

4. This is a generally accepted idea in the scholarship on the issue. Among the abundant number of studies that deal with things from this angle these offer very clear introductions and overviews: J.L. Nelson, 'Society, Theodicy and The origins of heresy. Towards a Reassessment of the Medieval Evidence' in: D. Baker (ed.), *Schism, Heresy and Religious Protest. Papers read at the tenth summer Meeting and the eleventh winter Meeting of the Ecclesiastical Historical Society* (Cambridge: 1972), and D. Lambert, *Medieval Heresy. Popular Movements from the Gregorian Reform to the Reformation* (Oxford: 1992) offer very clear introductions and overviews, and among others H. Grundmann, *Religiöse Bewegungen im Mittelater. Untersuchungen über de geschichtlichen Zusammenhänge zwischen der Ketzerei, den Bettelorden und den religiösen Frauenbewegungen im 12. und 13. Jahrhundert und über die geschichtliche Grundlagen der deutschen Mystik* (Berlin: 1935); idem, *Ausgewählte Aufsätze, I. Die Religiöse Bewegungen*, Schriften der Monumenta Germaniae Historica 25, 2. (Stuttgart: 1977); R. Manselli, *Studi sulle eresie del secolo XII* (Rome: 1975); J. Le Goff (ed.), *Hérésies et sociétés dans l'Europe pré-industrielle 11e-18e siècles.* (Paris: 1968), and R.I. Moore, *The Formation of a persecuting society: Power and Deviance in Western Europe, 950-1250* (Oxford: 1987); idem, *The First European Revolution, ca. 970-1215* (Oxford: 2000); idem, *The Origins of European Dissent.* (Oxford: 1985); idem, 'Heresy, Repression and Social Change in the Age of Gregorian Reform', in S.L. Waugh and P.D. Diehl (ed.), *Christendom and its Discontents: Exclusion, persecution, and Rebellion, 1000-1500* (Cambridge: 2002), 19-46, and B.J. Russel, *Dissent and Reform in the Early Middle Ages* (Berkeley: 1965) can be mentioned as some among the classic works on the topic.
5. Moore, *The Origins of European Dissent*, 47-52, mentions in this respect the monastic life in Camaldoli and Vallombrosa and the foundation of the Carthusian order and those of Citeaux, Tiron and Savigny.

sacramental acts of simoniac, unworthy clergy. Especially Gregory VII went very far in denying their validity up until the point where, as Moore states it, 'the pope was not a Donatist, but he often seemed to behave like one'.[6] Gregory very eloquently and passionately instigated apostolic communities to take action against their simoniac ministers and to reject their sacraments. Most significantly in this respect was his rehabilitation of the heretical Ramihrdus who had been burned for refusing to accept the sacrament from 'unworthy' clergy.[7]

However, turning apostolic groups against the sacraments of unworthy priests opened the door for establishing an unbridgeable opposition between the spiritual and intentional dimension of religion and the sacramental Church. Since unworthy clergy could be found everywhere, including on the papal throne. In fact, the Donatist-like point of view could very easily lead to a principal distrust of the church as a sacramental order as such, a distrust that could only catalyse further the conception of a strong opposition between the spiritual and sacramental aspects of faith. Peter Damian had already perceived this problem when as a papal legate at the time of the Patarene turmoil in Milan he refused to accept that the sacramental turned ineffective in the hand of simoniac clergy.[8]

Peter Damian's reaction to the problem is highly significant of the embryonic institutionalism that was already coming to the surface of the reform. When comparing Peter Damian's *Liber Gratissimus* to Humbert of Silva Candida's *Contra Simoniacos*, it can be stated that, their different positions concerning the issue of reordination notwithstanding, they clearly put forward the coincidence of the institutional and the sacramental Church, by both stressing the fact that only within the Church is a valid ordination is possible. Peter Damian explicitly stated that both the minister and the faithful need to be subordinated to the Church and to God.

What was at stake in the tension between the Patarene convictions and the view of Peter Damian was the operation of the sacraments independently from the Church. The impossibility of the reformers to arrive at a unanimous point of view regarding this matter[9] reflects the tension

6. Moore, *The Origins of European dissent*, 62.
7. Lambert, 'Medieval Heresy', 37.
8. Moore, *The Origins of European dissent*, 61.
9. Pope Leo IX whose pontificate initiates the Gregorian reform, does not conduct a consistent policy regarding this issue. Moreover, not all sacramental acts are treated in the same way and as to the condition of the ministers, opinions also differ to whether the minister for example is a heretic or only somehow deviant. Peter Damian, whose exposition on the problem in his *Liber Gratissimus* is not very coherent, and Humbert of Silva Candida, the Roman ideologists of the beginning years of the Reform, do not hold the same views. Whereas simoniacs in Peter's view are not heretics, according to Humbert they have to be reordained. In his *Adversus Simoniacos* that was moreover written against the *Liber Gratissimus*, heretic consecrations are considered to be invalid. Because simoniacs are heretics,

within the reform between its spiritualist and institutional tendencies. On the one hand, the spiritualist tendency within the reform rejected the validity of sacraments that had been administered by simoniac priests and in its most radical circles even rejected the concept of the sacrament as such altogether. On the other hand, this radical stand threatened the *ex opere operato* nature of the sacraments that increasingly became identified with the operation of the institutional Church itself. Indeed, making the effect of the sacraments somehow dependent of the minister's personal condition or intentions ran counter to the idea of an objective sacramental order and led to a kind of sacramental ungovernability. For, it would make the objective sacramental order dependent of the particular minister of the sacraments.

The institutional paraphrase of the sacramental effect and the organisation of the Church as a clerical body would gradually solve this tension between spiritual and institutionalist views. By making the institutional body of the Church into the locus of salvation, the threat of ungovernability to a large extent disappeared. The legitimacy of the institutional body could no longer be affected by a cleric's bad intentions. In the long run, this development of course only again radicalised the spiritual opposition and estranged the spiritual idealists among the reforming party from this ever growing institutionalist tendency within the reform.[10]

3. Cluny's view of reality

Peter the Venerable's criticism of the Petrobrusians is mainly an attack on two things. First, Peter strongly opposes to their spiritualist rejection of all visible tokens of faith. Second, he criticises the particular role inner spiritual life gets with Peter of Bruis and his followers. This is no surprise. In fact, heresies such as the Petrobrusian undermined the ecclesiological views Cluny stood for. These views come most exemplary forward in the meaning Cluny attributed to its liturgy and to herself. Her liturgy and her self-image were based upon the idea of the sacred nature of visible things in this world

---

their consecrations are as a consequence also invalid. Their doctrinal conflict was consequently continued by Atto of Vercelli and Anselm of Lucca on the one side and Deusdedit and Amatus of Oleron on the one. For an overview of the various points of view, please see L. Saltet, *Les réordinations. Etude sur le sacrament de l'ordre* (Paris: 1907), 181-207.

10. For a more detailed account on this particular matter, please see: D. Bauer, 'From Ivo of Chartres to the Decretum Gratiani: The Legal Nature of a Political Theology Revolution' in P. Andersen, M. Münster-Swendsen and H. Vogt (ed.), *Law Before Gratian. Law in Western Europe c. 500-1100. Proceedings of the Third Carlsberg Academy Conference on Medieval Legal History* (Copenhagen: 2007), 123-139; idem, 'On the Historical Genesis of Legal Proceduralism' in: E.J.F.M. Broers, B.M.C. Jacobs and R.C.H. Lesaffer (ed.), *Ius Brabanticum, Ius commune, Ius Gentium.* (Nijmegen : 2006), 209-220.

are directly and literary related to transcendent reality. It is important to mention these things for two reasons. First, precisely the lack of a more clear distinction between transcendent and secular reality determines Cluny's understanding of justice, the right order of power and politics and her view of the relation between the temporal and ecclesiastical powers. Second, the differences between the Cluniac and the Gregorian ways of understanding run parallel to the latter's equally different views concerning the status of secular reality and its relation to transcendent reality. In this paragraph will be briefly dealt with some of the relevant aspects of the Cluniac view of reality. In the fourth paragraph, some fundamental elements of Gregorian view will be presented.

The foundation of Cluny was deeply rooted in the legacy of the Carolingian world. Her foundation in 911 was one among the many attempts, as also in Gorze and Aurillac, to pick up the thread of the reform politics of Louis the Pious and Benedict of Aniane,[11] after the disintegration of the Carolingian empire had stabilized and the storms of the Norman invasions had calmed down.

Benedict of Aniane had issued, with the support of Louis the Pious, the *Capitulare monasticum* at the council of Aachen in 817 in order to reinstall the strict observance of the rule of Saint Benedict.[12] However, one major difference did exist between the original rule of Saint Benedict and the rule of Aachen. Benedict of Aniane had put significantly more stress on liturgy and less on labour than Saint Benedict had done. Precisely this fundamental difference is being further developed in Cluniac monasticism. Rather than changing it, Cluny expands the existing liturgy and liturgical customs that had emerged in the Carolingian world. The celebration of All Saints for example was a custom that had come up in England during the sixth century and that had spread around the Carolingian empire in the next century. This custom was taken up in Cluniac liturgy and supplemented, by abbot Odilo (962-1049), with a general commemoration of the dead after All Saints. Hugh of Cluny (1024-1109) adds commemoration days on the Monday after the feast of the Holy Trinity and on 31 January. All Saints and the commemoration of the dead fit into the self-attributed role of Cluny as a go-between between heaven and earth. The commemoration and burial of the dead, helping the deceased by prayers, masses and alms and the importance

11. I. Rosé, 'La presence clunisienne à Rome et dans sa region au Xe siècles réformes et écclésiologie monastiques d'Odon à Maïeul' in G. Spinelli (ed.) *Il monachesimo italiano dall'età longobarda all'età ottoniana: Atti del Convegno di studi sull'Italia benedittina Nonantola (Modena), 10-13 settembre 2003* (Cesena : 2006), 231-271, 250.
12. M. Pacout, *L'Ordre de Cluny : 909-1789* (Paris : 1988), 47.

that is being attached to the veneration of relics make Cluny in the first quarter of the eleventh century into a very important funerary centre.[13]

The assessment of the role played by sacraments as the visible, material presence of sacrality, first and foremost applies to the material Cluny itself. The monastery of Cluny actually operates herself as a sacrament. Through her liturgy, her cult of the dead and of relics and her function as a burial ground, Cluny serves as a material means of salvation. In performing that function, Cluny stands above any kind of institutionally determined effect that could also bear relevance to salvation.

In contrast with the anti-feudal strategy of many of the early Gregorians who would directly attack the interrelation of temporal and ecclesiastical power as the root of all evil, the Cluniac ambitions are directed at making the monastery a refuge and a material place of salvation. Cluny never attacks the feudal structure or the imperial sacred prerogatives, on the contrary. From the idea of the right order, Cluny takes a relatively independent position towards the two powers.[14] A haven of salvation, Cluny had obtained the papal admission to offer a safe place to those who were banned from the Christian community by the Church. The most famous example of people who were thus accepted into the monastery of Cluny is obviously that of Peter Abelard who, after having being condemned and mentally destroyed at the council of Sens (1141) under the instigation of Bernard of Clairvaux, found his way to Cluny where he was accepted into the hospitality of abbot Peter the Venerable. Cluny provides the banned with the *medicamentum indulgentiae et salutis* (medicine of indulgence and salvation) and guarantees them the *dilectio sanctae fraternitatis* (love of holy brotherhood). First and foremost she is the *causae salutis, divinae miserationis et pietatis refugium, et apostolicae benedictionis* (the cause of salvation, of divine sympathy and a refuge of piety and apostolic blessing).[15]

---

13. D. Iogna-Prat, *Ordonner et exclure. Cluny et la société chrétienne face à l'hérésie, au judaïsme et à l'Islam 1000-1150* (Paris : 1998), 219-222; M. De Valous, *Le monachisme clunisien des origines au XVe siècles, vie intérieure des monastères et organisation de l'ordre* (Paris : 1970), 372.
14. H.E.J. Cowdrey, *The Cluniacs and the Gregorian Reform* (Oxford: 1970), 266, states that Cluny can however not be regarded as a third force next to the pope and the emperor. In this respect he refers to the special link that existed between Cluny and Rome under which it directly resorted and the influence of Gregorian universalism. As however will be seen when entering upon Peter the Venerable's *Contra Petrobrusianos*, Cluniac universalism is of a fundamentally different nature than Gregorian universalism. This does however not imply that Cluny was not influenced by the universalist ambitions of the Gregorian reformers, it just had another concept of universalism.
15. Wollasch, J. 'Der Einfluss des Mönchstums auf Reich und Kirche', *Reich und Kirche vor dem Investiturstreit. Gerd Tellenbach zum 80. Geburtstag* (Sigmaringen: 1985), 45.

The Cluniac reform is an internal monastic reform that does not meddle in the feudal community of the day.[16] In this way, Cluny displays a fundamentally different approach towards lay power than many of the early Gregorians would do. Cluny's attitude towards the *Eigenkirchenwesen* clearly illustrates this. Some interesting conclusions concerning this issue can be drawn from research on Cluny's attitude towards the *Eigenkirchen*, donations and the buying and selling of churches. The research brings Cluny's conservative politics to light, a position that Cluny moreover shares with other non-Cluniac eleventh century monasteries. As feudal lords, Cluny makes use of the existing feudal mechanism to safeguard its position and from that motivation accepts the *Eigenkirchesnwesen* and the lay right to *Eigenkirchen*.[17] Cluny never seems to react against lay intrusion into ecclesiastical affairs and never takes part in the attempts of forcing feudal lords to donate the churches they possessed to monasteries. The admonition to donate churches is part of the general formulation that went with the donation of goods and was a traditional feudal way of enlarging the property of the monastery. Therefore, this admonition does certainly not fit in with the idea of an external attack on the feudal system.[18]

On the political field, Cluny has to be situated within the ideological framework of the cooperation between the papal and royal/imperial power and within the context of feudal society. Politically, Cluny plays a conservative role. It aims at preserving the traditional *ordo* based upon this cooperation. In the context of this *ordo tranquilitatis* the alliance of the two powers is vital. The legitimacy of this idea of tranquillity and order was partly rooted in a sense of securing social stability and partly in the solemn and sacred nature of the alliance that functioned as a kind of metaphysical reality and as the necessary guarantee for the maintenance of a transcendent sense of order and justice.

The transcendent nature of order and justice in the Cluniac world is not a 'merely' theoretical reality, but is also directly reflected in the politics of the day. Because of her transcendent dimension, the *tranquilitas ordinis* has to be clearly distinguished from any actual institutional situation. In this sense, it does not always or necessarily imply a politics of compliance with

---

16. H.-E. Mager, 'Studien über das Verhältnis der Cluniacenzer zum Eigenkirchenwesen' in G. Tellenbach (ed.) *Neue Forschungen über Cluny und die Cluniacenser* (Freiburg: 1959), 169-217, 189.
17. H.-E. Mager, 'Das Verhältnis der Cluniacenser zum Eigenkirchenwesen', 174-178, compared Cluny with a number of other monasteries: St. Martin des Champs (1059), Domëne (1057), La Charité-sur-Loire, St. Flour (between 1000-1030), Notre Dame de Longpont (1061), St. Mont (middle of the eleventh century), St. Bertin, St. Christoph en Halette (1061), St. Leu d'Esserent, Redon and Conques.
18. Mager, 'Das Verhältnis der Cluniacenser zum Eigenkirchenwesen', 186; G. Constable, 'Cluny und der Investiturstreit' in Ch. Stiegemann and M. Wemmhof *Canossa 1077: Erschütterung der Welt: Geschichte, Kunst und Kultur am Anfang der Romanik* (München: 2006), 143-148, 147.

the actual papal-imperial strategies. This can be illustrated by the fact that Peter the Venerable (1092-1156) supported Roger II and the Kingdom of the two Sicilies on the basis of the *pax* established although Roger II was at that point a common enemy and competitor in Southern Italy of both the pope and the emperor.[19]

The same sense of peace between the two powers as an expression of the right order can also be found with for example Burchard of Worms, Ivo of Chartres and Gerhoch of Reichersberg. It was moreover the framework in which the reform popes before Gregory VII operated, with the cooperation of Leo IX and Henry III[20] as a well known example. Catalysed however by the escalation of the Investiture Contest that lead to intensified claims on the exclusive possession of sacrality by both powers,[21] the papacy would break away from the traditional idea of the alliance between the two powers. The soteriological function that had been traditionally attached to the peace between pope, king or emperor would therefore gradually shift to the Holy See.

The opening *canones* of DI XVI[22] and Ivo's correspondence in contrast however clearly fit in with the Cluniac views. Discord between *regnum* and *sacerdotium* is directly connected with the fact that without this unity, the Church cannot flourish (letter CCXIV)[23] Thus, the concord between the two powers is viewed as contributing to the construction of the *Regnum Christi.* For, the latter is the ultimate goal of choosing to act on the basis of *misericordia* and *iustitia,* as it is said in Ivo's Prologue.[24]

---

19. J.-P. Torell, and D. Bouthilier, *Pierre le Vénérable et sa vision du monde: sa vie, son oeuvre, l'homme et le démon* (Leuven: 1986), 84-86.
20. H.E.J. Cowdrey, *Pope Gregory VII 1073-1085* (Oxford: 1998), 686. Before his ascension, Leo IX was imperial bishop of Tours, a position that he would maintain after he had become Pope Leo IX. The politics of mutual support between the pope and the emperor can be illustrated by the fact that in 1049 Leo IX excommunicated the leaders of the anti-imperial upraise in Lorraine and Baudouin of Flanders: G. Tellenbach, *The Church in Western Europe from the tenth to the early twelfth century* (Cambridge: 1995), 191.
21. Tellenbach, *The Church in Western Europe from the tenth to the early twelfth century*, 337.
22. [Decretum, Ivo] For example DI XVI [2] (Ms. London, Royal 11 D VII, fo. 298r° Episcopi in protegendis populis-emendare anathemathizentur; Migne, Patrologia Latina 161, 16.2; also in *Decretum Burchardi*, Migne, Patrologia Latina, 140, 537-1053, 15.1).
23. [Ivo of Chartres' letters have been partially edited: Yves de Chartres, *Correspondance*, J. Leclercq (ed.) (Paris: 1949). For practical reasons, I'm referring to the complete collection in the Patrologia Latina series] Ivo, letter CCXIV, Migne, Patrologia Latina, 162, 218: 'Videmus enim scissum regnum et sacerdotium... In tanta scissura, in tanta procella florere et fructificare non potest mater ecclesiae...'
24. *Iustitia* refers to the rigid application of law, whatever the circumstances. *Misericordia* refers to the dispensation from the application of law on pastoral grounds in view of what serves salvation best and taking circumstances of time,

Ivo, as well as Burchard of Worms,[25] defend the ecclesiastical supremacy and the independent competence of the Episcopal power in ecclesiastical matters. This hierarchy needs however to be set in the framework of the fundamental need of unity of the two powers. With Ivo this is for example expressed in the moral image of the ideal king. The moral nature of the king speaks from the role he needs as keeper of the ecclesiastical and royal peace.[26] Again, upholding the law is mentioned in one breath with the moral qualities a king needs to possess and with the maintenance of peace. Thus, the justification of the royal coercive power derives from the integration of this power in the soteriological unity of *regnum* and *sacerdotium*.

Within the pregregorian context, the concept of power has in this sense a sacred dimension. An example to illustrate the supra-institutional nature of the concept of the peace can be found in the work of Gerhoch of Reichersberg. With radical spiritual reformers, the argument of the unity between the powers will get increasingly compelling when they will get more and more isolated once the institutional course of the reform will start prevailing. This is also the case for Gerhoch of Reichersberg when he mentions the idea of the unity in his *Opusculum ad Cardinales*.[27] From his initial focus on the suppression of the Church by temporal power in the beginning of the twelfth century, the attention clearly shifts to the defence of the moral unity of the two powers after the second half of the twelfth century.

---

place and persons into account. For the edition and thorough analysis of Ivo of Chartres' Prologue, please see B.C. Brasington, *Ways of Mercy. The Prologue of Ivo of Chartres* (Munster: 2004).

25. M. Kerner, *Studien zum Dekret des Bischofs Burchard von Worms* (Aachen: 1970), 177.

26. Ivo, letter CXVIII, 1333 : 'Cum enim in regibus praecipae vigere debeat pietas, mansuetudo, justitiae, ad pietatem pertinere credemus, quod ad divinum cultum etiam usque ad nos aliquos facultatem vestrarum ramusculos extendi sui multiplicet... Non enim ad hoc instituuntur reges, ut leges frangant; sed distortores legum gladio, si aliter corrigi non possunt, feriant.'

27. Gerhoch mentions the idea of a 'council' as representing the ecclesiastical unity. Should the pope agree to appear before this council, he might free himself from the rumours on his conspiracy against the emperor. Gerhoch Gerhoch, *Opusculum ad Cardinales*. D. Van den Eynde and P. Rijmersdael (ed.), *Gerhohi praepositi Reichersbergensis. Opera inedita*. Vol. I. (Rome: 1957), 337: 'Nunc autem, quia idem iuravit simulque principes et multi episcopi cum eo iuraverunt prout voluerunt, nisi vos pietatis in conciliis vel in consiliis audientiam ad excusandam opinionem conspirationis.'

4. The case of Peter the Venerable's *Contra Petrobrusianos hereticos*

Although the Petrobrusians are only known through Peter's work and his correspondence and by a record in Abelard's *Introductio ad theologiam*, this heresy clearly illustrates the radical spiritualist character of many of the apostolic movements of the day. The heresy of Peter of Bruis and his 'successor' Henry of Lausanne that spread from around 1119 in the South of France shows a great resemblance with for example the movements of *pauperes Christi* in Lombardy. Moreover, the strong anti-clerical preaching of Henry of Lausanne (died around 1148, imprisoned in Toulouse) would stimulate the emergence of the Cathars.[28]

The anti-formal character of this heresy is strongly expressed in that they refuse to worship the cross. Very significantly, they do so on the basis of the distinction between *instrumentum* and *res invisibilis*. The *instrumentum*, or the – by definition – external or objectively given sign, is the material, visible cross that refers to Christ, who is the *res invisibilis*, the invisible reality. From the same point of view, they hold it useless to build churches as a place of worship or to do good works for the souls of the deceased because nothing can be added anymore to their merits.[29] According to the Petrobrusians, it is equally useless to baptise small

28. The Petrobrusian issue is thoroughly presented by Iogna-Prat, *Ordonner et exclure*, 103-152, further by J. Châtillon, J. 'Pierre le Vénérable et les Petrobrusiens' in R. Louis, J. Jolivet, J. and J. Châtillon, (ed.) *Pierre le Abélard et Pierre le Vénérable : les courants philosophiques, littéraires et artistiques en occident au milieu du xiie siècle. Colloques internationaux du Centre nationale de la recherche scientifique* (Paris: 1975), 165-167. K.A. Fink, *Papsttum und Kirche im abendlandischen Mittelalter* (München: 1981), 116-117; J.-P. Torell, 'L'Eglise dans L'oeuvre et la vie de Pierre le Vénérable', *Revue Thomiste*, 77 (1977), 352-392. J.C. Reagan, 'Did the Petrobrusians Teach Salvation by Faith Alone?' *The Journal of Religions*, 7 (1927), 81-91; J. Fearns, 'Peter von Bruis und die religiöse Bewegung des 12. Jahrhunderts', *Arbeiten zur geschichte des Kirchenkampfes* 48 (1966), 311-335. Very handy and accurate in this respect is also R. Nelli, *Dictionnaire des heresies méridionales* (Toulouse: 1968), 245-246 for Peter of Bruis and 159-162 for Henry of Lausanne (or Henri Henriciens). For the close but complex and not easily to assess relation between Peter of Bruis and Henry of Lausanne, please see among others especially Moore, *The Origins of European Dissent*, 82-114, further: Manselli, *Studi sulle eresie*, 79-109.
29. *Petri Venerabilis Contra Petrobrusianos heritocos*, Corpus Christianorum Continuatio Medieavalis (Turnhout: 1968), 56: 'Affirmatis vanum esse orare vel quicquam boni facere pro defunctis, quia eos vivorum bona iuvare non possunt, qui totum meritum suum, cui nil addi possunt, secum quando hinc transiere tulerunt.

children[30] or to preach the gospel to children because they cannot understand it yet, [31]and it impossible to be saved by someone else's faith.[32]

Central to Peter the Venerable's exposition is the search for what determines the economy of salvation. For the Petrobrusians salvation is rooted in personal faith, in one's intentions. In this respect, baptising small children or teaching them the faith is useless because they obviously do not know yet what is going on. It is equally senseless to add something to other people's merits or possible to be saved by someone else's faith. In this way, merit and faith are being treated as something personal. The spiritualist dimension of the Petrobrusian heresy is thus expressed in the concept of a personal faith that needs no mediation through visible signs, such as crosses and church buildings, in short, through sacraments.[33]

To Peter the Venerable in contrast, it is on the contrary the universal nature of the Church that makes salvation possible. In this framework, Peter refers to the impersonal nature of faith, as for example in depicting the roles of Adam and Christ: 'by the crime of one man we were condemned, by the justice of one man we were saved'.[34] Against the Petrobrusian key-function of personal faith, Peter puts the membership – through baptism – to the Church as a necessary precondition for salvation. When *fides* is being used in the sense of personal faith, it is not presented as a necessary precondition for salvation. Peter uses *fides* to prove that one can be saved by the faith of others, and in this sense opposes to the personal faith argument.[35]

30. *Petri Venerabilis Contra Petrobrusianos*, 13: Responsio contra id quod dicunt heretici parvulos non posse baptizari'.
31. *Petri Venerabilis Contra Petrobrusianos*, 49: 'Quomodo enim predicandum est evangelium quod non intelligunt nuntiandum quod non percipiunt, intimandum quod non advertunt.'
32. *Petri Venerabilis Contra Petrobrusianos*, 42: 'Hoc certe videndum est, si fide, quod negatis, alterius alter salvatus est, or, elsewhere [43] : Cui cum maxime vos credere dicatis, aut aliorum fide alios tandem posse salvari concedite aut de evangelio esse que posui, si potestis, negate.'
33. The word 'sacrament' does not refer yet to the seven sacraments and their specific meaning. The seven sacraments would only become 'official' in Peter Lombard's *Quattuor libri sententiarum* (between 1152 and 1159) after a time of formation that ended around 1145-1150. Apart from in Peter Lombard's work, they appear first in the *Sententiae divinitatis* (around 1141-1147), a book of sentences from the school of Gilbertus Porretanus, and the *De sacramentis* of a certain magister Simon (influenced by the *Sententiae divinitatis*). On their development, see for example B. Geyer, 'Die Siebenzahl der sakramente in ihren historischen Entwicklung', *Theologie und Glaube* 10 (1918), 325-348.
34. *Petri Venerabilis Contra Petrobrusianos*, 51 or elsewhere, against the Petrobrusian contention that it is impossible to be saved by the faith of others [43]: 'Iuste inquam, quoniam, qui aliena fide aliorum corpora curata demonstro, ab eodem animarum corporum conditore aliorum fide aliorum, animas purgari ostendo.'
35. *Petri Venerabilis Contra Petrobrusianos*, 50: 'Nulla est fides in parvulis christianorum, sed nec est aliqua fides in parvulis Iudeorum. Salvantur tamen

Elsewhere, *fides* is perceived in the same way as the sacraments in general. As the sacraments it functions *ex opere operato*. It is in no way connected with personal conviction or with any kind of intentionality.[36]

Yet, the *universa ecclesia* and the sacraments do not coincide. Peter states – a statement that points out to a very significant inconsistency in Peter's line of argument – that neither baptism without faith, nor faith without baptism, has any value. First, it seems evident to Peter that baptism can save a person without that person having a *propria fides*. In this sense, Peter defends the formal soteriological context that founds the *ex opere operato* functioning of the sacraments. In the same passage, Peter however states as well that the *propria fides* can save without the sacraments! For, it is inconceivable that the many saints and martyrs that were not baptised would not have been saved.[37] This apparent inconsistency is very revealing for the fundamental difference between the Cluniac Church and the institutional Church. *Iustitia* and *universa ecclesia* do not yet function as synonyms of the institutionally conceived sacramental Church, as they would come to do in Gregorian political thinking. This finding fits in with the fact that to Peter, no fundamental difference existed between pope and abbot[38] and with the general Cluniac attitude towards Rome. Rome was first and foremost the place where the apostle Peter was buried and because of this very important relic it was an important religious centre.[39] Therefore, the Petrine worship and the pilgrimage to Rome constitute an important means of attaining the Cluniac ideal of holiness.[40] However, the worship of Peter related to the universal Church and not to the Holy See.[41] Thus, in Cluniac ecclesiology the supra-institutional *universa ecclesia* is distinguished from the visible, institutional Church.

---

aliena fide cum suscepta circumcissione, salvantur et isti aliena fide cum suscpto baptismate.'

36. *Petri Venerabilis Contra Petrobrusianos*, 50: 'sine fide ... vel in baptismate, impossibile est placare deo.'
37. *Petri Venerabilis Contra Petrobrusianos*, 46-47: 'Quod vero propria fides sine baptismate salvet, auctoritate vel ratione existimo persuadendum.'
38. W.H. Principe, 'Monastic, Episcopal and Apologetic Theology of the Papacy, 1150-1250' in C. Ryan (ed.) *The Religious Roles of the Papacy: Ideals and Realities, 1150-1300* (Toronto: 1998), 117-170.
39. Rosé, 'La presence clunisienne à Rome et dans sa region au Xe siècles réformes et écclésiologie monastiques d'Odon à Maïeul'; E. Sackur, *Die Cluniacenser in ihren kirchlichen und allgemeingeschichtlichen Wirksamkeit bis zur Mitte des elften Jahrhunderts*, 2 vol. (Darmstadt: 1965), II, 443.
40. R. Morgen, 'Monastic Reform and Cluniac Spirituality' in N. Hunt (ed.) *Cluniac Monasticism in the Central Middle Ages* (London: 1971), 33-56, 20.
41. F. Neiske, 'Das Verhaltnis Clunys zum Papsttum' in G. Constable, G. Melville and J. Oberste (ed.), *Die Cluniazenser in ihrem politisch-sozialen Umfeld* (Münster: 1998), 279-320, 317.

In *Contra Petrobrusianus*, the issue of justice is being discussed in relation to the idea of *misericordia.* This theme appears in his criticism of the radical spiritualist statement that celebrating mass is pointless.[42] In his answer to this point, he tries to explain why God should be worshipped. Peter's point of departure is the reconciliation, from the angle of God's goodness, of divine *misericordia* with the righteous punishment of man. In his goodness God spares mankind from being subjected to *iustitia* through *misericordia.* The problem of the dispensation that is at the heart of the relation between *misericordia* and *iustitia* in Ivonian canon law[43] is theologically rephrased by Peter in the question whether *misericordia* does not devaluate *iustitia*, or in how *iustitia* is still being preserved notwithstanding God's *misericordia.* Again, Peter's primary concern is soteriological, just like with Ivo. This perspective clearly shines through the question of how it is possible that man can deserve *misericordia* while keeping *iustitia* intact[44] or in the statement that this dispensation in no way diminishes the operation of justice.[45].

From the soteriological motivation of Peter's exposition, it is not surprising that the most radical proof of God's *misericordia* lies in the incarnation. In this instance, Peter articulates the core of Cluniac liturgy. This liturgy enacted salvation as it was established by the glory of Christ. Hence the great importance of Easter in Cluniac liturgy, the stress that was put on the fact that Christ procured our salvation, and the fact that this feast is a theological synthesis of both Christological convictions and ecclesiology.[46] Also the fact that the celebration of the discovery and elevation of the Cross was primarily a celebration of Christ's majesty[47] fits in to these liturgical goals of Cluny.

The veneration of the majesty of Christ is immediately connected with the sacrament of the Eucharist. The Eucharist is a daily repetition of the *Imperium Christi*, the reign of Christ.[48] The realist conception of the

---

42. *Petri Venerabilis Contra Petrobrusianos*, 86: *Contra id quod dicunt missam nichil esse nec celebrari debent.*
43. Brasington, *Ways of Mercy*, 41-67.
44. *Petri Venerabilis Contra petrobrusianos*, 99: 'dum in eterno consilio suo quereret, qualiter misero salva iustitia misereri valeret.' Peter finds the solution to this problem, that is of lesser importance in this framework, in the valuation of good works and the glorification of God that he wanted to justify in the first place: 'hoc potissimum occurit, quo et iustia servaretur, et homo liberaretur, et gratia augeretur, et Deus glorificaretur.'
45. *Petri Venerabilis Contra Petrobrusianos*, 99: 'In qua dispensatione misericordia misereretur , iusitie nil detraheretur…'.
46. A. Härdelin, 'Pâques et Rédemption. Etude de théologie monastique au XIIe siècle', *Collectanea Cisterciensa* 43 (1981), 3-19; 5, 14.
47. D. Iogna-Prat, 'La croix, le moine et l'empereur : dévotion à la croix et théologie politique à Cluny' *Etudes clunisiennes* (Paris: 2002), 74-92, 453.
48. Iogna-Prat, 'La croix, le moine et l 'empereur', 452.

Eucharist and the image of a triumphing Christ constitute the core of Peter's criticism of the Petrobrusian contention that it is pointless to build churches, to pray for the death or to do good works on their behalf. For, on a theological level, Peter's criticism is constituted on the basis of the transition from the material sign, like a church or the Eucharistic bread, to the sacramental reality it refers to. He conceives this transition in such way as to maintain its soteriological nature. In order words, without building churches or worshipping the cross, salvation is not possible. Thus, a 'materialistic' interpretation of transcendence goes side by side with a non-institutional, transcendent idea of the reign of Christ. The power of Christ is supra-institutional.

5. Canon law doctrine: the institutional Church

In order to address the changing views of power, justice and order with the Gregorians, it is very clarifying to confront the ideas and background of *Contra Petrobrusianos hereticos* with particular evolutions in canon law doctrine. Particularly the interrelation between the Ivo's *Panormia* and *Decretum*, the *Decretum Gratiani* and the 'Gregorian collection' *Collectio Canonum* of Anselm of Lucca[49] (CC) is highly revealing in this respect.

Anselm's collection serves as a kind of declaration and legitimisation of the ambitions of the Reform and represents one of the first attempts to fit in canon law doctrine into this program. In other words: the collection formulations the basic principles of the Reform in legal terms.[50] In comparison to Ivo's *Panormia* and *Decretum,* the *Collectio Canonum* combines an explicit corporatist view of the Church[51] as well as a thorough proceduralist interpretation of canon law tradition. As the example taken from marriage law with Gratian will show, in a proceduralist view justice is no longer viewed as something exclusively transcendent. On the contrary, it is interpreted in terms of validity. A decision is 'right' because it had been carried out correctly for example. Thus, a view of justice comes into the limelight that in the first place has an institutional dimension and directly relates to the institutional organisation of the Church.

The same shift to proceduralism bearing on a proceduralist organisation of legal doctrine reoccurs in the *Decretum Gratiani.* The

49. P. Fournier, and G. LeBras, *Histoire des collections canoniques en occident. Depuis les Fausses Décrétales jusqu'au Décret de Gratien*, 2 vol. (Paris: 1931-1932); K. Cushing, *Papacy and Law in the Gregorian Revolution* (Oxford: 1998).
50. Cushing, *Papacy and Law in the Gregorian Revolution*, 143.
51. The view of the Church as an institutional and legal corpus is strongly reflected in the systematic exclusion of the laity from the Church and in the only negative formulation of its duties. This is coherent with the politics of Gregory VII: Blumenthal, *Gregory VII*, 269.

principles of organisation in the *Decretum Gratiani* differ especially from the *ratio* of the *Panormia* in that various *canones* are systematically set in a proceduralist context.[52] For example, sacramental realism-type *canones* that also figure in *Panormia* are either reshifted to the *De consecratione*, or they are rearranged in the corpus of the *Decretum Gratiani* in a procedural context, and therefore do no longer represent sacramental realism.[53]

Also in the *Collectio Canonum*, this general shift can be found.[54] Very interesting, especially from the angle of the development of the *De ecclesia* theme in going from the Ivonian collections to the *Decretum Gratiani,* is CC V, *De ordinationibus ecclesiarum et de omni iure ac statu illarum* (on the legal status of churches effected by their ordination). In very briefly comparing the setting of *canones* that figure both with Ivo and with Anselm of Lucca, it can be concluded that the transition from the Ivonian collections to Gratian's *Decretum* in this field is being confirmed. The stress that in Gratian's *Decretum* is put on validity is in Anselm's work found with *De ecclesia* theme. CC V only gives little attention to the consecration of holy places as such,[55] a theme that in the Ivonian collections played an important role. Instead the issue of the validity of consecrations comes to the fore: what consecrations and foundations are legitimate ones is the central question.

This does however not mean that the emergence of institutionalist concepts of power, law and order need to be completely separated from views as held by Peter the Venerable and Ivo of Chartres. For the concordance between the *Collectio Canonum* and the *Decretum Gratiani* concerning this matter only seems to apply to the parts of the *Decretum Gratiani* that made up the latter's first recension.[56] For, sacramental realism as it can be found concerning *De ecclesia* in the Ivonian collections is in fact reinforced in *De consecratione* that was added to the first recension of

---

52. On this transition between the *Panormia* and *Decretum* of Ivo, please see: Bauer, 'The Twelfth Century and the Emergence of the Juridical Subject – Some Reflections'.
53. A good example is the rearrangement of Ivo, *Panormia* V [12] (Paris, bib. Nat. 2472 Fo. 67v° Sciscitantibus vobis si sacerdote – hunc mundum) in C. 15 q. 8 c. 5. This canon is removed from a series of *canones* on *purgatio*, purgation to a context in which no longer purgation as such is relevant. Instead, the canon serves in the framework of the effect of the competences and rights that are brought into effect by the ordination.
54. For a more detailed account, please see: D. Bauer, 'How to interpret Canonical Collections as a Historical Source? Proposal of a Method and an example of 'Juridisation'', *Proceedings of the Twelfth International Congress of Medieval Canon Law*, Città del Vaticano, forthcoming.
55. For example CC V [23] Ut dedicationes ecclesiarum et sacerdotum singulis annis solleniter celebrentur et, si de consecratione ecclesiae dubitatur, iterim consecretur.
56. I'm following Anders Winroth's reconstruction of the first recension of the *Decretum Gratiani*: A. Winroth, *The making of Gratian's Decretum* (Cambridge: 2000).

the *Decretum Gratiani*. Furthermore, in the *Decretum Gratiani*, the significant passages of marriage law[57] that are, unlike those in *De consecratione,* present in the *Decretum*'s first recension, expresses the traditional context of sacramental realism.

Precisely in the way Gratian deals with marriage, in contrast with Ivo, it becomes very clear that sacramental realism played a decisive role in the elaboration of institutionalism. In this sense, it also played a considerable role in the construction of the new views of justice, power, law and order. First, sacramental realism is reinforced in the *Decretum Gratiani* when dealing with marriage. Second, with Ivo a tension remains between the objective, sacramental nature of marriage and its intentionalist foundation. With Gratian this tension disappears throughout his central aim of letting the institutional ratification coincide with the enactment of the sacramental effect of marriage. Thus, Gratian expresses within canon law doctrine the coincidence of the sacramental *ex opere operato* with the development of institutional procedure: the ratification of marriage.

One example can illustrate this. In C 27, Gratian presents a view of the foundation of marriage in which the opposition between the *copula* and the consensus theory is rubbed out. In order to achieve this goal, Gratian presents a number a distinctions spelling out the various aspects or stages of the marriage process. The *matrimonium initiatum* results from the *desponsatio,* the engagement. This *matrimonium initiatum* is consumed, *consummatum*, by intercourse and thus perfected. The *matrimonium ratum* refers to the ratification of the marriage that fully establishes the sacrament of Christ and his Church and is therefore called *perfectum*.[58]

With Ivo, who may be regarded as one of the most radical representatives of the consensus theory,[59] no legal difference existed between marriage and engagement. Both are being established by mutual consent and are therefore unbreakable. Gratian on the contrary distinguishes clearly between them as they are given different grounds. The *desponsatio* expresses the mutual consent, marriage is based upon intercourse and public ratification. In analysing this distinction, the fundamentally different roles that are played by consensualism with both canonists come to the fore.

57. C. 27 q. 2 c.34/39; C. 28 q. 1 are present in the first recension: Winroth, *The Making*, 222.

58. C 27. q. 2 c. 34 : 'Sed sciendum est, quod coniugium desponsatione initiatur, commixtione perficitur. Unde inter sponsum et sponsam coniugium est, sed initiatur; inter copulatos est coniugium ratum.'; C. 27 q. 2 c. 39: 'Ad matrimonium perfectum subintelligendum est, tale videlicet, quod habeat in se Christi et ecclesiae sacramentum.... Quod sponsiali coniunctione est initiatum, et offitio coporalis conmixtionis est consummatum.'

59. H.J. Reinhardt, *Die Ehelehre der Schule des Anselms von Laon. Eine Theologie- und kirchengeschichtliche Untersuchung zu den Ehetexten der frühen Pariser Schule des 12. Jahrhunderts* (Münster: 1974), 78.

Ivo's consensualism as giving consent out of free will, is with Gratian reduced to the *desponsatio* and subsequently rendered virtually irrelevant. The marriage is only initiated by the *desponsatio*, but perfected by intercourse and finally as *matrimonium perfectum* by its official ratification that only takes place between two persons that are legally capable to enter into a contract. It is the official exchange of the mutual consent. Thus, the legal relevance of the *desponsatio* is being reduced and at the same time the meaning of the legal qualification of the consensus as the basis of marriage shifts from the free agreement of the parties to the act of ratification. In this sense the fundamental consensualist moment as it existed with Ivo has virtually disappeared.

The *matrimonium ratum* is further dealt with in C. 28 q. 1 dictum post c. 18 on how to qualify marriages between infidels.[60] Gratian addresses this problem by applying the difference between *legitimum* and *ratum*: a marriage can be legitimate but not ratified, ratified but not legitimate and legitimate and ratified.[61] *Legitimum* means: according to customs and law.[62] When a marriage is contracted according to current laws, is it legitimate. The fact that the parties may be infidels is irrelevant in this respect. This does however not automatically imply that the marriage is ratified, *ratum*. With regard to the ratification, that fact that the parties are faithful or infidels is highly important as a ratified marriage is only possible within the faith.[63]

The official nature of the ratification directly and simultaneously refers to its sacramental and institutional nature. Through its ratification, a marriage establishes the sacrament of Christ and of the Church. In other words, the institutional, official character of the ratification enacts its sacramental effectiveness. Therefore, it is precisely the ratification that makes a marriage into a bond that cannot be dissolved. It makes the marriage between faithful parties firm, invulnerable and unbreakable.[64] Thus, the source of the sacramental effectiveness of marriage lies in its ratification. The strong coincidence of the institutional and the sacramental Church comes clearly forward in this instance. The sacramental effectiveness is rephrased in terms of institutional acts that are developed as procedures. Whereas with Ivo the tension between the objective nature of marriage and its intentionalist basis remains intact, Gratian succeeds in

60. C. 28 q. 1 dicum post c. 18: 'an coniugium sit inter infideles'.
61. C. 28 q. 1 dictum post c. 18: 'Coniugium enim aliud est legitimum et non ratum, aliud ratum et non legitimum, aliud legitimum et ratum.'
62. C. 28 q. 1 dictum post c. 18: 'Legitimum coniugium est, quod legali institutione vel provinciae moribus contrahitur.'
63. C. 28 q. 1 dictum post c. 18: 'Non est ratum coniugium, quod sine Deo est.'
64. C. 28 q. 1 dictum post c. 18: Hoc inter infideles ratum non est, quia non est firmum et inviolabile... Inter fideles vero ratum coniugium est ; quia coniugia, semel inita inter eos, ulterius solvi non possunt.

merging together the need of an objective legitimacy to marriage with its intentionalist foundation, the consensus. The consensus between the parties and the objective confirmation of the marriage are in this sense caught together in the moment of ratification.

Thus, with Gratian the institutional order is just because it functions as a secular-type version of the traditional *ex opere operato* structure of the sacraments. The differences between the Cluniac and Gregorian concepts of what is justice and of what is the right order of power are thus reflected in the different status of the institutional and legal framework of the Church. In the Cluniac context, justice and power are ultimately transcendent realities, whereas in the Gregorian context they are paraphrased into an institutional context, a context that however derives its legitimacy from its being a paraphrase of transcendent justice and order.

WITHOUT WERE FIGHTINGS, WITHIN WERE FEARS

POPE GREGORY VII, THE CANONS REGULAR OF WATTEN AND THE REFORM OF THE CHURCH IN THE DIOCESE OF THÉROUANNE (C. 1075 - C. 1100)

Brigitte Meijns

1. Introduction

During the episcopacy of John of Warneton, which began in the summer of 1099 and ended with his death on 27 January 1130, the diocese of Thérouanne was a focal point of Church Reform in the North of France.[1] This dynamic Bishop advocated the introduction of the Cluniac customs in the Benedictine abbeys situated within his diocese, and he played an important part in the establishment of several convents and abbeys, among which was Dunes Abbey.[2] Having himself been a canon regular in Mont-Saint-Eloi, he was responsible for the transformation of a series of collegiate churches into communities of canons regular, living according to the Rule of Saint Augustine.[3] A student of Ivo, abbot of Saint-Quentin in Beauvais

1. For a recent and comprehensive biography of John of Warneton in English, see Walter of Thérouanne, *Walteri Archidiaconi Tervanensis Vita Karoli comitis Flandrie et Vita Domni Ioannis Morinensis Episcopi*, ed. J. Rider, Corpus Christianorum, Continuatio Mediaeualis, 217 (Turnhout, 2006), XXXV-XLII.
2. M. Dubuisson, J.-B. Lefèvre and J.-F. Nieus, 'Une lecture nouvelle des sources relatives aux origines pré-cisterciennes de l'abbaye des Dunes (1107-1138)', *Revue d'histoire ecclésiastique*, 97 (2002), 59-88 and 457-494, especially 477-480.
3. B. Meijns, *Aken of Jeruzalem? Het ontstaan en de hervorming van de kanonikale instellingen in Vlaanderen tot circa 1155* (Louvain, 2000), vol. 2, 748-769 and 795-803; B. Meijns, 'La réorientation du paysage canonial en Flandre et le pouvoir

(before 1079-1091) and later Bishop of Chartres (1091-1115), he remained very interested in Canon Law.[4] The *Collection in Nine Books* is commonly ascribed to John.[5] He possibly finished this collection, which is partly based on the *Collectio Atrebatensis* in the MS. Arras 425,[6] when he was archdeacon of Arras, between the start of 1096 and the summer of 1099. John probably inspired his young archdeacon and future hagiographer, Walter, to compose the *Collection in Ten Parts* (c. 1123), a revision of his own *Collection in Nine Books* which depends heavily on Ivo's *Panormia.*[7] Both canonical collections include decrees promulgated at the reform councils from Gregory VII up to Calixtus II, thus effectively promoting the cause of reform.[8] John was supported by a veritable 'reform circle', which included not only the Countess of Flanders, Clémence, and several abbots and provosts from his diocese, but also Anselm, Archbishop of Canterbury, the papal legate Hugo, Bishop of Die, and other reforming prelates from nearby dioceses, such as Lambert of Arras, Clarembald of Senlis, Godfrey of Amiens and Ivo of Chartres.[9] According to the saint's *vita*, written

---

des évêques, comtes et nobles (XIe siècle-première moité du XIIe siècle)', *Le Moyen Âge. Revue d'histoire et de philologie*, 112 (2006), 111-134, especially 116-117.

4. Walter of Thérouanne, *Vita Domni Ioannis Morinensis Episcopi*, (ed. Rider), 129 § [2] and 132 § [5].
5. For references to the manuscripts of this unpublished collection and further litterature: L. Fowler-Magerl, *Clavis Canonum. Selected Canon Law Collections Before 1140. Access with data processing*. Monumenta Germaniae Historica, Hilfsmittel 21 (Hannover, 2005), 207-209; L. Kéry, *Canonical Collections of the Early Middle Ages (ca. 400-1140). A Bibliographical Guide to the Manuscripts and Literature*. History of Medieval Canon Law 1 (Washington DC, 1999), 262-263.
6. Cf. Fowler-Magerl, *Clavis Canonum*, 206-207; Kéry, *Canonical Collections*, 279.
7. Cf. Fowler-Magerl, *Clavis Canonum*, 209-214; Kéry, *Canonical Collections*, 263-264.
8. P. Fournier and G. Le Bras, *Histoire des Collections canoniques en Occident depuis les Fausses Décrétales jusqu'au Décret de Gratien*. Bibliothèque d'Histoire du Droit, 4-5 (Paris, 1931-1932), vol. 2, 259-306; R. Somerville, *The Councils of Urban II* (Amsterdam, 1972), 56-64; J. Gilchrist, 'The Reception of Pope Gregory VII into Canon Law (1073-1141) Part II', *Zeitschrift für Rechtsgeschichte. Kanonistische Abteilung*, 66 (1980), 192-229, especially 209-211; R. Somerville and B.C. Brasington, *Prefaces to Canon Law Books in Latin Christianity. Selected Translations, 500-1245* (New Haven and London, 1998), 111-117; L. Waelkens and D. Van den Auweele, 'La collection de Thérouanne en IX livres à l'abbaye de Saint-Pierre-au-Mont-Blandin: le codex Gandavensis 235', *Sacris Erudiri*, 24 (1980), 115-153; R. Somerville, 'The councils of Pope Calixtus II and the Collection in Ten Parts', *Bulletin of Medieval Canon Law*, 2 (1981), 80-86.
9. Walter of Thérouanne, *Vita Domni Ioannis Morinensis Episcopi*, ed. Rider,131-132 § [5], 136 § [8], 139-140 § [11] and XXXIX-XL n. 86 with references to the correspondence between John of Thérouanne and other reforming bishops; Simon of Saint Bertin, *Gesta abbatum Sancti Bertini Sithiensium*, ed. O. Holder-Egger, Monumenta Germaniae Historica, 13 (Hannover, 1881), 647, § 57.

shortly after John's death by Archdeacon Walter, Pope Paschal II counted John *inter charissimos.*[10] All these elements made the diocese of Thérouanne during the reign of John of Warneton into a pioneer of innovation within the Church.

However, this had not always been the case. John's four immediate predecessors had either been driven from office, or been deposed.[11] It all began at the Council of Poitiers in January 1078, when the aged Bishop Drogo was deposed after an episcopacy of more than 45 years. He died in August of that same year. His successor, archdeacon Hubert of Thérouanne, was not at all reform-minded.[12] This stubborn character very quickly managed to be at loggerheads with just about everyone, including Count Robert I of Flanders and Pope Gregory VII. After an attempt on his life, he retreated to the Abbey of Saint Bertin in 1081. Following this, Count Robert proposed a candidate of his own, Lambert, the cantor of the comital chapter of Saint Peter in Lille, whom he installed in the cathedral by force, despite the resistance of the clergy and the people of Thérouanne.[13] Notwithstanding several letters of Gregory VII and the excommunication for simony of Lambert at the Council of Meaux in 1082, the count continued to support the bishop and to persecute his opponents. The situation escalated when two knights looted the cathedral and maimed the bishop. Shortly afterwards, at the end of 1083, Lambert died, after having been bishop for barely two years. Peace and quiet more or less returned to the diocese under his successor, Gerard, the former archdeacon of Cambrai.[14] Still, Gerard was suspended at the Council of Nîmes in 1096 because of suspected simony at the time of his appointment. He was deposed in 1099, after which he retreated among the canons regular of

10. Walter of Thérouanne, *Vita Domni Ioannis Morinensis Episcopi*, ed. Rider, 144 § [14]: 'Sane apud beatę memorię Paschalem papam tantam obtinuerat familiaritatem ut eum inter charissimos semper habuerit.'

11. For this turbulent history: A. Giry, 'Grégoire VII et les évêques de Thérouane', *Revue historique*, 1 (1876), 387-409; H. Van Werveke, *Het Bisdom Terwaan van den oorsprong tot het begin van de veertiende eeuw*, Recueil de travaux publiés par la Faculté de philosophie et lettres de l'Université de Gand 52 (Ghent, 1924), 45-48; É. De Moreau, *Histoire de l'Eglise en Belgique*, vol. 2 (Bruxelles: , 1945-1952), 65-68; H.E.J. Cowdrey, *Pope Gregory VII. 1073-1085* (Oxford, 1998), 345-348 and 410-413.

12. N. Huyghebaert, 'Un légat de Grégoire VII en France: Warmond de Vienne', *Revue d'histoire ecclésiastique*, 30 (1944-1945), 187-200.

13. C. Verlinden, *Robert Ier le Frison, comte de Flandre. Etude d'histoire politique*, Universiteit te Gent, Werken uitgegeven door de Faculteit der Wijsbegeerte en Letteren 72 (Antwerp, Paris and The Hague, 1925), 119-124; Cowdrey, *Pope Gregory VII*, 346-348.

14. C. Dereine, 'Gérard, évêque de Thérouanne (1083-1096), face aux moines exempts. Le cas des prieurés de Nieppe, Andres et Framecourt', *Mémoires de la Société d'histoire de Comines-Warneton et de la région*, 10 (1980), 249-262.

Mont-Saint-Eloi, where his successor, John of Thérouanne, had also lived for some time.

In this article, I will examine how an originally conservative and turbulent diocese developed into a pioneer of reform in the space of a few decades. The topic will be approached by looking at the reception of the decrees concerning simony, that is the buying and selling of clerical offices, objects and liturgical acts, and nicolaitism, the non-observance of celibacy by members of the clergy, which had been promulgated by Gregory VII at the Lenten Synods of 1074 and 1075.[15] Even though both customs had been firmly rooted in the diocese of Thérouanne, married, concubinal and simoniacal priests were henceforth banned from saying mass, and the faithful were urged to avoid all contact with these clerics, who were deigned to be unworthy. Several contemporary sources allow us to discover how the new guidelines were implemented in the diocese of Thérouanne. A crucial role was reserved for the young community of canons regular in Watten, on the Flemish coastal plain. Canons of this new type revealed themselves to be ardent supporters of Church reform, as a result of which they repeatedly clashed with the conservative ecclesiastical establishment, despite continued papal support and exceptional privileges. In what follows, I will argue that the priory of canons regular of Watten served as a catalyst of Church reform, slowly but steadily creating the climate in which the reform-minded bishop, John of Warneton, could develop his activities without hindrance

2. The first community of canons regular in the county of Flanders

Around 1070, a Flemish wandering priest called Odfrid settled in Watten on a hill on the coastal plain to the north of Saint-Omer.[16] There, he wanted to

---

15. A small selection from the vast literature concerning the 11th and 12th century Church reform: A. Fliche, *La réforme grégorienne,* 2 vols (Louvain, 1924-1937); G. Tellenbach, *The Church in western Europe from the tenth to the early twelfth century* (Cambridge, 1993); G. Constable, *The Reformation of the Twelfth Century* (Cambridge, 1996); W. Goez, *Kirchenreform und Investiturstreit 910-1122* (Stuttgart: , 2000); I.S. Robinson, 'Reform and the Church, 1073-1122' in: *The New Cambridge Medieval History, IV, c. 1024-c.1198. Part I,* ed. D. Luscombe and J. Riley-Smith (Cambridge, 2004), 268-334 (with extensive bibliography).
16. C. Dereine, 'Les prédicateurs apostoliques dans les diocèses de Thérouanne, Tournai et Cambrai-Arras durant les années 1075-1125', *Analecta Praemonstratensia*, 54 (1983), 171-189, especially 173-175; idem, 'étude critique des chartes accordées par Robert I (1072) et Robert II (1093) de Flandre à l'abbaye de Watten', *Revue bénédictine*, 93 (1983), 80-107, especially 80; B. Meijns, 'De *pauperes Christi* van Watten. De moeizame beginjaren van de eerste gemeenschap van reguliere kanunniken in Vlaanderen (vóór 1072-ca. 1100)', *Jaarboek voor Middeleeuwse Geschiedenis*, 3 (2000), 44-91; B. Meijns, '*Inaudita novitas*

bring the *vita apostolica* into practice with a small group of followers by living in poverty, celibacy and close community, according to the Rule of Saint Augustine. The life he envisioned was that of the canons regular.[17] This new type of canons owed their existence to a reform movement within the canonical order which considered the traditional life of canons as far too lax. Ever since the Carolingian Church reform, all canons lived according to the *Institutio canonicorum*, promulgated by Louis the Pious at the Council of Aachen in 816. Even though the Rule of Aachen advocated community life as an ideal, it allowed private property and offered the possibility to live in private houses, thus undermining the *vita communis*. However, floating along on the waves of the general 11th century Church reform, certain canons in Italy and Southern France began to think that canonical life might also benefit from a reinterpretation. The reformers harked back to the dawn of Christianity. The preachings of Christ and the lives of the Apostles as well as the first Christians in Jerusalem provided an ideal to be followed. Hoping to attain the ideal of *Cor unum et anima una* – one of heart and one of soul – they renounced all private property and lived a true *vita communis*. To distinguish themselves from their colleagues who remained faithful to the Rule of Aachen, henceforth called canons secular, the reformers called themselves canons regular and chose one of the rules attributed to Saint Augustine as a guiding principle for their new communities.

Around 1070, at the time when canons regular took up residence in Watten, this form of canonical life was a conspicuous novelty in the area. Not only was the priory of Watten the first foundation of regular canons within the diocese of Thérouanne, it was also the first within the entire county of Flanders, which comprised the present day Belgian provinces West-Vlaanderen and Oost-Vlaanderen and the French departments of Nord and Pas-de-Calais. A few years later, another community of regular canons would originate in Mont-Saint-Eloi near Arras, in the south of the county.[18]

---

canonici ordinis. L'accueil des idées de réforme canoniale dans les milieux canoniaux du comté de Flandre pendant le dernier quart du onzième siècle', *Revue Mabillon, Revue internationale d'histoire et de littérature religieuses. Nouvelle Série*, XVIII (2007), 39-71.

17. C. Dereine, 'Vie commune, règle de Saint-Augustin et chanoines réguliers au XIe siècle', *Revue d'histoire ecclésiastique*, 41 (1946), 365-406; Idem., 'Chanoines', *Dictionnaire d'histoire et de géographie ecclésiastiques*, 12, 1953, col. 375-405; J.C. Dickinson, *The origins of the Austin canons and their introduction into England*, (London, 1959); C.W. Bynum, 'The Spirituality of the Regular Canons in the Twelfth Century' in: *Jesus as mother: Studies in the Spirituality of the High Middle Ages* (Berkeley/Los Angeles/London, 1977-1980); J. Châtillon, *Le mouvement canonial au Moyen Âge. Réforme de l'église, spiritualité et culture. Etudes réunies par P. Sicard*, Bibliotheca Victoriana 3 (Paris and Turnhout, 1992).

18. A. De Cardevacque, *L'abbaye de Mont-Saint-éloi 1068-1792* (Arras: 1859); O. Barubé, *L'abbaye du Mont-Saint-éloi des origines au XIVe siècle* (Poitiers, 1977); B. Meijns, '*Inaudita novitas canonici ordinis*', 42-46.

In Mont-Saint-Eloi John of Warneton sought an apostolic life before becoming archdeacon of Arras in 1096 and bishop of Thérouanne in 1099.[19] Chronologically, the foundation of Watten was preceded by similar initiatives during the 1060s in Paris and the south of the archdiocese of Rheims.[20] In 1072 the priory of Watten received charters of confirmation from Bishop Drogo of Thérouanne and Count Robert I of Flanders. A crucial role in the foundation process was played by the old Dowager Countess Adela and by her son Count Robert. Everything leads us to suspect that Watten was founded with their explicit approval.[21] The difficult start of the priory can be assessed thanks to the detailed foundation chronicle, the *Exordium Guatinensis ecclesiae*, or *The Beginnings of the Church of Watten*, written by an anonymous local canon in the closing years of the 11th Century.[22] Although this foundation chronicle was composed a generation after the events it describes, by an author who had not himself lived through those early days, it is still a precious source. According to his own words, the author spoke with older brothers who remembered the beginnings, and he also had the archive of his priory at his disposal. Moreover, several elements from his story are confirmed by other, independent sources. Like the authors of similar *historiae fundationis*, the anonymous canon from Watten also had a clear aim: to commemorate the difficult first years and the persistence of the first brethren, for the benefit of later generations.

3. Opposition to the Gregorian fervour of the brethren of Watten

It was precisely the novelty of their way of life which was at the core of the conflict in which the priory of Watten was involved during its early years. From the start, the canons regular were staunch defenders of the Gregorian reform in an area where the latest ideas within the Church and within the canonical order had barely penetrated. The foundation chronicle shows that the brethren's radical ideas and Gregorian fervour were met with a downright lack of understanding and violent resistance.[23] According to the

19. Walter of Thérouanne , *Vita Domni Ioannis Morinensis Episcopi*, ed. Rider, 130 § [4].
20. Meijns, '*Inaudita novitas canonici ordinis*', 42-46.
21. Meijns, 'De *pauperes Christi* van Watten', 57-62.
22. *Chronica monasterii Watinensis*, ed. O. Holder-Egger, MGH, Scriptores, 14 (Hannover, 1883), 161-175. Following the example of Dereine, 'étude critique', 83, I refer to this chronicle by using the initial words of the text: *Exordium Guatinensis ecclesiae*. P. Ruyffelaere, 'Les *historiae fundationum monasteriorum* et leurs sources orales au XIIe siècle', *Sacris Erudiri*, 29 (1986), 223-247, especially 234.
23. *Chronica monasterii Watinensis*, ed. Holder-Egger, 171 § 18: 'Nam huic successit incommodo totius fere provinciae contra nos, maxime autem clericorum, conflata

Exordium, the conflict erupted after the Lenten Synods of 1074-1075. The canons of Watten were blamed for the fact that they followed the reform decrees more strictly than all others. In accordance with the prescriptions, the community of Watten refused any contact with married priests who celebrated mass, and with clerics guilty of simony. However, this attitude was not appreciated by the *clerici vicini.* The scapegoat became Prior Odfrid, who suffered abuse and insults on a daily basis. Moreover, the opponents kept threatening to destroy the priory. The author of the *Exordium* strongly voiced the fear that had entered the hearts of the Watten canons: 'Without were fightings, within were fears'.[24] Not even a single hour was spent in safety. We feared rocks from one direction, arrows from the other, and all-consuming flames from elsewhere'.[25] The quotation from the second letter of Paul to the Corinthians (2 Cor 7, 5) – *foris pugnae, intus timore*, 'without were fightings, within were fears' – he complemented with the image of a community threatened by stones, arrows and arson. If he is to be believed, the enemies of Watten intended nothing less than the complete destruction of the priory. However, according to the author, God provided a shield for its defence, in the person of the Dowager Countess Adela, a lady inspired by heaven itself.[26] Ever since the priory had been founded, she had

---

suspicio, quia mandatorum apostolicorum plus aemulatores pre ceteris videbamur, videlicet de non suscipiendis ad missas faciendas uxoratis sacerdotibus, de incestuosis et simoniacis vitandis, tum etiam de aliis capitulis, quae in decreto Gregorii papae septimi distinguuntur, servandis, atque ob hoc velut incentorem huius commotionis domnum Odfridum odiis, opprobriis ac maledictionibus insectabantur, ut, preter illa quae ubique disseminando verbum Dei foris patiebatur convicia, comprovinciales et clerici vicini caedes, incendia, exterminium exitiale cotidie domi nobis comminarentur.' 'This misfortune was followed by a suspicion, stirred up against us by the entire (church) province, but most of all by the clerics, because we seemed more eager than others to follow the apostolical mandates concerning the non acceptance of married priests celebrating masses, concerning the avoidance of incestuous and simoniacal clerics and all other topics mentioned in the decree of Pope Gregory VII. Therefore they pursued master Odfrid with hatred, reproaches and abuse, as if he were the inciter of the commotion, so that, besides the outcries he endured by preaching the Word of God everywhere in the outside world, the inhabitants of the province and the nearby clerics threatened our home on a daily basis with bloodshed, arson and fatal destruction.'

24. Cf. 2 Corinthians 7,5 in the King James Version of the Bible: 'For, when we were come into Macedonia, our flesh had no rest, but we were troubled on every side; without were fightings, within were fears'.
25. *Chronica monasterii Watinensis*, ed. Holder-Egger, 171 § 18: 'Ita foris pugnae, intus timores, vix aliqua securi inter vivendum hora. Hinc, ut aiunt, lapides, inde sagittas, aliunde consumpturas omnia flammas timebamus.'
26. On Adela's generosity towards Watten: *Chronica monasterii Watinensis*, ed. Holder-Egger, 168 § 11: 'femina caelitus inspirata' and 168 § 12; Cf. N. Huyghebaert, 'Les femmes laïques dans la vie religieuse des XIe et XIIe siècles dans la province ecclésiastique de Reims' in: *I laici nella "Societas christiana' dei secoli XI e XII. Atti della terza Settimane internazionale di studio, Mendola 21-27*

been very closely involved. The widow of count Baldwin V had personally followed the construction of the monastic buildings and she had more than once saved the community from financial disaster. Now, Adela conceived the idea of asking Pope Gregory VII himself to grant the priory a written confirmation.[27] Despite her advanced age, she and Odfrid crossed the Alps to see the pope. Adela and Odfrid met the pope in the abbey of Nonantola, close to Modena in Emilia-Romagna. The bull in favour of Watten, which Gregory VII gave to Prior Odfrid, has been preserved in the Watten cartulary.[28] At that time, the pope was on his way home after the encounter with the German King Henry IV at Canossa in January of that year.[29] The moment when the bull was composed, 28 April 1077, allows us to conclude that the canons had for at least two years, maybe even three, stubbornly persevered in obeying the Lenten decrees. Armed with the bull and, no doubt, comforted by the remarkable contents of the document, Adela and Odfrid returned to Watten.

But the problems did not abate. On the contrary, their enemies became even more enraged when they learned about the contents of the papal bull. Indeed, next to the usual apostolic protection the pope had granted all Priors of Watten the *potestas ligandi atque solvendi* (the power of binding and loosing), as well as the authority to preach the Word of God everywhere (the *licentia praedicandi*).[30] According to the *Exordium*, both prerogatives met with the displeasure of the clergy of Thérouanne. Especially the fact that Odfrid had now the power to bind and loose, was unacceptable to them. They accused the Prior of Watten of usurping episcopal power: henceforth, the bishop would exert episcopal authority only in name; in reality, all authority would lie with the canons of Watten, as a result of the stipulations of the papal privilege.[31] The world turned upside down! The only thing the

---

agosto 1965. Miscellanea del Centro di Studi Medioevali 5, (Milan, 1968), 346-389, here, 374-383.

27. *Chronica monasterii Watinensis*,ed. Holder-Egger, 171 § 18.

28. J. Ramackers, *Papsturkunden in Frankreich, Neue Folge, 3. Artois*, Abhandlungen der Akademie der Wissenschaften zu Göttingen, Philologisch-Historische Klasse, Dritte Folge, 23 (Göttingen, 1940), 34-36 nr. 3; J. Ramackers, 'Analekten zur Geschichte des Papsttums im 11. Jahrhundert', *Quellen und Forschungen aus italienischen Archiven und Bibliotheken,* 25 (1933-1934) , 46-61, here 56-60.

29. A. Mercati, 'Gregorio VII a Nonantola', *Studi Gregoriani*, 1, Rome, (1947), 413-416; Cowdrey, *Pope Gregory VII*, 158-166; Cf. C. Stiegemann and M. Wemhoff, *Canossa 1077. Erschütterung der Welt. Geschichte, Kunst und Kultur am Aufgang der Romanik. Band I. Essays* (München, 2006).

30. Cf. *infra* n. 39.

31. *Chronica monasterii Watinensis*, ed. Holder-Egger, 171 § 19: 'Nec clam [in conventiculis] per se conferentes, capita cleri atque ipsum episcopum concitant, auctoritatem ligandi atque solvendi Romano libellatico prepositum nostrum suscepisse accusant, huiusmodi privilegio, si roboratum sit, ius episcopali destrui, de cetero solo nomine episcopum militare, Guatinenses imperare, summa imis commutari, inversa omnia, caput in caudam, nichil iam deesse preter infulas

Watten brothers did not yet have, was the episcopal ornaments; this was, according to the *Exordium*, the lament of the opponents. Those same opponents called for a thorough investigation of the document in question during a meeting of the clergy in the presence of the old Bishop Drogo of Thérouanne. When this opportunity presented itself, the brothers from Watten duly produced their papal bull. After it had been read aloud, the document was snatched from them, and tucked away in the book-case of the bishop, out of their reach.[32] Odfrid, who was considered to have been the perfidious composer of the document, was showered with insults, and was sent away by the crowd, without having been heard.[33]

Now that the priory had been 'beheaded', so the *Exordium* tells us, the community became even more the target of abuse and reproaches, public insults, threats, terror and ridicule.[34] But the author admired the constancy, *constantia*, of the orphaned canons who manfully resisted so much disaster. Not at any moment did they stray from their strict way of life, the *canonica vita*, which was considered to be the *regia via*, the 'royal way'.[35] Some visited Bishop Drogo and asked him why he had made the community a laughing-stock, and why he had allowed its existence to be threatened by the machinations of the enemy. Had the bishop forgotten that in 1072, he

---

episcopales.' 'They no longer held secret meetings, but they incited the heads of the clergy and even the bishop himself. They accused our prior of having accepted the authority to bind and loose by the Roman document. If this privilege were to be corroborated, episcopal right would be destroyed and, henceforth, the bishop would hold his function only nominally, while those from Watten would command. The highest would be exchanged for the lowest, the inversion of everything, the head would become the tail. The only thing they would still lack, were the episcopal ornaments.'

32. *Chronica monasterii Watinensis*, ed. Holder-Egger, 171 § 19: 'Defertur, legitur et velut adulterinum cum violentia atque iniuria, sine iure, sine iudicio trahitur, rapitur et in armario episcopi recluditur.' 'The document was presented, read aloud and, as it were not genuine, with violence and injury, without justice, without a judicial sentence, carried off, robbed and shut up in the closet of the bishop.'
33. *Chronica monasterii Watinensis*, ed. Holder-Egger, 171 § 19.
34. *Chronica monasterii Watinensis*, ed. Holder-Egger, 171 § 20.
35. *Chronica monasterii Watinensis*, ed. Holder-Egger, 171 § 20: 'Consolabatur tamen in filiorum qui residui erant constantia, quia viriliter resistentes omnibus quae acciderant infortuniis, canonicae vitae a regia via non exorbitabant, [...] episcopum adeunt, rogant, expostulant, incusant, cur scilicet Guatinensem ecclesiam ludibrio habitam sine lege fecisset, cur iniquorum machinatione destruere moliretur quo ipse fecisset...' 'Yet, the constancy of the remaining brethren was as source of consolation, because they manfully resisted all adversities they encountered and because they did not stray from the royal way of the canonical life [...] they went to the bishop, asking him, begging him and disapproving why he had made the church of Watten a laughing-stock without any law and why he exerted himself, along with the machinations of enemies, to destroy what he himself had made.'

himself had issued a charter confirming the existence of the community?[36] They begged the bishop to return the privilege. The property of the abbey, which had apparently been confiscated, was to be returned, and their possessions were to be reconfirmed. In short, the bishop was to keep from further thwarting the attempts of the disciples, now that their father, Odfrid, had been sent away in disgrace.[37] This approach was successful. It seems that the bishop was finally prepared to reinvestigate the matter, and to give the canons a hearing. In order to fully understand the exact contents of the papal bull, they sent for Ingelrannus, a secular canon from the church of Our Lady in Saint-Omer.[38] Ingelrannus had often stayed at the papal court of Gregory VII and was well-acquainted with the contents of apostolic privileges. At a new gathering of the Church of Thérouanne, he explained the text with great acuity. The opponents had no other option than to give in and leave the canons in peace.

4. The bull of Gregory VII and its remarkable contents

At stake in the conflict described above was the observance of the new guidelines issued by the reform-minded papacy, and hence of the ideas of the Gregorian reform. The bull of Gregory VII provoked a culmination of the conflict. The content of this document confirms the *Exordium*. Gregory

36. Cf. the charter of confirmation from Bishop Drogo (1072): Saint-Omer, *Bibliothèque Municipale*, ms. 852, f° 166 v°-167v°; *Chronica monasterii Watinensis*, ed. Holder-Egger, 167-168 § 11.

37. *Chronica monasterii Watinensis*, ed. Holder-Egger, 172 § 20.'

38. *Chronica monasterii Watinensis*, ed. Holder-Egger, 172 § 20: 'Intererat huic altercationi filius sanctae Romanae ecclesiae I[ngelramnus] Sancti-Audomarensis canonicus, quem in sacro palatio cum venerandae memoriae Gregorio papa septimo non parvo tempore commoratum et novimus et splendide peregrinatum vidimus. Qui Romuleos apices, reserata carta [...] acumine clariori quid continerent intuitus, rata interpretatione sine difficultate resolvit et, oppilato refragantium ore, Guatinensi ecclesiae, tultum privilegium resignari habundanti ratione convicit. Sic igitur restituti ac grate postliminium reversi, deinceps habundanti ratione libertatem nostram a nemine rescivimus cauponari.' 'During the conflict I[ngelrannus], a son of the holy Roman church and a canon of Saint-Omer, was present, of whom we know that he often stayed in the holy palace with Pope Gregory VII, of venerable memory, and whom we saw travelling with distinction. After the document was produced, he [...] scrutinized the contents of the Roman letter with a clear acuity and he interpreted and explained it without any difficulty. After the opponents had been silenced, he convincingly showed that the protection charter had to be given back to the church of Watten. Thus restored and gratefully returned [to our rights] we thereupon learned with abundant reason that no one was allowed to violate our freedom.' More on Ingelrannus: Giry, 'Grégoire VII et les évêques de Thérouane', 387-409; Huyghebaert, 'Un légat de Grégoire VII', 195; Verlinden, *Robert Ier,* 116-122; De Moreau, *Histoire de l'Eglise*, 2, 65; Cowdrey, *Pope Gregory VII,* 345-348.

VII did grant the priors of Watten the *potestas ligandi atque solvendi*, as well as the *licentia praedicandi.*[39] The power of binding and loosing, the power given by Christ to his Apostles according to the Gospel of Matthew (Mt. 16, 19 and 18, 18), refers to the sacrament of confession.[40] As direct heirs to the apostles, the bishops of the Early Church obtained the authority to absolve penitents and the power to spread the Word of God.[41] During the early Middle Ages, the bishops entrusted their diocesan clergy with these duties.[42]Forming a part of the *cura animarum*, these powers were closely connected as preaching was meant to incite the auditor to repent of his or her sins.[43]

---

39. J. Ramackers, *Papsturkunden,* 35 nr. 3: 'Qua de causa hoc libertatis donatiuum sub nomine dotis concedimus et perhenniter confirmamus ex parte Iesu Christi domini nostri sanctique Petri apostoli ac nostri uidelicet omnes prepositos illius habere potestatem ligandi atque soluendi ac ubique uerbum Dei predicandi, ut cotidie in illo loco celebretur memoria nominis mei'. 'For that reason we confer this gift of freedom under the name of a dowry/gift and we eternally confirm, on behalf of Jesus Christ Our Lord, of the Apostle St. Peter and on our behalf, that all provosts of that place shall have the power to bind and loose and the power to spread the Word of God everywhere, in order that the memory of my name shall be celebrated there daily.' Cf. U-R. Blumenthal, *Gregor VII. Papst zwischen Canossa und Kirchenreform* (Darmstadt, 2001), 41 and 257; H. Seibert, 'Kommunikation – Autorität – Recht – Lebensordnung. Das Papsttum und die monastisch-kanonikale Reformbewegung (1046-1124)' in: *Vom Umbruch zur Erneuerung? Das 11. und beginnende 12. Jahrhundert – Positionen der Forschung*, ed. J. Jarnut and M. Wemhoff, (Munich, 2006), 11-29, especially 21.
40. P. Bernard, 'Confession (du concile de Latran au concile de Trente)', *Dictionnaire de Théologie catholique*, (Paris: , 1911), vol. 3, col. 894-925, especially col. 894-898; J.-B. Belt, 'Absolution, d'après l'écriture sainte', *Dictionnaire de Théologie catholique* (Paris, 1909), vol. 1, col. 138-145 especially col. 138-140.
41. On the attribution of the power of binding and loosing to the successors of the Apostles, cf. Jonas of Orleans, *De institutione regia*, ed. J.P. Migne, *Patrologia Latina* 106, (Paris, 1851), col 286: 'Quod potestas et auctoritas absolvendi et ligandi sacerdotibus, id est successoribus apostolorum, a Christo sit attributa, evangelica patenter declarat lectio, quod et vestrae sapientiae non ignorat plenitudo'. G. Le Bras, *Institutions ecclésiastiques de la Chrétienté médiévale*, Histoire de l'Eglise, 12, (Paris, 1964) 366-367.
42. Since the Merovingian Council of Vaison (529, canon 2) preaching was considered to be an obligation, not only of the episcopacy but also of the entire priesthood. *Les canons des conciles Mérovingiens (VIe-VIIe siècles)*, ed. J. Gaudemet and B. Basdevant (Paris, 1989), vol. 2, 190-191. On the delegation of the power of binding and loosing from the bishops to the priesthood, see the treatise by Bernold of Constance, *De presbyteris*, ed. F. Thaner, MGH, Libelli de Lite 2, (Hannover, 1892), 142-146 which discusses the origin of this assignment. The treatise was written in answer to a question from the canons regular of Rottenbuch in Bavaria. More on Bernold, cf. *infra.*
43. G.G. Meersseman, 'Eremitismo e predicazione itinerante dei secoli XI e XII' in: *L'eremitismo in Occidente nei secoli XI e XII. Atti della seconda Settimana internazionale die studio. Mendola, 30 agosto-6 settembre 1962*, Pubblicazioni dell'Universita' Cattolica del Sacro Cuore. Contributi - serie terza, varia 4.

In the case of Watten, it is not surprising that the conferral of these powers would have been badly received by the local clergy, who grudgingly had to accept a serious competitor when it came to preaching, hearing confessions and granting absolution to the penitents. Not only did the parochial clergy, in all probability, consider the activity of the prior of Watten as an undesirable infringement on their assignment, the situation might also have resulted in a lack of income for them.[44] Moreover, as the priory of Watten was an important centre for the dissemination of reforming ideas, one might assume that the preachings of Odfrid dealt with the attack on simony, nicolaitism and lay interference. When treating these issues in his sermons, he, just as other penitential preachers, inevitably had to criticise the current state of affairs in the local church, especially the lifestyle of the clergy and the problem of clerical marriage or concubinage. In this conservative diocese, his message would have been unwelcome and rejected. In addition, the bishop and his entourage also would have been displeased with the situation as the direct papal intervention had crossed the episcopal prerogative to grant authorisation to preach in the diocese and to impose penitence.[45]

Even if conferring these powers to a prior of a community of canons regular was remarkable, it was not completely unheard-of in those days. Wederic, a priest and a monk of the Ghent abbey of Saint Peter, is believed to have received the *licentia praedicandi* from Gregory VII. One of the results of his preaching tour in Flanders and Brabant was the conversion to monastic life of six knights, culminating in the foundation of the Benedictine abbey of Affligem (before 1083) just over the Flemish border in the Duchy of Brabant.[46] On the basis of this, Gregory VII is considered to

---

Miscellanea del centro di Studi Medioevali 4, (Milan, 1965), 164-179 and following disscussion on 180-181; E. Werner, *Pauperes Christi. Studien zu sozial-religiösen Bewegungen im Zeitalter des Reformpapsttums* (Leipzig, 1957), 41-52; H. Leyser, *Hermits and the New Monasticism. A study of Religious Communities in Western Europe 1000-1150* (New York, 1984), 69-77.

44. On the opposition of the secular clergy to itinerant preachers and to pastoral functions fulfilled by monks or canons regular: L. Raison and R. Niderst, 'Le mouvement érémitique dans l'ouest de la France à la fin du XIe siècle et au début du XIIe', *Annales de Bretagne. Revue publiée par la Faculté des Lettres de Rennes*, 55 (1948) 1-46, here 26-30; Dereine, 'Les prédicateurs apostoliques', 184; B. Beck, *Saint Bernard de Tiron, l'ermite, le moine et le monde* (Cormelles-le-Royal, 1998), 202-211.

45. Werner, *Pauperes Christi*, 190 who refers to a sermon of Bernard of Clairvaux warning the faithful only to receive preachers sent by the pope or the bishop ordinary and not to put their trust in foreign or unknown preachers; Meersseman, 'Eremitismo', 164-179.

46. *Chronicon Affligemense*, G.H. Pertz, ed. (MGH SS, IX) (Hannover, 1851), 407-408: 'Horum unus fuit Wedericus, sacerdos et monachus s. Petri Gandensis coenobii, [...] qui apostolicae auctoritatis licentia Flandriam et Brabantia provincias

be the first pope to license public preachers.[47] Urban II followed in his footsteps, commissioning the wandering preacher Robert of Arbrissel (†1116) to preach in 1096 and Paschal II granted Bernard of Thiron († 1116), another *Wanderprediger*, the *licentia praedicandi*, the right to hear confession, to impose penances and to baptize in 1101.[48] Another example is Norbert of Xanten († 1134) to whom Pope Gelasius in all probability conferred the preaching licence in 1118.[49] According to the *Exordium*, Odfrid had also been a wandering preacher before he decided to establish a community of canons regular in Watten.[50]

However, there is one crucial difference between the above mentioned examples and the prior of Watten. In the cases of Wederic, Bernard of Tiron, Robert of Arbrissel and Norbert of Xanten, the bestowal of the *licentia praedicandi* is recorded in chronicles or hagiographical sources, written some time after the facts. In the case of Watten, we dispose over the pontifical privilege itself conferring the authority to preach and absolve sins. Moreover, in this case, the grant was not a singular event and the beneficiary was not just a specific person. By extending the privilege to Odfrid's successors as priors of Watten, Pope Gregory VII wanted to guarantee the continued existence of reform preaching in this part of Christendom, thus giving publicity to the long term new papal policies and the Gregorian standards of moral and spiritual life.

Equally the power of binding and loosing could be entrusted to certain pious persons by the pope. For instance, Aibert (†1140), a priest-monk from

---

circuibat, verbum Dei disseminando et populum Dei a peccatis sua praedicatione convertendo. Cf. Dereine, 'Les prédicateurs apostoliques', 171-189, here 175-178.

47. Meersseman, 'Eremitismo', 164-179; Leyser, *Hermits*, 75; P.G. Jestice, *Wayward Monks and the Religious revolution of the Eleventh Century* (Leiden - New York - Cologne, 1997), 280-282.

48. *Robert of Arbrissel. A Medieval Religious Life.*, trans. B. L. Venarde (Washington, D.C., 2003), 14 § 13, from the *First Life* by Baudri of Dol; Cf. J. Longère, 'Robert d'Arbrissel prédicateur' in *Robert d'Arbrissel et la vie religieuse dans l'ouest de la France. Actes du colloque de Fontevraud 13-16 décembre 2001, ed.* J. Dalarun (Turnhout, 2004), 87-104, here 88-89; Beck, *Saint Bernard de Tiron,* 204-206 and p. 374-377 § 59 according to the *vita* by Geoffroy le Gros; Cf. J. von Walter, *Die ersten Wanderprediger Frankreichs. Studien zur Geschichte des Mönchtums*, 2 vols (Leipzig, 1903-1906); Werner, *Pauperes Christi*, 45, rejects the authenticity of the pontifical permission to preach and dismisses it as an invention of the hagiographers to legitimize the activities of their heroes because, according to this author, the reform papacy did not want to collaborate with the movement of apostolic poverty. Raison and Niderst, 'Le mouvement érémitique', 22-30; Leyser, *Hermits*, 75.

49. However, the next year, Calixtus II is said to have refused to renew the licence Gelasius had granted to Norbert in 1118. Meersseman, 'Eremitismo', 164-179; Leyser, *Hermits*, 74-75; Dereine, 'Les prédicateurs apostoliques', 179-182.

50. *Chronica monasterii Watinensis*, ed. Holder-Egger, 65-166 § 4-5; Dereine, 'Les prédicateurs apostoliques', 173-175.

Crespin and hermit in Scopignies in the County of Hainaut, was granted by Paschal II and Honorius II the right to hear confession and grant absolution. In 1131 Innocent II confirmed the conferral of this authority in a privilege destined for Aibert's hermitage.[51] Gaucher of Aureil († 1140), a hermit-preacher from the Limousin obtained from Urban II the permission to absolve sinners (*consulendi peccatores*) in Limoges c. 1095-1096.[52] More contemporary to Odfrid was Bernold of Constance († 1100), a monk of the German Benedictine abbey of St. Blasien and later Schaffhausen, and a fervent supporter of the Gregorian cause, who upon his priestly ordination in 1084 received from Cardinal Odo of Ostia, the later Pope Urban II, the power to reconcile penitents (*ad suscipiendos penitentes ex apostolica auctoritate*).[53] According to some scholars this included the rare power to absolve the excommunicated.[54] It is not clear whether Odfrid and his successors might also have possessed this far-reaching power, which is normally an exclusive right of the bishop, or whether they were only entitled to absolve penitents after confession.

But there was more. In the same document, Gregory VII called the community of Watten 'a refuge and a place of consolation and support for any believer whomsoever'.[55] Anyone who wanted to do so could go to

51. *Patrologia Latina*, ed. J.-P. Migne (Paris, 1851), 95, col. 104: 'Quia veridica relatione comperi te a praedecessoribus meis sanctissimis viris Paschali et Honorio licentiam accepisse poenitentiam dare, et absolutionem facere confitentibus peccata sua, eamdem tibi potestatem auctoritate Dei et beati Petri apostoli et nostra concedimus, rogans dilectionem tuam ut memor sis nostri in orationibus tuis.' 'Because I have learned from a reliable account that you have received from my predecessors, the most holy men Paschal and Honorius, the licence of imposing penances and granting absolution to the penitents for their sins, I concede thee this power by the authority of God, of the holy Apostle Peter and ourselves, asking you, our beloved one, that you will remember us in your prayers.' Dereine, 'Les prédicateurs apostoliques', 182-185.
52. J. Becquet, 'L'érémitisme clérical et laïc dans l'ouest de la France' in: *L'eremitismo in Occidente*, here 197; Longère, 'Robert d'Arbrissel prédicateur', 89.
53. *Die Chroniken Bertholds von Reichenau und Bernolds von Konstanz, 1054-1100*, ed. I. S. Robinson, MGH, Scriptores Rerum Germanicarum, n.s., 14 (Hannover, 2003), 338-339 (ad annum 1084).
54. According to I. S. Robinson, 'The Friendship Network of Gregory VII', *History*, 1-22, here 21, Bernold could absolve from excommunication those who had been previously excommunicated by Gregory VII for their adherence to Henry IV; Cowdrey, *Pope Gregory VII*, 266, on the other hand, refers in this case to the reconciliation of excommunicated clergy.
55. J. Ramackers, *Papsturkunden,* 35 nr. 3: 'Primum quidem, ut locus ille in Dei seruicio ad refugium et solacium ac sustentacionem quorumcumque fidelium constitutus in sua stabilitate permaneat nec ulli potestati seculari aut ecclesiastice eum destruere uel incrementum, edificacionem et munitionem illius contradicere aut prohibere liceat.' 'First, that this place, which is constituted as a refuge and a place of consolation and support for any believer whomsoever, should remain firm

Watten and be absolved of his or her sins. Moreover, the bull stated that no authority – secular or ecclesiastical – could destroy or damage the priory. This stipulation is in accordance with the suggestion by the author of the *Exordium* that its opponents intended the destruction, and hence the disappearance, of the community. In response, Gregory VII not only put Watten under his apostolic protection, but also made it a place offering protection to those in need, with Rome's blessing. Were those 'needful' other like-minded persons, other supporters of the reform who found it hard to survive in a predominantly conservative environment? Armed with this remarkable privilege from the pope, Watten could really develop into the beating heart of the reform in Thérouanne.

The proclamation by Gregory VII of Watten *ad refugium et solacium ac sustentacionem quorumcumque fidelium* reminds us of the charter of Pope John XIX for Cluny in 1024, in which the famous abbey was proclaimed to be a refuge.[56] A look at the charters issued by Gregory VII shows us that he also explicitly granted the status of *refugium* to the abbeys of Saint Victor in Marseille (1081) and of San Salvatore in Fucecchio in the Italian diocese of Lucca (1085).[57] In both cases Gregory VII deployed the monks as agents of reform and both monasteries were important centres for

---

and that neither secular nor ecclesiastical authority is permitted to destroy the place or its growth and [is permitted] to contradict or prohibit its edifice and defences.'

56. H. Zimmermann, *Papsturkunden 896-1046*, Österreichische Akademie der Wissenschaften. Philosophisch-Historische Klasse. Denkschriften, 177, Veröffentlichungen der Historischen Kommission, 4 (Vienna, 1985), 1052-1054 n° 558: 'Decernimus etiam et illius cuius vice quamvis indigni fungimur, auctoritate sanctimus, ut isdem locus omnibus ad se ob salutem confugientibus sit misericordiae sinus, sit totius pietatis et salutis portus. Obtineat in eo locum iustus, nec repellatur poenitere volens iniquus... Sit autem omnibus ibi advenientibus causa salutis hic et in perpetuum divinę miserationis et pietatis refugium et apostolicę benedictionis et absolutionis presidium.' Cf. H. E. J. Cowdrey, *The Cluniacs and the Gregorian Reform* (Oxford, 1970), 153-155 : 'On behalf of the apostle whose vicar we, though unworthy, are, we appoint and ordain that [Cluny] and all places that are subject to it shall be a haven of mercy and a harbour of all grace and salvation to everyone who flees to it in order to be saved. May the righteous man find a place there and may the unrighteous man, who wants to do penance, never be turned away... To all who come there, may it be an aid to salvation, both here and in eternity. May it be a refuge of God's mercy and pity, and a guardian of apostolic blessing and absolution'. K. A. Frech, J. F. Böhmer, *Regesta Imperii. III. Salisches Haus 1024-1125, Fünfte Abteilung. Papstregesten 1024-1058. 1. Lieferung: 1024-1046*, Österreichischen Akademie der Wissenschaften – Regesta Imperii – und der Deutschen Kommission für die Bearbeitung der Regesta Imperii bei der Akademie der Wissenschaften und der Literatur. Mainz (Cologne-Weimar-Vienna, 2006), 26-28 nr. 42 with references to the specific litterature.
57. L. Santifaller, *Quellen und Forschungen zum Urkunden- und Kanzleiwesen Papst Gregors VII*, Studi et Testi, t. 190 (Vatican City, 1974) 234-237, especially 237 (Marseille) and 265-267 (Fucheccio); U-R. Blumenthal, *Gregor VII*, 329.

the propagation of the new ideas.[58] Was the priory of regular canons in the diocese of Thérouanne to play a similar role? In any case, the characterisation of the place as a refuge by the pope apparently constitutes an unusual act during his twelve-year pontificate.

5. The identity of the opponents

According to the *Exordium*, the Watten canons encountered opposition 'from the entire province, but most of all from the clerics.'[59] Apparently, the village priests and clergy with a lifestyle that was no longer tolerated by Rome felt uncomfortable and even threatened by the vicinity of a watchdog of the reform. Even more so now the prior of Watten had been granted the right to disseminate the new ideas and the community had been named a sanctuary, where the faithful could find consolation and support! As the author also mentions, the most violent reaction came from the *clerici vicini*, which probably refers to the conservative canons of the cathedral chapter of Thérouanne. The episcopal see of Thérouanne was situated a mere 20 kilometres south of Watten. It is hardly surprising that these opponents easily succeeded in using Bishop Drogo for their own purposes. The old bishop himself came from another era, when lay investiture and priestly marriage and concubinage were accepted practices, not punished by severe ecclesiastical sentences. Moreover, at that time, because of his advanced age, Drogo left his Archdeacon, Hubert – who would succeed him on the episcopal see – to deal with many of his cases. As already stated in the introduction, Bishop Hubert (1078-1081) was violently opposed to any reform. All in all, the author of the *Exordium* dealt rather charitably with the aged Drogo.[60] The abuses then rampant in the diocese of Thérouanne, he ascribed to the dotage (per simplicitatem) of the old shepherd of souls, who was no longer able to keep his flock on the straight and narrow.

---

58. E. Magnani Soares-Christen, 'Saint-Victor de Marseille, Cluny et la politique de Grégoire VII au Nord-Ouest de la Méditerranée' in., *Die Cluniacenzer in ihrem politisch-sozialen Umfeld*, Vita Regularis: Ordnungen und Deutungen religiösen Lebens im Mittelalter 7, ed. G. Constable , G. Melville and J. Oberste (Münster, 1988), 321-347; Cowdrey, *Pope Gregory VII*, 307 and 659-673.
59. *Chronica monasterii Watinensis*, ed. Holder-Egger, 171 § 18: 'Nam huic successit incommodo totius fere provinciae contra nos, maxime autem clericorum, conflata suspicio...'
60. *Chronica monasterii Watinensis*, ed. Holder-Egger, 171 § 18

6. Papal interests in the diocese of Thérouanne

The champion of reform, Gregory VII, plays an important role in this story. His interest in the situation in Thérouanne becomes clear from several letters included among his correspondence. On 10 November 1076, he sent letters to the Dowager Countess Adela and to her son, Robert I.[61] He appealed to them to take measures against the practice of simony and against priests and other clerics who persisted *in fornicatione* and were still celebrating mass.[62] Thanks to his 'man on the spot', canon Ingelrannus of Saint-Omer, Gregory VII was well aware of the fact that the ecclesiastical establishment of Thérouanne, with at its head the aged bishop and his influential archdeacon, were not kindly disposed towards the ideas of Church reform.[63] From the words of the pope to Adela one can also deduce that Archdeacon Hubert had revealed himself as an advocate of nicolaitism, holding sermons in favour of clerical marriage.[64] The pope's trust in these two men was not overwhelming. A year earlier, on 25 March 1076, Gregory VII had accused Bishop Drogo of Thérouanne of simony, because he had asked payment for administering Holy Oil.[65] The pope also warned Adela against Hubert, who had been accused of heresy by a papal legate in Montreuil in the summer of 1076.

Pope Gregory was very favourably disposed towards the *vita apostolica* pursued by Odfrid and his companions. At the Lateran Council of 1059, the pope – at that time still Archdeacon Hildebrand of the Roman Church – had defended this new movement, and more specifically some

61. E. Caspar, *Das Register Gregors VII* (Berlin-Dublin-Zürich, 1967), 309 nr. IV,10 (Adela) and 310-311 nr. IV,11 (Robert); Verlinden, *Robert Ier*, 115-124; Cowdrey, *Pope Gregory VII*, 345-348 and 410-413.

62. *The Register of Pope Gregory VII, 1073-1085. An English Translation*, ed. and trans. H. E .J. Cowdrey (Oxford, 2002), 219-220, nr. 4.10 (to Adela): 'It has come to our ears that certain of your people are uncertain whether or not priests and deacons or others who minister at the sacred altars and who persist in fornication should do duty at mass' Op. cit., p. 220-221 nr. 4.11 (to Count Robert): 'It has come to the apostolic see that in the land under your rule those who are called priests but are given over to fornication have no shame when singing mass to handle the body and blood of Christ, not heeding what madness or what crime it is at one and the same time to touch the body of a harlot and the body of Christ.'

63. *The Register*, ed. and trans. Cowdrey, 221, nr. 4.11: 'These words of ours, unpolished though they are, read often with our common faithful follower Ingelrannus, who has for long stayed with us in the sacred palace, or with other lovers of truth...'

64. *The Register*, ed. and trans. Cowdrey, 220, nr. 4.10: ' you should neither pay attention to the words of Archdeacon Hubert nor approve of any of his sayings, because, as I have heard, he has fallen into heresy by his wicked disputations and has been publicly found guilty at Montreuil by Hubert, the legate of this holy Roman see.'

65. Santifaller, *Quellen und Forschungen*, 110-113 nr. 114.

Roman clerics who had renounced all worldly possessions to lead an apostolic life.[66] Moreover, the recent biography of Gregory VII by Ute-Renate Blumenthal shows that the pope was probably himself a canon regular, and not a monk.[67] As was the case with the canons regular in the South of Germany, and especially in Bavaria, Gregory VII might also have deployed the brethren of Watten to propagate the new reform ideas.[68] In any case, the canons regular with their apostolic ideals, their orientation towards the outside world and their eagerness for pastoral work were excellent means to transmit the higher standards of the reform church. According to a papal bull of Urban II from 1099 in favour of Watten, this community was 'on very friendly terms' (*intra familiarissimos)* with the Church of Rome, and because of its 'great dignity', Gregory VII had granted the young community a bull in 1077.[69] A charter of Bishop Gerard of Thérouanne of 10 October 1085, written in all probability in the Watten *scriptorium*, contains in the *datatio* an explicit reference to the exile of the pope and deplores his sad fate.[70] Moreover, a miracle story written c. 1091 by the same author as the *Exordium*, testifies to the solicitude of the Watten brethren to dutifully celebrate the anniversary of Gregory VII.[71]

However, a close reading of the *Exordium* also reveals that some laypersons and clerics from the diocese of Thérouanne did feel considerable

66. A. Werminghoff, 'Die Beschlüsse des Aachener Konzils im Jahre 816', *Neues Archiv*, 26 (1902), 669-675; J.C. Dickinson, *The Origins of the Austin canons*, 29-33; Dereine, 'Vie commune', 390-392; J. Leclercq, 'Un témoignage sur l'influence de Grégoire VII dans la réforme canoniale', *Studi Gregoriani*, 6 (1959-1960), 173-188; Ch. Dereine, 'La prétendue règle de Grégoire VII pour chanoines réguliers', *Revue bénédictine*, 71 (1961), 108-118.
67. U.-R. Blumenthal, *Gregor VII.*, 31-43.
68. Cf. Cowdrey, *Pope Gregory VII*, 249-253.
69. J. Ramackers, *Papsturkunden,* 38-39, 5: '[...] eo quod beate memorie Gregorii pape predecessoris nostri auctoritate simul et solacio patet fore fundatum, quam eciam cum habitatoribus et omnibus ad eundem pertinentibus intra familiarissimos sancte et uniuersalis matris Romane ecclesie comperimus esse susceptum et tanta dignitate ditatum, ut prelatos eiusdem loci episcopali more ubique in diuini uerbi administratione in ligandi soluendique potestate quandam prerogatiuam sublimior(is) gratie pater idem insigniret.'
70. Saint-Omer, *Bibliothèque Municipale*, ms. 852, f° 38v°-39: 'Fecimus autem hanc traditionem anno Incarnationis dominice millesimo LXXXVto, indictione VIII, sexto idus octobris, beato Gregorio papa pro fide christiana et religione catholica ab Henrico apostata et Guiberto heresiarcha jam in exilium expulso...'
71. *Miraculum sancti Donatiani,* ed. O. Holder-Egger, MGH, Scriptores, 14 (Hannover, 1883) 181; in his bull of 1077, Pope Gregory VII had, immediately after conferring the power of binding and loosing and the authority to preach, expressed the desire to be commemorated daily in the community of Watten. Ramackers, *Papsturkunden,* 35-26, 3 (cf. *supra,* n. 39); U.-R. Blumenthal, *Gregor VII*, 41; H. Seibert, "Kommunikation", 25.

goodwill towards the young community.[72] They expressed this through donations, or by entering the community. By slightly dramatizing the difficulties which the community undoubtedly experienced in the beginning, the perseverance of Odfrid and his little flock of followers seemed to be even more impressive. Still, there is little doubt that feelings must have run high, since other sources also indicate that there was a conservative clergy.

7. The priory of Watten after Odfrid's resignation

During the summer of 1079, Odfrid resigned his position as prior, in the interest of his community and on the advice of Gregory VII.[73] The year before, the prior had become involved in a bitter dispute with the new bishop, Hubert, regarding the choice of an abbot for the comital abbey of Bergues. After having consulted the papal legate Warmund of Vienne, and with the consent of some of the monks of Bergues, Odfrid had proposed a reform-minded candidate. However, this candidate, who was also endorsed by the Count, had been viewed unfavourably by Bishop Hubert, who had excommunicated both the man in question and Odfrid. In this turbulent period, Odfrid clearly emerged as the advocate of reform in the diocese of Thérouanne, but the enmity with Bishop Hubert finally forced him to resign in order to safeguard the survival of his community. Odfrid's abdication is the last historical event mentioned in the *Exordium*. Indeed, the *Exordium* probably served as a kind of *apologia*, intended to defend the deeds of the man who had founded Watten, and who had consequently clashed with the ecclesiastical establishment.[74] However, Bishop Hubert initially refused to accept the resignation of the prior, because he feared that Odfrid would rant even more furiously against *fornicarii*, married and concubinal clerics, if he were to be discharged from his obedience to the diocesan bishop.[75] Apparently, to Hubert, the preaching prior of Watten was still slightly less dangerous than the *Wanderprediger*. The *Exordium* does not mention what happened next to Odfrid. Other sources mention his death on 22 November

72. *Chronica monasterii Watinensis*, ed. Holder-Egger, 166-168 § 6-12; B. Meijns, 'De *pauperes Christi* van Watten', 59-62.
73. *Chronica monasterii Watinensis*, ed. Holder-Egger, 173-175 § 23-28; Huyghebaert, 'Un légat de Grégoire VII', 187-200; B. Meijns, 'De *pauperes Christi*', 69-72.
74. P. Ruyffelaere, 'Les *historiae fundationum monasteriorum*', 234.
75. *Chronica monasterii Watinensis*, ed. Holder-Egger, 175 § 27: 'Cavebat enim in hoc, ne quasi contra fornicarios eundem, quibus ipse [= Hubertus] patrocinabatur, infestiorem et audaciorem redderet, si absolutum subiectione a se removeret, quos multociens continentiae zelo severa correptione confuderat.'

1085 or 1086, near Ghent. The monks of the Ghent abbey of Saint Peter buried him in their abbey church.[76]

Without the help of the voluble author of the *Exordium*, the history of the priory after Odfrid's abdication in 1080 is much more difficult to reconstruct. Hardly anything is known about the administration of Odfrid's successor, Alfwin, which probably only lasted about six years.[77] His successor, Bernold, who stood at the head of Watten for a period of nearly twenty years, and maybe even a quarter of a century, appears much more often in the sources.[78] Bernold was one of the first followers of Odfrid and he had been present from the very beginning.[79] Under Bernold, the priory not only enjoyed a substantial expansion of its property, but it also benefited from the generosity of the count and countess of Flanders.[80] In the meantime, the community had established a solid reputation with regard to the new canonical lifestyle. *Circa* 1092, Odo of Orléans, the famous master of the cathedral school of Tournai, visited the community with some like-minded companions to find inspiration.[81] He described the way of life in Watten as much stricter than that of Mont-Saint-Eloi, that other nucleus of

76. *Ex miraculis S. Richarii*, O. Holder-Egger, MGH, Scriptores, t. 15, 2 (Hannover, 1888), 919 § 1; Ph. Grierson, *Les Annales de Saint-Pierre de Gand et de Saint-Amand. Annales Blandinienses – Annales Elmarenses – Annales Formoselenses – Annales Elnonenses*, Commission royale d'Histoire, Recueil de Textes pour servir à l'Etude de l'Histoire de Belgique (Brussels, 1937), 30.
77. Alfwin served as parish priest before the parochial church of Watten was turned into a community of canons regular. *Chronica monasterii Watinensis*, ed. Holder-Egger, 164 § 1; O. Bled, 'Inventaire de reliques du monastère de Watten en 1079', *Bulletin de la Société académique des Antiquaires de la Morinie* 19 (1957-1962) 149-152.
78. The first contemporary mention of Bernold as provost (or abbot, as he is sometimes called) of Watten dates from 4 August 1089 as he is present, together with his brethren, at the elevation of St. Walburga in Veurne (A. Miraeus and J.F. Foppens, *Opera diplomatica et historica* 3 (Louvain, 1734), 20-21 nr. 20). According to Simon of Saint-Bertin in his *Gesta abbatum Sancti Bertini Sithiensium*, ed. Holder-Egger, 651 § 82, Bernold attended the consecration of the abbey church of Saint Bertin on 1 May 1106. Bernold's successor, Arnold, makes his first appearance as a signatory of a comital charter for Watten in 1114 (F. Vercauteren, *Actes des comtes de Flandre 1071-1128*, Commission royale d'Histoire, Recueil des Actes des Princes belges (Brussels, 1938), 153-155 n. 65). However, the *Vita secunda* of Bishop Arnulf of Soissons by Abbot Hariulf of Oudenburg notes the presence of a *Bernoldus praepositus Guatenensis* at the funeral of Arnulf of Soissons in Oudenburg in August 1087 (*De S. Arnulfo confessore*, ed. G. Cuypers, *Acta Sanctorum, Augusti* III (Paris and Rome, 1867), 253).
79. *Chronica monasterii Watinensis*, Holder-Egger, ed., p. 167 § 10; Saint-Omer, *Bibliothèque Municipale*, ms. 852, f° 166 v°-167v°: charter of confirmation from Bishop Drogo of Thérouanne (1072) enumerating the initial gifts to the community of Watten, including the gift of some land made by a 'Bernoldus'.
80. Meijns, 'De *pauperes Christi*', 72-78.
81. Herman of Tournai, *The Restoration of the Monastery of Saint Martin of Tournai*. Ed. and trans. L. N. Nelson (Washington, D.C., 1996), 19 § 4.

reform in the south of the county. Bernold frequently appears as a signatory of charters concerning important religious events in the diocese. He was present when Bishop Gerald of Thérouanne founded a new community of canons regular on the Flemish coastal plain in Eversam in 1091, and when Bishop John in 1100 reformed the chapter of Lo into a community of canons regular. [82] From the last decade of the 11th century, his name often appears in connection with the abbots of Saint Bertin and Ham, in what we might call the recently established reform circle of the diocese of Thérouanne.[83] It was this small reform circle of *abbates religiosi* which pleaded the cause of Archdeacon John with Pope Urban II.[84] and which continued to protect his interests once John had become bishop of Thérouanne.[85]

8. Conclusion

When in the summer of 1099, John of Warneton was appointed bishop of Thérouanne, a wind of change was blowing through the diocese.[86] The

82. P. Callebert, 'Ontstaan en vroegste geschiedenis van het kapittel te Eversam (1091-1200)', *Handelingen van het Genootschap voor Geschiedenis te Brugge*, 107 (1970), 166-216, here 192; *Cartulaire de l'abbaye de Saint-Pierre de Loo de l'ordre de Saint-Augustin (1093-1794)*, ed. L. Van Hollebeke (Brussels, 1870), 3-4, n. II.
83. Bernold appears for the first time in the company of the abbots of Saint Bertin and Ham-en-Artois when he signed the episcopal foundation charter of Eversam in 1091 (cf. *supra*, preceding footnote). The next year, the trio was delegated by the council of Rheims to Count Robert I for mediation in the conflict between the count of Flanders and the Flemish clergy (Lambert of Saint-Omer, *Lamberti Genealogia comitum Flandriae*, ed. L. C. Bethmann, MHG, SS, IX (Hannover, 1851), 311). The three prelates in all probability attended the Council held in Rome 24-30 April 1099, where the nomination of a new bishop of Thérouanne was discussed in the presence of Urban II (cf. *infra*, next footnote). In 1100 all three of them signed the charter of Bishop John confirming the installation of canons regular in the collegiate church of Lo (cf. *supra*, preceding footnote). Cf. H. Sproemberg, 'Clementia, Gräfin von Flandern' in: *Mittelalter und Demokratische Geschichtsschreibung. Ausgewählte Abhandlungen*, Forschungen zur Mittelalterliche Geschichte 18 (Berlin, 1971), 192-220, here 197-201.
84. Cf. Simon of Saint Bertin, *Gesta abbatum Sancti Bertini Sithiensium*, ed. Holder-Egger, 647, liber II § 57; Walter of Thérouanne, *Vita Domni Ioannis Morinensis Episcopi*, ed. Rider, 134 § [7] (*abbates religiosi*).
85. Walter of Thérouanne, *Vita Domni Ioannis Morinensis Episcopi*, ed. Rider, XXXIX-XLI and 139-140 § [11].
86. One wonders if the relatively high productivity of canonical collections in the Northwest of France and specifically in the dioceses of Arras and Thérouanne during the last decade of the 11th century and the first decades of the 12th century, is not related one way or another to the fierce resistance against the new papal policies in this region one generation earlier. The *Collectio Atrebatensis*, the

community of Watten had become firmly established, and the difficult start was once and for all a thing of the past. But now the new bishop and his entourage also felt great goodwill towards the idea of reform within the Church. Moreover, the bishop owed his appointment to a small but tenacious reform circle, which included the prior of Watten. The continued existence and the success of this stronghold of reform was to a large extent due to the support of Pope Gregory VII himself. By granting exceptional privileges to Odfrid, a former itinerant preacher, and his successors in his bull of 1077, he succesfully established an active nucleus of reform in an area where reform had not yet taken root and he succeeded in giving effective publicity to the new papal policies. Not only did he count on the cooperation of the local prior for spreading the new ideas by granting him the *licentia praedicandi*, the Watten community also served as a refuge for penitents wanting to confess their sins, and possibly also for those who were persecuted for their Gregorian convictions. Consequently, the community of regular canons in Watten was not only a pioneering institution as far as the canonical way of life in the diocese and in Flanders was concerned, it also kept the flame of Church reform burning. To use the words of I. S. Robinson in his article 'The Friendship Network of Gregory VII', it looks like the modest priory of Watten on the Flemish coastal plain was yet another 'pocket of enlightenment' from which the reform movement spread.[87]

Collection in Nine Books and the *Collection in Ten Parts* all herald reform ideas and distribute the new papal legislation. Noteworthy is the ninth part of the *Collection in Ten Parts*, ascribed to archdeacon Walter of Thérouanne, which is entirely dedicated to penance, the confession of sins, satisfaction and reconciliation (cf. Somerville and Brasington, *Prefaces to Canon Law Books*, 164). Together with the fourth part of this collection, which contains the Rule of Saint Augustine, this concluding chapter is the result of the personal initiative of the compiler while the other parts of his collection are derived from Ivo's *Panormia*. Fournier and Le Bras, *Histoire des Collections canoniques*, 297-298 and 303.

87. Robinson, 'The Friendship Network', 22: 'Yet in this dark world there were, after all, pockets of enlightenment: among the canons of Constance and St. Omer [he refers to Ingelrannus] and the lower clergy of Milan and Piacenza, in the unlikely person of the steward of the church of Lyons.'

OUTLAWRY AND ECCLESIASTICAL POWER IN MEDIEVAL NORWAY

Anne Irene Riisøy

1. Introduction

When a person had committed crimes like murder, treason or arson and was sentenced to outlawry, he thus became a person without the protection of the law. This had several consequences. For instance the outlaw was expelled from the country, he could be killed with impunity and risked forfeiture of his property. It was possible to regain full legal rights through the king's pardon. However this was not without cost and normally the outlaw had to pay heavily in order to be reintegrated into society. The most common consequences of outlawry, for example a sentence decreed at the assembly involving the expulsion of the outlaw and the possibility that the outlaw could be killed with impunity and have his property confiscated, were most likely also used as punishment during heathen times.[1]

1. According to the glossary to *Norges gamle Love indtil 1387. Femte Bind* (Abbreviated NgL V), ed. Gustav Storm and Ebbe Hertzberg (Christiania 1895), 676, *útlagr*, *útlægr*, *útslægr* means '... fredløs, stillet udenfor loven' i.e 'outlaw, placed outside the law'. Thus Hertzberg, who was responsible for the glossary, disagrees with Vilhjálmur Finsen, who in the glossary to *Grágás* was of the opinion that the terms *útlagr* and *útlegð* allude to *leggia*, *leggja*, i.e 'lay out/ lying out', not of *lög*. Most scholars follow Hertzbergs interpretation, and so do I. Anglo-Saxon sources offer additional evidence concerning this interpretation and also support the view that outlawry was actually used as a punishment in Viking age Norway. A recent study by Sara M. Pons-Sanz, *Norse-derived vocabulary in late Old English Texts. Wulfstan's works. A case study* (Odense 2007) offers a through discussion of these problems; see especially 61-62, 80-83. The Anglo-Saxon legal term *utlah*, which is linguistically akin to *útlagr*/*útlegð* must, when it was first borrowed by the Anglo-Saxons, have been connected with *lagu*. It is not likely that *utlah* has been connected with *leggja*/ 'laying out' because traces of such a

However, Christianity, which gained political acceptance in Norway during the first decades of the eleventh century, gradually exercised influence over the concept and applicability of outlawry. These aspects are first of all reflected in the oldest Christian Laws, which were enacted at the four regional assemblies (Gulathing, Frostathing, Eidsivathing and Borgarthing) during the eleventh century and with new law added during the twelfth century.[2] For instance penance became a factor in which a sentence of outlawry might be mitigated or abolished, outlawry became linked to un-Christian behaviour and in addition the outlaw was at times denied a Christian burial.

2. Confession, penance and reintegration of the outlaw

While the concepts of sin, repentance and penance were unknown in pre-Christian society, they influenced, and to a certain extent also fused with, the concept of crime and secular punishment at an early stage of Christianity. Some paragraphs in the oldest Christian laws show that a criminal act was also considered a sin, because in various ways confession and penance were linked to secular punishment. An introduction of this new and revolutionary way of thinking in the law codes most likely represented an attempt to make these concepts known outside a confined ecclesiastical circle, as well as a wish for cooperation between native law and the

---

conception has not been found in the extant forms. Pons-Sanz argues that 'the connection which probably existed in the Anglo-Saxons minds between útlah/útlaga "outlaw(ed)" (as well as inlagian "to reverse a sentence of outlawry") and lagu justifies the analysis of these terms as members of the lagu word-field.' Besides, the 'OE lagu in its earliest records (none older than the tenth century) is solely associated with the Scandinavian newcomers and their legal practice.' Thus *utlah* like *lagu* have a possible Old Norse origin, and are generally accepted as such.

2. In recent years questions concerning the dating of the Christian Laws, and when they were first written down, have been debated. See for instance Magnus Rindal, 'Dei eldste norske kristenrettane' in *Religionsskiftet i Norden. Brytinger mellom nordisk og europeisk kultur 800-1200 e.Kr.*, ed. Jón Viðar Sugyrðsson et al., (Oslo 2004), 103-137. The oldest group was probably codified in the first half of the eleventh century, and the references to the 'Olaf-text', found in several paragraphs in the *Old Christian Law of the Gulathing*, are to the Saint King Olaf Haraldsson (king 1015-1028, dead 1030). St. Olaf brought with him several bishops and priests from England, and among them was the Anglo-Saxon bishop Grimkjell who is mentioned as co-initiator of the Olaf text. Recently Torgeir Landro, *Dei eldste norske kristenrettane: innhald og opphav*, unpublished hovedoppgave, (Bergen 2005) has argued that during the years between 1050 and 1150 continental law was incorporated. In the 1160s and 70s the *Old Christian Law of the Gulathing*, the *Magnustext* (after King Magnus Erlingsson), and the *Christian Law of the Frostathing* were thoroughly revised.

penitential system. Thus, in *the Old Christian Law of the Gulathing* while the outlaw lost his property expulsion from the kingdom might be avoided if he went to confession and did penance: 'ganga til skripta ok bæta við Krist'.[3] The Christian laws of the eleventh and twelfth centuries have distinct local features, and this rule seems to be absent from the other contemporary Christian Laws. However, in the mid-thirteenth century, it again appears in several paragraphs in the new Christian laws from all over the country.[4]

Most likely the influence on this legal dualism came from Anglo-Saxon church law, where one and the same act often was defined as a crime as well as a sin. Absalon Taranger has convincingly argued that when King Olaf Haraldsson stayed in England before he became king in 1015, violations of the Anglo-Saxon church law most commonly led to ecclesiastical as well as secular punishment.[5] Regarding this period Olav Tveito is even more specific, and he argues that Archbishop Wulfstan of York (elected Archbishop 1002, died 1023) exercised a considerable impact on the oldest Norwegian Church laws. Thereby the archbishop's vision of establishing 'a holy society' is echoed.[6]

The interaction between law and theology, which is expressed in the Norwegian Christian laws, was, as succinctly put by Thomas Pollock Oakley, a common approach when new ideas were introduced in early medieval Europe. Oakley further states that:

> In contrast to our present practice, the secular laws of that time constantly reiterated that crimes were sins, and that secular penal law had a religious, as well as a punitive purpose. In addition to being wrongs against individuals or the State, crimes were regarded as defiling the soul of the committer.[7]

---

3. For instance rules concerning burial in the church yard, G 23, and incest, G 24, *Norges gamle Love indtil 1387. Förste Bind* (Abbreviated NgL I), ed. R. Keyser and P. A. Munch (Christiania 1846). NgL I, 13-15. For general references see *'[go to confession and] do penance', 'b. við Crist'* in the glossary in NgL V, 129.
4. See references in NgL V, 583, '*skript*'.
5. Absalon Taranger, *Den angelsaksiske kirkes indflydelse paa den norske* (Kristiania 1890), 299-300. See also Thomas Pollock Oakley, *English Penitential Discipline and Anglo-Saxon Law in their Joint Influence* (New York 1923), 145.
6. Olav Tveito, 'Erkebiskop Wulfstan av York og de eldste norske kristenrettene', *Norsk Teologisk Tidsskrift*, 3 (2007). I would like to thank Tveito for bringing this relevant and interesting article to my attention.
7. Thomas Pollock Oakley, 'The Cooperation of Medieval Penance and Secular Law', *Speculum. Journal of Medieval Studies*, VII (1932), 516-518. Regarding Anglo-Saxon penitentials and Anglo-Saxon law Oakley *English Penitential Discipline and Anglo-Saxon Law* has thoroughly demonstrated how these interplayed with each other.

Ideally the laws and sanctions of church and king should be complementary, and violators of the Christian Laws should make amends, both secular and ecclesiastical. Thus, when the fourth Lateran Council in 1215 decreed that people should go to confession once a year, this rule was implemented in the Christian laws of the mid-thirteenth century. People who abstained from confession for three winters, were declared outlaws, and some manuscripts explicitly connect breaking this rule to heathen practice '*heidin dom*'.[8]

3. Outlaw and un-Christian

Yet another interesting distinction between Christian and heathen behaviour appears and outlaws were explicitly linked to the latter conduct. According to the *Old Christian Law of the Borgarthing* an outlaw not only lost legal protection and absolutely all he owned, he was also often expelled to a heathen country. Some provisions add that the act of becoming an outlaw is a refusal to be a Christian. Thus the outlaw chooses to be a heathen, and therefore he shall never again be allowed in a country where Christians live.[9] We also find traces of precisely this line of thought in the *Old Christian Law of the Eidsivathing*.[10] Stubborn resistance towards the church's commands normally led to outlawry of which expulsion from the country was an important part. Presumably this expulsion also assumed an element of purification because the country was thus delivered from all non-Christian beings.

Again Anglo-Saxon church law is a possible source of inspiration, and again we have to turn to an explanation put forward by Absalon Taranger to place these rulings in a convincing historical context. In Anglo-Saxon England, in the first decades of the eleventh century, persevering opposition to the Church commands normally led to expulsion from the country which was thus delivered from un-Christian beings.[11] In the Norwegian Christian laws we also find this idea manifest in prohibitions to have heathens in the country. Even someone who gave the heathen food risked heavy fines.[12]

---

8. NG 22, *Norges gamle Love indtil 1387. Andet Bind* (Abbreviated NgL II), ed. R. Keyser and P. A. Munch (Christiania 1848), NgL II, 318; cf. NB I 14, NgL II, 299; NG II, NgL II, 332-333.
9. Amongst them outlawry because of incest in the first degree, B I 15, NgL I, 350; murder of newborn B I 3, NgL I, 340; refuse to baptize newborn within 12 months, B I 4, NgL I, 341; divorce without proper cause B II 6, NgL I, 355, cf. B III 6, and failure to pay tithe, B I 11, NgL I, 346.
10. E I 52, NgL I, 392 on incest and E I 27, NgL I, 384, concerning meat eating on Fridays during 'imbru daga'.
11. Taranger, *Den angelsaksiske kirkes,* 299-300.
12. Anne Irene Riisøy, *Sex, rett og reformasjon*, unpublished Ph.D thesis, University of Oslo, (Oslo 2006), 90. G 22, NgL I, 13, see translation in *The Earliest Norwegian*

Determined resistance towards the Church's commands was interpreted as dissociating oneself from Christianity and the will of God. Thus outlawry and an association with paganism was not an unlikely outcome. This idea found resonance in other sources and in later periods as well. According to Gabriel Turvill-Petre, Icelandic Folk-tales occasionally associate outlaws with heathens. The outlaw might for instance change colour if he heard the name of God, and even his horse could not stand the sign of the Cross.[13]

4. Christian burial – or not

Outlaws also risked being expelled from the Christian community after death. The Christian laws have detailed provisions regarding burial in consecrated ground. This privilege was, however, denied to certain categories of people, primarily outlaws. The relevant paragraphs in the various Christian laws provide a list of these people: shameful truce breakers, traitors, convicted thieves, hired assassins, robbers (all of which were defined as outlaws in specific paragraphs in the secular parts of the law codes), people who died while excommunicated, people who committed suicide, people who preached the wrong faith, usurers, and people who were not baptized when they died.[14] *The Old Christian Law of the Eidsivathing* attaches a wolf-epithet to particularly heinous categories of outlaws:

Laws, Being the Gulathing Law and the Frostathing Law, ed. and transl. Laurence M. Larson (New York 1935), 61.

13. Gabriel Turville-Petre, '*Outlawry*' in Sjötíu Ritgerðir. Helgaðar Jakobi Benediktssyni (Reykjavík 1977), 775-776.

14. Paragraphs in the oldest Christian laws: G 23, NgL I, 13-14, *The Earliest Norwegian Laws, Being the Gulathing Law and the Frostathing Law*, ed. Larson, 51; E I 50, NgL I, 391; F II 15, NgL I, 135-136 has a more general rule see *The Earliest Norwegian Laws, Being the Gulathing Law and the Frostathing Law*, ed. Larson, 232 'Every Christian shall be buried at the church and his body must normally be brought to the church within five nights, unless he was by intent his own banesman or had cast aside his Christian faith while he was still living [...]' The paragraphs on burial in the Old Christian Law of the Borgarthing do not mention anything about whether outlaws should be allowed Christian burial or not. The priest seems to have had some veto if money had not been paid for the burial, cf. B II 21, NgL I, 361. Otherwise, the primary concern in early medieval Borgarthing seems to have been whether people were buried according to their social standing or not, it was prohibited to bury a corpse in a part of the church yard preserved for his superiors, B I 9, B II 18, B III 13, NgL I, 345, 359-360, 368. All the Christian laws from the mid-thirteenth century list specifically various categories of people denied Christian burial. NB I 8, NgL II, 296; NG I 16, NgL II, 314-315; NB II 10, *Norges gamle Love indtil 1387. Fjerde Bind* (Abbreviated NgL IV). ed. Gustav Storm (Christiania 1885). NgL IV, 166; J 16, NgL II, 350.

murderwolves, firewolves (arsonists) and 'wolves who attack people with violence in their own homes'.[15]

In the secular sections of the law books from the Gulathing, Frostathing and the Icelandic *Grágás*, as well as in the Icelandic sagas (also called the family sagas), we occasionally find outlaws designated in wolf-terms or in wolf-compounds. The wolf-epithet seems to be reserved the most heinous categories of outlaws and it also appears to be an older designation which became outdated during the thirteenth century at the latest.[16]

The Christian laws of the mid-thirteenth century basically exclude the same categories of people from Christian burial, while they also introduce a few exceptions to these rules. If a person called on the priest before dying and confessed, then the priest had the power to grant permission for a Christian burial. However, convicted thieves, murderers, robbers, and people who were not baptized were not allowed any reprieve.[17] To be

---

15. E II 40, NgL I, 405. 'morðuargar','brænno vargar', 'heimsoknar vargar', cf. E I 50, NgL I, 391. *Morð*, which is cognate with the English 'murder', indicates a reprehensible kind of manslaughter. If the killer concealed the deed and did not publish what he had done as soon as possible he had committed a *morð*, thus he had also forfeited his legal immunity. See reference to relevant legislation in NgL V, 452-453, *morð*. An arsonist was a particularly cowardly felon; see also G 98, NgL I, 46-47, *The Earliest Norwegian Laws, Being the Gulathing Law and the Frostathing Law*, ed. Larson, 105. A person's legal protection was supposed to increase at home, thus attack on people at home was particularly reprehensible. Moreover, *heimsókn* also implies that the attack was violent, and that the *heimsoknar vargar* not only caused material damage but also personal injury. See more references in NgL V, 277 and an interesting discussion of this crime in a wider Western European context by Rebecca V. Colman, 'Hamsocn: Its Meaning and Significance in Early English Law', *American Journal of Legal History*, XXV, 1981, 95-110.
16. I have categorized all relevant information regarding outlawry in the Norwegian and Icelandic legislation, and there seems to be a parallel chronological development in Norway and Iceland, since the wolf-terms, with one or two exceptions, disappear in the mid-thirteenth century laws. While wolf-terms in connection with outlaws occur in the Icelandic sagas/family sagas (describing mostly events that took place in Iceland in the 10th and early 11th centuries, but written down in the thirteenth and fourteenth centuries), none are found in the Sturlunga Saga. In the Sturlunga Saga (events that took place 1117-1264) only more modern 'nyare' terms for outlaws are found according to Gunnhild Vatne Ersland, *'... til død og fredløshed ...' Fredløysas innhald og funksjon på Island frå 1117 til 1264*, unpublished hovedfagsoppgave (Oslo 2001), 20.
17. NB I 8, NgL II, 296; NG I 16, NgL II, 314-315; NB II 10, NgL IV, 166; J 16, NgL II, 350, which were all codified in the period c. 1250-1273. In 1999 an argument was put forward that thoroughly revised Christian laws were codified during King Håkon Håkonsson's reign, around 1250, and that the last revision took place in 1267 and 1268, during Magnus the Law-Amenders reign. Anne Irene Riisøy and Bjørg Dale Spørck, '*Dateringen av nyere Borgartings kristenretter*', *Collegium Medievale*, 12 (1999). The classification presented here differs from the traditional

denied burial in consecrated ground was an additional punishment and the principle of double punishment was problematic according to Roman law which Gratian adhered to and further developed. A person sentenced to outlawry was punished again if he or she was also refused a Christian burial. Ideally a member of the church who had repented, confessed, and thus become reintegrated into the community of all Christians was entitled to a Christian burial. Secular authorities however, were of the opinion that an impending threat to be buried in un-consecrated ground would deter potential criminals. According to Gratian's *Decretum*, Christian burial was allowed if secular authorities assented as well.[18] This view is reflected in the mid-thirteenth century Christian laws, because regarding outlaws henceforth the king's approval was also required to obtain a Christian burial. In addition, the outlaw's heir was also obliged to compensate for the deceased outlaw's crimes.[19]

In an age where the belief in the resurrection of the body on the last Day of Judgement was firmly dependent upon whether the deceased had received a Christian burial or not, this was a critical issue for the outlaw as well as his family. A diploma which has survived from 1492 relates that a family had not complied with the dean's command to unearth an outlaw, Sveinung Aslaksson, and remove his corpse from the churchyard. Later, the bishop of Stavanger laconically notes that the outlaw's body 'shall have to rest in the churchyard because it is buried together with the corpses of other good Christians.'[20] The bishop's resignation reflects the provisions enacted in the mid-thirteenth century Christian laws; dead bodies buried illegally, and whose bones were impossible to distinguish from the bones of other

one, because since Jens Arup Seip's research from 1937-1942 it has been usual to assume that the last codification of a Christian Law was around 1370. Jens Arup Seip, *Sættargjerden i Tunsberg og kirkens jurisdiksjon* (Oslo 1942). Of the scholars who discuss the problem, Eldbjørg Haug supports Seip's dating. Eldbjørg Haug, 'Konkordat-konflikt-privilegium. Sættargjerden som indikator på forholdet stat-kirke fra Magnus lagabøter til Chrisitan I (1277-1458)' in *Ecclesia Nidrosiensis 1153-1537: Søkelys på Nidaroskirkens og Nidarosprovinsens historie*, ed., Steinar Imsen (Trondheim 2003), 105. I still adhere to my classification presented in 1999, see Riisøy, *Sex, rett og reformasjon, 15-18.* Regardless of which stand one takes in this debate, it is however clear that this rule was introduced during the thirteenth century. In addition, Archbishop *Jon Raude* issued his own *Christian Law* in 1273. Arne Bøe, '*Kristenrettar*' *Kulturhistorisk leksikon for nordisk middelalder* XX (1964), 300.

18. Bertil Nilsson, *De sepulturis: Gravrätten i Corpus Iuris Canonici och i medeltida nordisk lagstiftning* (Stockholm 1989), 260.
19. NB I 8, NgL II, 296; NG I 16, NgL II, 314-315; cf. NG II (Anhang I.), NgL II, 330; NB II 10 NgL IV, 166; J 16, NgL II, 350-351.
20. DN I, nr. 975 [1492]. '[...] maa liggæ nu framdeles i kirkæ gardh som kommen er med andhrom godæ kristnæ manne liik'.

Christian people had to remain in the churchyard.[21] If a corpse was illegally buried, those responsible were not only fined, the Christian laws also prescribed that they had to pay for the re-consecration of the churchyard. In this case, the influence of Canon Law is evident. Bertil Nilsson has pointed out that this issue was debated in Norway at the latest around the year 1200, because in a letter now lost, the archbishop of Niðaros had asked pope Innocent III for advice. In the pope's reply we learn that

> [...] people with whom we shall not keep company while they are alive, we shall not keep company with while they are dead. Those who previously were excluded from the church and who are not reconciled with the church at the time of death shall not receive Christian burial. Therefore, corpses of excommunicated, if it happens that they are buried in the churchyard, either through force or violence, or otherwise, shall be dug up.[22]

In the letter the pope also stressed that corpses with whom one should not keep company even in death, were to be removed if only it was possible to identify them. Thus, it was imperative that the deceased who were part of the Christian community, in life as well as in death, were not removed from the church yard. Outlaws fit nicely in the category of 'people with whom we shall not keep company' neither in life nor in death. Excommunicates which were specifically singled out by the pope could be regarded as a kind of spiritual outlaws. Moreover the link between an incorrigible excommunicate and an *ipso facto* outlaw is attested in the Christian laws, possibly from the late twelfth century. The Christian Law of the Frostathing stipulates that an excommunicate, who did not repent and concluded his affairs within a specific time, should be summoned by the bishop's bailiff before a thing and declared an outlaw.[23]

---

21. NG 16, NgL II, 315; NG II 12, NgL II, 330; NB 8, NgL II, 296-297; NB II 10, NgL IV, 167; J 16, NgL II, 351.
22. Nilsson, *De sepulturis,* 40 refers to DN XVII, no. 10 [1200]. *Diplomatarium Norvegicum I-XXI* (Christiania 1847-), DN XVII, no. 10 [1200] is translated into Norwegian in LatDok no.39, *Latinske dokument til norsk historie: fram til år 1204,* ed. and trans. Eirik Vandvik (Oslo 1959), 125-127. The translation into English is my responsibility. The pope answers a request from Archbishop Eirik, then living in exile in Denmark because of the quarrel with the king. As Vandvik points out, the contact with the pope was most likely initiated because of the excommunication of King Sverrir and his followers. For a more thorough discussion of the Archbishops' exile, see Ólafía Einarsdóttir, 'Erik Ivarsson of Trondheim. Archbishop in exile in Absalon's Lund 1190-1202', in *International Scandinavian and Medieval Studies in Memory of Gerd Wolfgang Weber* (Trieste 2000), 367-381.
23. F III 21, NgL I: 154, *The Earliest Norwegian Laws, Being the Gulathing Law and the Frostathing Law*, ed. Larson, 254. This rule is also found in, J 60, NgL II, 382.

5. Outlawry, secular law and ecclesiastical influence

So far only the Christian laws have been brought into this discussion but when and how did ecclesiastical ideals influence a sentence of outlawry when someone had committed crimes under secular law? Earlier secular parts of the regional law-books have been preserved from the Gulating and the Frostathing, while those from the eastern part of the country have been lost.[24] In the secular parts of the provincial laws of the Gulathing and the Frostathing, penance does not in any way seem to have had an influence on a sentence of outlawry; in fact penance is not mentioned at all here.

However, by the late twelfth century penance had clearly become an issue when crimes under secular law had been committed. In a letter of reply (dated 1161-1172) from Pope Alexander III to the archbishop of Niðaros penance for homicide is stipulated:

> Regarding manslaughter, we advice you that when a man, whoever he is, is killed, his killer shall be imposed penance for seven years or more, according to circumstances, unless anyone kills on behalf of a legal prince and legally, that is to uphold justice, or when he kills in ignorance.[25]

In a similar manner penance for homicide is included in the late twelfth century penitential of St. Þorlákur of Skálholt. According to Sveinbjörn Rafnsson this paragraph could possibly depend on the above mentioned papal reply.[26]

In 1274 King Magnus, nicknamed the Law-Amender, codified a secular law code which was applied to the whole country (two years later this law was adapted to the conditions in the cities). Here we find a few references to confession and penance, although not specifically mentioned in the context of outlaws.[27] However from the turn of the fourteenth century onwards, diplomas which have survived show that penance had become an important factor also in legal practice. In order to receive the king's pardon

---

24. In an early fourteenth century manuscript from the Old Christian Law of the Borgarthing a few paragraphs which contain rules otherwise found in the secular laws sections in the other regional laws are enacted. These paragraphs are concerned with control of women's sexuality, compensation as well as revenge killings, and the formation of marriage and women's right to divorce. Anne Irene Riisøy, 'Komparativt blikk på "verdslig" rett i Eldre Borgartings kristenrett', in *Østfold og Viken i yngre jernalder og middelalder*, ed. Jón Viðar Sigurðsson, et al. (Oslo 2003).
25. *Latinske dokument til norsk historie,* ed. Vandvik, 72-73, § 2. The translation into English is my responsibility.
26. Sveinbjörn Rafnsson, 'The Penitential of St. Torlakur in its Icelandic context', *Bulletin of Medieval Canon Law* (1985), 26.
27. NgL V, 583: L VII 57, script, *skrift*; L IV 16; L II 1 *skriptgangr*.

in cases of outlawry, three parallel sets of criteria had to be met: compensation had to be paid to the victim or heirs of the deceased, this being in addition to a heavy penalty to the king and the performance of penance by the wrongdoer. Moreover, the old expression that the outlaw should go to confession and pay his dues to Christ/God is included in the diplomas. In fact, the procedure regarding outlaws who were allowed to regain their legal rights had developed into an administrative routine during the reign of king Håkon V (1299-1319).[28]

6. Summary

With the arrival of Christianity the new Christian legislation used outlawry as a punishment for the most severe crimes. They kept the older elements, for instance forfeiture and expulsion, while at the same time some new elements were introduced. A refusal to go to confession and do penance was obviously not a good idea; stubborn resistance towards the commandments of the church was interpreted as dissociation from Christianity and the will of God. According to the Christian laws such people lost the opportunity to have their sentence mitigated, and besides, they were outlawed not only from the living but also from the Christian community of the dead.

Although there were periods of conflict between the Church and the Kingdom regarding the administration of justice under Christian Law,[29] they had a shared sense of purpose, the upholding of law and order in a Christian society. It seems to have been realized that ecclesiastical and secular sanctions combined were possibly the best way to enforce law.

28. Lars Hamre, 'Landsvist', *Kulturhistorisk leksikon for nordisk middelalder*, XXI (1977), 259-263. Steinar Imsen, 'Kunsten å konstruere. Noen kritiske merknader til Erling Sandmos avhandling "Slagsbrødre. En studie av vold i to norske regioner i tiden fram mot eneveldet', *Historisk Tidsskrift*, 77 (1998), 489-490.

29. Anne Irene Riisøy, *Stat og kirke: rettsutøvelsen i kristenrettssaker mellom sættargjerden og reformasjonen*, unpublished hovedoppgave (Oslo 2000).

THE CONFLICT IN THE STAVANGER CHURCH AROUND 1300 AND THE INTERVENTION OF HÅKON MAGNUSSON

Eldbjørg Haug

1. Introduction

In the 1290s a conflict between Bishop Arne of Stavanger (1269 – 1303) and the chapter of the cathedral concerning the tithe from Finnøy flared up. Two similar conflicts occurred at the same time in the archdiocese and the diocese of Skálholt in Iceland. The conflict in Stavanger has not received the same attention as the conflicts between church and state during the reigns of Magnus the Lawmender (1263 – 1280) and his son Eirik Magnusson (1280 – 1299);[1] but they are all important to understand the

1. The general histories on the Norwegian church in the Middle Ages treat the conflict sin Stavanger: Anton Christian Bang, *Den norske Kirkes Historie* (Kristiania: 1912); Rudolf Keyser, *Den norske Kirkes Historie under Katholicismen*, II vols. (Christiania: 1856-1858); Oluf Kolsrud, *Noregs kyrkjesoga I. Millomalderen* (Oslo: 1958 †). See also A. W. Brøgger, *Stavangers historie i middelalderen* (Stavanger: Dreyer, 1915); Knut Helle, *Stavanger fra våg til by* ([Stavanger]: Stabenfeldt, 1975), for the conflict in Iceland see Magnús Stefánsson, "Eigenkirche, -nwesen, 1. Island," in *Lexikon des Mittelalters* (Brepolis Medieval Encyclopaedias - Online, 1977); "Islandsk egenkirkevesen," in *Rett og historie: Festskrift til Gudmund Sandvik* (Oslo: 1995); *Staðir og staðamál: Studier i islandske egenkirkelige og beneficialrettslige forhold i middelalderen I*, vol. 4, Skrifter (Bergen: Department of History, 2000). On the conflict in Nidaros see Lars Hamre, edited by Eldbjørg Haug, and Steinar Imsen, "Striden mellom erkebiskop Jørund og domkapitlet i Nidaros. English Summary," in *Ecclesia Nidrosiensis 1153 - 1537: Søkelys på*

internal church conflicts. Both the pope and the king were involved in the case in Stavanger. These circumstances give it a broader perspective and an important role in the political history of the 1290s. Moreover, it concerned core issues in the church law and ecclesiastical legal procedure both at home and in a European context. In short, the conflict deserves a closer study.

The aim of this article is to provide a case study with a particular emphasis on the legal issues of the conflict. The hypothesis is that the cause of the conflict was a reorganisation of the Stavanger church connected to a long-term secularisation of the chapter. There is no doubt that the chapter in Stavanger was a secular one towards the end of the 13th century; the pertinent question is whether or not the chapter was regular from its beginning. Although the actual conflict was an internal church conflict it was a public case and belonged to the ecclesiastical *forum externo*.[2] The article further argues in favour of the conflict being so bitter because the secular power was involved, but also that this in the end presented the solution.

Most of the primary sources to the conflict are preserved in contemporary documents of the event, some as drafts, some as copies and some as certified documents. All the evidence from Stavanger was transferred from Norway to Denmark by the Icelandic scholar Arní Magnusson, but is now in the Norwegian National Archives. The documents are published in *Diplomatarium Norvegicum*. They are mostly written in Latin to serve as evidence in canonical civil proceedings. And many of them deserve an external diplomatic analysis, a task which goes beyond this piece of work; the description of the parchments in DN gives some clues as to which documents to study in further detail. Diplomas in ON are published with photos and translations to Norwegian by Finn Hødnebø and Erik Simensen.[3] There are no medieval narratives on the case in Stavanger.

The records of the conflict started in 1292 when Duke Håkon Magnusson issued a letter of protection to the chapter and protected the

Nidaroskirken og Nidarosprovinsens historie, ed. Steinar Imsen (Trondheim: Tapir, 2003 †).

2. Viz Joseph Goering, "The Internal Forum and the Literature of Penance and Confession," in *The History of medieval Canon Law in the Classical Period, 1140-1234: From Gratian to the Decretals of Pope Gregory IX*, ed. Wilfried Hartmann and Kenneth Pennington, *The History of Medieval Canon Law* (Washington, D.C.: The Catholic University of America Press, 2008), 380.

3. Finn Hødnebø, ed., *Norske diplomer til og med år 1300*, vol. 2, Corpus codicum Norvegicorum medii aevi (Oslo: Selskapet til utgivelse av gamle norske håndskrifter, 1960); Erik Simensen, *Norske diplom 1301-1310*, vol. X, Corpus codicum Norvegicorum medii aevi. Quarto series (Oslo: Selskapet til utgivelse av gamle norske håndskrifter / Norli, 2002).

rights of his *special* clerics.[4] The letter has traditionally been interpreted as given on the request of the canons as an intervention in their ongoing dispute with Bishop Arne. This article argues for another interpretation.

2. The context

The bishop's part of the tithe from Finnøy had been given perpetually to the Stavanger chapter by Bishop Thorgils (1254-1276) more than 30 years before the conflict started. In the ninth year of his pontificate (1263- spring 1264) he gave his tithe to the *mensa* of the residing canons in Stavanger with the advice and consent of King Magnus the Lawmender. His reason for this reallocation was the poverty of the chapter's prebends.[5] That laymen had a saying in church affairs like this was on the one hand not in accordance with canonistic doctrine. A reallocation of the income of a church office belonged in principle only to the church, in 1264 as well as in 1295. On the other hand the king's consent may be considered as an element of royal patronage of the Stavanger church.

The bishop's part of the tithe from Finnøy was the cause of the conflict according to the parties. Let us therefore look further into the background of the disputed issue.

Wherever the tithe was paid, it was paid in full from farming and / or fishing by the farmers to the local church. It was normally divided in four – one part to the bishop, his *mensa* and his see, one part to the parish priest's *mensa*, one to the *fabrica* of the church, and one to the poor. The tithe was the Norwegian bishops' main income; they were not feudal princes. In Stavanger it seems that the tithe was divided in three parts, and that the bishop took the *fabrica*-part.[6] The obligation to pay the tithe annually was introduced by King Sigurd Magnusson called *Jorsalfar* (1103 – 1130) because he had been a pilgrim to *Jorsal,* the ON for Jerusalem. He had then promised to introduce the tithe. It is assumed that this was a tithe on property, and that the annual tithe was introduced in connection with the

---

4. DN I no. 80 (AM fasc. 27 no. 1 a). The dispositio of the letter: 'ver hafum tækit korsbrœðr j Stafangre kæra vini vara. ok hæimilegha klærcka. suæina þæirra alla þa sem til komusens hœyra huærsdagslega. ok allt þat goz. sem þæir æiga eða æigande verða j lannde eða lausum œyri. vttan garðs oc jnnan. loghlega j huæriu sem huært er tiundir garða. æignir æingia garða. akra ok allt þat sem þæirra kanna læikr a j guðs walld. oc vart fullkomet traust til allra retra mala.'
5. DN II no. 13. Eldbjørg Haug, "Thorgils, bishop, d. 1276: bishop of Stavanger 1254-1276," Brepols Publishers, www.brepolis.net.
6. DN IV no. 23. The late Lars Hamre has informed me on the three-part division of the tithe in Stavanger, but has not discussed this divison in his authoritative article on the subject, Lars Hamre, "Tiend. Noreg," *Kulturhistorisk leksikon for nordisk middelalder* XVIII (1974).

establishment of the church province.[7] King Sigurd had also founded the Stavanger see c. 1125, but it is hard to imagine that the bishop in Stavanger had a permanent see if he had to constantly visit his diocese to earn a living. The presumed three-partite division of the annual tithe in the diocese also supports an earlier introduction there than in the other bishoprics. The annual tithe was probably of the same age as the permanent episcopal see.

There is no information on the reasons for King Magnus giving his advice and consent to Bishop Thorgils' reallocation of the tithe from Finnøy. Some indications may be found in the concordat between the Norwegian church and king called the Settlement of Tønsberg (1277). King Magnus then promised that he and his men would pay the tithes. He also accepted a new scale for the tithe with a tax on all products, even trade and shipping.[8] Most scholars have assumed that the king's promise of tithes was no new admission; King Håkon Sverresson (1202 – 1204) gave the same pledge in his reconciliation letter to the Norwegian church and the kings had probably given the tithe on a regular basis since then.[9] One might, however, doubt that there was nothing new in this paragraph of the Settlement. The kings as well as the tenants on royal farms may have paid the tithes, but it was always paid to the local church. Who cashed it in? Was it the bishop's bailiff or the parishioner? Or was it rather the church patron? The reason that the concordat gives a statement concerning the rights to the tithe was probably that the practice had been somewhat ambiguous.

And one of the ambiguities may have been at Finnøy. Here, at the manor Hesby we find the residence of the sheriffs of Rygjafylke from the 13th century and throughout the Middle Ages – and a church, situated on the king's land. Most of Finnøy actually belonged to the king, a fact which can be dated back to the sole rule of King Magnus the Lawmender from winter / spring 1264: The old baron and sheriff Bård of Hesby had died during King Håkon Håkonsson's last campaign in Scotland. He had been one of Duke Skule Bårdson's men, but changed his loyalty to King Håkon when Skule demanded to be acclaimed as king. Hesby may have been a part of the land of Duke Skule or his family; his daughter Margaret was married to King Håkon and was the mother of King Magnus.[10]

Hesby's change of ownership and sheriff may be a clue to King Magnus' consent: the tithe-privilege was given in 1263, immediately before the campaign to Scotland, or in the spring 1264 when Bishop Thorgils returned to Norway with the body of the late king and King Magnus became

7. Ibid.
8. NGL II: 474 – 475 is a translation of the Tønsberg Concordat from Latin to Old Norse with the new scale for the tithe.
9. NGL I: 444 f.
10. For more on this aspect, see Ludvig Daae, "Munaan Biskopssøn og Fru Ragnrid Skulesdatter," *Historisk tidsskrift (Norwegian Historical Review)* 3. rk. III (1895).

the sole ruler. Up to this time the patron over the Hesby church had been the sheriff and Bård of Hesby had probably not let a part of the tithe pass on to the bishop. It is overall doubtful that the bishops of Stavanger had received this tithe before. The bishop's part of it had probably mostly gone to the local patron up to this time as a relic of the *Eigenkirchenwesen* in Norway.[11]

According to the Law of the Countryside a new king should give a vow to look after peace and justice for the sake of the church and the people after he had been received as a king and hailed. He also pledged to keep the laws which were set by St. Olav,[12] i.e. the ecclesiastical laws. King Magnus may on his hailing have promised to keep up the old letter of reconciliation of his grandfather. He may also have promised to abstain from his patron rights to churches on behalf of himself and his men, the same principle as is later seen in the Concordat of Bergen and the Settlement of Tønsberg.

Another question is *why* the tithe of Finnøy became a hot issue between the bishop of Stavanger and his chapter. The founder of the 'Norwegian Historical School', Rudolf Keyser, put the blame on Bishop Arne for being greedy.[13] The archaeologist A. W. Brøgger had another explanation in his history on Stavanger (1915): the main cause of the conflict was that the bishop lacked funds to rebuild St. Swithun's cathedral. He pointed to the fire in Stavanger in 1272 which caused severe damage to the old Romanesque basilica. The choir was totally destroyed, while the pillars in the nave still remained. The bishop held the responsibility of repairing the churches, including of course the cathedral, and it is interesting that the bishop's part of the tithe from Finnøy was the *fabrica* part. In case the revenues of the actual church were insufficient, the bishop, the chapter, the clergy of the cathedral, and the inhabitants of the diocese ought to contribute to its support. For the support of his cathedral, as for its erection, the bishop could ask for a special aid from his clergy (*subsidium charitativum*).

Bishop Thorgils had started to rebuild the cathedral and extend its choir, but the incomes were limited. Bishop Arne needed more means to

---

11 Note, however, that in 1963 a lead seal mould from Bishop Eirik of Stavanger was found between the stones of an alter base in the foundations of an old church at Hemsedal. Odd Sandaaker has read its rather illegible legend as 'Henricus episcopus Finensis', i.e. Eirik, bishop of Finnøy (Odd Sandaaker, "Biskopen av Finnøy," *Historisk tidsskrift (Norwegian Historical Review)* 63 (1984)). I do not follow Sandaaker in Bishop Eirik using such a title, but the mould may have a connection to the tithe from Finnøy, and also to the conflict between the kings Magnus Erlingsson and Sverre; Bishop Eirik was in the vanguard of King Magnus.

12 L.II.viii. NGL II: 29. Eldbjørg Haug, "St. Olavs lov og unionskongene i senmiddelalderen," in *Årsrapport och Återblick: Tävlingen om det Sporrong Lönnrothska Priset XIX, Norges Høyesterett, Oslo 14-15 juni 2003*, ed. Jacob Sundberg (Stockholm: Institutet för offentlig och internationell rätt, 2003).

13 Keyser, 85.

restore, build, and extend it. Both bishops tried to raise money by collecting indulgence privileges; pilgrims who attended the damaged cathedral on certain feast days, including the three feasts of St. Swithun, could reduce their penitence in Purgatory with 40 days.[14] But the privileges did not reach far enough.[15] Brøgger's explanation of the conflict has been adhered to by historians and has some merit. An example is the use of the chapter's church of St. Mary which was situated next to the cathedral. Valuables belonging to this church played a role in the conflict because the bishop's men had removed them to the cathedral. A chalice and bells are mentioned, indicating that the decors were liturgical items used in the celebration of the mass. The reason behind the removal may have been that they were believed initially to have belonged to the cathedral and were moved to St. Mary's when the cathedral took fire.

But when Bishop Eivind of Oslo issued an indulgence privilege to the Stavanger cathedral 17 April 1289, he did not mention damage to the cathedral any more, in contrast to the older privileges. The same is seen in the indulgence privilege from Pope Nicholas IV (7 October 1290).[16] The reconstruction was at this time obviously finished. A possible explanation to why the conflict manifested itself when the cathedral was finished is that the canons had agreed in all *fabrica*-tithe being used for a common goal up to this point, but objected when the bishop continued to take it for his *mensa*. Still this is not a sufficient explanation of the conflict; a counter-argument is that the canons maintained that they had enjoyed the tithe for 30 years or more. Let us therefore take a closer look at the background of the strife and start with the tension between church and king which led to the Settlement of Tønsberg.

Its point of departure was a matter of legislation. Archbishop Jon Raude of Nidaros had objected when King Magnus presented a new church law to the Frostating as a part of his legislation. On the one hand the archbishop considered the Norwegian ecclesiastical laws to be subject to his

14. DN III nos. 14 – 15, 17 – 19, 23, 25. On the veneration of St. Swithun in Norway see DN XII no. 81 and a discussion in Eldbjørg Haug, "Fra byens grunnleggelse? Nylesning og nytolkning av Stavanger-privilegiet og dets bestemmelsers tradering (English Summary)," in *Stavanger Museums Årbok 2004*, ed. Anne Tove Austbø (Stavanger: Stavanger Museum, 2005), 68 note 128.

15. Isl. ann.: 139 f. P. A. Munch, *Det norske folks historie* (Christiania: 1852-1859), 310 ff; Brøgger, 49 f., 52-100; Gerhard Fischer, *Domkirken i Stavanger: Kirkebygget i middelalderen* (Oslo: Dreyer, 1964); Øystein Ekroll, Jirí Havran, and Morten Stige, *Middelalder i stein*, vol. 1, Kirker i Norge (Arfo, 2000), 116-125; Christopher Hohler, "The Cathedral of St. Swithun at Stavanger in the Twelfth Century," *The Journal of the British Archeological Association* Third series volume XXVII (1964); "Remarks on the early cathedral of Stavanger and related buildings," in *Universitetets Oldsaksamlings Årbok* (Oslo: 1967).

16. DN III no. 25, VI no. 56.

authority; King Magnus maintained on the contrary that his royal office gave him the authority as a legislator also in matters which concerned the church, but also that king and church should cooperate. 1 August 1273 King Magnus and Archbishop Jon thus entered into the Bergen Concordat. On behalf of the church the archbishop renounced the traditional claims of the Norwegian church: a major voice in the election of idoneous kings and the sacrifice of the new king's crown to St. Olav. On the other hand the king guaranteed the church several rights and privileges which had been disputed since the time of King Sverre (1177 – 1202). Significant for the later conflict in Stavanger is that the king accepted ecclesiastical jurisdiction in several specified cases, such as jurisdiction in all cases which concerned clerics and canon law. The church also received several economic privileges, in particular tax exemption. The archbishop obtained the right of exemption for one hundred of his men, while the suffragans enjoyed the same immunity for forty men. The king also renewed and confirmed older rights and privileges for the church.[17]

Both parties agreed that the Concordat should be confirmed by the pope, and Archbishop Jon Raude brought it with him when he went to the Council of Lyon (1274). When he returned, he brought back the message from the pope that he did not ratify the Concordat.[18] The Archbishop must have been behind this, reopening the issues on which he had former agreed with the king. A tense situation between church and state followed.[19]

Bishop Thorgils had attended the meeting in Bergen 1273 and sealed the Concordat, but did not live long enough to see the end to the stalemate in the relationship church – king. When the church and the king met again in Tønsberg in the summer 1277, Arne had succeeded Thorgils as bishop of Stavanger and sealed the new concordat, the Settlement of Tønsberg, as one of two suffragans. This time the parties did not involve the pope.

---

17. Eldbjørg Haug, "Konkordat - konflikt - privilegium: Sættargjerden som indikator på forholdet stat - kirke fra Magnus Lagabøter til Christian I (1273 - 1458)," in *Ecclesia Nidrosiensis 1153-1537: Søkelys på Nidaroskirkens og Nidarosprovinsens historie*, ed. Steinar Imsen, *Senter for middelalderstudier, NTNU. Skrifter* (Trondheim: Tapir, 2003), 88 f.
18. NGL II: 62.
19. Haug, "Konkordat - konflikt - privilegium: Sættargjerden som indikator på forholdet stat - kirke fra Magnus Lagabøter til Christian I (1273 - 1458)," 89 ff. It is interesting to note that the Icelandic Annals do not record the refusal from the pope, but give considerable attention to the collection of the papal six-year tithe which the archbishop started to collect immediately after his return to Norway, and the gift which he brought back from King Philippe of France to King Magnus, a thorn from the crown of Christ. Gustav Storm, ed., *Islandske Annaler indtil 1578* (Christiania: Det norske historiske Kildeskriftfond, 1888), 332, 29, 49, 69, 139, 194, 259, 332.

The Settlement follows the Concordat of Bergen closely, confirming the ecclesiastical jurisdiction in cases which had the privilege of forum *ratione personae*, i.e. caused by the personal status of the actual person.[20] There are, however, some small amendments in favour of the king's position which are significant to the later conflict in Stavanger; the king and his men now promise always to follow canon law in all cases which *undisputedly* are ecclesiastical (cases *mero iure*), a modification contrasting the king's former promise in the Concordat of Bergen. The Norwegian historian Jens Arup Seip interpreted this as a result of the king's reconsideration or caused by pressure from his lay counsellors who would not in every circumstance accept canon law as binding. For Archbishop Jon the amendment was so important that when he referred to it in the provincial statute of 1280, he changed the words to read 'all cases of the same kind which belongs to the jurisdiction of the holy church according to the Law of God.'[21]

The authority of the Norwegian church reached its peak with the Settlement of Tønsberg. But in 1280 King Magnus suddenly died. The minor king's guardians represented a reaction against the church's growing power and had their own agenda. The barons went against the new tithe scale. In their legislation they prohibited the provosts to hold jurisdiction while at the same time practising the cure of souls within their deanery. They went against the Settlement's principles and took an ultra-royalist position in abandoning them according to the legalist theory of concordats: the Settlement was a privilege given by the grace of King Magnus and should not be extended beyond his lifetime.[22] And they started to tax the church. In 1281 the barons finally broke with Archbishop Jon Raude who went in exile to Skara in Sweden where he died towards the end of 1282.

The deterioration in the relations between church and kingdom also affected Stavanger. From 1226 and onwards the bishops had enjoyed the income not only from the landed properties of the church and see, and the tithe, but also the taxes and fines from its possessions. This was the result of King Håkon Håkonsson's renewal of the so-called Stavanger Privilege. He

20. R. Génestal, *Le privilegium fori en France du decret de Gratien a la fin du XIVe siecle*, 2 vols., vol. 35, 39, Bibliotheque de l'ecole des hautes etudes / Sciences religieuses (Paris: Ernest Leroux, 1921), tom. I: II-X.

21. NGL II: 462 – 467; III: 229 – 237. Jens Arup Seip, *Sættargjerden i Tunsberg og kirkens jurisdiksjon* (Oslo: 1942), 167f. On the settlement also see Lars Hamre and Eldbjørg Haug (ed.), "Ein diplomatarisk og rettshistorisk analyse av Sættargjerda i Tunsberg," *Historisk tidsskrift (Norwegian Historical Review)* 82, no. 4 (2003 (†)); Halvdan Koht, "Sættargjerda i Tønsberg 1277," *Historisk tidsskrift (Norwegian Historical Review)* 5. R. 2 (1916).

22. Seip, 110-143, 174-180; Hamre and Eldbjørg Haug (ed.), "Ein diplomatarisk og rettshistorisk analyse av Sættargjerda i Tunsberg," 387; Haug, "Konkordat - konflikt - privilegium: Sættargjerden som indikator på forholdet stat - kirke fra Magnus Lagabøter til Christian I (1273 - 1458)," 98.

confirmed the cathedral's possession of Stavanger with all its underlying parts and rights, including the levy, the *leidang*-tax, which in 1226 still was a personal obligation, and the fines from the cathedral's possessions. By this privilege the bishop of Stavanger was ensured a jurisdiction over the possessions of the cathedral and the see which was not restricted to the subordinate clerics. He had in fact more income from these possessions than the king's sheriffs had from their office; they enjoyed immunity from taxation for themselves and three men and were otherwise paid with the fines. In other words, on the one hand the Stavanger privilege went further than the later Settlement of Tønsberg. On the other hand the Settlement had confirmed the church in its older privileges, thus also the Stavanger Privilege.

But all older privileges to the church were overlooked by the minor king's government of barons. The Law of the Country from 1274 presumed that the *leidang*-tax should be paid as a property tax on land, not as an individual tax. Magnus the Lawmender had, however, not matriculated the land of the church. The barons did this now against many clerical protests.[23] Moreover, the barons demanded *leidang*-tax from the clergy, paid according to the matriculation of their possessions. But when the government tried to tax Bishop Arne's men, he told them to abstain from paying. The episode is told in *Bishop Arní's saga*, which also informs us that the baron Audun Hugleiksson called a moot in the churchyard of St. Mary's and outlawed the men of the bishop. They left the country, and their properties were given to the local baron Gaute of Talgje.[24]

Bishop Arne may have referred to the Settlement of Tønsberg which had given the suffragans immunity of taxation for themselves and forty of their men.[25] The Stavanger Privilege had let the tax on church properties go to the bishop. When this source of income now disappeared Bishop Arne needed to replace it. The reconstruction of the cathedral was not finished, and the costs were great.

The crusade tax of clerical incomes for six years had been collected by Archbishop Jon Raude until his death, but had not been forwarded. Towards the end of 1285 Pope Honorius IV therefore sent his chaplain Huguccio to Scandinavia to collect the balance owed.[26] While Huguccio was in Scandinavia he seems to have become close to the Norwegian king; he was

23. NGL, L III § 6; DN III nos. 6, 20. Seip, 147 f.
24. *Arna saga biskups*: 93-94.
25. NGL II: 465 i.m.
26. DN I no. 75. P. A. Munch, ed., *Pavelige Nuntiers Regnskabs- og Dagbøger* (Kristiania: 1864), 156; Yngve Brilioth, *Den påfliga beskattningen af Sverige intill den stora schismen* (Uppsala: 1915), 101-104.

among the king's delegates to Scotland in 1292.[27] But the papal collection of the six years' tithe put another strain on Bishop Arne. This may have been the situation when he decided to achieve a larger part of the tithe for his *mensa*, the tithe from Finnøy. The situation invited to such a step also from another point of view: the canons who earlier had received the tithe may still have been exiled. In circumstances like this it was the bishop's duty as 'Shepherd of the Church' to take care of the rights of his men.

The conflict between the church and the barons came, however, to an end in the middle of the 1280s and the political climate changed. The church gave up their new tithe scale around 1290. In Stavanger the cathedral was finished and the church had not the same need as before for resources. Without a common external enemy the conflict between bishop and chapter started to develop.

3. The principles

The conflict in Stavanger was a civil case between two ecclesiastical institutions and belonged to the *forum externo*. Bishop Arne was the *judex a quo* (lower authority), but the canons considered that he had deprived them of what rightfully belonged to them and 10 December 1294 appealed his ruling to the pope. Gratian and the decretalists had established the Roman see as a court of first instance, and the right of appeal to the pope was universal and unrestricted. At any stage in a dispute, with or without an initial process in a local court, an aggrieved party could appeal to the pope. Arne consequently wrote an *apostolos* through Abbot Eirik in Munkeliv monastery in Bergen who forwarded it directly to the pope.[28]

It was, however, impossible as well as impractical to bring any litigation for the Rota in Rome. In response to the aggrieved party the pope often empowered one or more local ecclesiastics to summon the parties, examine witnesses, evaluate the evidence, and reach a judgment by the pope's authority. The delegated judges had the right to commission sub-

---

27. Cf. Rymer, Foedera 1: III: 1112: I: 777 f.; DN XIX no. 372. 361-64, 373-379, no. 377.

28. DN IV nos. 8, 9. Jane E. Sayers, *Papal Judges Delegate in the Province of Canterbury, 1198-1254: A Study in Ecclesiastical Jurisdiction and Administration* (London: Oxford University Press, 1971), 2-8; Charles Duggan, "Papal Judges Delegate and the "New Law"," in *Decretals and the Creation of "New Law" in the Twelfth Century: Judges, Judgements, Equity, and Law*, ed. Charles Duggan, *Collected Studies Series* (Aldershot: Ashgate, 1998), 172-180.
The *apostolos* was sent by the Stavanger chapter's nuncio *Nicholas dictus Albus* which is Latin for white. He probably belonged to the Danish Hvide-family; 'Hvide' is Danish for white. The contemporary Lund canon John Albus belonged to this family.

delegates to collect evidence and mandate the execution of sentence by the local ordinary which is seen in the case of Stavanger. The pope first authorised only one *iudex delegatus*, the already mentioned abbot in Bergen. Later the pope authorised three judges delegate, the bishops of Oslo and Hamar, and the abbot of the Cistercian monastery Hovedø nearby Oslo. Worth noting is that the commission went to the judges in their respective offices. While Bishop Eivind of Oslo took part in most court sessions, Bishop Thorstein used the opportunity given a delegated judge to authorise a canon to replace him in some of them. Abbot Halle of Hovedø died while the case still versed for the court, but was replaced by his successor Bård.

While Bishop Thorgils' reason for the perpetual reallocation to the common table of the residing canons in Stavanger was the poverty of their prebends, Bishop Arne emphasized that it was a alienation which was prejudicial to great harm of the *mensa* and the see. In other words he raised the legal issue how far a bishop could go in prejudicing the rights and properties of his office. This was widely discussed in the Middle Ages, not only in Norway, and concerned the kingdom and its rights as well as those of the church. If Bishop Thorgils' transfer of the tithe from Finnøy could be considered as a privilege a characteristic feature would be that it could be revoked. In the Middle Ages we often see that privileges are given only for the life time of the donor.[29] A king's gift of royal property would, however,give the receiver the allodium rights.[30]

Related to these issues were: How should the office of the bishop be regarded? Both canon law and canonistic doctrine set rather narrow limits in the disposal of the bishop's *mensa* and the rights of the office. A bishop should be considered as a guardian who temporarily administered the rights and properties of his office, in line with any beneficiary. He neither owned the rights of his office nor had a lordship of them, he *administered* them. Bishop Arne could apply the Latin maxim *nemo plus iuris ad alium transferre potest quam ipse habet* (nobody can give away a greater right than he possesses).[31]

Moreover, a bishop was always bound by the prohibition of alienation. Movable or real property or a property right could not be sold or otherwise transferred from the church unless it was remunerated with a gift or rights of the same value. But also in the case of an exchange the alienation should be

29. Lars Hamre, review of Grethe Authén Blom: Kongemakt og privilegier i Norge inntil 1387, *Historisk tidsskrift (Norwegian Historical Review)* 49, no. 2 (1970): 195.
30. Grethe Authén Blom, "Replikk [reply to the critic of Lars Hamre and Gudmund Sandvik]," *Historisk tidsskrift (Norwegian Historical Review)* 49 (1970): 227.
31. Hamre: 195.

approved by a superior.[32] This was the legal reason for Bishop Arne; the tithe from Finnøy was given contrary to the canonical institutes of alienation and to great harm for him and his church.

The chapter's position was another. They could point to tithes which had formerly been given to monasteries like Munkeliv, and also the tithe from four churches which the archbishop had granted the canons in Nidaros when he founded their common table.[33] Although the canonical prohibition of alienation was absolute it was possible to circumvent. There were three valid reasons: *urgens necessitas, evidens utilitas* and *christiana necessitas* (cogent necessity, evidently useful, and a deed of Christian love). As a cogent necessity one can find shortage of food or clothes for a priest. Bishop Thorgils' transfer to the chapter's common *mensa* was motivated by the poverty of the prebends and fits in with this reason. But it could also be considered as evidently useful to the church that the canons had the necessary means to perform their duties. This explanation points to a possible reorganisation of the chapter, from a regular to a secular one, an issue which is discussed below.

4. Abbot Eirik of Munkeliv as *iudex delegatus*

Pope Boniface VIII answered the chapter's appeal by empowering Abbot Eirik to investigate the case and give his verdict.[34] During normal circumstances the metropolitan would have been a more obvious choice as *iudex delegatus*, but Archbishop Jørund's (1288-1309) simultaneous conflict with his chapter in Nidaros forbade him to be the judge.

In the beginning of September 1295 the abbot sub-delegated four priests to summon Bishop Arne to Bergen within a set limit of time to answer some questions; the procedural rules in canon law followed the same deadlines for being summoned to a legal hearing as in Roman civil law and secular Norwegian law. The priests ignored, however, the abbot's instruction. Later reports show that at least some were in the bishop's vanguard.[35]

Bishop Arne sent an appeal to Pope Boniface VIII in which he disputed the competence of Abbot Eirik. The appeal is not preserved, and neither the reason for it nor its date are known. It was later revealed that the

32. "Gåve," in *Kulturhistorisk leksikon for nordisk middelalder* (København: Rosenkilde og Bagger, 1960); "Kongegåve," in *Kulturhistorisk leksikon for nordisk middelalder* (København: 1964) vol. IX.
33. DN III no. 4. Cf. Jeremiah Francis Kelliher, *Loss of privileges* (Washington: Catholic University of America Press, 1964), 5 f. on the time limit of a privilege.
34. DN IV no. 11.
35. DN IV no. 16.

same person had presented the case on behalf of both parties to the pope.[36] Two Nidaros canons stayed at the university in Bologna in 1296 and may have helped in presenting the bishop's appeal – and the other side's complaints – to the Curia.[37] As already mentioned a similar conflict in the archdiocese occurred at the same time as the conflict in Stavanger, and the canons may have inspired each other.

The canons tried to avoid Bishop Arne's appeal; they explained that the abbot had been part in a case with the bishop 'which was settled', but probably glossed over the larger context; the explanation may have been a matter of principle:

On 24 May 1295 the abbot had acted as Duke Håkon's judge delegate in a royal court in Ryfylke, a region in the Stavanger diocese. The case was a dispute between the local priest and the inhabitants concerning the salmon fisheries at Fakstad.[38] Bishop Arne had given this farm to the canons of the chapter in 1283 on the condition that they annually commemorated his day of death with a mass and offered 12 marks to the church and the same to the poor.[39] The conflict over the fisheries was a mixed case which involved laymen as well as the church. Later in the Middle Ages the king's law speaker and the bishop's official often presided together in cases like this when they were brought to court.[40] In 1296 an objection to the abbot's competence may have been related to him acting as a royal judge; there had been a manifest conflict concerning ecclesiastical jurisdiction during the minority government of King Eirik Magnusson which was not resolved yet. Moreover, that a conflict concerning the title rights of the bishop's gift had been appealed to a *royal court* was probably against Bishop Arne's principles and may have been the reason for him disputing the abbot's competence.

The bishop's appeal had met no reaction when the abbot of Munkeliv sub-delegated the canon Åke in the Church of the Apostles in Bergen and Bishop Thorstein of Hamar to hear and resolve the case at issue. Åke was high in rank, educated at a European university, and is often referred to as

36. DN IV no. 22. The bishop's appeal was sent around Easter 1296 at the latest. Pope Boniface VIII's four letters are issued 11 November 1296. Rome could be reached in 10 weeks from Norway if everything went well, but approximately six months should also be given to the administrative procedure at the curia.
37. Åke Sällström, *Bologna och Norden intill Avignonpåvedømets tid*, vol. 5, Bibliotheca historica Lundensis (Lund: 1957), 167 f.
38. DN II no. 35.
39. DN II no. 21.
40. Cf. DN II no. 222; Eldbjørg Haug, *Provincia Nidrosiensis i dronning Margretes unions- og maktpolitikk: With an English Summary*, 2nd ed., vol. 54, Skriftserie fra Historisk institutt (Trondheim: Historisk institutt, NTNU, 2006), 72.

magister (master). He was the chancellor of Duke Håkon Magnusson. Bishop Thorstein asked, however, to be excused.[41]

The bishop had an agent, Bartholomew of Poland,[42] who on 2 October 1296 arrived at Abbot Eirik's with some letters of unknown content. The abbot referred him, however, to the chancellor and the already mentioned bishop of Hamar. Master Åke in vain summoned Bishop Arne.[43] His judgement by default of which only a fragment is preserved ruled that the tithe from Finnøy should go into the hands of the canons of the cathedral 'subject to the ownership of [...]', the fragment does not say of what. The bishop should within a month pay the canons the tithe from the last two years. Those who in spite of the verdict harmed the chapter were threatened with excommunication or interdict.[44]

A judgement should be promulgated orally and publicly, and the verdict was pronounced in the bishop's own cathedral. The chancellor followed up by issuing a copy of the verdict. But Bishop Arne declared publicly that he would not obey the ruling of the chancellor, and sent his servants to Finnøy with his letter in which he demanded the annual tithe to be paid;[45] the bishop had appealed the case to the pope and may have complained about the abbot sub-delegating a cleric who exerted a secular profession; a debate was going on if such a person could enjoy the privilege of forum.[46] Two years later more is learnt of the case. The priest Eirik called 'guest' had on the instruction of Bishop Arne taken the tithe-share of the

41. Thorstein is mentioned as a canon in this draft (DN IV no. 16), but it has been assumed to be an error for the bishop of Hamar. The date of this sub-delegation (27 September 1296) is given in the record, but must also be wrong; Pope Boniface VIII refers to the chancellor's ruling in a new mandate given only two months later. A travel to Rome took around 10 weeks, and the papal bureaucracy should be given at least half a year to handle the case. In his judicial verdict issued before 24 November 1296 Master Åke says that Bishop Arne had been summoned thrice. The time limit for serving a writ gives room for only one subpoena from Master Åke after September 27. There is the possibility that the verdict refers to two subpoenas from the abbot. But a better explanation is that also the date of the sub-delegation is wrong; a date around Easter 1296 fits better. Bishop Thorstein took later part in the papal court. On Pope Alexander III's decretal on sub-delegation in the judicial process, see a summary in Duggan, 178 a).

42. Bartholomew is a rare name in Norway, but during these years three persons carry the name. The agent may be identical with the public notary Bartholomew Ortolani who records some of the documents in the case of King Erik Menved of Denmark vs. Archbishop Jens Grand (DD 2: V no. 42 19 June 1299). None of the documents from Norway concerning Bartholomew of Poland require that he was present when they were written.

43. DN IV nos. 15, 16.

44. DN VII no. 27. The preserved text of the fragment is only on the right side of the parchment.

45. DN IV nos. 15, 16, 27.

46. Génestal, 183-195

priest as well as the *fabrica*-share which belonged to the chapter, and refused the Eucharist on Easter Sunday to those who did not pay the tithe to him.[47]

Now Duke Håkon intervened. 24 November 1296 he confirmed the judgement of his chancellor and ordered the inhabitants of Finnøy to pay their tithe to the canons. Everyone who paid to anybody but the canons should give the double tithe and a fine to the duke of 13 mark and 8 ørtug, which was the law's most severe penalty. He also asked Basse Guttormsson and Amund Sigurdsson, local barons and members of his *hirð* (the royal retinue and bodyguard), to support the canons and the farmers in this case. Anybody who took the tithe with brute force would be outlawed.[48] Master Åke followed up by prohibiting Bishop Arne to do anything in conflict with his verdict. And having the sub-delegated apostolic authority he threatened him with interdict or excommunication if he did not follow his ruling.[49]

5. New issues

The duke's intervention was a lay intermingling in the internal affairs of the church. The reason for the bishop ignoring the chancellor's verdict may be that 11 November 1296 Pope Boniface VIII authorised three judges, the bishops of Oslo and Hamar, and the Cistercian abbot of Hovedø monastery, to summon all parties and take all conflicts into consideration. The judgement of the chancellor should either be verified or judicially declared null and void. The commission also said that the ombudsmen of both parties agreed in the procedure (*de vtriusque partis procuratorum assensu*), but this was later denied by the bishop.[50]

The sole cause to the conflict was not any longer the tithe from Finnøy; other issues had been raised concerning beneficial rights, inheritances, and ownership to decors, churches, and properties.[51] The duke added to the conflict by giving the canons a building site next to St. Olav's monastery.[52] Let us examine closer what happened outside the courtroom.

The first reported incident was the banning of the canon Ingemund of Skagen. The bishop had dismissed him from his office and benefice because

47. DN IV no. 23. This indicates that Eirik Gæstr was the parish priest at Finnøy, his epithet that he belonged to the 'guests', the lowest rank of the *hirð*.
48. DN I no. 84.
49. DN IV 15.
50. DN IV nos. 11, 22.
51. DN IV nos. 11, 14, 41, 42, 44, 47.
52. DN III no. 41, IV no. 26; on the date (27 February 1297) see Asgaut Steinnes, "Datering etter styringsår under Eirik og Håkon Magnussøner 1280-1299," *Historisk tidsskrift* 31 (1937): 37.

he had mingled in worldly affairs. The bishop also accused him of serious crimes – unjustified, according to Ingemund. But if this was true, the canon had abused his privilege of forum and could not refer to canon law for protection.[53] The excommunicated canon nevertheless appealed his case to the pope who 11 November 1296 commissioned it to his papal judges delegate.[54] The concurrence in time with the appeal from Bishop Arne suggests that the excommunication and dismissal had taken place approximately one year before.

By interacting with Ingemund who was now a banned person the members of the chapter had been excommunicated *ipso facto*.[55] The argument of the counterpart being excommunicated *ipso facto* is often seen in the evidence from the conflict. Sometimes, as in this case, the argument is founded in canon law. The Provincial Statute of Archbishop Jon 1280 had adopted these cases from the Decretals, but was also inspired by the list of cases for excommunication *ipso facto* which the pope used to post on the door of the Lateran church every Maundy Thursday.[56]

Ingemund's case had nothing to do with the tithe from Finnøy, but was probably based on a dispute over property. The knight Sigurd of Randaberg had given the farm Sunnanå (Vikedal) to St. Swithun's church, probably on the condition of masses on his anniversaries. When he died, Sunnanå was held by the canon Ingemund and his brother Åsmund as a pawn, but the owner had the right to redeem it. The case had been pending for the secular court because Ingemund and Åsmund disputed the redemption of the church. In 1292 Archbishop Jørund therefore recalled the former verdict and ruled that Sunnanå belonged to the Stavanger church, and that the brothers should be compensated for their expenses.[57] Three years after the ruling the case seemingly had become a part of the conflict between Bishop Arne and the chapter.[58]

The chapter's position in this was that they had the right to incomes from gifts to the church on the condition of anniversaries. The masses were mostly sung by a canon who usually received one half of the interest from the gift as a compensation for his service. Most wills also emphasized such

53. See the essay in this volume by Bruce Brasington, *Frustra legis auxilium invocat: Uses and Transformations of a Medieval Legal and Political Maxim*.
54. DN IV no. 13.
55. DN IV no. 22.
56. See DN IV no. 24; F. Clacys Boúaert, "Bulle *In Cœna Domini*," *Dictionnaire de Droit Canonique* III; Erik Gunnes, "Left Papers in EG's Archive," (The Norwegian National Archives, without year); Haug, "Konkordat - konflikt - privilegium: Sættargjerden som indikator på forholdet stat - kirke fra Magnus Lagabøter til Christian I (1273 - 1458)," 99.
57. DN II no. 31.
58. The chapter and the bishop had a common ownership to Sunnanå in 1319, DN III no. 116.

a division between the church and the canons. Still disputes over inheritances connected to the properties Hodne, Rossavik, Mjølhus, and Orstad, all farms in present-day Rogaland, occurred in the conflict.[59] When Ingemund, supported by the chapter, later complained of Bishop Arne having stolen his grain, this was probably the canons' rents from Sunnanå. The bishop's men allegedly also stole grain from the canons, no reference, but it was probably thought to be rents from disputed properties.[60]

The canons also claimed a collecting box on the cathedral's main altar. This was the altar of Swithun with its precious relic of an arm from the saint. It is hard to believe that the canons demanded the oblations to the saint itself, the box was rather meant to reward the priest who actually celebrated the mass.

A report further illustrates the conflict over beneficial rights. The bailiff of the local sheriff (Basse Guttormsson) and another Stavanger-man stated 10 February 1298 that they had been at the bishop's quay when his men arrived with firewood which the canons had bought. The canons read Duke Håkon's protection letter from 1292,[61] the bailiff proclaimed that anybody who opposed it by removing the wood were subject to the most severe fine of the law for 'breaking the duke's letter' (*brefabrót*) and summoned the perpetrators to appear for the duke's court within a month. Alas, in vain. Master Steinar, the schoolmaster, took God as his witness in obliging 'another letter and jurisdiction'; the wood should be removed to the house of the bishop. The letter which Steinar referred to presumably was from the bishop while 'another jurisdiction' was the ecclesiastical one; the duke's men should not intervene in that. The wood was removed, 'against the will of the canons.'[62]

20 of the bishop's men took part in the theft. The referred report told that the canons had bought the wood from Sigmund at Helle, situated in Forsand, south-east of Stavanger and in the opposite direction of Finnøy. Such an act was not titled in any law, and the removal of the firewood must have another explanation than mere robbery. From where the bishop's men had taken the wood is not known, but it is hard to believe that Sigmund had been involved in its removal. No excuses are given in the evidence left to us, the interlocutory and final rulings were that it should be given back to the canons or compensated for. And this was done in the end.[63] Access to firewood may have been considered a beneficial right for those who celebrated mass in an unheated cathedral, something the canons were short

59. DN IV no. 25. Eldbjørg Haug, "Den første abbeden på Utstein og Arnbjørn av Heimnes," *Ætt og heim* (2006).
60. DN IV no. 48.
61. See note 4.
62. DN II no. 39. Concerning the year see DN IV no. 26 and RN II no. 906 note 1.
63. DN IV no. 38.

of and had on their agenda. From the papal Camera is learnt that the papal minor penitentiaries had a certain amount of firewood as a right.[64] The bishop and his men may have believed that the chapter sought to readjust their unfair deal by taking the law into their own hand. This may also be an example of other products thån grain, butter or milk being paid as the tithe.

6. The papal judges delegate in action

Pope Boniface VIII's mandate reached Norway in the spring 1297. On May 27 the papal judges delegate commissioned Abbot Arnfinn of Utstein monastery and the rectors Arnbjørn of Tjore and William of Høle in their capacities as office-holders to serve Bishop Arne with a summons to meet personally or with a deputy in Oslo on the first *thing* day after the feast of St. Mary's nativity (8 September) and give his answer to the complaints from the chapter. The papal judges foresaw the possibility that the bishop would avoid receiving the citation; he could claim the summons invalid if he had not received it within the fixed limit of time. If so happened they should read the subpoena publicly in the Stavanger cathedral.[65]

The sub-delegates followed the instruction, but Bishop Arne did not appear in court. A second session was scheduled in mid-April, the subpoena probably sent from Oslo around 10 February 1298. For the second time the bishop was a no-show. The papal judges delegate therefore ruled (21 April 1298) that he had showed contumacy, but still considered their verdict as interlocutory due to his rank. He should compensate the chapter for the costs of their case. He should also be summoned a third time to answer the complaints of the chapter and the canon Ingemund, and this time the ruling should be peremptory.[66]

Bishop Arne had, however, this time sent two of his men to the court session in Oslo. 7 May 1298, somewhat more than a fortnight after the judges had given their interlocutory judgement, the priests Salomon and Torberg read an appeal from the choir of the cathedral in Oslo. The weather and the wind had obstructed them, and they had therefore arrived in Oslo a couple of days too late to meet before the papal judges delegate in the conflict between Bishop Arne on the one hand and the chapter of Stavanger and the former canon Ingemund on the other. They had asked for the documents in the case, but they were denied them. On behalf of Bishop Arne they objected to the judgement of 21 April 1298 because the canons

64. DS IV no. 3532. Eldbjørg Haug, "Penitentiaries, Scandinavian," *International Encyclopaedia for the Middle Ages-Online. A Supplement to LexMA-Online* (2007),
65. DN IV 17.
66. DN IV no. 20.

Kjetil and Jon *ipso facto* had fallen into the church's ban by interacting with the excommunicated Ingemund. They had also used the help of the secular power against the church and its clerics. Bishop Arne had appealed his case from the former papal judges to the Apostolic Curia, but the same person had presented the case on behalf of both parties. They therefore considered the pope's authorisation of judges null and void. They appealed the case to be settled by the pope and submitted themselves to the protection of the Apostolic See.[67]

The third session of the court was set to the first thing day after Trinity (June 1).[68] The appeal of Bishop Arne's deputies was vehemently opposed by the leader of the Stavanger chapter, Canon Kjetil, and Canon Ingemund of Skagen; their plea is extensively referred in the final verdict of 13 June 1298. They maintained that Salomon was not in a position to be an authorised agent because he was a temple defiler who had taken decors and bells from the church of St. Mary. He was excommunicated *ipso facto* for having violently pulled Canon Kjetil through the church and churchyard, and thereafter incarcerated him. Torberg had also fallen into excommunication for turning his back to these and other crimes against the chapters. – The canons pointed to central elements in the canonical privileges which they claimed had been violated. They furthermore denied that all interested parties and all judges had been present when the canons Kjetil and Torberg read their appeal, that the judges had refused to hear them, that the canons had called for the secular arm, and that the judges had been appointed contrary to former prescripts which only concerned the tithe of Finnøy; that case was not tried now. It was moreover not true that the case was treated by the Roman Curia. The canons Kjetil and Ingemund therefore finally asked that the court proceeded with the case, in spite of the appeal and the bishop's absence.[69]

The papal judges delegate considered the appeal of the bishop a frivolous one, and went to action.[70] Bishop Arne was sentenced for having shown contumacy by not appearing in court after having received a third subpoena. He was to pay the chapter 15 marks to compensate their expenses. The chapter was confirmed in its possession of fields next to the church of St. Olav in Stavanger and the above-mentioned collecting box on St. Swithun's altar.[71] The income from Hodne, Rossavik, Mjølhus and Orstad should be divided equally between the bishop and the chapter.

---

67. DN IV no. 22.
68. DN IV nos. 20, 21.
69. DN IV no. 24.
70. DN IV no. 30. The so-called frivolous appeals were made for no other reason than to retard the execution of a sentence justly pronounced. Canon law's prohibition can be traced back to Roman civil laws.
71. DN IV no. 25.

The promulgation and execution of the verdict was handed over to the canon and rector of the church in Kinsarvik Thorkel, Bård of Avaldsnes, probably the rector of St. Olav's church, and the former mentioned rector Eirik of Gand.[72] Subject to excommunication authorised by the pope those who had stolen the firewood from the chapter should give it back or compensate for it within a month. The sub-delegates should instruct Bishop Arne to return the chalice, the books and the other decors which he had taken from the church of St. Mary within the same time limit, and before September 29 he should compensate the damage which he had inflicted upon the chapter. The executors should report to the judges on their progress with the case.[73] Concerning the grain which was stolen from the canon Ingemund the priest Bileiv and his helpers should give it back or compensate him, also this subject to excommunication.[74]

Having been convinced by the leading canons of Stavanger the delegated judges still had doubts concerning the process. A week after their sentence they with reference to the appeal of Bishop Arne's agents summoned him to appear in court on the first day of thing after St. Mary's nativity if he had proofs to show in the case.[75]

The bishop stayed in an accomodation in Tønsberg in July 1298 when the rector Eirik of Gand and the Stavanger canon Olav asked for access to his pension to read the sentence. He refused, and Canon Kjetil read it out loud and clear in the presence of witnesses outside the bishop's lodging.[76] Arne did not appreciate the disrespectful way in which his subordinate Eirik had treated him. He dismissed him from his office and the benefice Gand and installed Ivar Steinvardsson, one of his followers, in the office.[77]

Bishop Arne also appointed Svein, another of his men, as vicar in Håland in the community Sola.[78] Bishop Thorgils had given this church to the chapter,[79] and Bishop Arne and the canons had entered into an agreement which probably concerned its incomes and collation rights. This settlement was now dismissed by the bishop. In stead he gave the new vicar the income from half the church properties, 'although it had been rented to a farmer'. No ordinary vicar is, however, mentioned, and it is possible that most of the incomes from the actual church had gone to the canons that paid a vicar to keep up the cure of souls. Canon Kjetil asked the sub-delegated

72. DN IV nos. 25, 27, cf. no. 36. St. Olav's church at Avaldsnes was a royal chapel, a collegiate church with four clerics (p. 31).
73. DN IV no 26.
74. DN IV no. 28.
75. DN IV no. 31.
76. 16 July 1298, DN IV no. 32.
77. DN V no. 37.
78. DN IV no. 23.
79. DN II no. 15.

judges and rectors Arnbjørn of Tjore, William of Høle, and Eirik of Gand to excommunicate Svein, but they did not considered themselves authorised to do so and 12 May 1298 asked the papal judges delegate for further instructions.[80]

The delegated executors were authorised to instruct seven of the bishop's men to pay back what they had stolen (grain, firewood) and excommunicate them without further ado. The problem was that such a procedure of excommunication was against canon law, which prescribed three admonitions before a ban could be executed. The excommunication was therefore appealed by the seven priests (13 September 1298).[81]

In March 1299 there was another court session in which Bishop Arne's deputy Bartholomew of Poland presented his part's litigation. The canons Kjetil and Jon answered it, but Bartholomew refused to say anything more. The reason may have been that the canons now presented arguments in a case in which Bartholomew had no instructions. Another explanation is that he was not present when the chapters' deputies presented their plea.[82]

7. The call for secular authorities

The papal judges delegate handed the execution of the judicial verdict over to the sheriff Basse Guttormsson of Rygjafylke and his men. The chapter was reinstated in the possession of the fields next to St. Olav's church. Basse kept the keys to the storehouse of the grain and should hand them over to the canons to ensure that the grain was not spoiled.[83] A report from the executors stated that ten priests had plundered several of the mansions belonging to the chapter and the canon Ingemund in spite of being warned while the case was pending. Assumingly they were acting according to instructions from Bishop Arne and had not taken notice of the threat of excommunication. The three executors had in vain instructed Bishop Arne to return the chalice, the books and the other decors which had been taken from the canons' church. The executors continued by naming the 20 persons who had taken part in the theft of firewood from the chapter. They were instructed to compensate the chapter within a month. 'Long overdue and on behalf of all of them Eirik Bratt did so.'[84]

The bishop of Hamar and the new abbot of Hovedø, Bård, instructed the rectors Thorkel of Kinsarvik and Arnbjørn of Tjore to reinstate their colleague Eirik in his office as rector of Gand (19 June 1299), and

80. DN IV no. 23.
81. DN IV no. 36.
82. DN II no. 51.
83. DN II nos. 48, 51.
84. DN IV no. 38.

excommunicate Ivar Steinvardsson who had taken over his office. Eirik was reinstated in the beginning of September, but only by the rector of Kinsarvik;[85] from now on Arnbjørn of Tjore ignored the mandates of the papal judges delegate.[86] We further note that William, the rector of Høle, was not any longer a sub-delegate, perhaps because he had excommunicated the laymen who had executed the judgement of the papal judges delegate.[87]

In their verdict of 19 June 1299 the papal judges delegate emphasised the rights of the chapter in the appointment of priests and other rights connected with canon law. This is new compared with the judgement of 13 June 1298 and may have been inspired by the case of Eirik of Gand. Even more prejudicial was, however, the Concord of Tautra which Archbishop Jørund had entered into with his canons on the Eve of St. John the Baptist (June 23) 1297. The Concord concerned issues which were special for the archdiocese, but also economic and beneficial rights of the chapter.[88] Although the Concord had the form of a *notitia* it was a precedent and created new particular law. Also another agreement from 1297 (May 2 or September13) between King Eirik Magnusson and Bishop Arne of Skálholt on the ownership to the Icelandic so-called *staðir* churches may have been relevant for the Stavanger case.[89]

The papal judges delegate recalled that the chapter of Stavanger for more than a year had enjoyed the rights which they had obtained from the verdict one year ago (see note 71). The verdict was confirmed, on the condition that Bishop Arne had the right to try the rights of the properties before a competent court. There had been court proceedings concerning the inheritances from Abbot Arnbjørn of Utstein and his relative, the baron Arnbjørn of Heimnes.[90] The judgement probably refers to offers whose context it had not been possible to account for.[91] Subject to excommunication and within a month the bishop should compensate the chapter of the harvests which he had taken from them. By September 29 (Michaelmas) he should pay them back the income from manors, oblations and donations connected to masses on death days which he wrongly had taken from them. If necessary the secular power should protect the chapter

85. DN V no. 37, 39.
86. T.a.q. 7 September 1299, t.p.q. 1 December 1299, cf. discussion RN II no. 1018. DN III no. 43.
87. DN IV no. 48.
88. DN III no. 39. More on this issue in Hamre, edited by Eldbjørg Haug, and Steinar Imsen, "Striden mellom erkebiskop Jørund og domkapitlet i Nidaros. English Summary," 187 ff.187 ff.
89. DI no. 167. Stefánsson, "Eigenkirche, -nwesen, 1. Island," passim.
90. Haug, "Den første abbeden på Utstein og Arnbjørn av Heimnes," 7-22.
91. '*Textus seu tabule pro offerenda portentur per ecclesiam secundum antiquam consuetudinem [in] capitulum. nisi aliter ordinetur per episcopum de consensu capituli.*' DN IV no. 47.

and the rights which the papal judges had assigned to them. The rectors Arnbjørn of Tjore and Jon of Hjelmeland were instructed to execute the rulings of the papal court together with the rector of Kinsarvik according to the demands of the chapter or face excommunication.[92]

It is worth noting that several local lords participated in the conflict. Count Jakob of Halland was present in the court session in Oslo c. 20 April 1298. He is particularly interesting for having found a refuge in the Stavanger region after having been accused of murdering the Danish King Erik Glipping and outlawed.[93] *Sub plica* in a vidimus of the ruling 19 June 1299 can be read 'in the presence of Count Jakob of Halland and many other good men.' The count took part in the secular judicial administration in Ryfylke and is an example of a refugee who reached a high position in exile. We also learn that the count and the *hirð* men Sigurd of Randaberg and Håkon of Reve were present in Bishop Arne's court when the ruling was read to him 3 September 1299.[94]

Obviously the case was now treated by the secular court, because the law speaker in Rygjafylke (the already mentioned Sigurd of Randaberg) and local secular jurors reported that Bishop Arne had been interrogated by the rector of Kinsarvik and admitted to be responsible for the acting of priests, clerics, and laymen against the canons.[95] They confirmed that the ruling of the papal jurors had been read to Bishop Arne in Latin and in a Norse translation, and gave a resume of the verdict. Moreover, they recalled that the bishop's men had been called to the local court meeting, but none appeared. The rector Arnbjørn of Tjore was summoned to meet in court on the 7th of September and bring the letter which he had former received on the execution of the sentence. He did not show up.[96]

8. The arbitration

Although the chapter to our knowledge had won on every single point which had been disputed, the conflict had created severe tensions within the Stavanger diocese. Four priests had ignored to communicate the subpoena from Abbot Eirik of Munkeliv in 1295, and two papal sub-delegates had

92. DN IV no. 41, 42, 44.
93. DN IV no. 24. Stig Andersen, another of the Danish outlaws, also stayed in Norway.
94. DN IV no. 41, 42, 44.
95. '[...] *þatt være hans boð oc vili a sem prestar, clærkar, oc leikmenn gerdo aa skada korsbrodra ofuer þeira at taka tiundir korn af akrom þeira vid, oc adra luti oc han sagde sik openberlegha þatt boditt hafua oc alltt annatt þatt sem korsbræðr seigia ser raghntt gortt uera, af ymisim monnom.*' DN II no. 54.
96. DN II no. 54, V no. 39.

defected from their duties and were assumingly in Bishop Arne's vanguard. Other clerics whom we do not know of may have done the same. A settlement in court with a winner and a loser was no good solution in a small community. The parties should continue to cooperate for a common cause.

This may be the reasoning behind Archbishop Jørund's effort of arbitration. 13 November 1299 he and Bishop Narve of Bergen announced that Bishop Arne and the chapter's deputies, the canons Jon and Kjetil, had compromised to leave the conflicts on the tithe of Finnøy, wills, donations for masses, other tithes, oblations, properties, the allocation of benefices and all the other matters which had been disputed and for a long time tried by papal judges delegate, to the arbitration of the same men. The parties promised to respect and abide with their decision, or face a punishment of £20 sterling.[97]

The arbitrators – and papal judges – issued their ruling 1 December 1299. With reference to there having been doubts about the former sentences in the cases of the Stavanger chapter vs. Bishop Arne, and to make sure that there should be no more disagreement they abolished their former rulings. Bishop Arne was instructed to revoke the excommunications and sentences concerning loss of office and benefices and not obstruct them any more of freely using them. Abbot Arnfinn of Utstein should absolve all laymen and clerics in Stavanger and the diocese who might have been excommunicated, to enable them to testify in the case. The bishop's part of the tithe of Finnøy should belong to the chapter's *mensa*, as decided by Bishop Thorgils. The ownership of the disputed fields next to St. Olav's should be left to the canon's *mensa*. Rents from gifts and oblations should be left to those whom it concerned and sanctioned by the canons. The collation and benefices to altars in the cathedral, the churches in Stavanger and the rural districts should be given by the bishop with the consent of the chapter. Properties left to the church for anniversaries should benefit those who fulfilled the will's conditions. Salaries to vicars or non-resident canons should not be diminished unless the bishop and the canons agreed. Donations whose contexts could not be established, should be dealt with according to old custom, and if changed by the bishop with the consent of the chapter. Other outstanding issues should be settled in court on the first thing day after the feast of St. Hallvard.[98] The document in settling the

97. DN IV no. 46.

98. DN IV no. 47. Two documents which may be connected to the sharing of properties conditioned on anniversaries of a man's death concern Abbot Arnbjørn's donation of 12 *månedsmatsbol* in Hodne and Olav of Foss's donation of what he owned in Rossavik (DN IV nos. 55, 56).

outstanding issues as well as regulating those which were never mentioned before may be inspired by the Concord of Tautra.[99]

According to the arbitration Bishop Arne now offered the chapter two farms as compensation. But the canons refused to accept anything before the bishop had recalled his sentences against them, and had paid them the 12 mark which they had been bequeathed by King Magnus Håkonsson.[100] Four priests in the diocese, among them the bishop's brother Aslak of Hundvåg and the former mentioned sub-delegated judge William of Høle, were each sentenced to pay 6 mark to the five *hirð* men who had been excommunicated by them for executing the judgement and taking back the grain which was stolen from the canons.[101]

The conflict should now be settled, but it seems as Bishop Arne had not given in yet. When 2 June 1302 the canon Jon on behalf of the canons registered a new donation letter from King Håkon in court he also demanded that Bishop Arne complied with the arbitration by recalling his rulings against some of them, gave a guarantee for the compensation of 60 mark *brent* (i.e. 'burnt' silver) to the canons, and paid them 12 mark according to the will of King Magnus Håkonsson. To protect themselves from the bishop and his men's encroachment of their rights Jon finally placed the canons and their properties under the protection of the pope and his judges delegate.[102]

This is the last evidence on the conflict; Bishop Arne died towards the end of 1303,[103] and 1 May 1304 two canons of Stavanger presented their election of a new bishop to Archbishop Jørund for his approval and consecration. The elect was Canon Kjetil who had been the spokesman of the chapter throughout its strife with Bishop Arne. To rest assured that the elect would follow up what he had achieved for his fellow canons he had given them an election pledge.[104]

The conflict in Stavanger over the tithe from Finnøy and beneficial rights thus ended with arbitration and a new bishop. Why the case took the direction from a papal delegated court via the intervention of seculars and ended with arbitration will be discussed below, but first we have to look into the organisation of the chapter.

99. DN III no. 39. Hamre, edited by Eldbjørg Haug, and Steinar Imsen, "Striden mellom erkebiskop Jørund og domkapitlet i Nidaros. English Summary," 207.
100. DN IV no. 49.
101. Peter of Fister and Thord of Soma are mentioned as well as the bishop's brother Aslak of Hundvåg and the already mentioned rector William of Høle, DN IV 48.
102. DN IV no. 54, cf. III no. 41.
103. DN IV no. 9.
104. DN II no. 73.

9. The secularisation of the chapter

The conflict in Stavanger is relevant to the organisation of the diocese and the secularisation of the chapter. The commonly held view is that the Norwegian chapters were not organised before the church province was established in 1152-1153, and that this was so late that they were secular from the start. According to Chrodegang's rule the chapter's leader should be a provost, but only a few provosts are mentioned in 13th century Norway.

One of them is Master Eirik who is mentioned as provost at Lista deanery in Stavanger diocese in 1280; Brøgger presumed that he was the schoolmaster and that Lista with the parish Vanse was the only canonry benefice in Stavanger which was connected to a particular function, that of the schoolmaster. But Lista had also a royal chapel and thus a royal chaplain. Not excluding Brøgger's interpretation I have suggested that the royal chaplain at Lista cumulated a canonry in the cathedral chapter and held the deanery as his prebend.[105]

Seip considered that provosts were not introduced in Norway on a general basis before 1273 when the Bergen Concordat was agreed upon. The tasks of the provosts were to take care of the administrative and economical affairs of the church within each deanery. The leader of the Nidaros chapter was normally a deacon, while archdeacons led the chapters of Stavanger, Bergen, and Hamar. The leader in Oslo was called archpriest. When Pope Celestine III in 1196 granted the chapter of Nidaros the ecclesiastical jurisdiction, he referred to the three archdeaconries and the deaconry that his predecessor, Pope Adrian IV, had established.[106] Only the Oslo diocese was partitioned systematically in deaneries. In the Bergen

105. DN XII nr. 8, 15, 17, 22. Brøgger, 168; Haug, "Fra byens grunnleggelse? Nylesning og nytolkning av Stavanger-privilegiet og dets bestemmelsers tradering (English Summary)," ; "Middelalderens lærdomsinstitusjoner i Stavanger-regionen" (paper presented at the conference "Universitetet - idé og institusjon", Utstein Kloster, 3 February 2006).

106. DN I no. 1. A Norwegian archdeacon Henricus is mentioned in the 1160s (*Regesta Norvegica* vol. I no. 116 with reference to the Pipe Rolls for the 11th year of Henry II). I have raised the questions if he is identical with the later Stavanger bishop and archbishop Eirik Ivarsson and/or has been the archdeacon of Shetland ("Fra Stavanger-kirkens tidligste historie," *Historisk tidsskrift (Norwegian Historical Review)* 88, no. 3 (2009): 478. The archdeacon Erling is mentioned in a document from 1170-1190, probably from Bergen, DN VIII no. 2. Archdeacon Andres of Shetland in mentioned in the Icelandic *Annales regii* as deceased in 1215 (Storm: Islandske Annaler: 124). Einar Molland, "Ærkedegn," *Kulturhistorisk leksikon for nordisk middelalder* 20 (1976): col. 573-575 Brian Smith raises the question in a forthcoming work if the archdeaconry came into existence when the secular disjunction between Shetland and Orkney occurred, after having studied the *syslumaðr* Gregory keeker, *viz*. Brian Smith, "Who was Gregory 'keeker'?," *Unkans* 2010, 4.

diocese the office of *hofud* priest ('head priest') are synonymous with the (Latin) *rector ecclesie*, and some of them were called provosts in the Late Middle Ages.[107] Bearing in mind that the rectors of Gand, Tjora and Høle were involved as sub-delegated judges in the conflict in the Stavanger diocese in the 1290s, a reasonable hypothesis is that they had the same function as their colleagues in the Bergen diocese.

We often meet the view that the Norwegian chapters were founded at the same time as the church province and never were regular. Margit Hübert, the only scholar who has presented a comprehensive study of the Norwegian chapters, saw the possibilities of another interpretation. She considered that there were regular priests at the episcopal sees of Selja, Nidaros, and Stavanger before 1152. In these places there were both monasteries and episcopal churches, and the priests acted as chapters.[108] We can say the same of the cathedrals in Iceland and Gardar, churches that never had chapters, but monks that certainly performed the necessary liturgical functions when the bishop celebrated the mass.[109] The Swedish diocese Skara, which was strongly influenced from the Norwegian region Viken, had a regular chapter according to the Augustinian rule in 1220.[110] Uppsala had a regular chapter that followed the Benedictine rule around 1200, and also in Denmark there were several regular chapters.[111]

In Stavanger there was a Benedictine monastery dedicated to St. Olav. It has been presumed that it was founded by the first bishop of Stavanger during King Sigurd Jorsalfar's rule (1103 – 1130); he founded the permanent see c. 1125.[112] It is, however, likely that the monastery was founded somewhat earlier. We recall that Stavanger possessed a precious relic of St. Swithun. The assumption that Bishop Reinald brought the relic to the cathedral when he became bishop of Stavanger has been challenged by the fact that there are no known translations of the saint between 1093 and 1050. Because the relic is a large one, it is more probable that it was

---

107. Sigríður Júliusdóttir, "The Major Churches in Iceland and Norway: A Study into the Major Churches in Skálholt Diocese and Bergen Diocese in the 11th to the 15th Centuries" (Cand. philol. thesis, Bergen, 2006), 52-77.
108. Margit Hübert, *Nogen undersøkelser om de norske domkapitler væsentlig indtil 1450*, vol. 6, Bidrag til norsk historie (Oslo: Grøndahl & Søns Boktrykkeri, 1922), 20; Lars Hamre, "Domkapitel. Norge," *Kulturhistorisk leksikon for nordisk middelalder* III (1958): col. 196.
109. Ívar Bárðarson and Finnur Jónsson, *Det gamle Grønlands beskrivelse* (København: Levin & Munksgaard, 1930).
110. Herman Schück, "Det augustinska kanikesamfundet vid Skara domkyrka: En studie om den västgötska kyrkan och des förbindelser under 1200-talet," in *Kyrka och rike - från folkungatid til vasatid*, ed. Herman Schück (Stockholm: 2005), 87-163.
111. Kauko Pirinen, "Domkapitel," *Kulturhistorisk leksikon for nordisk middelalder* III (1958): 186 f.
112. Edv. Bull, "Et kloster i Stavanger," *Stavanger Museums Årskrift* (1910).

translated to Norway before the Conquest, with 1093 as *t.a.p*. The relic belonged to the church in Stavanger before 1100 and thus before the establishment of the permanent episcopal see. There was a need for priests in liturgical and pastoral functions connected to this relic, and the first priests at the shrine may have formed the core group of the monastery in Stavanger.[113]

Moreover, the monastery may also have functioned as the first chapter of the cathedral. It is tempting to point to the well-known influence from English mission in the Christianisation of Norway. But the influence went beyond mere conversion; the Anglo-Saxon saints and the liturgies according to *Regularis Concordia anglicae nationis* are good examples of Wessex' influence in the establishment of a Norwegian church. According to this Anglo-Saxon church reform (c. 975) the Benedictine monasteries functioned as chapters for the cathedrals.

A chapter's free election of bishops is supposed to be its most important task, and the one which gave the canons power. But the religious in St. Olav's monastery had no right in this respect before the church province was established in the middle of the twelfth century. Moreover, the Norwegian kings continued to appoint bishops also after 1153. Worth noticing is that in the neighbouring Scandinavian kingdoms the king's right to present bishop candidates and consent in their election continued in the 13th century, although not unopposed.

During the civil wars in Norway (1130-1240) there was a severe conflict between church and state during the rule of King Sverre. His son and successor Håkon Sverresson was reconciled with the church, but his rule was short. In the Fourth Lateran Council 1215 the free election of bishops was established as canon law, but it is hard to believe that the kings never intervened in the election after the Council, at least in presenting candidates.[114] The civil wars may have delayed the secularisation of the chapter of Stavanger.[115] The peaceful conditions from 1240 and onwards

113. Hohler, "The Cathedral of St. Swithun at Stavanger in the Twelfth Century," 94, 115; "Remarks on the early cathedral of Stavanger and related buildings," ; Michael Lapidge, *The Cult of St Swithun*, vol. 4.ii, Winchester Studies (Oxford: Clarendon, 2003), 792; Haug, "Fra byens grunnleggelse? Nylesning og nytolkning av Stavanger-privilegiet og dets bestemmelsers tradering (English Summary)," 33 – 36; a concise resume of the old view and a critic of mine in Knut Helle, "Stavanger by og Utstein kloster," *Historisk tidsskrift (Norwegian Historical Review)* 87, no. 4 (2008): particularly pp. 593 - 598; Haug, "Fra Stavanger-kirkens tidligste historie," 464 f.

114. The earliest record from the Norwegian province concerns the Sodor see, DN XIX no.128, 9 November 1219.

115. Hübert, 19 f; Hamre, "Domkapitel. Norge," col. 195 f; Eldbjørg Haug, ed., *Utstein kloster og Klosterøys historie* (Rennesøy: Stiftelsen Utstein Kloster, 2005), 119 - 122; "Middelalderens lærdomsinstitusjoner i Stavanger-regionen" ; Esben

seem to have encouraged an inrush to the chapters from the higher echelon of society. Many of them were highly qualified men who as secular canons were used by the kings in the daily affairs of the kingdom; several of the Stavanger canons can be identified in the king's service.

As late as 1236 an agreement between Bishop Askell of Stavanger (1226-1254) and Archbishop Sigurd (1231-1252) concerning the diocese's contribution to a new archbishop's travel expenses to Rome was confirmed by the Stavanger chapter and testified on the Stavanger side by Bishop Askell, Bishop Nicholas of Gardar, the abbot 'N' in the monastery (of St Olav) and the prior 'E''at the same place, on the Nidaros side by three canons of the archiepiscopal see.[116] Bishop Nicholas was probably identical with the archdeacon 'N' who was one of the addressees in the Stavanger Privilege (t.p.q. 1226 - t.a.q. 1223); he is mentioned immediately after Bishop Askell and before the chapter. The bishop had obviously a connection to the Stavanger church and has been considered as the leader of the Stavanger chapter. We should, however, not exclude that he was identical with Archdeacon Nicholas of Shetland who is only mentioned in 1226 and must then have stayed in Norway.[117] The pope demanded that all similar agreements between the metropolitan and his suffragans should be confirmed by the chapters,[118] so the record from Stavanger is an indication of the monastery of St. Olav still playing a role in the administration of the Stavanger church. We also note that no archdeacon is mentioned in the chapter during its conflict with Bishop Arne. Rather than the chapter being either regular or secular a better explanation is therefore that its secularisation was a process; most of its canons were regular well into the 13th century.

In the later Middle Ages the chapter was, however, secular. Duke Håkon's donation to the canons of sites in his common land east of St. Mary's church shows that around 1300 the canons had a need for building plots other than the monastery. That the donation was a part of the conflict

---

Albrectsen, "Abelslægten og de schauenburgske hertuger," in *De slesvigske hertuger*, ed. Carsten Porskrog Rasmussen, Inge Adriansen, and Lennart S. Madsen (Aabenraa: Historisk Samfund for Sønderjylland, 2005), 7.

116. Heinrich Kalteisen and Alexander Bugge, eds., *Erkebiskop Henrik Kalteisens Kopibog* (Christiania: Det Norske Historiske Kildeskriftfond, 1899), 192.

117. DN I no. 51; DN I no. 9. Odd Sandaaker, "Håkon Håkonsson og Stavanger-privilegiet," *Historisk tidsskrift (Norwegian Historical Review)* 49 (1970): 292; Brian Smith, "Archdeacons of Shetland 1095-1567," in *Ecclesia Nidrosiensis 1153-1537: Søkelys på Nidaroskirkens og Nidarosprovinsens historie*, ed. Steinar Imsen (Trondheim: Tapir, 2003), 161 identifies the archdeacon of Shetland with the Archdeacon Nicholas who attended the meeting in Bergen 1223 (Marina Mundt, ed., *Hákonar saga Hákonarsonar etter Sth. 8 fol., AM 325,4o og AM 304,4o*, vol. 2, Norrøne tekster (Oslo: Kjeldeskriftfondet, 1977), cap. 89 (86): 376).

118. DN I no. 21.

indicates that the bishop had disputed this right.[119] But the buildings of the monastery still seem to have been used by the chapter. When 27 February 1297 Duke Håkon gave them a plot, it was described as 'the plot limited by the fence east of their house, downwards from the churchyard to the creek, and from the fences at the hospital field to the lane by the churchyard of St. Swithun.' This description fits with a plot east of the site where St. Olav's monastery used to be. Put together this is evidence for the monastery still being the chapter's house.[120] From the middle of the 14th century records show that the chapter had their common table in the 'refectory', an expression which is found in no other episcopal see and points to the old monastery. A relatively late secularisation contributes to explain Bishop Thorgils' reallocation of resources to the chapter caused by the 'poverty of the prebends'. His reallocation of the tithe from Finnøy was probably motivated by the new challenges which the secularisation of St. Olav's monastery meant.[121]

10. The intervention of Håkon Magnusson

We have seen that the conflict between bishop and chapter in Stavanger was not kept in the ecclesiastical court, that it reached a stalemate, and that sub-delegated clerics presumably not taking part in the conflict ended up in one or the other camps. Bishop Arne did not accept the papal commission and abided neither by its judgement nor by its arbitration for reasons that are somewhat obscure. In the last document concerning the strife the parties are encouraged to voluntarily follow the ruling of the papal judges concerning the tithe issue. To a certain extent both parties were right. In such a situation there is a need for something totally different, an instance from outside. Pope Boniface VIII with his own problems was too far away. Could the answer come from the new king, the former Duke Håkon, or was he too much involved on the side of the chapter?

We recall that Duke Håkon gave the canons several plots next to the monastery and the church of St. Mary. We also remember his protection letter of 1292. In this document he calls them his 'special' clerics. This is a feudal element which indicates that the canons had an homagial relationship to the duke.[122] When Håkon had succeeded his brother as king, he renewed

---

119. DN III no. 41, IV 54.
120. '*tuft ser til gardz austr þar sem stoua þeirra stenðr, niðr fra kirkiu gardenom allt till beksens, oc fra gardenom uid spitals akren fram till gotunnar uid Suithuns kirkiu garð.*' DN III no. 41, IV no. 26.
121. DN IV nos. 335, 340; Haug, ed., *Utstein kloster og Klosterøys historie*, 158.
122. '*Uær uilium at þer vitið at ver hafum tækit korsbræðr j Stafangre kæra vini vara. ok hæimilegha klærcka. suæina þæirra alla þa sem til komusens hæyra*

the letter (1 June 1300).[123] And King Håkon really had a special relation to the canons in Stavanger. The king had the patron rights to at least five churches in the diocese of which four were later institutionalised in the royal chapel clergy.[124] Some members of the chapter were priests in the royal chapels and held them as their prebends. In this way Håkon Magnusson's special clerics had a double loyalty, to the king and to the bishop.

The king's protection did, however, not solve the conflict in Stavanger. Nor did his threat of severe fines from those who chose to pay the tithe from Finnøy to the bishop's bailiff solve anything. But something completely different seems to have softened the bishop: King Håkon renewed the Stavanger Privilege. The evidence is found in a record from 1450, when King Christian I renewed the Stavanger Privilege after his election and coronation as Norwegian king.[125] Håkon Magnusson must have issued his renewal after he became king in 1299 and before Bishop Arne died towards the end of 1303.

Norwegian historians of the 20th century found it inconceivable that King Håkon Magnusson had renewed the Stavanger Privilege, in spite of the wording of Christian I's renewal document. A renewal of the Stavanger Privilege would be inconsistent with his protection letters which favoured the canons in the internal church conflict.[126]

Apparently scholars have not taken into consideration that Bishop Arne followed up his duties to the royal house along with the other bishops. One duty was to follow the king in war and when he met with other sovereigns. The latter was called *stefnuleiðangr* and is mentioned several

---

huærsdagslega. ok alt þat goz. sem þæir æiga eða æigande verða j lannde eða lausum æyri. vttan garðs oc jnnan. loghlega j huæriu sem huært er tiundir garða. æignir æingia garða. akra ok allt þat sem þæirra kanna læikr a j guðs walld. oc vart fullkomet traust til allra retra mala.' DN I no. 80. Hamre and Eldbjørg Haug (ed.), "Ein diplomatarisk og rettshistorisk analyse av Sættargjerda i Tunsberg," 401.

123. DN I no. 91. There were some adjustments: The canons' men should normally pay fines directly to the king when the penalty concerned the king's law, i.e. *Landsloven*.

124. The royal chapels were St. Olav's at Avaldsnes, St. Peter's at Sørbø, St. Lawrence's at Eigersund, and St. Lawrence's at Lista. The church at Finnøy was another royal church, as pointed out above.

125. DN IV no. 924; NGL 2: I no. 22. In Haug, "Fra byens grunnleggelse? Nylesning og nytolkning av Stavanger-privilegiet og dets bestemmelsers tradering (English Summary)," 11-16 I have shown that the preserved Stavanger Privilege AM fasc. 26 no. 1 is not the original letter from King Håkon Håkonsson. Anne-Marit Hamre has suggested to me that it has been cut out of a book. Something more has been written above and below the preserved document. The writing seems to be from the 13th century. Does this parchment originate from a book in King Håkon Magnusson's chancery? Does the lost text refer to his renewal of his grandfather's privilege?

126. I have discussed their views in chap. II of ibid., 49-53.

times in the sagas (written in the 13th century) and also in canon 3 of the *canones Nidrosienses* (from 1060s – 1070s). When called upon the king's good men gathered in Tønsberg in the latter part of the 13th century.[127] A call for a *stefnuleiðangr* was also the reason why Bishop Arne stayed in Tønsberg in the summer 1298. The bishops are seldom mentioned in connection with such meetings, along with a lot of other laymen, but Bishop Arne reportedly from Denmark excommunicated the rector Eirik of Gand 1 September 1298, and must have been a part of the king's retinue.[128]

The Stavanger Privilege must have been renewed after Håkon Magnusson's succession to the throne and before Bishop Arne died. There are several occasions when this might have occurred. The first is the day of his coronation which probably was 1 November 1299.[129] The anointment of a new king was an ecclesiastical act, an initiation of the church in line with the consecration of a bishop. It is inconceivable that Bishop Arne was absent. The coronation was also an occasion for the renewal of old privileges as well as giving new ones. The church of St. Mary in Oslo was privileged on this day, and the privilege was renewed 22 June 1302. Bishop Arne was present at the renewal, and this event has been suitable for renewing the Stavanger Privilege.[130] The third occasion was September 1302, when King Håkon issued an amendment to the Law of the Country in which he changed the rules of succession to the throne in order to allow his daughter to succeed him. At the same time he struck at the barons, accusing them of misrule during his and his brother's childhood. Bishop Arne was the second in rank to seal the charter.[131] He had at this time become one of the king's bosom friends.

We cannot say which day Håkon Magnusson renewed the Stavanger privilege; both the coronation and the renewal of the privilege to the church of St. Mary in Oslo point to these occasions as suitable. A renewal as late as in 1302 may explain why nothing more was heard about the conflict in Stavanger. That the Privilege was renewed is, however, more important than when it happened. It has probably more than weighed up for the bishop's

127. Jan E. G. Eriksen and Per Toresen, *Gamle Tønsberg: Middelalderbyen*, vol. V, Gamle Tønsberg (Tønsberg: 1976), http://www-bib.hive.no/tekster/tunsberg/middelalderbyen/del8.html.
128. The Danish magnate Erik of Langeland who was married to the queen dowager's sister Sophia in her second marriage, and the Danish refugees Count Jakob of Halland and Marsk Stig Andersen were excluded from the safe conduct, while Ogmund Krøkedans should stop at Åby. DD 2: IV no. 327. Arild Huitfeldt, *Danmarckis Riges Krønike*, Folio ed. (København: 1595-1603/1650-52) vol. I: 310-11. – Bishop Arne's whereabouts are reported in DN V no. 37.
129. Gustav Storm, "De ældre norske Kongers Kroningsstad " *Historisk tidsskrift (Norwegian Historical Review)* 3. Rk. IV (1898): 399-406.
130. DN I no. 92; *Akershusregisteret* no. 591.
131. NGL III no. 14.

part of the tithe of Finnøy. Once more the bishop received the *leidang*-tax.[132] The end to the conflict in this way seems to be a situation in which the king has solved the legal dilemma, and internal conflict in the church, by renewing an old privilege.

11. Conclusion

This article presents itself as a case study of an ecclesiastical strife within the Stavanger church in Norway. As a case for an ecclesiastical court in the *forum externo* it is also a study of a delegated judicial process from the pope. The background to the strife was a serious conflict between church and kingdom in Norway over jurisdiction and economic rights. Norwegian church leaders, among them Bishop Arne, took a strict stand to leave out the seculars from intermingling in ecclesiastical jurisdiction in 'all cases of the same kind which belongs to the jurisdiction of the holy church according to the Law of God.'[133] When his conflict with the chapter in Stavanger in the course of events took the direction from the ecclesiastical court to intervention of laymen this may have been a matter of principle for Bishop Arne: the *privilegium fori* had been given to the entire clerical state, and could not be renounced by an individual privately.[134] But canon law did not explicitly prohibit papal judges delegate to sub-delegate laymen to execute their rulings. A settling by amicable arbitration was welcomed by the church. If the case should be settled in this way the participation of seculars seemed necessary.[135]

Initially a hypothesis was put forward: that the cause of the conflict in the Stavanger church over the bishop's tithe from Finnøy was a reorganisation connected to a long-term secularisation of the chapter. After having sifted the evidence of St. Olav monastery it offers itself as the regular chapter, and continued to be the house of the secular one in the Late Middle Ages.

Finally we once more see that money oils the machinery. The renewal of the Stavanger Privilege by King Håkon V meant more to the bishop's

132. That he also received the local tax *utskyld* which was privileged to the church in the Late Middle Ages should not be excluded, cf. Haug, "Fra byens grunnleggelse? Nylesning og nytolkning av Stavanger-privilegiet og dets bestemmelsers tradering (English Summary)," 43 f.

133. NGL II: 462 – 467; III: 229 – 237. Seip, 167f. On the settlement also see Hamre and Eldbjørg Haug (ed.), "Ein diplomatarisk og rettshistorisk analyse av Sættargjerda i Tunsberg," 381-431; Koht: 379-396.

134. Kelliher, 11 with reference to C. 12, X, de foro competenti, II, 2 (Innocent III, 1206).

135. Duggan, 175.

mensa than his tithe from Finnøy and offers itself as a solution to the internal church conflict; it levelled the ground for an amicable settlement between the bishop and the chapter, giving both parties a better economic foundation than before.

THE *HAULDR*: PEASANT OR NOBLEMAN?

Jo Rune Ugulen

1. Introduction

When King Canute of Denmark invaded England in 1015, he was, among many others, opposed by the ealdorman of Northumbria, Uhtred. Uhtred was the son of Waltheof, ealdorman of Bamburgh, and belonged to a kindred that had ruled the Rock of Bamburgh since the 9th century. In 1007 he was appointed ealdorman of Northumbria by King Æthelred II, and soon after he married the daughter of a wealthy and powerful inhabitant of York, Styr Ulfsson. This brought Uhtred into conflict with one of Styr's enemies, Thurbrand, who bore the cognomen Hold. Thurbrand was a Northumbrian magnate belonging to one of the most prominent Anglo-Danish families in York. When Sweyn Forkbeard invaded England in 1013, Uhtred joined him. But when Æthelred II returned to England in 1014 after Sweyn's death, he tried to win Uthred back to his side by offering him his daughter, Ælgifu, in marriage. Uhtred repudiated his first wife, and promptly married Ælgifu. When Canute invaded in 1015 Uhtred thus supported his new brother-in-law, Edmund Ironside, against the invading Danes. Canute, on the other side, entered into an alliance with Uhtred's sworn enemy, Thurbrand Hold. Uhtred soon had to give up his resistance to the invading forces, and surrendered to Canute, but was killed by Thurbrand with tacit support from the king in 1016.[1] This fuelled one of the best known feuds in English history. Thurbrand himself was killed by Uhtred's son, ealdorman Ealdred of Bamburgh in 1019.[2] Ealdred was subsequently killed by Thurbrand's

1. Ann Williams, Alfred P. Smyth, and D. P. Kirby, *A Biographical Dictionary of Dark Age Britain: England, Scotland and Wales, c.500–c.1050* (London: Seaby, 1991), 227 and 230–231.
2. Ibid., 227.

son, Carl, in 1038,[3] while several of Carl's sons were later killed by Waltheof, the son of earl Siward of Northumbria and a daughter of Ealdred.[4] However, it is not this feud that I'm going to focus upon, but the story might still work as an introduction to the main subject of this paper, as the cognomen of the Thurbrand killed in 1019, Hold, is corresponding to the Old Norwegian and Old Norse term of *hauldr*.

2. The *hauldr* in Norwegian historiography

In Norwegian historiography the *hauldr* is largely described as an *odelsbonde*, an allodial peasant, and often as *the* symbol of the free peasant society in the Viking Age and the Early Middle Ages. For instance Norwegian historian Andreas Holmsen wrote in his classic textbook from the late 1930's, later reprinted several times well into the 1990's, that the 'normal person still is [around 1100] everywhere the allodial peasant or the *hauldr*.' Holmsen adds that the concept *hauldr* can not have meant the same in every part of the country, but that he reckons the *hauldr* to be a peasant, is hardly worth discussing. He continues to write that the concept everywhere points to the man who is sitting free and independent on the farm that his kindred has owned for generations.[5]

Historian Ingvild Øye contends in the first volume of the recent Norwegian agricultural history, that the *hauldr* was an integral part of what she calls the real peasant society, although she also advocates that the distinction between a *hauldr* and a *bonde* (peasant) in the Gulating law shows a social and judicial division of peasant society in the early medieval era. She also points to the fact that a similar distinction existed in Trøndelag according to the Frostating law, between the hauldr and the so-called *årbårne menn*. The distinction seems not to have been as clear in the eastern parts of Norway, where this was seemingly not taken into effect until the

3. Ibid., 117.
4. Frank Merry Stenton, *Anglo-Saxon England*, Third ed., Oxford History of England (Oxford/New York: Oxford University Press, 1971; reissued paperback edition 1998), 390, note 1. The main source for this story is an anonymous chronicle from around 1090, called 'De obsessione Dunelmi, et de probitate Uchtredi comitis, et de comitibus qui ei successerunt'. It is published in *Symeonis Monachi Opera Omnia: Historia Ecclesiæ Dunhelmensis*, ed. Thomas Arnold, vol. 75:1, *Rerum Britannicarum Medii Ævi, Scriptores* (London: Her Majesty's Stationery Office, 1882; reprint, London: Klaus Reprint Ltd., 1965). The feud itself is thoroughly analysed by Richard Fletcher in his book *Bloodfeud: Murder and Revenge in Anglo-Saxon England*, published in 2003.
5. Andreas Holmsen, *Norges historie fra de eldste tider til 1660*, 4. utgave (Oslo/Bergen/Stavanger/Tromsø: Universitetsforlaget, 1977; reprint 1991), 180.

Landslaw from the 1270's.[6] Most other contemporary Norwegian historians maintain this view, that the *hauldr* was an integral part of Norwegian peasant society, and that he first and foremost was an allodial peasant.[7]

I'm not quite convinced that this is entirely correct. I tend to agree more with the overview of the social groups presented in a book written by Ole Georg Moseng, Erik Opsahl, Gunnar Pettersen and Erling Sandmo from 1999, where the *hauldr*, together with *årbåren mann*, *bonde* og *rekstegn*, is placed in a group referred to as 'fully free outside public hierarchies', and not directly into peasant society.[8]

3. An Old English source

From the first part of the 10th century there exist a list of the size of wergeld-fines in the Scandinavian kingdom of York and Northumbria, the so-called *Norðleoda laga* ('the law of the people of the north').[9] *Wergeld* is the term for the fixed amount, or blood-price, payable by a killer and his kin to his victim's kinsmen. The amount or the size of the wergeld was also an important mark of social status.[10] Thus *wergeld* is the equivalent of the similar custom (*gjald*, pl. *gjöld*) we find in the Norwegian regional laws, and later in the Landslaw.[11]

6. Ingvild Øye, 'Landbruk under press 800–1350,' in *Jorda blir levevei: 4000 f. Kr-1350*, by Bjørn Myhre and Ingvild Øye, *Norges landbrukshistorie* (Oslo: Det Norske Samlaget, 2002), vol. 1, 258.
7. See for instance *Bjarkøyretten: Nidaros eldste bylov*, trans. Jan Ragnar Hagland and Jørn Sandnes, Norrøne bokverk (Oslo: Det Norske Samlaget, 1997), 107. Jón Viðar Sigurðsson, *Norsk historie 800–1300: Frå høvdingmakt til konge- og kyrkjemakt*, vol. 1, Samlagets Norsk historie 800–2000 (Oslo: Det Norske Samlaget, 1999), 206–207. Knut Helle, *Gulatinget og Gulatingslova* (Leikanger: Skald, 2001), 117. Cf. Jo Rune Ugulen, 'Haulden: Bonde eller aristokrat?', in *Rettstekstar i mellomalderen - Idé og praksis*, ed. Jørn Øyrehagen Sunde, *Rettshistoriske studier (Institutt for offentlig retts skriftserie, nr. 6/2006)* (Oslo: Institutt for offentlig rett, UiO, 2006), 57–58.
8. Ole Georg Moseng et al., *Norsk historie I: 750–1537* (Oslo: Tano Aschehoug, 1999), 91.
9. *Die Gesetze der Angelsachsen*, ed. Felix Liebermann, Herausgegeben im Auftrage der Savigny-Stiftung ed., 3 vols. (Aalen: Scientia, 1960; reprint, Unveränderter Neudruck der Ausgabe 1903–1916), vol. I, 458–461. The text itself only survives through an early 11th century collection, ascribed to archbishop Wulfstan of York (1002–1023), but which in part must rely on an older copy. Cf. Dorothy Bethurum, 'Six Anonymous Old English Codes,' *Journal of English and Germanic Philology* XLIX, no. 4 (1950).
10. John A. Cannon, ed., *The Oxford Companion to British History*, Revised edition ed. (Oxford: Oxford University Press, 2002), 973, s. v. 'wergeld'.
11. See for instance Helle, *Gulatinget og Gulatingslova*, 117.

The law referred to, is:[12]

> [1] Norðleoda cynges gild is XXX þusend þrymsa: fiftene þusend þrymsa bið þæs wergildes, XV þusend þæs cynedomes; se wer gebirað magum ok seo cynebot þam leodum.
> [2] Arcebiscopes ok æþelinges wergild is XV þusend þrymsa.
> [3] Biscopes ok ealdormannes VIII þusend ðrymsa.
> [4] Holdes ok cyninges heahgerefan IIII þusend þrimsa.
> [5] Mæsseþegnes ok worldþegnes II þusend þrimsa.
> [6] Ceorles wergild is CC ok LXVI þrimsa, þæt bið II hund scill'. be Myrcna lage.

To quote Sir Frank Stenton: This 'early list of Northumbrian wergilds shows a grading of ranks to which there is no exact parallel elsewhere.' In addition the wergelds are expressed in terms of *þrymsa*, an ancient unit of account, instead of the much more common *shilling*. One such *þrymsa* probably corresponds to three silver pennies. At the bottom of this list one finds that the life of a *ceorl* was valued to 266 *þrymsa*, a sum which comes quite near the wergeld of a Mercian *ceorl*.[13] A *ceorl* was the term for the lowest class of free men.[14] Above them we find the *thegn*, who in English historiography is counted among the aristocracy. The thegn has here a wergeld on 2000 þrymsa, a sum also assigned to the mass-thegn or priest. In other Anglo-Saxon laws it was usual that the thegn was valued at six times the wergeld of a ceorl, but here we find that the thegn is valued even higher. In Anglo-Saxon times a thegn was a title reserved for those who owned more than five *hides* of land, and who had the obligation to serve the king as a warrior.[15] Above the thegn, with a wergeld of 4000 *þrymsa*, we find the king's *high reeve*, and what Sir Frank Stenton refers to as 'noblemen of an exalted class who are described as "holds"'.[16] The office of high reeve must either be of higher rank than, or simply correspond to the so-called *shire-reeves* (*scirgerefa*), the later sheriffs, who were the highest-ranking royal official in a county,[17] and probably quite similar to the later Norwegian *syslemann*. However, Hector Chadwick points to the fact that a high reeve also can be equal to an earl, and shows that the Northumbrian earl Osulf in the mid-10th century refers to himself both as *dux* and *hæhgerefa*.[18] Above

12. *Die Gesetze der Angelsachsen*, vol. I, 458–461.
13. Stenton, *Anglo-Saxon England*, 508–509.
14. Cannon, ed., *The Oxford Companion to British History*, 182–183, s. v. 'ceorl'.
15. Ibid., 916, s. v. 'thegns'.
16. Stenton, *Anglo-Saxon England*, 509.
17. See for instance Cannon, ed., *The Oxford Companion to British History*, 791–792, s. v. 'reeve'.
18. Hector Munro Chadwick, *Studies on Anglo-Saxon Institutions* (Cambridge: At the University Press, 1905), 231–233, cf. 237–239.

these we then find *ealdorman* (approximately corresponding to earl, but from time to time it is used of sub-kings, *subreguli*) [19] and bishop with a wergeld of 8000 *þrymsa*. Then archbishop and a king's son (*ætheling*) with 15000 *þrymsa*, before finally we find the king himself valued to 30000 *þrymsa*. This list thus gives us information of an otherwise rather obscure class within the Northumbrian aristocracy or nobility, ranking between thegn and ealdorman.

4. Conclusion

I have gone through most of the available Old Norse and Norwegian sources such as chronicles and sagas, legal texts, charters and diplomas, in addition to a few other references to the *hauldr* in English sources. This material is not included here, but for those of you who read Norwegian and who are in need of further reference, most of it is published in an article that came out as part of the anthology *Rettstekstar i mellomalderen* in 2006.[20] What I have concluded with, is that there is not much that can be said to be absolute conclusive. There is still a lot of uncertainty concerning the correspondence of these terminologies, and thus much will remain tentative. But one conclusion that in my opinion can be drawn, based on the sources available to us today, is that the Norwegian *hauldr* was not simply a peasant, or an allodial one for that matter. Beside this the Norwegian source material, mainly the laws, is very ambiguous. The contemporary Anglo-Saxon sources do however indicate that the *hauldr*, as the term was used by the Vikings on the British Isles in the 10th century, was a comparatively high-ranking bigshot. I subsequently have to disagree with Andreas Holmsen in that the *hauldr* was the 'normal person' in 12th century Norway. If it is at all possible to speak of a 'normal person' in the Middle Ages, it is likely that this person was neither landowning or high-ranking, as the *hauldr* seems to have been. The fact that the *hauld*'s wergeld in the Gulating law formed the basis of the wergeld for the remaining social groups, does in my opinion tell us more about the social group that drew up the lawcode, than it does of 'normal persons'. It is reasonable to assume that those who controlled the land as well as the use of the land, at the same time were powerful enough to use this power to draw up law as well as to enforce it.

That the *hauldr* largely is defined as an allodial peasant by most Norwegian historians, I find terminologically unfortunate. Of course the *hauldr* was a farmer (a *bonde*) – at least as long as he was involved in agriculture. As long as medieval Norway was an agrarian society, it was at the same time a peasant society, and everyone from slave to king was

19. Cannon, ed., *The Oxford Companion to British History*, 317, s. v. 'ealdorman'.
20. Ugulen, 'Haulden: Bonde eller aristokrat?', 61–72.

wholly embedded in this peasant society. But I find it somewhat difficult to place the *hauldr*, the *bonde* and the slave into a peasant society based on the wergeld lists in the laws. In my opinion the wergeld does not tell us anything about peasant society as such, but it rather tells us about social stratification in society in its entirety, and not just as a peasant society. Very interesting concerning this matter is a paragraph in the Gulating law usually referred to as G200. There it is said that the son of a *lendmann* (from the 1270's termed baron) should have the right of a *hauldr* if he didn't get land. This might imply that the real difference between a *hauldr* and a *lendmann*, was that the *lendmann* had received land from the king, whereas the *hauldr* had not. This is supported by the fact that later in the same paragraph it is said that a *skutilsvein* (a class referred to as knights from the 1270's) should have the same rights as a *hauld*. Royal service, or not, thus seems to be what separates the *hauldr* from the *lendmann's* son and *skutilsvein*.

When it comes to the term *hauldr* it seems to be anachronistic by the latter half of the 13th century. In the Norwegian Landslaw I've found the term only in four places, and as a byname or cognomen it seems to have stopped being used at some time during the 12th century. Most places where we find *hauldr* as a cognomen outside of England, it is used by people who must have been of high rank in the regional aristocracy, and hardly ought to be characterized as mere local bigshots. A question is whether it is possible, based on the meagre amount of sources, to see a development of the meaning of the concept of *hauldr* from the Viking Age until around 1300. Based on English sources from the 10th century I find it reasonable to acknowledge the *hauldr* as a powerful man not only locally, but also on a 'national' level, as they appear as warlords worthy of being mentioned by name when they fell in battle against the English. It is not unreasonable to transfer a similar status across the North Sea to contemporary 10th century Norway. That the term in itself becomes rarer and rarer throughout the 12th and 13th centuries in Norway, indicates that it gradually became anachronistic. Powerful men who at the same time did not perform royal service were probably uncommon around 1200. That the size of this social group is diminishing is also indicated by a paragraph in the Landslaw (Landsleigebolken, ch. 61) where it is said that twelve *haulds* should be appointed witnesses in disputes concerning commons, but if *haulds* are not to be found, twelve of the best among free men (*bønder*) should be appointed. In another paragraph concerning whaling (Landsleigebolken, ch. 64), the term *hauldr* is even defined,[21] a fact that support the idea that the *hauldr* is a vanishing concept, or that the definition in this particular case

21. A *hauldr* is he who has inherited *odelsgods* from both mother and father, and whose ancestors have possessed before them, and where the *odel* of another man has not been infused by means of buying or distant inheritance (*utarv*). See *Norges gamle Love*, II, ed. Rudolf Keyser and P. A. Munch (Christiania, 1848), 146. Cf. *Magnus Lagabøters landslov*, ed. Absalon Taranger (Kristiania, 1915), 158.

should be seen as special. On the other hand, it might also indicate that the meaning of the concept had in fact changed into what many historians claim that the *hauldr* was: an allodial peasant (*odelsbonde*). The definition of a *hauldr* in this chapter on whaling might just as well be an expression of a more expanded meaning of the concept, as a more limited meaning. That the real meaning of concepts of this type changes and develops throughout time is not uncommon. The Anglo-Saxon title of *ealdorman* was in 9th century Wessex used as a term for a royal servant, although a quite powerful one. A century later the ealdorman had evolved into something much closer to a hereditary position under far less royal control than before;[22] a similar development occured with other Anglo-Saxon terms such as *gesith* and *thegn* from the 7th to the 10th century.[23]

The term does not disappear completely in Norway though. Occasionally it is found in late medieval charters, such as one from 1446 where we are told that a man called Salmund at Vinje in 1430 had bought land from 'hauldborne menn' who had owned the land from time immemorial ('frå haug og heidni').[24] As late as 1634 the Norwegian chancellor Jens Bjelke in his book of explanations to the Norwegian lawcode, *Termini Juridici*, says that a *hauldr* is a man who is more than a common man.[25]

I'm not claiming that with this paper I have found *the* solution to what a *hauldr* was or has been. I do however feel that I have argued reasonably for the case that there has to have been a rather extensive development in the meaning of the concept from the 10th towards the 13th century. I thus find it relatively safe to express my support of what was said by Hector Munro Chadwick as early as 1905: 'The person with the wergeld (...) corresponding to the freeman of the continental laws, was originally the *bóndi*. The *höldr* or *hold* had a double wergeld and must be regarded as a nobleman'.[26]

22. Henry Royston Loyn, 'The Term Ealdorman in the Translations Prepared at the Time of King Alfred', *The English Historical Review* 68 (1953), 524.
23. Henry Royston Loyn , 'Gesiths and Thegns in Anglo-Saxon England from the Seventh to the Tenth Century', *The English Historical Review* 70 (1955).
24. *Diplomatarium Norvegicum: Oldbreve til Kundskab om Norges indre og ydre Forhold, Sprog, Slægter, Sæder, Lovgivning og Rettergang i Middelalderen*, ed. Christian Christoph Andreas Lange et al., 22 vols. (Christiania / Oslo: Norsk historisk Kjeldeskrift-Institutt, 1847–1995), vol. XXI, no. 434.
25. Jens Ågessøn Bjelke, *Termini Juridici*, ed. Sigurd Kolsrud (Oslo: Norsk historisk Kjeldeskrift-Institutt, 1952), 121.
26. Chadwick, *Studies on Anglo-Saxon Institutions*, p. 399.

POWER, LAW, AND THE ADMINISTRATION OF JUSTICE IN ENGLAND 900-1200

John G. H. Hudson

1. Introduction

This paper is one of a series that I have been writing as attempts to compare the nature and practices of law in England in c. 1200 with those in the tenth century. They seek to provide the argument for my volume of *The Oxford History of the Laws of England* covering the period from Alfred's code to Magna Carta. Put in a different way, they are a series of meditations or explorations as to why I am very largely convinced by Patrick Wormald's picture of law and justice in late Anglo-Saxon England, less convinced by his view of the determinative contribution of that period to the later development of English law.[1] Implicit in my paper, therefore, is the question of the periodisation of legal as opposed to other forms of history.

Distinctions between law and power, with underlying assumptions concerning right and might, influence much historiography. There is a tendency to see law, legal history, as somehow detached from the history of the real workings of politics and society, particularly if it can be referred to as 'old fashioned, black letter, legal history'. Patrick Wormald took pride in not being a 'Legal Historian' in the 'orthodox capitalised sense.' I remember Rees Davies commenting at dinner – tongue firmly in cheek, I hope – that the legal historians were sat well away at the end of the table. The legal historians can fight back – I think it is Sir John Baker who notes that you can tell works of legal history written by historians, because they

1. See esp. the essays collected in his *Legal Culture in the Early Medieval West* (London: 1999).

feel obliged to use 'and Society' in the titles, or at least the sub-titles of their books, whereas the lawyer legal historian knows that the relationship of law to society is considerably too distant to require such tokenism.

One reaction amongst historians interested in the areas formerly the preserve of the legal historian has been to shift the focus to the analysis of disputing. Here, all too often, however, the distinction between law and power has simply been collapsed, with an abandonment of the normative, a simple concentration on the political or the social. This shift has occurred partly under the influence of social anthropology, and of works such as Comaroff and Roberts' *Rules and Processes.*[2] Those historians analysing disputes have particularly seized on the processual element within this study, and the relative subordination of rules to processes; they have been in danger, however, of neglecting the role that Comaroff and Roberts allow to rules even within the societies they study, let alone considering the different distribution of power in medieval ones.

At the same time, some writers on legal theory have been considering the relationship of law and power. Even those with a quite formalist or positivist view of law will admit that legal rules have an open texture, particularly apparent in hard cases, and in such circumstances non-normative elements will intrude. Other jurisprudential approaches, be they those of Marxists or of the legal realists break down the law/power distinction still further. Most recently, the movement known as 'Critical Legal Studies' has emphasised that power is embedded in law; that there is ambiguity in all legal rules; that such ambiguity necessarily involves interpretation, and interpretation will involve power and interests; therefore, even when rules seem to produce regular answers to legal problems, such answers are not definitive.[3]

Such ideas and approaches in history and in jurisprudence underlie this paper. At the same time they suggest many themes that I will not today pursue. In particular there are the broadest of questions, for example the role of law in the perpetuation or reproduction of social relations and of inequalities of power. One might also investigate how exercise of power was legitimated by reference to law, or the ideological bases upon which the power of law rested, or how some degree of routinised sense of obedience to the law developed. I will concentrate instead on the administration of justice. I want to discuss how royal servants derived power from their role in justice and their knowledge of law; how these administrators affected the development of law; and how royal administration of justice affected the distinction between law and the forceful assertion of power.

---

2. J. L. Comaroff and S. Roberts, *Rules and Processes: the Cultural Logic of Dispute in an African Context* (Chicago: 1981). See also J. Hudson, 'La interpretación de disputas y resoluciones: el caso inglés, c. 1066-1135', *Hispania,* lvii (1997), 885-916.
3. See e.g. M. Kelman, *A Guide to Critical Legal Studies* (Harvard: 1987).

2. Personal power derived from law

Personal power could be derived from law and from the workings of justice in various ways. The position of a king might be strengthened by his acting as legislator, not merely through the introduction or reinforcement of regulations but also through the recalling of great law-givers of the past, most notably Moses but also, for example, the Roman emperors.[4] Kings and others could also present themselves in a fashion resonant of great archetypes when acting as judge.

At the same time, control of a court offered obvious opportunity for personal advancement through the assertion of influence or the acceptance of bribes or other perks. Take the late Anglo-Saxon case of a merchant named Flodoald who had a household servant, whom he liked greatly. The man was seized by the king's reeve, Eadric of Colne, for an offence.[5] It was ordered that the accused be held by some king's thegns until his lord came and the servant was then to go to trial by hot iron. If cleared, he was to go free, if found guilty, to suffer capital punishment.[6] Hearing that his servant was being held in chains, Flodoald went swiftly to ask Eadric to waive the ordeal and keep the aforesaid household servant on servile terms.

As this case shows, an official position could bring power and profit. What historians regard as the efficiency of English royal administration may often have rested on petty tyrannies, based on local influence and local knowledge. A famous example is Robert Malarteis, probably mentioned in the 1130 Pipe Roll and described as follows by the chronicler Orderic Vitalis:

> A certain minister of King Henry, who was more particularly a servant of the devil with wolf-like fangs, appeared on the scene. [...] His name was Robert and he was nicknamed "Malarteis", from the Latin meaning 'ill-doer'. The nickname was well deserved, for he seemed to have no function except to catch men out. [...] he accused all equally, whenever he could, striving with all his might to harm everyone. [...] If he could find no valid reason for condemning them, he became an inventor of falsehood and father of lies through the devil who spoke in him.[7]

---

4. See esp. P. Wormald, '*Lex scripta* and *Verbum Regis*: Legislation and Germanic kingship from Euric to Cnut', in his *Legal Culture in the Early Medieval West*, 1-43.
5. See Lantfred, *Translatio et miracula S. Swithuni*, c. 25, M. Lapidge, *The Cult of St Swithun* (Oxford: 2003), 308-10. For a tentative suggestion as to the identity of Eadric, see Lapidge, *Cult of St Swithun*, 308 n. 229. Calne, Wiltshire, was a royal estate.
6. See Lapidge, *Cult of St Swithun,* 310 n. 232, on this phrase.
7. *English Lawsuits from William I to Richard I*, ed. R. C. van Caenegem (2 vols, Selden Society, 106, 107; 1990-1), no. 204. PR 31 HI, 49, 104, has a Malarteis excused Danegeld in Huntingdonshire and Bedfordshire, the exemption suggesting

Such abuses, and complaints concerning them, would of course continue well beyond our period.

Others might derive power from their skill at pleading in court.[8] It appears that certainly until the later twelfth century, court proceedings amongst laymen allowed a fair amount of room for general argument. Robert Malarteis's victim in Orderic's account was a man named Bricstan. He denied criminal charges against him, but 'the opposing party charged him with lying and made fun of him, for he was short in stature, somewhat corpulent, and had what one might call a homely face.'[9] There were more subtle arguments, notably the pleading of exceptions, that is reasons why the defendant should not be obliged to make a formal defence against the claim or accusation; however, even these do not seem to have required any specialised knowledge.[10] Rather what was needed was the combination of practical intelligence and eloquence that is referred to in legal and other contexts – at least in the higher levels of society – as 'courtoisie'.[11]

A key element here was authority gained from verbal as opposed to physical assertion. Verbal skill could take various forms, of differing degrees of specialisation. The use of subtle and specialised arguments was often a dividing line between the ecclesiastical and the lay. Let us examine the trial of William of St Calais, bishop of Durham, following his failure to support King William Rufus against rebels in 1088. We have a Durham account, by a cleric, which puts direct speech into the mouths of various leading figures,[12] and allows us to differentiate various types of discourse. First there are the arguments of the churchmen, Bishop William on one side, Archbishop Lanfranc of Canterbury on the other. Bishop William expounded his versions of the facts of the case, but also drew on canon law for arguments. For example, he stated that 'I am prepared to answer as one despoiled, if this is canonically adjudged, for I shall in no way transgress the law of my order in this suit,' knowing full well that the canons indicated that he should not plead whilst despoiled. Lanfranc put forward arguments that were sometimes technical, as when distinguishing William of St Calais' bishopric and his fief, but sometimes based on strategic use of common

that he held an official position. A similar man, Benjamin, the king's sergeant, appears in Norfolk in 1130 Pipe Roll rendering account of £4 5s, that he might keep the pleas which belong to the king's crown; PR 31 HI, p. 91; he appears as a king's serjeant witnessing a charter in *Sir Christopher Hatton's Book of Seals*, ed. L. C. Loyd and D. M. Stenton (Northamptonshire Record Society and Oxford, 1950), no. 407.

8. P. A. Brand, *The Origins of the English Legal Profession* (Oxford: 1992), 3-5.
9. *English Lawsuits*, ed. van Caengem, no. 204.
10. See J. G. H. Hudson, 'Court cases and legal argument in England, *c.* 1066-1166', *Transactions of the Royal Historical Society,* 6th Series 10 (2000), 91-115.
11. See P. R. Hyams, 'Henry II and Ganelon', *Syracus Scholar*, 4 (1983), 22-3.
12. *English Lawsuits*, ed. van Caenegem, no. 134.

sense. When Bishop William said that he was not going to act in any way that was not canonical and according to his order, that it seemed to him that ecclesiastical custom demanded that he should plead his case robed before people who were themselves robed, and that should reply canonically to his impleaders, Lanfranc replied bluntly that 'we can certainly discuss the king's and your business dressed as we are; clothes do not hinder the truth.'

The lay arguments are of a rather different nature, certainly from the technical ones put forward by the churchmen. Laymen felt that they should act honourably, for example by observing any safe conduct that had been provided for the bishop. Some of their speeches suggest a sense of due process, as when Roger Bigod said to the king 'you should tell the bishop what you want to accuse him of and afterwards if he is willing to answer us, let him be judged on his reply; if not, act according to your barons' counsel.' But they were firm in their rejection of William's appeal to canonical principle, preferring again a form of common sense equivalence. Thus Hugh de Beaumont told Bishop William: 'If I cannot today judge you and your order, you and your order will never again sit in judgment over me.' Technicality they may have regarded as the preserve of the churchman, if laudable when used for purposes of which they approved: thus having heard Lanfranc's arguments, they shouted – concerning William – 'Arrest him, arrest him, for the old blood hound [i.e. Lanfranc] has spoken well.' Such clamour differs from the threat to draw their swords that was the lay response to some of the arguments of Anselm and of Becket, but it still shows the Durham writer differentiating the subtle arguments of the churchmen from the more straightforward views of the laity.

As the twelfth century moved on, specialist language and argument came to be used not just by learned churchmen but by a new group of experts in secular law. Now it needs to be pointed out that expertise in aspects of law and justice were not new. A famous Canterbury story tells of Bishop Æthelric of Chichester's appearance at a trial at Penenden Heath: 'a very old man most learned of the laws of the land, [...] brought in a cart at the king's order to discuss and expound these old customs of the laws.'[13] From the *History of the Church of Abingdon* we learn that the first Norman abbot

> was helped greatly by two monks of this church, who were indeed brothers, the older called Sacol, the younger Godric; with these also was Ælfwig, then the priest in charge of the church of the neighbouring royal village of Sutton.[14] These men were so eloquent concerning

13. *English Lawsuits,* ed. van Caenegem, no. 5B.
14. *Historia ecclesie Abbendonensis*, ed. J. G. H. Hudson, 2 vols (Oxford: OUP, 2002, 2007), ii. 4. Domesday Book, i. fo. 59^{r} states that '*Aluui* the priest holds one hide from the abbot' of Abingdon in Sutton. *Alwius* and *Aluui* are forms for the Old English name Ælfwig, or possibly Ælfwine.

> matters of this world and remembered past events so well that others, on every side, easily approved a judgment they pronounced as correct. In addition, at that time many other English pleaders were retained in the abbey, whose arguments no wise man opposed.[15] With these men protecting the public affairs of the church, its opponents became tongue-tied.

Likewise Hervey de Glanvill, father of Henry II's justiciar Ranulf de Glanvill, possessed a type of specialised legal knowledge. From lengthy experience, he could tell a court that

> every time a case arose in the shire courts involving any man of the eight and a half hundreds [of Bury St Edmunds] whosesoever man he was, the abbot St Edmunds or his steward and officials took that case with them for hearing in the court of St Edmund and, whatsoever the allegation or charge, with the exception of treasure trove and murder, it was dealt with there.[16]

Another expert of a different aspect of procedure was Hervey 'the monk', who appears in the twelfth-century *Ramsey Chronicle*. An account of a dispute settlement tells us that 'Robert of Yaxley has sworn fealty to Abbot Robert [of Thorney] as Hervey le Moigne has best known to set it out, namely that he be faithful to [the abbot] and all of his men as to his lawful lord, and that never against the abbot will he make any claim or suit, and that never at any time will he harm him or anyone of his men and that he will keep the aforesaid agreements for ever.'[17] Hervey le Moigne was also one of four men named amongst those making a judgment in another land case, and one of three named men involved in the settlement ceremony of a third case.[18]

However, these Herveys' knowledge concerned specific rights and procedures. The skills of the Abingdon pleaders consisted of eloquence and memory. By the later twelfth century, the forms of specialised knowledge had changed or perhaps multiplied. Legal knowledge was becoming more distant from common social norms, expressed in an increasingly specialised register of language, and applied from a position of particular power. As royal justices, the specialists could, for example, decide what evidence and what stories were relevant to a hearing, ruling out of court material that would earlier have been accepted. The late twelfth-century law-book known as *Glanvill* tells us in the context of arrangements concerning debt that

15. On such men, see Brand, *Legal Profession*, 9-13.
16. *English Lawsuits*, ed. van Caenegem, no. 331.
17. *English Lawsuits*, no. 272.
18. *English Lawsuits*, nos. 187, 269. Hervey also witnessed *English Lawsuits*, nos. 175, 268.

> it should be noted in this connection that it is not the custom of the court of the lord king to protect or warrant private agreements of this king concerning the giving or receiving of things as a gage, or other such agreements, whether made out of court or in courts other than that of the lord king; it follows that if such agreements are not kept, the court of the lord king will not concern itself with them, and is therefore not bound to pronounce upon the rights or privileges of the several prior or subsequent creditors.[19]

Tellingly, such a view not only rendered of no legal standing some previously acceptable practices, but was likely to increase business for the king's court, where legally binding arrangements could be made.

Now in the instance just cited the sophisticated legal argument was one produced by a royal justice, and it may be the case that in the period from c. 1176 to the mid-thirteenth century, royal justices held a particular advantage in court in terms of legal expertise, before the emergence of the legal profession in the second half of the thirteenth century.[20] This was particularly important as a further key change under Henry II was the degree of central control over the administration of justice. In part this was because of clear institutional change, for example the development of frequent visitations of the general eyre, visitations of justices sent out on circuits by the king to hear a wide range of cases in the localities. However, it was also a result of less immediately obvious change, notably the emergence of a group of regular royal justices who seem to have been responsible not merely for presiding over but also deciding cases.[21] Some caution must be exercised here. Actually showing that earlier cases were decided not by those presiding but by the suitors who made up the courts is not easy. The decisions pronounced by royal justices in the Angevin period might rest heavily on the verdict of inquests by local men. However, the basic shift in role does appear to have taken place. This would make considerably more influential any judicial views or specialised knowledge that they possessed. In addition, justices increasingly served outside the areas in which they had personal interests and knowledge, perhaps making them less open to local considerations and local custom. If the increasing specialisation of legal knowledge was a feature of much of twelfth-century Europe, it took a particular form in England, and one closely associated with the activities and interests of royal justices.[22]

---

19. *Tractatus de Legibus et consuetudinibus regni Anglie qui Glanvilla vocatur*, Bk x c. 8, ed. G. D. G. Hall (Edinburgh: 1965), 124; see also Bk x c. 18, ed. Hall, 132.
20. However, see below, p. 159-60, on sophisticated legal devices.
21. P. A. Brand, '"Multis vigiliis excogitatam et inventam"; Henry II and the creation of the English Common Law', in his *The Making of the Common Law* (London: 1992), 77-102, esp. 80-6.
22. S. M. G. Reynolds, 'The emergence of professional law in the long twelfth century', *Law and History Review*, 21 (2003), 347-66.

3. Power and legal development

Amongst Henry's justices was a close knit core, centred on Richard de Lucy, Ranulf de Glanvill, and Hubert Walter.[23] In this section of my paper I want to deal with this group in the context of power and legal development. This topic could be examined in various fields, for example the development of notions and classifications of crime. It has been shown in various periods that a judicial regime could classify as crime an activity previously not considered illegal but rather the subject of a variety of views based, for example, on custom and social position.[24] A similar process may have occurred in land law in the twelfth century, and it is upon this that I wish to concentrate. Whereas various legal historians, most notably Milsom, have argued for the replacement in this period of one set of fundamental legal ideas concerning landholding by another, Steve White has very plausibly argued that a variety of attitudes to a subject of landholding co-existed.[25] What then happened was that royal justices came to back one of these views, and their activities separated it from its competitors, rendering it the royally enforced land law.[26]

The view that came to predominate was one that supported the free tenant's rights in land as opposed to the discretionary power of the lord – or rather of any lord apart from the king. Why was this? There have to be a variety of explanations. For example, in part it was that tenants had already enjoyed considerable customary rights in the time of Henry I, sometimes backed by royal intervention.[27] However, further elements of the explanation may lie in the circle of Henry II's justices. Many of these came from the middle ranks of society, and they looked to men of knightly status to work their new remedies. The justices of higher status often came from families with a tradition of royal administrative service.[28] Now of course there had been administrators of similar status before, but they may have

---

23. Far from all the justices of Glanvill's time were East Anglian; for example they included John of Oxford; Roger son of Reinfrid, who had Devon lands; Alan de Furnellis, who also seems to have had a link to Devon and Cornwall; Roger of Wheatfield to Oxfordshire.
24. See esp. E. P. Thompson, *Whigs and Hunters* (London: 1975).
25. S. F. C. Milsom, *The Legal Framework of English Feudalism* (Cambridge: 1996); S. D. White, 'The discourse of inheritance in twelfth-century France: alternative models of the fief in *Raoul de Cambrai*', in *Law and Government in Medieval England and Normandy: Essays in Honour of Sir James Holt*, ed. G. S. Garnett and J. G. H. Hudson (Cambridge: CUP, 1994), 173-97.
26. See J. G. H. Hudson, 'Anglo-Norman land law and the origins of property', in *Law and Government*, ed. Garnett and Hudson, 198-222.
27. See J. G. H. Hudson, *Land, Law, and Lordship in Anglo-Norman England* (Oxford: 1994).
28. See R. V. Turner, *The English Judiciary in the Age of Glanvill and Bracton, c. 1176-1239* (Cambridge: 1985), 25-6.

been more numerous under Henry II, and as already argued they now exercised greater central control of judicial proceedings.[29] It may be that their ideology of royal service had been cultivated by the Becket dispute. Certainly the opening of Richard fitzNigel's *Dialogue of the Exchequer* shows thought, perhaps anxiety, about the subject from the point of view of the ecclesiastical administrator:

> To the powers ordained by God it is necessary to be subject and obedient with all fear. For all power is from Lord God. Therefore it does not seem absurd or foreign from ecclesiastical men in serving kings, as supreme, and other powers to preserve their rights, especially in those matters that are not inconsistent with truth and honour.[30]

It may be that this circle had views potentially antagonistic to the greater lay aristocracy, as when the *Dialogue* described lords as the natural enemies [*domesticis hostibus*] of their men, and the king as the protector of the men.[31] And if, as Paul Brand has persuasively argued, the significant shift in the influence of royal justice came in the 1170s rather than the mid-1160s,[32] it may be significant that it occurred after the death of the co-justiciar Robert, earl of Leicester, in 1168, leaving as sole justiciar his colleague, Richard de Lucy; the man of administrative family had thus outlived the great magnate.

The circle of justices around Richard de Lucy, Ranulf de Glanvill, and others may also have had a more intellectual interest in the practices and perhaps the substantive elements of law than had their predecessors. Whilst there is no strong evidence for any of the circle of Ranulf de Glanvill having contact with Bologna or the other Continental centres of the academic study of the learned laws,[33] theirs was a literate court culture. And from marginal entries in some manuscripts of their key text, the lawbook Glanvill, we know that they debated points of law.[34]

---

29. Note also Walter Map, *De nugis curialium*, distintio i. c. 10, ed. and trans. M. R. James, rev. C. N. L. Brooke and R. A. B. Mynors (Oxford: OUP, 1983), 12: 'This court sends out beings whom it calls justices, sheriffs, undersheriffs and beadles, to make strict inquisition. These leave nothing untouched or untried, and, bee-like, sting the unoffending – yet their stomach escapes uninjured.'
30. Richard Fitz Nigel, *Dialogus de Scaccario*, Prefatio, ed. and trans. C. Johnson, rev. F. E. L. Carter and D. E. Greenway (Oxford: OUP, 1983), 1.
31. *Dialogus*, Bk ii. c. 10, ed. Johnson *et al.*, 101.
32. Brand, '"Multis vigiliis"'.
33. R. V.Turner, 'Who was the author of *Glanvill*? Reflections on the education of Henry II's Common Lawyers', *Law and History Review*, 8 (1990), 97-127, esp. 117, takes a rather different line. Whilst he is convincing in stating that a significant number of Henry's justices must have had some practical knowledge of at least canon law, the evidence for study of law at Bologna or elsewhere on the Continent is extremely limited.
34. *Tractatus de Legibus*, ed. Hall, xliii-xlv.

We do not know the name of the author of the book, but it is likely that he came from the circle of Ranulf de Glanvill or of Geoffrey fitzPeter, both of East Anglian origin. Seven justices are named as commenting on legal matters. Four have clear East Anglian or East of England origins: Ranulf himself; Richard de Lucy, holder of East Anglian and Essex estates; Hubert Walter, son of a Norfolk knight of middling status, and nephew of Ranulf de Glanvill; Hugh Bardolf, son of a Lincolnshire knight.[35]

Now most people, I think, would accept that these shared origins have a significance in the way that administration worked in Angevin England, but does the East Anglian element have any further significance for the development of the Common Law? Evidence must be circumstantial, but it has often been noted that a characteristic of the Angevin reforms concerning landholding was that they were open to all holders of free land, not to a more narrowly selected social group. In addition, it has been noted that a significant preponderance of the demand for justice in the royal courts, as recorded in the plea rolls, came from the east of England, which was the area with the largest proportion of free population. Did this situation influence the royal justices when considering which of the various models of landholding they should enforce, thereby making it the basis of Common Law property?

In addition, local experiences may have increased any antagonism royal justices felt to locally privileged areas. Jocelin of Brakelond's chronicle may give some indication of their attitudes:[36]

> After Abbot Hugh's death, the custodians of the abbacy wanted to dismiss the reeves of St Edmund's town and replace them with their own nominees, claiming that this right belonged to the king when the abbacy was in his hands. But we made a complaint about this, and sent our messengers to Ranulf de Glanvill who was then the justiciar. He replied that he knew quite well that the town owed an annual payment of £40 to our sacristy for the lighting of the church. He also said that Abbot Robert had appointed his own candidates as reeves whenever he chose [...] Therefore it should be no cause of surprise that the king's servants now required the same right on the king's behalf. He spoke severely, calling us simpletons to have allowed our abbot to act in this fashion [...][37]

35. See entries in *Oxford Dictionary of National Biography*.
36. See also *The Chronicle of Jocelin of Brakelond*, ed. and trans. H. E. Butler (Edinburgh: 1949), 64-5, for a fine being imposed by itinerant justices. The abbot looked to the king to reverse their decision.

37. *Jocelin of Brakelond*, ed. Butler, 72-3.

Jocelin also tells us that Abbot Samson at first relied on his own opinion in the external business of the monastery:

> This surprised the monks and angered the knights, who condemned his arrogance and in some measure discredited him at the king's court, saying that he would not bother himself with the views of his free tenants. He excluded from his private circle of counsellors all the greater tenants of the abbey, both lay and literate, without whose advice and assistance it was thought that the abbey could not properly be governed. For this reason Ranulph de Glanvill, the justiciar of England, was at first suspicious of Samson and less well disposed towards him than he should have been, until evidence convinced him beyond doubt that the abbot was conducting both the internal and the external affairs of the abbey skilfully and wisely.[38]

Such local experience may have encouraged the view of privileged areas expressed for example in the Assize of Clarendon's provision that its measures be enforced 'even in the Honour of Wallingford.'[39] The argument for the importance of the justices' East Anglian origins thus can explain certain features of both administrative and substantive legal development in a plausible fashion.

However, there are plenty of possible objections to the argument. The evidence is scanty – to say the least. Counter arguments could be placed: Ranulf de Glanvill's father had protected the privileges of Bury rather than sought their limitation.[40] Even middle-ranking lords might have favoured greater control of their free tenants. It is safer only to conclude that the mentality of the royal administrator, and perhaps their social rather than their geographical origins, had an important effect on the pattern of legal development.

4. Law, power, and disputing

How did these developments in the field of the administration of royal justice change the place of law within the wider field of disputing? Important distinctions were made throughout our period, for example between law and power. The contrast could be a general one, for example between war and law, as when the Prologue of *Glanvill* stated that

> Not only must royal power be furnished with arms against rebels and nations that rise up against the king and the realm, but it is also fitting

38. *Jocelin of Brakelond*, ed. Butler, 26-7.
39. Assize of Clarendon, c. 11, *Select Charters and Other Illustrations of English Constitutional History*, ed. W. Stubbs (9th edn., Oxford: 1913), 171.
40. *English Lawsuits*, no. 331.

> that it should be adorned with laws for the governance of subject and peaceful peoples.[41]

Geoffrey of Monmouth had King Arthur state the following in response to the oppressive seeking of tribute by the Roman ruler: 'Nothing that is acquired by force and violence is justly possessed by anyone. He has done us violence in that he brings an unreasonable case by which he considers us to be tributaries to him by right.'[42] Such distinctions do not mean that the dividing line between law and force was the same as ours. In some areas, one might argue, medieval law allowed less force that does modern; killing in self-defence was still classified as homicide, requiring a pardon rather than producing an acquittal.[43] In other areas, more force might be allowed. Even in the thirteenth century a disseised tenant might eject a recent and unjust disseisor, even using a certain amount of force, although this should not involve violence against the disseisor's person or personal property.[44] However, willing as some disputants were to use extra-curial methods, there remainedan awareness of the distinction between self-help and legal process.

Furthermore, some methods of pursuing disputes, whether in or out of court, could certainly be classified as wrong. Asser has King Alfred investigating unjust sentences by his men – 'whether through ignorance or because of some other malpractice (that is to say, either for love or fear of the one party or for hatred of the other, or even for lust for money [*pecuniae cupiditate*]).'[45] Nevertheless, the classification of an action as legal or illegal may not always have been clear, or the same deed might be classified as a different type of action by the different parties, a classification with implications for legality. A gift might have been classified as a bribe or as a payment for aid. It is unclear that the Clare family would have agreed with the *Liber Eliensis*'s condemnation of its actions early in Henry I's reign. The lineage had been made noble

> by their reputation for valour and the sheer number of their progeny and , wherever a meeting of nobles took place, their procession was supported by a huge entourage which was terrifying. Moreover, it was no longer safe in their presence, for anyone at all from among the magnates to compete with them over the reception of guests or the conduct of lawsuits [in causis tractandis], since frequent killings were

41. *Tractatus de Legibus*, Prol., ed. Hall, 1.
42. Geoffrey of Monmouth, *The Historia regum Britannie of Geoffrey of Monmouth, i. Bern Burgerbibliothek, MS 568*, ed. N. Wright, 114.
43. N. D. Hurnard, *The King's Pardon for Homicide before A.D. 1307* (Oxford: 1969).
44. J. G. H. Hudson, *The Formation of the English Common Law* (London: 1996), 211-12.
45. Asser, *Life of Alfred*, c. 106, ed. W. H. Stevenson (Oxford: 1904), 93.

> carried out at court by their hands and on many occasions they had struck terror into the king's majesty.[46]

Displays of might, if not killings, might be considered proper exercise of lordship, of what is sometimes described as 'maintenance.'[47]

Similarly, the suitors of a local court might take on a very different appearance to the two parties. Take another dispute described by Jocelin of Brakelond, this time between Bury and Christchurch Canterbury. Canterbury supported its position with charters, but the abbot of Bury responded that

> 'Whatever may be said of the charters, we are in seisin and have been so up to his time, and on this matter I desire to place myself on the verdict of two counties, to wit, Norfolk and Suffolk, that they allow this to be true.' But Archbishop Baldwin, after consultation with his men, said that the men of Norfolk and Suffolk had a great love of St Edmund and that a great part of those counties was under the abbot's jurisdiction [dictione], and therefore he refused to stand on their judgment [arbitrio].[48]

Throughout the period, therefore, distinctions were drawn between legal and extra-legal methods of disputing, but on occasion the distinction may have depended on the viewpoint of a particular party.

Was there, then, change within our period in the place or the sharpness of the border between the legal and the extra-legal? Let us begin with the use of force. The extra-judicial pursuit of vengeance, particularly through violence to the person, was increasingly restricted. Alfred's efforts to see that judicial pursuit of claims preceded vengeance were followed by the considerably greater restrictions on the scope of vengeance contained in Edmund's laws. By the twelfth century, Orderic Vitalis was commenting that Henry I,

> an unbending judge, [...] accused Ivo [de Grandmesnil], who was unable to clear himself of waging war [*guerram*] in England and burning the lands of his neighbours,

46. *Liber Eliensis*, Bk ii c. 142, ed. E. O. Blake (Camden Society, 3rd Series 92, 1962), 226.
47. See P. R. Hyams, 'Warranty and good lordship in twelfth century England', *Law and History Review*, 5 (1987), 449-53.
48. *Jocelin of Brakelond*, ed. Butler, 51-2. Note also the advice concerning postponement of a plea in the *Leges Henrici Primi*, c. 49. 2a, ed. and trans. L. J. Downer (Oxford: OUP, 1972), 162: 'At times it is better, depending on the presence or absence of friends or enemies, to postpone the plea, and at other times to proceed with the plea, even when it could be deferred.'

> which is an unaccustomed crime in that country [*quod in illa regione_crimen est inusitatum*] and can be atoned only by a very heavy penalty [*ultione*].[49]

Feud was being seen as a characteristic of Wales and Ireland, not England.[50] In thirteenth-century Common Law there were severe restrictions on self-help involving even limited violence in reply to theft or assault.[51] Although juries might modify the verdict upon an accused in order to reflect their own standards,[52] they did so within the context of the increasingly specialized legal and judicial rules propounded by royal justices, in the ways already discussed.

Other changes may also have increased the degree to which the legal was a category discrete from other aspects of culture and society. Take the manuscript contexts in which Anglo-Saxon laws were preserved. Those from before 1066 are often in a religious setting, combined, for example, with homilies and other such works. It is only after the Conquest that we have the appearance of what Wormald has termed 'Legal encyclopedias', that is manuscripts containing lawcodes and nothing but lawcodes.[53] Similarly the author of *Glanvill* was much more a legal specialist than the great composer of the late Anglo-Saxon codes, Archbishop Wulfstan, extensive as the latter's legal knowledge was.[54] And it is to such specialisation that we must relate the increasing tendency to narrow down the matter relevant to a lawsuit, [55] whilst also increasing the sophistication of the arguments used in court.[56]

5. Conclusion

Some final concluding remarks comparing the situation in c. 1200 with that in c. 900 and picking up on points made in my introduction: We have seen

49. *The Ecclesiastical History of Orderic Vitalis,* Bk xi. c. 2, ed. and trans. M. Chibnall (6 vols, Oxford: OUP, 1969-80), vi. 18-19. He was probably writing between 1135 and 1145; *Ecclesiastical History*, ed. Chibnall, vi., xviii.
50. See J. G. H. Hudson, 'Faide, vengeance et violence en Angleterre (ca 900-1200), in *La Vengeance, 400-1200,* ed. D. Barthélemy, F. Bougard, and R. Le Jan (Rome: 2006), 340-82.
51. See D. W. Sutherland, *The Assize of Novel Disseisin* (Oxford: 1973), 122-3.
52. See T. A. Green, *Verdict according to Conscience* (Chicago: 1985), esp.p. 31 on social resistance to official judicial ideas of homicide; Hurnard, *King's Pardon*; also e.g. Sutherland, *Novel Disseisin,* p. 122.
53. P. Wormald, *The Making of English Law: King Alfred to the Twelfth Century. I: Legislation and its Limits* (Oxford: OUP, 1999), 224.
54. Furthermore, *Glanvill*'s thinking of law comes across very much in a secular fashion, in contrast to the theological embedding of Wulfstan's legal thought.
55. Also returnable writ.
56. See Hudson, 'Court cases and legal arguments', 110.

much continuity, but at the same time there has been a distinct shift in the nature of law, related to changes in the administration of justice. Some hardening had occurred in the border between judicial and extra judicial methods of disputing. This was probably a gradual process, whereas a restriction of the range of arguments that could be used in court may have occurred more rapidly in the Angevin period.[57] It may well be that more cases, for example concerning inheritance, were determined by hardening legal rules, leaving fewer hard cases where other considerations might intrude.[58] Furthermore, particularly from the later twelfth century, legal rules grew more distanced from many ordinary social norms. Law cannot be wholly detached from society, but the relationship is not unchanging.

The distancing of the legal from the social moreover allowed skilled practitioners to play with law in ways that the legal norms did not intend but which achieved the ends that the practitioners' clients desired.[59] In Northampton in c. 1190 it was laid down that 'no-one can gage land to any one for a long term or a short one unless the gagor and he who took the gage will swear that they do not do this to defraud the lords or the kin of their rights.'[60] Dying men appear to have been making limited term land grants so that, when the grant ended, the grantor's heir would have the reversion, freeing him from paying relief. [61] Such devices became a characteristic of late medieval conveyancing, and one not generally accessible to the non-specialist. Likewise, certainly by 1250, perhaps by 1200 at least some court processes were becoming less comprehensible to non-specialist participants. This change gave law a new autonomy, and thus a new type of power. Such autonomy, and such professionaliszation, is also connected to the development of new types of sources, more discretely legal than those on which this paper has been based. It is as a result of both these different

57. Note also the development of the returnable writ, on which see Hudson, *Formation of the English Common Law*, 143.
58. See Hudson, *Land, Law, and Lordship*, esp. c. 4.
59. Note also the divergence of criminal law from social attitudes, the ferocity of the law being tempered by jury modification; see esp. Green, *Verdict according to Conscience.*
60. *Borough Customs,* ed. M. Bateson (2 vols, Selden Society, 18, 21; 1904, 1906) i. 288; such grants might also be used to avoid wardship if the heir were a minor.
61. For other devices, see e.g. S. J. Bailey, 'Warranties of land in the thirteenth century', *Cambridge Law Journal* 8 (1942-4), 293 and n. 145, on the avoidance of claims to provide exchange. See also the 1217 Magna Carta, c. 43 (*Select Charters*, ed. Stubbs, 343), which specified that 'it is not permitted to anyone to give his land to any religious house thus that he resume it to hold from the same house, nor is it permitted for any religious house to receive the land of anyone thus that they hand it over to him from whom they accepted it to hold. Moreover, if anyone [...] gives his land to any religious house in this way and is found guilty of it, his gift will be utterly voided and that land fall to his lord of that fee.' A church never died and therefore the lord lost his rights of relief and wardship, whilst the marriage of a church was obviously an impossibility.

sources and the changed nature of law that a different type of legal history is now often written of the later middle ages. The appearance of the words 'and society' in a title may distinguish not only the historian legal historian from the lawyer legal historian, but also the historian of law before and after the thirteenth century.

In Coronam Regiam Commiserunt Iniuriam: The Barons' War and the Legal Status of Rebellion, 1264-1266

Matthew Strickland

1. Introduction

On 4 August, 1265, a little to the north of the town of Evesham, the forces of Earl Simon de Montfort were overwhelmed by a royalist army led by Prince Edward and Montfort's former ally Gilbert de Clare, earl of Gloucester. Before the battle, they had agreed not to take Earl Simon prisoner or ransom him, but to seek him out and slay him on the field of battle.[1] Accordingly, Simon and many of his leading supporters were cut down without quarter and the earl's body was severely mutilated.[2] His head and testicles were sent as a grisly trophy to the wife of the marcher lord

My thanks are due to colleagues at the Law and Power conference for their helpful comments on the subject of this paper, and in particular to Professors John Gillingham and John Hudson for reading earlier drafts of it and making valuable suggestions for its development.

1. *The Chronicle of Pierre Langtoft*, ed. T. Wright, 2 vols (Rolls Series, London, 1866-1868), II, 144-5; O. De la Laborderie, J. R. Maddicott and D. A. Carpenter, 'The Last Hours of Simon de Montfort: A New Account', *EHR*, cxv (2000), 378-412, at 408.
2. *Chronicon vulgo dictum Chronicon Thomae Wykes* (Wykes), *Annales Monastici*, ed. H. R. Luard, 5 vols (Rolls Series, London, 1864-69), iv, 174; *The Chronicle of William Rishanger of the Barons' Wars* (Rishanger), ed. J.O. Haliwell (Camden Society, London, 1840), 35-7.

Roger Mortimer, one of Earl Simon's most bitter opponents.[3] Montfort's fate has rightly been seen as the inception of a major shift in the crown's response to baronial rebellion, whereby comparative leniency in the punishment of armed opposition - by disseisin, fine, imprisonment or exile - increasingly gave way during the reigns of Edward I and Edward II to the infliction of the death penalty for bearing arms against the king.[4] My intention here, however, is to look back beyond Evesham to the beginning of the war the year previously, and to examine what light a series of formal letters exchanged between the rebels and royalists on the eve of the battle of Lewes, fought on 14 May, 1264, shed on perceptions of the legitimacy, or otherwise, of resistance to the king, and on the legal framework in which hostilities were viewed.

2. Royal authority and baronial rights

It has been argued by legal historians such as S. H. Cutler that later thirteenth- and early fourteenth-century France witnessed the gradual development of royal authority at the expense of the long established baronial right to wage private war. Still more significant, the legitimization of resistance to the king himself through the formal act of defiance, which had thitherto placed an erstwhile vassal beyond the charge of treason, increasingly gave way before developing concepts of sovereignty, buttressed by Roman law and its concepts of the *crimen maiestatis*, drawn from texts such as the *Lex Julia Maiestatis* and the *Lex Quisquis*.[5] From the 1250s, jurists were arguing that as the king of France recognized no superior, he was thus *princeps* in his kingdom and enjoyed the imperial rights set out in civil law; not only did he thus have a monopoly on the right to wage war, but any war levied against him was treason, punishable by death and total forfeiture. Thus the Bologna-trained jurist Jean Blanot argued in his *Commentaria super Titulum de Actionibus*, c. 1256, that a

3. Rishanger, *Chronica*, 37; *The Metrical Chronicle of Robert of Gloucester*, ed. W. A. Wright, 2 vols (Rolls Series, London, 1887), II, lines 11, 727- 11, 735.
4. J. G. Bellamy, *The Law of Treason in England in the later Middle Ages* (Cambridge, 1970), 23-58; J. Gillingham, 'Killing and Mutilating Political Enemies in the British Isles from the Late Twelfth to the Early Fourteenth Century: A Comparative Study', *Britain and Ireland, 900-1300: Insular Responses to Medieval European Change*, ed. B. Smith (Cambridge, 1999), 114-34, at 131-2; J. R. S. Phillips, 'Simon de Montfort (1265), the Earl of Manchester (1644) and Other Stories: Violence and Politics in Thirteenth- and Early Fourteenth-Century England', *Violence in Medieval Society*, ed. R. W. Kaeuper (Woodbridge, 2000), 79-90.
5. S. H. Cutler, *The Law of Treason and Treason Trials in Later Medieval France* (Cambridge, 1981), 4-15. For the crime of majesty in Roman law itself, F. S. Lear, *Treason in Roman and Germanic Law* (Austin, 1965), 3-72, and cf. 108-122.

baron taking up arms against the king of France was guilty of treason, 'because he is deemed to have acted directly against the *princeps*, for the king of France is a *princeps* in his own kingdom, since he does not recognize a superior in temporal matters'.[6] Drawing on Blanot, Guillaume Durand in his *Speculum Juris*, c. 1271, stated still more explicitly that levying war against the king of France was treason.[7] Nevertheless, the transition from theory to practice was slow and halting; the *Etablissement* of Louis IX still recognized the legitimacy of war, even against the king, if a *deni de justice* could be proved, while early Valois legislation such as that of Philip the Fair in 1304 merely echoed earlier Capetian ordinances concerning private war in asserting that 'wars, homicides, burning of towns or houses, attacks and assaults on fields or ploughs', as well as challenges to duel or battle, were forbidden only when the king himself was engaged in war.[8] Even such strictures could be relaxed, and private war remained a jealously guarded right of French nobles well into the fourteenth century.[9]

But what of England? The *De Legibus et Consuetudines Angliae*, initially compiled in the 1220s -1230s before its subsequent revision by Henry Bracton, reveals a familiarity with Roman law among Henry III's justices.[10] 'Bracton' too applied the maxim '*Rex superiorem non*

---

6. Joannes de Blanosco, *Commentaria super Titulum de Actionibus in Institutis* (Mayence, 1539), fols. 44v – 51vr; Cutler, *The Law of Treason*, 10-11.
7. Gulielmus Durandus, *Speculum Juris* (Frankfurt, 1592), Lib. IV, Pars III, *De Feudis*, no. 29 (p. 310); Cutler, *The Law of Treason*, 12. One wonders how far knowledge of events in England between 1263 and 1267 helped to sharpen the attitudes of French jurists such as Durand in regarding the levying of war against the king as treason.
8. *Etablissements de Saint Louis*, ed. P. Viollet, 4 vols. (Société de l'histoire de France, Paris, 1881-6), II, 75-7; *Ordonnances des rois de France de la troisième race*, ed. E. J. de Laurière *et al.*, 22 vols (Paris, 1723-1849), I, 390-2, and for further legislation in 1352 and 1361, II, 511-12, III, 525-7. On the legislation on private war see R. Cazelles, 'La règlementation royale de la guerre privée de St Louis à Charles V et la precarité des ordonnances', *Receuil de droit francais et étranger*, xxxviii (1960), 530-48, at 545; and M. Vale, *The Angevin Legacy and the Hundred Years War, 1250-1340* (Oxford, 1990), 112-13.
9. Vale, *The Angevin Legacy*, 113-139; R. W. Kaeuper, *War, Justice and Public Order. England and France in the Later Middle Ages* (Oxford, 1988), 188-190. As late as 1361, Edward III himself could argue for the right of individuals in France to make private war to recover outstanding ransom payments even at a time of peace between the two kingdoms. The king of France, however, took a very different view; not only did he imprison one William Bulmer without trial – the action which had caused Edward III's response – but subsequently executed him for having ridden in arms in the kingdom of France at a time of peace (P. Chaplais, *Some Documents Regarding the Fulfilment and Interpretation of the Treaty of Brétigny* (Camden Miscellany, xix), 22; M. H. Keen, *The Laws of War in the Late Middle Ages* (London and Toronto, 1965), 232-3).
10. For the dating of Bracton see P. Brand, 'The Age of Bracton', *The History of English Law: Centenary essays on Pollock and Maitland*, ed. J. Hudson

recognoscens est imperator in regno suo' to the king of England, to whom he gave the imperial title of *vicarius Dei.*[11] It has been argued that the period of Henry III's personal rule between 1234 and 1258, and particularly the years 1245 to 1255, witnessed the growth in his own absolutist notions of kingship, and that the influence at court of men like the great canonist Henry of Susa, or of royal officials such as William of Kilkenny and John of Lexington, '*in iure canonico et civile peritus et circumpectis*' 'may have contributed to Henry III's political notions which were approaching Roman imperial ideas of authority'.[12] In this, moreover, the king may have sought to emulate his brother-in-law Frederick II, whose *Liber Augustalis* of 1231 had drawn directly on Roman law for its draconian rulings on treason and heresy, and whose imperial protonotary, Peter de Vinea, had visited England in 1235.[13] By contrast, however, David Carpenter has contested the view of Bracton as advancing more absolutist theories of kingship, and argues that Henry, unlike Frederick, did not regard himself as above the law.[14] That the king was exposed to such thinking, however, is suggested by Henry's own admission to Frederick II, following the fall of Peter des Roches in 1234, that he had been too influenced by Peter's inflated views of monarchical authority, among which was the view that the power of the king's *voluntas* allowed him to injure his subjects at will.[15] As Michael Clanchy has suggested, it may be no coincidence that the teaching of Roman Law was prohibited in London soon after Peter's dismissal.[16]

(*Proceedings of the British Academy*, 89, 1996), pp. 65-89; R. V. Turner, *The English Judiciary in the Age of Glanvill and Bracton, c. 1176-1239* (Cambridge, 1985), 231-6, 268-9.

11 . *De Legibus et Consuetudinibus Angliae*, ed. G. E. Woodbine and tr. S. E. Thorne, 4 vols (Cambridge, Mass., 1968-1977), and for statements on king's power; II, 33 (fos. 5b-6), 109 (f. 34), 167 (f. .55b). See also F. Schultz, 'Bracton on Kingship', *EHR*, lx (1945), 136-176. In this, however, 'Bracton' was merely following the statement of 'Glanvill' that 'the lord king can have no equal, much less a superior' (*dominus rex nullum potest habere parem multo minus superiorem*); *The Treatise on the Laws and Customs of the Realm of England commonly called Glanvill* (Glanvill), ed. G. D. G. Hall (London, 1965), 84 (VII:10).

12. M. T. Clanchy, 'Did Henry III have a Policy?',*History*, liii (1968), 203-216; idem, *England and its Rulers, 1066-1307* (3rd edn., 2006), 211-218; Turner, *The English Judiciary*, 233. Both Lexington and Kilkenney were keepers of the king's seal.

13. *The Liber Augustalis*, tr. J.M. Powell (New York, 1971), 9, 85, 151; E. H. Kantorowicz, 'Petrus de Vinea in England', *Mitteilungen des Osterreichischen Instituts fur Geschictsforschung*, li (1937), 43-88; Turner, *The English Judiciary*, 233-4.

14. D. Carpenter, 'King, Magnates and Society: the Personal Rule of Henry III, 1234-58', *Speculum*, lx (1985), 39-70, reprinted in D. Carpenter, *The Reign of Henry III* (London, 1996), 75-106, at 76-9.

15. *Treaty Rolls preserved in the Public Record Office*, I, ed. P. Chaplais (London, 1955), no. 15; Powicke, *Henry III*, 145; Carpenter, 'King, Magnates and Society', 77. On Peter's fall see N. Vincent, *Peter des Roches* (Cambridge, 1996), 429-65.

16. Clanchy, *England and its Rulers*, 212.

Whatever the reality of Henry's own beliefs, moreover, some hostile contemporaries continued to regard both the king's *legistae*, trained in civil and canon law, and his 'alien' kinsmen with deep suspicion as fomentors of absolutist pretensions.[17]

Yet for all such perceptions, it would seem that in reality Roman law had comparatively little influence on concepts of treason in thirteenth-century England. 'Bracton' adds little to 'Glanvill''s brief definitions of treason, which he had already labelled as '*crimen quod in legibus dicitur lese maiestatis*'.[18] The charge of lèse majesté itself is already visible at least by the 1190s,[19] though arguably Henry III's reign may have witnessed a wider use of the of the charge, and thereby an extension of the scope of treason or capital offences.[20] Among a range of examples we may note the royal justice Henry of Bath, summoned before the king's court in 1251 to answer charges of infidelity, treason and '*laesa majestas*' arising from his greed and corruption in office,[21] while in the Parliament of April 1260, Henry accused Simon de Montfort himself of perjury and lèse majesté.[22] As Powicke noted,

17. *Matthæi Parisiensis monachi Santi Albani, Chronica Majora* (Matthew Paris, *Chronica Majora*), ed. H. R. Luard, 7 vols (Rolls Series, London, 1872-83), V, 130. Similarly, the barons complained to the pope in 1258 that the king's half-brothers had 'damnably whispered to him that a prince was not subject to laws, however much he was in himself, so putting the king outside the law' (*Annales Monastici,* I, 463; Clanchy, 'Did Henry III have a Policy?', 209).
18. Glanvill, 3, 171, 176-7; Glanvill included amongst these the killing of the king, the betrayal of the realm or army, breach of the king's peace.
19. Thus, for example, Roger of Howden notes that in 1194, one of the charges brought against Gerard de Camville, a partisan of King Richard I's rebellious brother Count John, was '*de laesione regiae maiestatis*' as he had refused a summons by royal justices to answer for harbouring thieves who had plundered the fairs at Stamford (*Chronica Magistri Rogeri de Hovedene*, ed. W. Stubbs, 4 vols (Rolls Series, London, 1868-71), III, 242). In the same year, a disseisin was described as being done '*in lesionem coronae domini regis*' (*Curia Regis Rolls: Records of the court held before the King's Justiciars or Justices* (*Rotuli Curia. Regis*), ed. F. Palgrave (London, 1835), I, 31; Turner, *The English Judiciary*, 272, n. 14.
20. In late 1220 or early 1221, the leading magnates of the king's council wrote to Pope Honorius, warning him to keep out of the kingdom Simon Langton, earlier expelled 'for his immense malice...and the crime of lèse majesty, and for disturbing the whole kingdom', and who had thirsted for the blood of King Henry and his *fideles* (*Foedera*, I, 171; Carpenter, *The Minority of Henry III*, 228; N.Denholm-Young, 'A Letter from the Council to Pope Honorius III, 1220-1221', *EHR*, lx (1945), 88-96.
21. Matthew Paris, *Chronica Majora*, V, 213-215, 223-4, 240; *Close Rolls, 1247-51*, 539; Powicke, *Henry III*, 335-6.
22. *Annales prioratus de Dunstaplia* (Dunstable), in *Annales Monastici*, ed. H. R. Luard, 5 vols (London, Rolls Series, 1864-69), III, 215.

> Injured majesty was a more far-reaching conception that injured lordship. It could comprehend the leader in a riot or a clipper of coin, and in particular it could comprehend all those who, in an unchartered area of trespass, incurred the royal displeasure by wounding his dignity, neglecting their official duties, or showing contempt for his authority.[23]

Such a fluid concept could be used to particular effect against ministers who had incurred royal displeasure; many of the numerous indictments against Hubert de Burgh, who fell in 1232 charged with treason against Henry III's royal person, could have been construed as lèse majesté, and Hubert seems genuinely to have feared for his life.[24] Similarly, greater emphasis on the crime of lèse majesté may explain the emergence in the 1230s and1240s of symbolic multiple punishments beyond drawing and hanging for those convicted of treason, a reflection of the growing distinction between high and petty treason. Thus in 1238, a squire convicted of attempting to assassinate Henry III at Woodstock was executed '*quasi regiae majestatis occisorem*'; after being drawn apart by horses at Coventry, his corpse was beheaded and divided into three parts, which were each dragged through a major city of the kingdom before being affixed to gibbets.[25] Similarly in 1242, though he had consistently declared himself '*immunis, purus et penitus inculpabilis...de crimine laesae majestatis*', William Marsh was convicted for a range of crimes including piracy and complicity in this earlier plot to murder the king, and was drawn and hanged before his body was disembowelled, his entrails burned, and his body quartered.[26] It seems very likely that in 1265 the mutilation of Montfort's body was an attempt to inflict an analogous punishment upon the corpse of a man deemed by his opponents to be a traitor.[27]

Nevertheless, while such concepts might help to widen the scope of treason or aggravate its punishment, English monarchs did not need to invoke principles of Roman law to punish armed rebellion with death or mutilation. As both John Gillingham and I have argued, Anglo-Norman and

23. Powicke, *Henry III*, 336. It may be, however, that a new label was being given to a much older offence.
24. For the charges and process against Hubert in 1232, *Matthei Parisiensis monachi Sancti Albani Historia Anglorum*, ed. F. Maddern, 3 vols (Rolls Series, London, 1866-9), II, 341-2; *Foedera*, I:1, 207-8; *Calendar of Patent Rolls, Henry III, A.D. 1223-1247* (London, 1906), 28-30; and for subsequent charges in 1239, including an alleged attempt to murder the king, Matthew Paris, *Chronica Majora*, VI, 63-74. His fall is treated in detail by C. Ellis, *Hubert de Burgh* (London, 1952), 126-69, and D. Carpenter, 'The Fall of Hubert de Burgh', *Journal of British Studies*, xix (1980), 1-17.
25. Matthew Paris, *Chronica Majora*, III, 498.
26. Matthew Paris, *Chronica Majora*, IV, 196.
27. B. Weiler, 'Symbolism and Politics in the Reign of Henry III', *Thirteenth Century England IX: Proceedings of the Durham Conference, 2001*, ed. M. Prestwich, R. Britnell and R. Frame (Woodbridge, 2003), 15-41.

Angevin kings had always claimed the right to punished rebellion, which they consistently viewed as *proditio et infidelitas*, by execution or mutilation. In reality, a combination of political expediency and an intense and consistent pressure by the nobility to limit de facto punishment of rebellion served to make actual cases of execution or mutilation the exception rather than the rule.[28] Thus in a letter of August 1265 demanding the surrender of a rebel garrison, probably that of Kenilworth, the king noted that although he 'ought to deal with them, generally and severally, judicially rather than mercifully, yet of his inborn benevolence' he has thought fit to counsel them, commanding them, as they would not be reputed public enemies or be disinherited, or lose their lives, that they go out of the castle and deliver it to the king immediately'.[29] Here, the king's legal right to exact the ultimate penalty is stressed, but clemency is proffered to men who have not yet been placed beyond the royal mercy by being labelled *hostes publicos*. Similarly, the Dictum of Kenilworth of 1266, which marked a key stage in the pacification of the rebellion begun in 1264, is a prime example of both the claims of royal power of execution and the tempering of such through acceptance of political reality. Thus in pronouncing a royal pardon for all who 'in the present disorders of the realm have offend against or done injury to him or the royal crown (*in ipsum vel in coronam regiam commiserunt iniuriam quamlibet vel offensam*)', the Dictum acknowledged the king's potential rights while at the same time pledging that he would not 'inflict any penalty or revenge against them in life, limb or imprisonment, exile or fine'.[30] After Evesham, the king had disinherited Simon de Montfort's supporters, but such was the strength of resistance that the baronial umpires replaced the king's initial judgement by the provision whereby rebels could ransom back their lands according to a sliding scale of their involvement in the hostilities. The principle was redemption, not disinheritance.[31] Only those who refused to accept the Dictum and return to the king's peace remained in danger of losing life or limb should they be captured.[32]

---

28. J. Gillingham, '1066 and the Introduction of Chivalry into England', *Law and Government in Medieval England and Normandy. Essays in Honour of Sir James Holt*, eds. G. Garnett and J. Hudson (Cambridge, 1994), 31-55, and reprinted in J. Gillingham, *The English in the Twelfth Century* (Woodbridge, 2000), 209-232; M. J. Strickland, *War and Chivalry. The Conduct and Perception of War in England and Normandy, 1066-1217* (Cambridge, 1996), 230-57.
29. *Calendar of Patent Rolls, 1258-66*, 488.
30. *Documents of the Baronial Movement of Reform and Rebellion, 1258-1267*, ed. R. E. Treharne and I. J. Sanders (Oxford, 1973), 320-1 (c. 5).
31. *Documents of the Baronial Movement*, 324, '*non fiat exheredacio sed redempcio*'.
32. Hence, for example, Robert de Wollerton, knight, was taken and hanged at Chene (Langtoft, II, 148-9). Similarly, Luke de Tany and his men gained a royal exemption from legal action while on crusade with the Lord Edward for having

Nevertheless, though it was frequently tempered, king's right to execute or mutilate was certainly far from merely nominal. In 1224, Henry III had ordered the execution of the garrison of Bedford, comprising around eighty knights and serjeants; the castellan, who had been one of Henry's own household knights, had kidnapped a royal justice, Henry de Braybrook, and the eight week siege proved costly in lives and money.[33] When soon after the outbreak of the war in 1264, the rebel stronghold of Northampton fell to a royal assault, the barons and their men in the town and castle were allowed to surrender, though the town itself was brutally sacked.[34] But King Henry was initially intent on hanging a group of Oxford students, who, having been expelled from that city by the king, had joined the defenders of Northampton, and fought fiercely under their own banner. In the event, however, he was dissuaded from this course by cooler heads who argued that since many of these students were the sons of the nobility, their execution would only serve to alienate the powerful men who were their fathers or kinsmen.[35] Others were less fortunate. Later in April, when the royalists marched to relief of Rochester castle, Prince Edward had those besiegers he captured mutilated by the loss of their hands and feet.[36] Similarly, when on his march to Lewes through the Weald one of his household was shot by an archer, Henry III had 315 local archers beheaded in his presence.[37] Most of these victims, of course, were men of lesser rank; they were not tenants-in-chief or other royal vassals but merely subjects, deemed to have violated the fealty owed by all men to the king.

---

beheaded a number of rebels when castellan of Tickhill and Knaresborough during the civil war (*Calendar of Patent Rolls, 1266-1272*, 442).

33. K. Norgate, *The Minority of Henry III* (London, 1912), 296-8; D. Carpenter, *The Minority of Henry III* (London, 1990), 363-7.
34. *The Chronicle of Walter of Guisborough* (Guisborough), ed. H. Rothwell (Camden Scoiety, lxxxix, London, 1957), 189-90. The Dictum of Kenilworth was later to distinguish between 'those who violently and maliciously' had held Northampton against the king ('*qui violenter et maliciose detinentes Northampton contra regem*), who were to regain their lands by paying five times their annual value, and those who had entered the town on De Montfort's orders 'but neither fought nor did harm, and who, 'if they fled to the church when they saw the king coming and this is proved by lawful men', were to pay only half the annual value of their lands (*Documents of the Baronial Movement*, 324-5, 332-5, c. 12, and c. 29.
35. Guisborough, 190, and for context see C. H. Lawrence, 'The University of Oxford and the Chronicle of the Barons' War', *EHR*, 95 (1980), 99-113.
36. Wykes, 147. One may compare Edward's actions in late 1265, when he had a number of men from Winchelsea hanged in reprisal for the burning of Portsmouth by the men of the Cinque Ports (*Annales de Waverleia*, in *Annales Monastici*, II, 367).
37. Wykes, 148; the chronicle of Battle abbey, printed in C. Bémont, *Simon de Montfort* (Paris, 1884), 375; D. Carpenter, *The Battles of Lewes and Evesham 1264/5* (University of Keele, 1987), 16.

In the case of such greater lords and vassals, however, the competing feudal ideology whereby taking up arms could be legitimized by the renunciation of homage was still very much alive.[38] A vassal might defy his honorial lord, as Fulk fitzWarin did Thomas Corbet, lord of Caus, in 1255 rendering him back his homage by a third party.[39] But men might also renounce their homage to the king himself.[40] King John had been defied in 1215 by his baronial opponents, while similarly in 1233, Gilbert Basset and a group of nobles defied Henry III before ravaging the land of the king's supporters, though they would not attack the person of the king himself.[41] The same year Richard Marshal responded to royal aggression by renouncing his homage to Henry III; and subsequently carefully set out a detailed justification of the circumstances in which he had done so.[42] In 1263, by contrast, the baronial reformers who had summoned Simon de Montfort back from France to be their leader adopted a more indirect approach, sending a letter to the king asking him to maintain the Provisions of Oxford, but following this by a defiance of all those who wished to oppose these measures, saving, however, the person of the king, the queen and their children.[43] The men to be defied were the king's 'evil counsellors', not the king.

Nowhere, however, is the manner in which such notions of defiance and renunciation of homage might co-exist and overlap with notions of

---

38. M. Bloch, 'Les formes de la rupture de l'hommage dans l'ancient droit féodal', in idem., *Mélanges historiques*, 2 vols (Paris, 1963), I, 189-209; Strickland, *War and Chivalry*, 231-5; and for the views of canon and civil lawyers see M. Ryan, Feudal Obligation and Rights of Resistance', *Die Gegenwart des Feudalismus*, ed. N. Fryde, P. Monnet and O. G. Oexle (Göttingen, 2002), 51-78.
39. R. W. Eyton, *Antiquities of Shropshire*, 12 vols. (London, 1854-1860), VII, 80-1; R. R. Davies, 'The Law of the March', *Welsh Historical Review*, 5 (1970-71), 1-30, at 15.
40. Thus in the *Romance of Fouk fitzWarin* an earlier Fulk fitzWarin (Fulk III) defies King John for withholding his inheritance and denying him justice.(*The Legend of Fulk fitzWarin*, in *Radulphi de Coggeshall Cronicon Anglicanum*, ed. J. Stevenson (Rolls Series, London, 1875), 328-9) It is striking that in its original verse form this romance dates from the later thirteenth century and appears to have been composed in the northern Shropshire marches (G. Burgess, *Two Medieval Outlaws. Eustace the Monk and Fouke fitzWarin* (Cambridge, 1997), 127-9).
41. *Memoriale fratris Walteri de Coventria*, ed. W. Stubbs, 2 vols (Rolls Series, London, 1872-3), II, 219; Matthew Paris, *Chronica Majora*, III, 246-7, 256, 271. For an example of a baronial defiance of a count in 1216 see T. Evergates, *Feudal Society in Medieval France. Documents from the County of Champagne* (Philadelphia, 1993), 75.
42. Matthew Paris, *Chronica Majora*, III, 249, 258.
43. *De Antiquis Legibus Liber. Cronica Maiorum et Vicecomitum Londiniarum*, ed. T. Stapleton (Camden Society, London, 1846), 53, '*et diffidaverunt omnes illos, qui contra ire voluerunt, salva persona Regis, Regine et liberorum suorum*'. For the context of these attacks, see D. A. Carpenter, 'King Henry III's Statute against Aliens, July 1263', *EHR*, cvii (1992), 925-944.

kingship and sovereignty more strikingly illustrated than by a series of three letters exchanged between the baronial opposition and the king and his supporters on 13 May, 1264, the eve of the battle of Lewes.[44] As John Maddicott has noted, this set of letters survives in at least six chronicles and other collections of documents, suggesting that they were originally widely circulated in some form of newsletter, and testifying to the significance which contemporaries attached to them. [45] Their dissemination was most likely have been part of the attempt, also witnessed by the production of the remarkable political tract *The Song of Lewes*, to justify the barons' defeat and capture of the king, his son Edward and Richard of Cornwall in the battle, an event which must have profoundly shocked many.[46]

The first letter consists of the response by Simon de Montfort and Gilbert de Clare to the king's rejection of their offer of peace. The leaders of the baronial opposition had been anxious to come to a negotiated settlement. Since the outbreak of hostilities on 3 April, the war had being going badly for them.[47] Montfort himself may well have realized that a direct confrontation with the king was the only way of securing both the immediate strategic position and the future of the reforms gained since 1258, but he also knew there would be many in his ranks who felt deep unease at the prospect of directly fighting against their own anointed sovereign.[48] The king's army, moreover, was a powerful one, reinforced by contingents brought by Anglo-Scottish nobles and by stipendiary knights.[49] Accordingly, Earl Simon had sent two delegations to the king at Lewes,

44 . I here follow the dating of these letters and the chronology of the pre-battle negotiations as suggested by David Carpenter, *The Battles of Lewes and Evesham* , 19-22, who argues convincingly that all three documents were issued on the same day, 13 May.

45. J. Maddicott, 'The Mise of Lewes, 1264', *EHR*, 98 (1983), 588-603, at 589 n.2, where full references are given to their occurrence in published and manuscript sources, and where he also notes that 'these letters appear in more chronicles than any other document for the period 1258-1265'.

46. Maddicott, 'The Mise of Lewes', 589; *The Song of Lewes*, ed. C. L. Kingsford (Oxford, 1890). As late as 10 June 1265, only a short time before his own destruction at Evesham, Simon felt it expedient to speak of 'the detestable battle of Lewes' in a propaganda letter to the men of Ireland (*Calendar of Patent Rolls, 1258-66*, 432; Powicke, *Henry III*, 498-9).

47. Though they still held the strategic key of London, they had suffered a major reverse at Northampton, their siege of Rochester had failed, and Gilbert de Clare's castle of Tonbridge had fallen to the king, while the royalists were moving to isolate Dover and gain control of the Cinque Ports (J. Maddicott, *Simon de Montfort* (Cambridge, 1994), 267-9).

48. At Northampton, the baronial leaders were said to have been 'not willing to fight against their lord', and royal justices were later informed that some individuals had fled from the ensuing fight once they saw the king's standard (*Continuation of William of Newburgh* (the Furness Chronicle), 542-3; C. Valente, *The Theory and Practice of Revolt in Medieval England* (Aldershot, 2003), 73 n.28.

49. Wykes, 149; Carpenter, *The Battles of Lewes and Evesham*, 22-3.

probably on 12 May. The first proposed that contested points in the Provisions of Oxford be put to the arbitration of a panel of ecclesiastical experts, and the second - in what was in a reality a fine to buy the king's peace and acceptance of the Provisions - offered a very substantial sum, perhaps as much as £30,000, by way of compensation for the damages already suffered by Richard of Cornwall and other royalists.[50] The chroniclers are divided as to how far Henry himself was inclined to accept these terms, or how far their rejection was at the urging of his brother Richard of Cornwall, but whatever the case, the barons' proposals were spurned.[51] Montfort and his supporters were now faced with the stark choice of abject surrender,[52] or pitched battle against the royal army. They chose the latter, fortifying their resolve by wearing the crosses of crusaders on their garments.[53] This was the context of the letter now addressed to King Henry, sealed by Earl Simon and Gilbert de Clare, on behalf of 'his barons and others of his faithful subjects who wish to observe their oath and fealty to God and himself'.[54]

3. The barons' letter

The king is assured that 'it is our wish to preserve the health and safety of your person with all our strength, and with the fidelity that is due to you',

---

50. J. P. Gilson, 'An Unpublished Notice of the Battle of Lewes', *EHR*, xi (1896), 520-22, at 521; *Song of Lewes*, lines 193-206; *The Historical Works of Gervase of Canterbury*, ed. W. Stubbs, 2 vols (Rolls Series, London, 1880), II, 236; Rishanger, 29-30; Wykes, 148-9; Maddicott, 'The Mise of Lewes', 588-91; Carpenter, *The Battles of Lewes and Evesham*, 20-2; Maddicott, *Simon de Montfort*, 269-71.
51. N. Denholm-Young, *Richard of Cornwall* (Oxford, 1947), 127-8.
52. According to the *Song of Lewes*, lines 250-2, Prince Edward is said to have replied to the baronial requests for a settlement, 'They shall have no peace unless they put halters about their necks, and deliver themselves up to us to be hanged or drawn'.
53. Rishanger, 26; *Flores Historiarum*, ed. H. R. Luard, 3 vols (Rolls Series, London, 1890), II, 495.
54. *Cronica Maiorum et Vicecomitum Londiniarum*, 64: 'Excellentissimo Domino suo Henrico, Dei gratia, illustri Regi Anglie, Domino Hibernie et Duci Aquitaniae, Barones et alii fideles sui, sacramentum suum et fidelitatem Deo et sibi debitam observare volentes, salutum et devotum, cum omni reverentia et honore, famulatum. Cum per plura experimenta liqueat, quod quidam vobis assistentes multa de nobis mendacia vestre dominationi suggesserint, et mala, quanta possunt, non solum nobis, sed etiam vobis et toti regno vestro intentantes; noverit vestra excellentia, quod salutem et securitatem corporis vestri totis viribus cum fidelitate vobis debita voluimus observare, inimicos nostros non solum, set et vestros et totius regni vestri juxta posse gravare proponentes, illis super predictis, si placet, non credatis. Nos enim vestri fideles semper inveniemur. Et nos Comes Lecestriae et Gilbertus de Clare, ad petitionem aliorum, pro nobis et ipsis presentibus, sigilla nostra apposuimus'..

and that the barons' aim was only 'to punish as far as lies in our power, not only our own enemies, but yours, and those of the whole of your kingdom'. Their letter is thus not a defiance of the king himself but, as in 1263, only of those malicious counsellors who have misled the king and endangered the realm. Such a topos was of long standing,[55] but in 1264 the interest lies in the fact that the barons' unnamed opponents, accused of misrepresenting the reformers' aims by their lies, were now formally challenged in an open declaration of enmity.[56] As Robert Bartlett has demonstrated, in parts of twelfth- and thirteenth-century Europe a state of mortal enmity was widely accepted as a legal status, provided it was openly declared through acknowledged rituals. Though often hedged in by restrictions of time and place, this advertised state of enmity nonetheless empowered both parties to engage in legitimate violence against the person, though usually not against the property, of the *inimicus capitalis*.[57] In England, by contrast, the law did not recognize the distinctive status of such enmities nor legitimize their accompanying expressions of violence.[58] Nevertheless, as Paul Hyams has shown, concepts of enmity were ubiquitous in thirteenth-century English culture, operating at all levels of society but particularly visible among the aristocracy. The language of enmity, moreover, increasingly entered into political discourse, with 'epithets like capital, mortal or public … used to intensify enmities and place their proponents in the firing line. Kings and political leaders used the notion to warn those who flouted their wills on especially serious issues that they were exposing themselves to summary treatment'.[59]

This trend becomes increasingly visible in the political struggles against John and Henry III. In May 1215, for example, the baronial opponents of King John who had taken control of London threatened other nobles that if they did not side with them against the king they would be treated as public enemies and war made upon them, their castles brought down, their homes and buildings burned, their warrens, parks and orchards

55. J. Rosenthal, 'The King's Wicked Advisors and Medieval Baronial Rebellions', *Political Science Quarterly*, lxxxii (1967), 595-618.
56. *Cronica Maiorum et Vicecomitum Londiniarum*, 64.
57. R. Bartlett, '"Mortal Enmities": The Legal Aspect of Hostility in the Middle Ages', T. Jones Pierce Lecture (Aberystwyth, 1998).
58. P. Hyams, *Rancour and Reconciliation in Medieval England*, (Ithaca, N.Y, and London, 2003), 58; 'Neither formal English law nor any post-Conquest custom…ever went this far. Mortal enmities were never privileged by medieval English law'.
59. Hyams, *Rancour and Reconciliation*, 58. For enmity and feud in England before the thirteenth century see J. Hudson, 'Faide, vengeance et violence en Angleterre (ca 900-1200)', *La Vengeance, 400-1200*, ed. D. Barthélemy, F. Bougard and R. Le Jan (École Francaise de Rome, 2006), 341-82.

destroyed.[60] Such concepts of enmity were again harnessed by the baronial reformers from 1258 both to enforce adherence to their programme and to give legitimacy to any military action needed so to do. Thus the oath taken in 1258 to uphold the Provisions of Oxford on behalf of the 'community of England', so central to attempts to legitimize the baronial reforms, included the pledge to hold any who opposed the Provisions as mortal enemies.[61] The king himself and leading members of the royal family were made to take this oath, so that by implication default would bring this status upon them, while Henry was made to order all the king's subjects to swear an oath of obedience to the baronial council.[62] This formula was subsequently renewed in the early summer of 1263 when the group of radicals who had summoned Earl Simon back from France to be their leader proclaimed at a meeting at London that they would hold as capital enemies all who declared themselves against the enactments of the Provisions.[63]

When in both 1263 and in 1264, Montfort's supporters had attacked the lands and castles of 'aliens' or other leading royalists, they were merely putting into effect the implications of such enmity. As Bartlett notes '*guerra* and *inimicitia mortalis* could be used as synonyms', just as the Melrose chronicler recorded that in 1263 the barons were preparing for '*guerra mortalis*'.[64] Montfort, and indeed his Poitevin opponents,[65] must have been familiar with notions of private war still firmly entrenched in France; as Philippe de Beaumanoir noted in his *Coutumes de Beauvaisis*, completed in 1283, 'gentil home puissant guerroier selonc nostre coustume'.[66] Nowhere, indeed, was this more true than in Gascony, where as seneschal from 1248 to 1252, Earl Simon himself had first hand experience of the prevalence and

60. Matthew Paris, *Chronica Majora*, II, 587, '*in omnes ipsos, quam in hostes publicos, arma dirigerent et vexilla*'.

61. *Documents of the Baronial Movement*, 100-101, 'E si nul fet encontre ceo, nus le tendrums a enemi mortel'; Wykes, 119, '*quod si quis dictis provisionibus contraire praesumeret, vel observare recusaret, hostis publicus censeretur*'.

62. *Calendar of Patent Rolls, 1247-58*, 664-5, 649; R. F. Treharne, *The Baronial Plan of Reform*, 1258-63 (2nd edn., Manchester, 1971), 77.

63. Dunstable, 221, '*quod omnes venietes contra statute Oxoniae, haberetur pro inimicis capitalibus*'; Wykes, 133, '*quasi capitals inimici eorum corporum et possessionum discrimine punirentur*'.

64. Bartlett, '"Mortal Enmities"', 4.; *Chronica de Mailros*, ed. J. Stevenson (Edinburgh, 1835), 192. The continuator of William of Newburgh similarly calls the hostilities of 1263 '*guerra manifesta*' (*Chronicles and Memorials of the Reigns of Stephen, Henry II and Richard I*, ed.R. Howlett, 4 vols (London, Rolls Series, London, 1884-90), II, 540-1).

65. For private war in Poitou, Powicke, *Henry III*, 166-7.

66. Philippe de Rémi, sire de Beaumanoir, *Coutumes de Beauvaisis*, ed. A. Salmon (Paris, 1900, repr. 1970), II, 354-65, at 357 (ch. 59:7); *The Coutumes de Beauvaisis of Philippe de Beaumanoir*, tr. F. R. P. Akenhurst (Philadelphia, 1992), 610-18 (ch. 59, c. 1673), and for the importance of a clear and public announcement of enmity, c.1675.

manifestations of this *droit de guerre*.[67] Yet in England itself, Anglo-Norman and Angevin kings had effectively prohibited 'private' war, even if 'Glanvill' assumes its occurrence and even imply its legitimacy.[68] Within Henry III's island realm, only the lords of the Welsh march, among whom Gilbert de Clare was one of the greatest, still enjoyed the right to wage war and make separate truces on their own authority, whether it be against the Welsh or against their fellow marchers.[69] Implicit in any recognition of this right by the crown was that it was limited to Wales and the March itself. Yet the marcher lords were quick to take advantage of internal discord within the kingdom, particularly between 1258 and 1265, to extend eastwards the areas covered by the *libertas Marchiae* to include areas of the border shires formerly under direct royal jurisdiction.[70] Given their prominence in Richard Marshal's rebellion of 1233, the troubles of 1263 and then in the war of 1264-5, it may also be that the marcher lords, several of whom were also substantial landholders in England itself, were equally exploiting a *tempus turbacionis* to push their right to carry *guerra* further into the kingdom against their enemies. [71]

Be that as it may, the nature of military activity carried east of the March appears to have been consciously more restricted in its forms than that waged in the March itself.[72] For war in the March might encompass not only the seizure of livestock on a large scale, but also riding with banners displayed, the seizure of booty, the ravaging and burning of lands and the slaying of men – a degree of hostility directed not simply against the

---

67. The nature of private war in Gascony during the later thirteenth and early fourteenth century is discussed in detail by Vale, *Angevin Legacy*, 112-39.
68. *Glanvill*, 104 (IX:1), 112 (IX:8); F. Pollock and F. W. Maitland, *The History of the English Law*, 2 vols (2nd edn., Cambridge, 1898), I, 301-2. The possible nature of such private war is discussed J. Gillingham, '1066 and the Introduction of Chivalry into England', in idem., *The English in the Twelfth Century* (Woodbridge, 2000), at 230-1; and Hudson, 'Faide, vengeance et violence en Angleterre', 370-72.
69. For discussion as to whether this right to wage war stemmed from the absorption by conquering Anglo-Norman nobles of the regalian rights of Welsh commote lordship, or was a privilege granted by the English crown as a necessary element for the successful defence and expansion of the border, or a mixture of both, see J. G. Edwards, 'The Normans and the Welsh March', *Proceedings of the British Academy*, xlii (1956), 155-178; R. R. Davies, 'Kings, Lords and Liberties in the March of Wales, 1066-1272', *Transactions of the Royal Historical Society*, 5th series, 29 (1979), 41-61; Davies, *The Age of Conquest*, 280-88.
70. Davies, *The Age of Conquest*, 276.
71. A useful contextual survey is provided by T. F. Tout, 'Wales and the March during the Barons' War 1258-1267', *The Collected Works of Thomas Frederick Tout*, 3 vols. (Manchester, 1932-34), II, 47-100.
72. For a valuable discussion of the nature of the violence perpetrated in 1264 -1265, see Valente, *The Theory and Practice of Revolt*, 76-78, who points out that some acts were little more than the seizure of grain or cattle, and though despoiling and burning occurred, killing was usually notable by its absence.

Welsh.[73] As such, 'private' warfare in the Marches went well beyond the notions of *guerre couverte* in France as understood by Beaumanoir and his contemporaries, which allowed war against the person of one's enemy and his kindred, but which seemingly forbade burning of buildings and crops, the seizure of booty and the taking of prisoners. These latter degrees of aggression were – or at least had become by the fourteenth century – recognized as pertaining only to public war, and thus were the prerogative of a sovereign.[74] The military actions of the baronial opposition in 1233 and 1263 seem to have ranged between these two forms. Thus in 1233, Richard Siward, Gilbert Basset and other marchers had launched expeditions from Netherwent deep into England, burning manors and laying waste the lands and other economic assets of Richard Marshal's opponents, but apparently not killing men.[75] Similarly in June 1263, after the Oxford parliament, the coalition of marcher lords now under de Montfort's leadership began hostilities '*in marchia Walliae*', with the seizure of the town and castle of Hereford, and the arrest of its bishop, Peter de Aigueblanche and his canons, who were despoiled of all their goods. It soon, however, became more

73. Evidence from the royal inquest in 1292 into the hostilities in the March between the earls of Gloucester and Hereford noted that Gloucester's men from his lordship of Glamorgan had three times ridden with the banner of the earl displayed against Hereford's lordship of Brecon; men had been slain, though the jury of inquest did not know the number, hundreds of cows, sheep and horses had been seized, and Gloucester had taken a third of all these spoils '*prout decet dominum tempore guerre habere secundum usum et consuetudinem Marchie*'. (*Rotuli Parliamentorum*, I (Record Commission, 1783), 70-77; Edwards, 'The Normans and the Welsh March', 173-4; and R. R. Davies, *Lordship and Society in the March of Wales, 1282-1400* (Oxford, 1978), 217-20. The case is discussed by J. E. Morris, *The Welsh Wars of Edward I* (2nd edn, Stroud, 1996), 220-238, and M. Prestwich, *Edward I* (London, 1988), 348-52.
74. Keen, *Laws of War*, 64, 68, 72-3, 79-80; Kaeuper, *War, Justice and Public Order*, 227-8. Cf *Coutumes de Beauvaisis*, chapter 32, c. 986; 'It used to be that when some gentleman who had jurisdiction over his lands took something belonging to another gentleman, the person whose property was taken did not only go and seek the thing which had been taken from him, with or without force, but took everything he could find belonging to the gentleman who had done this to him, both on his lands and on the lands of the man who had done it to him. And because this was the legal commencement of a private war, and the cause of mortal hatred, such retaliation (*contregagemens*) is forbidden by the power and authority of the sovereign the King of France'.
75. Wykes, 76, who notes that Siward's burning of the manors of Earl Richard of Cornwall and of the bishop of Winchester was done '*ut domini sui Ricardi Marescalli et complicium surorum vindicaret injurias*', while both he and the Osney annalist, 76, stress that such actions were carefully targeted and not indiscriminate. For Siward and his martial activities, see D. Crouch, 'The Last Adventure of Richard Siward' *Morgannwg*, xxxv (1991), 70-130.

widespread, involving the despoliation or burning of manors of 'alien' clergy and of leading royalists as well as the seizure of royal castles.[76]

Yet though burning occurred, the reformers may well have regarded such actions as no more than forms of legitimate distraint against the enemies of the king and the community of the realm, analogous to the 'distraint and distress' envisaged by Magna Carta in 1215 in clause 61 against the lands, castles and possessions, but not the person, of the king.[77] For whereas in 1233 Richard Marshal and his men had defied Henry III and regarded themselves as in a state of open war against him, in 1263 the baronial opposition used a formal declaration of enmity towards enemies of the Provisions to attempt to legitimize their warfare. To stress that that their actions were undertaken on behalf of, and hence with the authorization of the king himself,[78] they had carried the royal standard with them at all times, while they labelled their opponents as transgressors of their oaths to the Provisions and as felons, whose goods could be seized wherever they were found. When they took castles, they had made the new constables who they installed swear an oath of fidelity to the king.[79] In reality, however, widespread spoliation – including attacks on the lands of Queen Eleanor and of the Lord Edward[80] – and the pursuit of individual vendettas occurred to the extent that de Monfort later deemed it expedient to gain royal pardons for the actions of some of his supporters.[81] As Henry III complained in his

---

76. Rishanger, 11; *Flores Historiarum*, II, 479; *Cronica Maiorum et Vicecomitum Londoniarum, 53; The Historical Works of Gervase of Canterbury*, ed. W. Stubbs, 2 vols (Rolls Series, London, 1878-80), II, 221-223 (the Dover chronicle); Wykes, 134-5, who notes that the queen's possessions, and those of Simon de Walton, bishop of Norwich, and John Mansel were especially targeted. For membership of this group of marchers, many of them *iuvenes* see Powicke, *The Thirteenth Century*, 172-4.
77. J. C. Holt, *Magna Carta* (2nd edn, 1992), 470-1.
78. The same had been true in 1258, when the reformers took the king in person with them against the Lusignans. According to an anonymous letter written in July, 1258, after the Oxford parliament, 'all the barons, together with the lord king, came with horses and arms to Winchester, ready to besiege the bishop-elect of Winchester's castle, Wolvesey, and after that his other castles, and the castles of the William de Valence, and to pursue them to the farthest limits unless they abandoned the error which they had conceived against the community of the realm on the provisions of the barons' (*Documents of the Baronial Movement*, 92-3).
79. *Cronica Maiorum et Vicecomitum Londoniarum*, 53, '*semper vexillum Domini Regis coram se detulerunt*'; Dunstaple, 222.
80. Wykes, 135; Dunstable, 223.
81. This was shown by the issuing of commissions of oyer and terminer in August, while Simon himself obtained letters of royal pardon for some of his followers (*Annales Monastici*, III, 224; Powicke, *Henry III,* 441; idem., *The Thirteenth Century*, 177). As the Dunstable annalist recorded, '*per consilium magnatum provisum fuit quod dominus rex omnibus spoliatis, conquerentibus de spoiliatoribus, plenam justitiam exhiberet per se et per justiciarios suos ad hoc*

gravamina presented to Louis IX in January 1264, his castles had been taken, his lands and those of his family and faithful men, both lay and clerical had been plundered and destroyed, 'all of which, and other infinite evils, have been occasioned by the edict for that oath, by which all who oppose their orders should be treated as capital enemies (*inimici capitales*) by all men of the realm'.[82] The royalist chronicler Thomas Wykes concurred, noting that '*articulus iste totum confundit negotium, cujus occasione totius guerrae et dissensionis materia sumpsit initium seu fomentum*'.[83] Royalists could hardly construe such attacks as anything other acts of war, a belief only reinforced by the barons' adoption of the language of mortal enmity. It was little wonder that in describing the Londoners' devastation of Richard of Cornwall's rich manor of Isleworth in 1264, the *Chronicle of the Mayors and Sheriffs* remarked that '*hoc fuit initium dolorum et origo mortalis guerre*'.[84]

4. The royalist defiances

The barons' letter prompted an immediate response from Henry's camp. Strikingly, this took the form not of a single reply by the king, but by two separate letters of defiance. The first was sent by Henry III himself, countering the barons' assurance of loyalty to the king by a rejection of their fealty and homage. The second was issued by Richard of Cornwall and the Lord Edward in their name and in that of 'all the other barons and knights who firmly adhere to the said King of England, with sincere faith and force', rejecting the allegations made in the barons' letter and defying them as public enemies.[85] Addressed to Simon de Montfort, Gilbert de Clare,

---

deputatos; prout continebatur in quadam forma, in scriptis redacta' (Dunstaple, 224).

82. *Documents of the Baronial Movement*, 254-5.
83. Wykes, 119-120.
84. *Cronica Maiorum et Vicecomitum Londoniarum*, 61.
85. *Cronica Maiorum et Vicecomitum Londiniarum*, 64-5: 'Ricardus, Dei gratia, Romanorum Rex semper Augustus, et Edwardus, illustris Regis Anglie primogenitus, ceterique barones, omnes et nobiles predicto Regi Anglie constanter sincere fide et devotionis operibus adherentes, Simoni de Monte Forti, Gilberto de Clare, ceterisque universis et singulis perfidie sue complicibus. Ex litteris vestris, quas illustri Regi Anglie, Domino nostro karissimo, transmisistis, accepimus nos esse diffidatos a vobis; quamvis hujusmodi verbalis diffidatio satis fuerit nobis ante realiter vestra hostili in rerum nostrarum incendiis et bonorum nostrorum depopulationibus prosecutione probata. Nos igitur scire volumus vos a nobis universis et singulis, tamquam hostes publicos ab hostibus diffidatos; qui deinceps personarum vestrarum et rerum dispendiis, ubicumque nobis ad hoc facultas affuerit, totis viribus nostris et mentibus insistemus. De hoc, autem, quod falso nobis imponitis, quod nec fidele nec bonum consilium ipsi Regi nostro damus, nequaquam verum dicitis. Et si vos, Domine Simon de Monte Forti vel Gilberte de

'and to all and each of the other accomplices in their perfidy' (*ceterisque universis et singulis perfidie sue complicibus*), Richard and Edward's reply reveals that they understood themselves to be foremost among those unnamed persons labelled by the reformers as the enemies of the king and kingdom. They responded in kind with a formal declaration of enmity against those who, by acts of open hostility, have in effect already declared war upon them:

> We have understood, by the letters you have sent to our Lord the illustrious king of England, that we are defied by you, although indeed this verbal defiance had been proved before by hostilities against us by the burning of our goods and the ravaging of our possessions. We therefore let you know that you are all defied as public enemies by each and all of us your enemies (*tamquam hostes publicos ab hostibus diffidatos*), and that henceforth, whenever occasion offers, we will, with all our might, labour to damage your property and your persons.

As to the charge of infidelity to the king, Richard and Edward give the barons the lie, and offer safe conduct to either Earl Simon or Earl Gilbert to come to the king's court formally to make such allegations. In the *curia regis* and before their peers, they will not only prove themselves innocent of such charges, but will prove the rebel earls to have lied 'like forsworn traitors'. This was, in effect, a formal appeal of the baronial leaders on a charge of treason. Richard and Edward cannot have expected their opponents to have accepted this individual challenge, but it served to cast the imminent clash of arms still more strongly in the light of a trial by battle and a judicial duel writ large. A state of mutual and public enmity had thus been formally declared between two parties, each claiming to be the true and loyal subjects of the king against his enemies.

It is, however, the king's own response that is the most striking. Montfort and his accomplices have, notes King Henry, raised *guerra et turbatio generalis* in his kingdom, and committed *incendia et dampna enormia*. The language of injured majesty, of treason, or reference to the barons as traitors or excommunicates, is notably lacking. Rather, the king notes that their actions are a manifest sign of their disregard for their fealty to the king, and that by attacking his faithful subjects and by threatening further injuries to them, they have shown they care nothing for the security of the king's person. Hence he rejects their assurances of loyalty, and defies

---

Clare, velitis hoc in Curia dicti Regis asserere, parati sumus vobis securum ad veniendum ad dictam Curiam procurare conductum, et nostre super hoc innocentie veritatem, et vestri, sicut perfidi proditoris, mendacium declarare per alium nobilitate et genere nobis parem. Omnes nos contenti sumus predictorum Dominorum sigillis, videlicet, Romanorum Regis et Domini Edwardi. Datum Lewes, xii [*recte* xiii] die Mai.'

them; 'we do not care either for your fidelity or your love, and we defy you as our enemies'.[86]

It is thus the king who defies the barons, not vice versa. The same had occurred in 1233, when Henry had defied Richard Marshal before attacking his castle at Usk, and only then – with great reluctance – did the Marshal respond with his own defiance of the king.[87] So too in 1264, it was only after receiving Henry's written defiance that Montfort and his supporters replied with their own *diffidatio* of the king. No text of this survives, and it may have only have been delivered orally.[88] As the chronicler Robert of Gloucester realized, Henry's renunciation of the ties of homage and fealty left Montfort and his men with no option than to fight,

> The King sent them word again, without greeting, this,
> That he cared nothing of their service, iwis,
> And that out of love and truth he put them each one,
> And that he would seek them out, as his pure fon.
> The barons knew no other rede, when they heard this,
> But bid God's grace and battle abide, iwis.[89]

Powicke believed that in labelling the King's enemies as depredators and thus liable to judgement, the Dictum of Kenilworth 'helped to destroy the doctrine that all war is alike and that *diffidatio* creates a state of open war'.[90] Such may have been the argument of the victorious royalists by 1266,[91] but it was not so in May 1264. Henry's letter placed Montfort and his supporters beyond his lordship, as he done Richard Marshal in 1233; and by

---

86. *Cronica Maiorum et Vicecomitum Londiniarum*, 64: 'Henricus, Dei gratia, etc, Simoni de Monte forti et Gilberto de Clare et complicibus suis. Cum per guerram et turbationem generalem in regno nostro, per vos iam subortas, necnon et incendia et alia dampna enormia, appareat manifeste quod fidelitatem vestram nobis debitam non observatis, nec de securitate corporis nostri in aliquo curatis; eo quod magnates et alios fideles nostros fidei constanter adherentes, enormiter gravastis, et ipsos pro posse vestro gravare proponitis sicut per litteras vestras nobis significastis, nos gravamen ipsorum nostrum proprium, et inimicos eorum nostros reputantes, precipue cum dicti fideles nostri, pro fidelitate sua observanda, contra infidelitatem vestram nobis viriliter et fideliter assistant, de vestra securitate vel amore non curamus, sed vos, tanquam nostros inimicos, diffidamus. Teste me ipso, apud Lewes, xij die Maii, anno regni nostri quadragesimo octavo.'
87. Matthew Paris, *Chronica Majora*, III, 258.
88. Wykes, 149, ' *unde comes et sui complices indignati, domino regi fidelitatem qua sibi tenebantur et sua prorsus homagia reddiderunt* '.
89. *The Metrical Chronicle of Robert of Gloucester*, ed. W. A. Wright, 2 vols (Rolls Series, 1887), II, lines 11,358-11,362; modernized English rendering in T. Beamish, *Battle Royal* (London, 1965), 136.
90. Powicke, *Henry III and the Lord Edward*, 555, n.1.
91. Compare Holt, *Magna Carta*, 170-1, for John's attempts to avoid the open acknowledgement of a state of war in 1215.

so doing, he recognized the barons' status as mortal enemies, with all the consequences which that implied.

But on the eve of the battle of Lewes, why would Henry seek to put his baronial opponents beyond his lordship, rather than attack, defeat, and then punish them as rebels and contumacious vassals? The fate of the garrison of Bedford in 1224 indicates that the king did not need to defy rebels before executing men of knightly rank. His renunciation of lordship, moreover, is all the more striking in that elements of the offences of which Henry accuses the barons emerge in formal indictments for treason only decades later. Though violation of the king's peace is not explicitly mentioned in Henry's letter, the charges of arson and plundering appear both in the indictments of David of Wales in 1283 and of William Wallace in 1305.[92] Henry's statement that 'you do not care in any way for our security' finds a striking parallel in Jean Blanot's argument that all war against the king is treason because it encompassed the death of the king; and anticipates the sentence against Wallace '*pro manifesta seditione quam ipsi domino regi fecerat...in mortem eius perpetrando*'.[93] That such was Henry's thinking is shown by a statement in 1266 that Simon de Montfort had moved war 'for the disherison of the king and the destruction of his crown'.[94] As Bellamy notes, 'this was approaching very close to the fourteenth-century treason of levying war against the king'.[95] Indeed, it is probable that had Simon lost the battle of Lewes and been captured, Henry would have placed him on trial on similar charges, including that of having raised a banner in war against the king. Though this charge seemingly finds its first explicit appearance in the indictment of Wallace, the chronicler Pierre Langtoft regarded the raising of his banner as summarizing Montfort's hostile intentions.[96]

Nevertheless, even in the wake of a crushing royalist victory, it is much more uncertain if Henry would have felt able to inflict any punishment greater than diseisin and banishment upon Earl Simon and his closest supporters. The king may thus have decided to take no chances. Severing his ties of lordship would not only free him from any further appeals to royal justice, but would also allow him to cut the Gordian knot of the reform programme and the Provisions of Oxford which had dogged him since 1258. By 1264 it must have been clear to all that the only way to enforce the annulment of the Provisions pronounced by the papacy and by Louis IX was to physically remove its chief proponents. The anonymous

---

92 . *Annales Monastici*, III, 295; *Chronicles of Edward I and Edward II*, I, 141.

93. *Chronicles of Edward I and Edward II*, I, 141.

94. *Calendar of Patent Rolls*, 1258-66, 532.

95. Bellamy, *The Law of Treason in England*, 27.

96. *Chronicles of Edward I and Edward II*, I, 141; Bellamy, *The Law of Treason in England*, 37. For Langtoft, see below.

author of the *Song of Lewes* recognized this when he wrote of Henry's rejection of Montfort's overtures before the battle:

> His death alone would satisfy the King,
> No ransom was allowed to save his head.
> They hoped thereby completely to confound
> The people, and disarm the greater part
> Of the whole country, for they thought that thus
> Disaster would then follow close at hand.
> Long may it be before this comes about![97]

Henry clearly felt that by putting the barons beyond his fealty and love, he was freeing himself from any constraints his lordship might have placed upon him in his subsequent conduct towards them. By unfurling the royal dragon standard 'portending the judgement of death',[98] Henry was declaring a war in which there was no obligation to spare the defeated or take prisoners for ransom.[99] Henry's renunciation of homage, moreover, was a direct reaction to, and overt rejection of, the reformers' claims to be acting on behalf of the king and the kingdom. At Lewes, there was to be no question that they were fighting in the king's name or under his banner. As Langtoft succinctly put it, 'Earl Simon unfolds his banner in the fields; the dragon is raised, the king defies the earl'.[100]

5. Conclusion

The series of letters exchanged before the battle of Lewes thus help to indicate something of the complexity of the relationship still existing between kingship and lordship, and between declarations of enmity and rebellion. One the one hand, levying war and raising a banner against the king were perceived by the crown, as they had long so been, as an offence

97. *Song of Lewes*, lines. 186-92; tr. Beamish, *Battle Royal*, 165.. The fact that de Montfort's standard bearer, William Blunt, was killed at Lewes suggests that Simon was deliberately targeted by the royalists, as he was to be at Evesham (Rishanger, 28).
98. Rishanger, 32, '*signo regio judicium mortis praecedente*'; Gilson Fragment, 521, '*in signum quod nulli parceretur partis adversae*'.
99. Rishanger, 30, notes explicitly that Richard of Cornwall not only defied the barons, but '*necnon ut Edwardus eosdem diffidaret callide procuravit, ad ultionem in barones exercendam totis conatibus insistens*'.
100. Langtoft, II, 142-3; '*Ly quens Symoun al chauns sa baner desplye;/ Le dragon est levé, le rei le quens defie*'. Cf 142-3, 'Simon de Montfort had discomfited the king's party, had thrown down the dragon (*Symon de Mountfort discomfit avayt/La parete le rays, le dragon avalait*).

punishable at the very least by forfeiture,[101] if not necessarily by harsher penalties including imprisonment, mutilation or even death. The king condemns violations of his peace, which are almost certainly deemed treasonous, reflecting less perhaps a growing influence of Roman law than the longstanding prohibition on private war in the kingdom since the Conquest, and hence the crown's claim to a monopoly on such levels of violence.[102] Yet on the other, the conflict is still perceived as a series of enmities. Henry III couches his own defiance in terms of taking sides with his friends and subjects against their enemies; 'Now we consider their injuries to be injuries done to us, and their enemies to be our enemies'.[103] Such a concept accords with Bartlett's suggestion that 'the violence of the state ... can be seen not as public violence reborn but as private violence writ large'.[104] Likewise, though the earl of Gloucester had been one of Montfort's leading supporters at Lewes, he was later to refute allegations of treason, sending letters patent to the king in 1266 protesting that he had never borne arms against Henry or the Lord Edward, except in self defence and against his own enemies.[105]

The continued existence, moreover, of the marchers' right to wage war must have served to further blur distinctions between licit defence and illicit rebellion. Edward's experiences of the volatility of the marchers in the 1260s must surely have informed his decisive and hard-line intervention into the conflict between Gloucester and Hereford in 1292. But as J.G. Edwards noted, Gloucester was punished by the king 'not for having made war, but for having done so after a royal prohibition', and similar clashes between marcher lords were to occur under Edward II.[106] It was this context

101. According to Rishanger, 65, Henry III informed those still resisting him '*quod quicumnque insurexerunt cum manu armata contra dominum suum agmine, ipso facto et jure amittere tenetur tenementum suum, quod tenet ab eodem*'.

102. This stance is clear in the order issued by Henry III to the sheriff of Westmorland in August 1265 that he was to proclaim the king's peace in cities, towns and churches, and prohibit 'anyone, under peril of life and limb and loss of his lands to go armed throughout the country, or to carry arms of offence (*arma hostilia*) in public, or plunder or run upon anyone without the king's special mandate or licence' (*Calendar of Patent Rolls, 1258-66*, 489).

103. *Cronica Maiorum et Vicecomitum Londiniarum*, 94,*'nos gravamen ipsorum nostrum proprium, et inimicos eorum nostros reputantes, precipue cum dicti fideles nostri, pro fidelitate sua observanda, contra infidelitatem vestramnobis viriliter et fideliter assistant'*.

104. Bartlett, 'Mortal Enmities', 14.

105. Rishanger, 60; '*quod nuncquam arma portaret contra dominum regem nec filium suum Edwardum, nisi se defendendo, sed inimicos suos, scilicet R. de Mortuo Mari et caeteros pro posse suo suppeditaret. Hoc fecit per consilium, quod notam proditionis sibi formidabat impositam*'.

106. Edwards, 'The Normans and the Welsh March', 174, n.1; J. C. Davies, *The Baronial Opposition to Edward II* (Cambridge, 1918), 39. Cf. *Rot. Parl.* I, 75; *Calander of Chancery Rolls*, 346.

which enabled Morgan ap Maredudd to make his peace with Edward I in 1295, following the collapse of the Welsh revolt, by claiming that he had not been fighting against the king, but only prosecuting a private war against the earl of Gloucester.[107]

Perhaps most crucially, by defying the barons in 1264, Henry was himself acknowledging the legal significance of *diffidatio* and the ability to alter the relationship not simply between an erstwhile lord and vassal, but even between an anointed king and his greater subjects. Such a stance was hardly in keeping with the implications of Bracton and Blanot's maxim '*rex in regno suo princeps est*' concerning the treasonous nature of bearing arms in the lands of a sovereign prince. Even when, in line with such theories, the punishment of armed opposition within Britain grew more ruthless under Edward I, the position of the kings of England themselves as homagers of the kings of France for their continental possessions undoubtedly did much to sustain the validity of defiance. For the king, in his capacity as duke of Gascony, might use the renunciation of homage to counter the increasing claims to sovereignty by the kings of France. Thus in 1294, Edward I reacted to Philip the Fair's confiscation of Aquitaine by renouncing his homage, and, as the chronicler Pierre Langtoft has his messenger tell Philip, 'when he shall have recovered his land to himself, he will claim to hold it of God Almighty'.[108]

Such defiance was, however, a high risk strategy. Philip the Fair declared that because Aquitaine was held by 'homage and fealty', Edward's renunciation of this homage meant that these lands were now forfeit, and that the king of France could recover them by force of arms.[109] Only two years later, Edward employed precisely the same arguments against John Balliol, king of Scots, who had renounced his homage; having had Balliol's defiance carefully enrolled by a notary public, he declared Balliol contumacious and Scotland to be a fief now legitimately forfeit to its rightful overlord.[110] But whereas Edward renewed his homage to Philip in 1303 and formally received back Aquitaine, Balliol was never given such an opportunity and his forfeiture was intended to be permanent. It was little

107. Prestwich, *Edward I*, 223-4. As Langtoft, II, 218-19, noted, 'The earl of Gloucester, I know not the reason, has lost in south Wales moor and dwelling, but to King Edward Morgan means nothing but well'.

108. Langtoft, II, 208-9. Subsequently, in 1298 Edward's jurists were to argue that Gascony was held as an allod, or that, if held as a fief, the king of France had forfeited his suzerainty over it by breach of the feudal contract and a *deni de justice*. See Powicke, *The Thirteenth Century*, 313, 650-3; H. Rothwell, 'Edward I's Case against Philip the Fair over Gascony', *EHR* , xlii (1927), 572-82; P. Chaplais, *English Medieval Diplomatic Practice*, 3 vols (London, 1975, 1982), I, ii, 422-30; Vale, *The Angevin Legacy*, 48-79.

109. Vale, *The Angevin Legacy*, 193.

110. E. L. G. Stones, *Anglo-Scottish Relations, 1174-1328* (London, 1965), 70-4, 106-108.

wonder then that following their victory at Lewes, the barons would not only extract a charter from the king whereby he remitted his ill-will to those who had earlier defied him, but would seek to regularize their position once more by performing homage and fealty to King Henry, thereby reversing the process of defiance.[111] When in 1267, Henry informed the Disinherited still holding out at Ely that whoever had raised arms against their lord deserved to lose the lands he held from him, the barons replied that although they had renounced their homage before Lewes, they had later performed homage anew to the king at London and sworn fealty to him, which they had inviolably maintained thereafter, and they had not subsequently borne arms against him.[112]

The distinction drawn by later jurists between *guerra* – the prosecution of private war or enmity – and *bellum*, waged by sovereign princes, was not as yet clearly visible in the England of the 1260s. In the eyes of most contemporaries the struggle between Henry III and his baronial opponents from 1264 was viewed as a *tempus gwerra*, [113] The Dictum of Kenilworth, issued on 31 October 1266, might refer to the conflict it sought to settle as a *tempus turbacionis*, but it too spoke of *guerra*, and other royal letters spoke of 'strong war'.[114] One can only guess the extent to which the Barons' War, in which the king had been defeated and captured by his own subjects, contributed to the increasingly uncompromising stance of French jurists such as Guillaume Durand in regarding the bearing of arms against the crown as treason. But in England, the king was as yet either unable or unwilling to pursue the full judicial implications of such arguments based on Roman law. Rather, the crown, as much as its baronial opponents, had sought to deploy the language of mortal enmity to vindicate extreme actions, and the royalists had intended that Lewes should be a *guerre mortelle* – war fought without respect to persons or ransom as if against the heathen or heretic. In the event, Henry III lost the battle of Lewes, and the annihilation of Simon de Montfort and his supporters had to await the bloodbath of Evesham, where the full implications of the status of enmity were to be so graphically revealed.

---

111. *Foedera*, I, 453; *Annales Monastici*, II, 359. Henry's pledge, made in return for the liberation of Edward and Richard of Cornwall, promises to observe the ordinances of June 1264, and to put aside any ill will toward Earls Simon or Earl Gilbert, adding, '*Hoc adjecto in eodem sacremento specialiter, et quidem expresse, quod occasione factorum praecedentium, tempore turbacionis et guerrae praecedentis, neminem occasionibimus aut inculpabimus de illis aut ex parte illorum, quos tanquam inimicos defidavimus*'.
112. Rishanger, 65.
113. H. W. C. Davis, 'The Commune of Bury St Edmunds', *EHR*, xxiv (1909), 313-17, at 314 and 316.
114. *Documents of the Baronial Movement*, 322-3, 324-5, 330-31. *Calendar of Patent Rolls, 1258-66*, 532.

ENFORCING OLD LAW IN NEW WAYS: PROFESSIONAL LAWYERS AND TREASON IN EARLY FOURTEENTH CENTURY ENGLAND AND FRANCE

John Gillingham

1. Introduction[1]

In March 1322, following the battle of Boroughbridge, at which Edward II's forces defeated rebels led by the greatest magnate in the realm, the king's cousin, Thomas, earl of Lancaster, no less than two dozen English nobles were hanged, and Thomas himself beheaded.[2] Nothing on this scale had been seen in England since the bloodbath by which the Danish King Cnut rid himself of his enemies more than three hundred years earlier in 1017. It gave a kind of plausibility to the claim made by a Westminster monk, probably writing c. 1327 in order to justify the regime of Isabella and Mortimer, that Edward II 'hated all the magnates with such mad fury that he plotted the complete and permanent overthrow of all the great men of the realm together with the whole English aristocracy'. In the words of the

1. For advice and help I am indebted to Matthew Strickland, Jennifer Ward and Paul Brand, the last of whom judiciously steered me away from less profitable lines of inquiry.

2. J. R. Maddicott, *Thomas of Lancaster 1307-1322* (Oxford, 1970). For the names and number of the other victims, and for the observation that the prolonged detention of their wives and children was 'more curious, brutal and seemingly unnecessary', see Natalie Fryde, *The Tyranny and Fall of Edward II, 1321-1326* (Cambridge, 1979), 61-64.

prose *Brut,* Edward II 'had brought the flower of chivalry unto death'.[3] To justify this reversion to a more brutal style of power politics, the king turned to the law and the emerging class of professional lawyers. Before the defeated rebels of 1322 were put to death, they were put on trial by one means or another and convicted of treason. Their offence, in legal terms, was that of 'levying war against the king'. The king and his friends, in particular the Despensers, father and son, now seemed to enjoy untrammelled power. In March 1323 Andrew Harclay, earl of Carlisle, was convicted of treason, drawn, hanged and quartered. By 1325 the author of the *Vita Edwardi Secundi* was paraphrasing Justinian: '*Nam quicquid regi placuerit, quamvis ratione careat, legis habet vigorem.*'[4]

But in 1326 the wheel of fortune turned. Edward's estranged wife, Isabella of France, returned to England with her lover, Roger Mortimer of Wigmore, and together they overthrew the old regime.[5] The two Despensers were tried and executed for treason; the earl of Arundel killed, apparently without any kind of formal judgement.[6] Edward II himself was murdered in 1327. The spate of treason trials and executions continued. The earl of Kent met his death in this way in March 1330 and then Roger Mortimer, earl of March, in November of that year. As Seymour Phillips has observed:

> Once used, it was all too easy to use the charge [of treason] again and again. The result was to raise the stakes in political controversy to unprecedented levels: anyone wishing to engage in violent opposition to the king had to be prepared to think the unthinkable and remove the king himself. [...] The genie of political violence, once out of the bottle, was to return to haunt the king and the magnates once again in the reign of Richard II and with increasing frequency in the future.[7]

3. *Flores Historiarum,* ed. H. R. Luard, 3 vols. (RS, 1890), iii, 200; *The Brut or Chronicles of England*, ed. F. W. D. Brie (Early English Text Society cxxxi, 1906), 224-5.
4. *Vita Edwardi Secundi*, ed. N. Denholm-Young (London, 1957), 136.
5. Roger Mortimer had surrendered on terms on 22 January 1322 and been sent to the Tower. Next year the king changed his mind and Roger was condemned to death. He drugged the constable of the Tower, John Segrave, and escaped on 1 August 1323, going to France and Isabella, E. L. G. Stones, 'The date of Roger Mortimer's escape from the Tower of London', *EHR* 66 (1951), 97-8.
6. 'The "trial" of the elder Despenser was clearly intended as a parody of Thomas of Lancaster's, May McKisack, *The Fourteenth Century* (Oxford, 1959), 86.
7. Seymour Phillips, 'Simon de Montfort (1265), the Earl of Manchester (1644), and Other Stories: Violence and Politics in Thirteenth- and Early Fourteenth-Century England', in ed. Richard W. Kaeuper, *Violence in Medieval Society* (Woodbridge, 2000), 79-89, 88.

2. The turning point

Indeed the number of political killings in late medieval England led Paul-Joachim Heinig to reckon that in this period England came second only to Italy as an arena of political bloodshed.[8] The execution of defeated political leaders was to remain part of the game of English power politics until the seventeenth century. This stands in stark contrast to the centuries before 1322 when defeated aristocratic rebels had in practice enjoyed the privilege of immunity of life and limb. For the previous two hundred years kings of England had consistently spared the bodies of high-status rebels, though they punished them in other ways, by imprisonment, banishment and confiscation of property – all punishments which, crucially, were reversible.[9] As Maitland put it, 'For two centuries after the Conquest, the frank, open rebellions of the great folk were treated with a clemency which, when we look back to it through the intervening ages of blood, seems wonderful'.[10] The bloodshed of Edward II's reign marked a violent turning point in English political life. As the early seventeenth-century poet and historian, Samuel Daniel, commented: 'And this is the first blood of Nobility that ever was shed in this manner since William the first, which being such, and so much as it was, opened veins for more to follow, and procured a most hideous revenge, which shortly afterward ensued. Thus is the beam of power turned, and Regality (now in the heavier scale) weighs down all'.[11]

Not surprisingly the legality of the trials of 1322-23, none of which were held in parliament, was called into doubt, both by near-contemporary chroniclers and by the families of the victims. According to the prose *Brut*, Thomas of Lancaster had been put to death 'without judgement of his peers'; according to the Lanercost chronicle, he was condemned 'without parliament or consulting greater or wiser counsel (*sine parliamento et sine maiori et saniori consilio).*'[12] In the account of the trial at Pontefract on 22

8. P-J. Heinig, 'Fürstenmorde. Das europäische (Spät-)Mittelalter zwischen Gewalt, Zähmung der Leidenschaften und Verrechtlichung', in *Reich, Regionen und Europa in Mittelalter und Neuzeit. Festschrift für Peter Moraw*, Historische Forschungen 67 (Berlin, 2000), 355-88, 360-1.
9. Kings were much less squeamish when punishing rebels of low social status.
10. F. Pollock and F. W. Maitland, *The History of English Law before the time of Edward I* (Cambridge, 1968), vol. 2, 506.
11. Samuel Daniel, *The Collection of the Historie of England* (London, 1618), 180.
12. *The Brut*, 221; *Chronicon de Lanercost*, ed. J. Stevenson, Bannatyne Club, 65 (Edinburgh, 1839), 244. That subsequently attempts were made to lend the authority of parliaments to the judgements of 1322-3 is suggested by a memorandum in the King's Bench records for 1325 noting that in the parliament of February 1324 it had been agreed that the records of the judicial proceedings should be entered on the rolls of parliament in perpetual memory of what had happened, and so that in future the king's subjects would fear to attempt such

March 1322 in the *Vita Edwardi Secundi,* when Thomas wished to speak in mitigation of his crimes, 'the judges refused to hear him, because the words of the condemned can neither harm nor be of any profit. Then the earl said: "This is a powerful court (*fortis curia*), and great in authority, where no answer is heard nor any excuse admitted".'[13] The king had already denounced him as a traitor on 11 March.[14] As Natalie Fryde put it, 'Lancaster was in fact being subjected to the usual summary process of martial law during which the defendant was never allowed to make a defence once his offence had been recognised by witnesses'.[15] In 1327 in parliament Henry of Lancaster argued that his brother should not have been convicted in this way, on king's record. The king, he claimed, had not unfurled his banner in 1322 and hence it was a time of peace not war, and consequently Thomas should have been judged by his peers, as was set down in Magna Carta.[16] Andrew Harclay's nephew petitioned Edward III that his uncle 'ne fuist attaint par enquest des piers' and had been condemned on the king's record 'encontre ley de tut temps usee'.[17] When the elder Hugh Despenser, earl of Winchester, was put on trial in 1326, he was told: 'This court denies you any right of answer because you yourself made a law that a man could be condemned without right of answer.'[18] Roger Mortimer was at least tried and condemned 'by his peers in parliament', but as Adam Murimuth wrote: 'he did not come before them, nor did he have the opportunity to reply. No wonder, since from time of Lancaster's death to the time of death of this earl, all nobles were put to death arbitrarily and without either right of reply or lawful conviction

---

traitorous and sinful acts. George Sayles, 'The Formal Judgments on the Traitors of 1322', *Speculum* 16 (1941), 57-63. The parliamentary roll for February roll for February 1324 does not survive.

13. *Vita Edwardi Secundi*, 126. For the speed with which Thomas came to be regarded as a martyred hero see Maddicott, *Thomas of Lancaster,* 329-30.
14. *Calendar of Close Rolls, 1318-23*, 522.
15. Fryde, *Tyranny and Fall,* 59, following the analysis in Maurice Keen, 'Treason Trials under the Law of Arms', in Maurice Keen, *Nobles, Knights and Men-at-arms in the Middle Ages* (London, 1996), 149-66, 164-5.
16. Printed from the chancery rolls by L. W. Vernon Harcourt, *His Grace the Steward and the Trial of Peers*, 327-9. Also cancelled on the same grounds were the judgements on Mortimers and Badlesmere, Harcourt, 299-300, 332-4. For discussion see T. F. T. Plucknett, 'The Origin of Impeachment', *Transactions of the Royal Historical Society,* 4th Series, 24, 1942, 47-71, 56-60. On the significance of unfurling banners, Keen, 'Treason Trials', 156-9, 164-5.
17. Harcourt, *His Grace the Steward*, 334.
18. Annales Paulini in *Chronicles of the Reigns of Edward I and Edward II*, ed. William Stubbs, 2 vols. (RS, 1882-3), 317-18.

(*omnes nobiles ad mortem traditi sine responsione et convicta legitima voluntarie perierunt*).'[19]

It is equally not in the least surprising that historians have long tried to explain the change. Edward I's executions of his Welsh and Scottish enemies, beginning with the execution of Prince David of Wales in 1283, have been said to show that he extended the scope of the law of treason so as to include rebellion within it. Hitherto, so Maitland argued, levying war against the king had not been regarded as high treason (*lèse-majesté*).[20] Rather, rebellion had been treated as feud, sometimes justifiable, especially if preceded by a formal renunciation of allegiance – *diffidatio*.[21] This long remained the orthodox interpretation. In what remains the standard work on the subject, J. G. Bellamy wrote: 'In the process at Shrewsbury against David ap Gruffydd in 1283 the English state trial had its origin and the *quasi* treason of levying war against the king took on a new status and importance.'[22] In the mid 1990s Matthew Strickland, David Carpenter and I all argued that this was mistaken.[23] No doubt in their own eyes, and in the opinion of many twelfth- and thirteenth-century contemporaries too, rebels had always felt they were within their rights when they took up arms against the king, especially if they tried to avoid fighting against the king in person, but we argued that from the kings' point of view they had always been regarded as traitors. If captured, their lives and limbs were in law at the king's mercy. The early fourteenth-century change that needs explaining was not in the scope of treason but in the procedures which led to conviction and, above all, in the conventions of punishment, for it was this that transformed the nature of English politics.

Whether we were right or wrong in our interpretation of twelfth- and thirteenth-century law, what is clear is that from 1322 the punishments

---

19. Adae Murimuth, Continuatio Chronicarum, ed. E. M. Thompson, RS, 1889, 62: 'ut versificaretur illa civilis sapientia, quod quisquis juris in alterum statuit etc, usus exstitit eo jure, et eadem mensura qua aliis mensi fuerant, erat remensum eisdem.'
20. Pollock and Maitland, *English Law,* ii. 502-8.
21. See Matthew Strickland's essay in this volume.
22. J. G. Bellamy, *The Law of Treason in England in the Later Middle Ages* (Cambridge, 1970), 24. 'In England war against the king became treason in the reign of the imperious Edward I', Richard Kaeuper, *War, Justice and Public Order England and France in the Later Middle Ages* (Oxford, 1988), 229-30.
23. D. Carpenter, 'From King John to the First English Duke: 1215-1337', in ed. R. Smith and J. S. Moore, *The House of Lords: A Thousand Years of British Tradition* (London, 1994), 28. J. Gillingham, '1066 and the Introduction of Chivalry into England', in eds. G. Garnett and J. Hudson, *Law and Government in Medieval England and Normandy* (Cambridge, 1994), 31-55, reprinted in Gillingham, *The English in the Twelfth Century.* Matthew Strickland, *War and Chivalry. The Conduct and Perception of War in England and Normandy 1066-1217* (Cambridge, 1996), 230-57. Not all have been entirely convinced, see Claire Valente, *The Theory and Practice of Revolt in Medieval England* (Aldershot, 2003), 23, 33, 36, 41, 48; Phillips, 'Simon de Montfort', 87 n. 45.

meted out to high-status enemies of the English crown became more brutal. Had this begun with the way Edward I dealt with his non-English enemies? In the view of the Osney annalist, David of Wales had been sentenced to an unheard-of death (*judicialiter adjudicatus est morti retroactis a temporibus inauditae*).[24] According to the Dunstable annals, a four-fold punishment was inflicted on him: to be drawn by horses to the place of execution, there hanged, then disembowelled and his entrails burned, finally his body cut into pieces and the pieces sent to different parts of England *ad terrorem malignantium*.[25] But there was a long history of the rulers of England treating members of Welsh princely families brutally without it 'contaminating' internal English politics.[26] More significant was Edward I's treatment of Scots in 1305-6, especially his execution of his own kinsman, the earl of Atholl in 1306 – the first earl put to death by an English king since William I had had Waltheof beheaded in 1076. Although the Scots did not see themselves as part of the English political community, and hence emphatically not as rebels, in terms of language and culture they were much more English than were the Welsh. Moreover by bringing William Wallace, the earl of Atholl, Sir Simon Fraser and others to Westminster and London, Edward I brought the brutal rituals of execution to the centre of the English political system.[27] Even so, there was some difference between anglicised Scots on the one hand and, on the other, men who had for years played a central role in English politics. Seymour Phillips has argued that what allowed the charge and penalty of treason to 'jump the species barrier' from Welsh or Scottish enemy to leading members of the English nobility was the execution/murder of Gaveston.[28] There can indeed be no doubt that the murder of Piers Gaveston in 1312 by a group of English earls, led by Thomas of Lancaster, resulted in Edward II being powerfully motivated by a desire for revenge.

But I am not persuaded that we can explain the new and bloodier structure of English power politics solely in terms of developments that

24. *Annales monastici*, iv. 294
25. *Annales monastici*, ed. H. R. Luard, 4 vols. RS 1864-9, iii, 293-4. The first of these was, according to the annalist, because he was a traitor to the king who had knighted him (*Quia proditor fuit domini regis, qui eum militem fecerat*).
26. Notably in the mutilation and hanging of hostages by Henry II and John. See John Gillingham, 'Killing and mutilating political enemies in the British Isles from the late twelfth to the early fourteenth century: a comparative study', in *Britain and Ireland 900-1300. Insular Responses to Medieval European Change*, ed. Brendan Smith (Cambridge, 1999), 114-34, 132; and Matthew Strickland, 'A Law of Arms or a Law of Treason? Conduct in War in Edward I's Campaigns in Scotland, 1296-1307', in ed. Kaeuper, *Violence in Medieval Society*, 39-77, 52-3.
27. Matthew Strickland makes these points in a forthcoming essay, 'Treason, Feud and the Growth of State Violence: Edward I and the "War of the Earl of Carrick", 1306-7'.
28. Phillips,'Simon de Montfort', 88.

occurred within Britain.

One problem with insular explanations is that they take no account of the fact that something similar was happening in the kingdom of France at about the same time. When Jourdain de l'Isle-Jourdain, lord of Casaubon, 'rebelle au roy' (the phrase used in the *Grandes Chroniques*), was stripped naked, drawn through the streets of Paris and hanged in 1323, a Parisian chronicler of the time noted, 'one cannot remember nor find written in the *gestes* of France that a man as high-born as my lord Jourdain has ever suffered such a death since the time of Ganelon'.[29] Cuttler's explanation for this was that the Roman concept of treason had negligible influence in France from the sixth to the eleventh century and then disappeared altogether until the reign of Louis IX. Hence he argued that it was only in the later thirteenth century that 'the Roman notion of lese-majesty began to play a truly central role not only in French thinking on treason but also in political life'. During the twelfth and thirteenth centuries what he called 'the intellectually inferior feudal notion of infidelity' had, he believed, allowed a noble to resort to war in defence of his rights.[30] In his view levying war against the king was not regarded as treason until 1315, when Robert de Béthune, count of Flanders, was accused of various treasons including 'entering into rebellion against us and waging war'. The presence of the count's peers in what Louis X called 'nostre cour garnie de nos pers et autres bons gens et grands de nostre conseil' may help to explain why Robert was sentenced only to forfeiture. 'At least as far as the peers were concerned, there was as yet no question of corporal punishment'.[31] Since it had always been possible for a king's friends to argue that rebels, by taking up arms against the lord's anointed, had aimed at his death, I think that in France too those who made war against the king ran the risk of being branded as traitors.[32] This, however, is a separate debate and this is not the place to pursue it any further.

What matters here is that given the generally accepted view that

29. S. H. Cuttler, *The Law of Treason and Treason Trials in Later Medieval France* (Cambridge, 1981), 46, 116, 144-5. It should be said that Jourdain's most high-profile offence seems to have been killing the royal serjeant who summoned him to court; according to one manuscript of the *Chroniques,* 'auquel il avoit bouté la masse enarmée des armes le roy parmi le fondement', *Les Grandes Chroniques de France*, ed. J. Viard (SHF) 10 vols., Paris 1920-53, ix, 17 n. 1.
30. Cuttler, *Law of Treason,* 8-9. Kaeuper, *War, Justice*, 229-31.
31. Cuttler, *Law of Treason,* 31, 95-6.
32. For instance William the Breton praised Philip Augustus's mercy (*O mira principis clementia),* when he put to death none of the five counts and twenty-five other greater nobles captured at Bouvines in 1214, though they were all his subjects and he could have had them executed *secundum leges et secundum terre illius consuetudinem tanquam rei lese majestatis* on the grounds that by fighting against him they had sought his death, *Œuvres de Rigord et de Guillaume le Breton*, ed. H. F. Delaborde, 2 vols. (Paris, 1882-5), 290-291.

Roman law had no more influence in England c.1300 than c.1200,[33] we are at present in the position of having two different explanations for a similar and more or less simultaneous change in *die Spielregeln der Politik*[34] in the two countries. This is, of course, not impossible, but even so I suggest it would be sensible to look for phenomena common to both kingdoms. And there is a development which they do have in common: the emergence of a professional judiciary. This suggests a different explanation for the increasing severity with which rebellion was punished in both England and France, not in a widening of the scope of the law of treason, but in the way a professional judiciary chose to implement the law, in other words in the relationship between the judges and the state.

3. The professional judges and the English trials

In what follows I have adopted Paul Brand's definition of a professional judge – that is, not just a man who was a full-time judge and was paid a salary, but also – and very importantly – someone who before his appointment as judge had been a career lawyer. In the case of England this meant a man who acted as a serjeant (i.e. an advocate) in the two central courts at Westminster, King's Bench and the Common Bench, after first having learned the law by being an apprentice present in the court of Common Bench. Professional judges in this sense, men who had spent their whole adult life in and around the courts of law, first emerged after c. 1290. By the end of Edward I's reign the serjeants of the Common Bench – a small group of about thirty – had become established as the main source of justices for King's Bench and the Common Bench; by 1330 this elite group of lawyers enjoyed a monopoly of appointments to them. As Brand argues, 'it seems likely that admission to this group was gained on the basis of proven technical competence'.[35] Highly significant too is Paul Brand's analysis of the social origins of these men. Most came from obscure families, 'from humble or poor rural backgrounds, from the ranks of those who leave little trace in the records'. Few, if any, of them came from

33. Bellamy, *Law of Treason,* 4-8, 11, 14; also Matthew Strickland's essay in this volume. But see Anthony Musson, 'Edward II: The Public and Private Faces of the Law', in *The Reign of Edward II: New Perspectives*, ed. Gwilym Dodd and Anthony Musson (Woodbridge, 2006), 140-64, 157.
34. For this term see Gerd Althoff, *Spielregeln der Politik im Mittelalter: Kommunikation in Frieden und Fehde* (Darmstadt, 1997)
35. 'Edward I and the Transformation of the English Judiciary' in Paul Brand, *The Making of the Common Law* (London, 1992), 135-68, 166. See also Paul Brand, *The Origins of the English Legal Profession* (Oxford, 1992), 94-119.

families in which Anglo-Norman was a normal language of everyday life.[36] A question is: how much would judges appointed from such groups sympathise with or respect the old conventions which had allowed aristocrats to 'get away' with rebellion when less mercy was commonly shown to men of lower rank? Or might professional lawyers have been inclined to think that the full rigour of the law should be applied to all impartially?

One of these new groups of professional judges played a key role in the trial *coram rege* of Thomas of Lancaster at Pontefract on 22 March. This was Robert Mablethorpe. When appointed a justice of the King's Bench in August 1320 he had had twenty years experience as a sergeant in the Common Bench.[37] According to the *Annales Paulini,* Mablethorpe was the judge assigned to the trial, sitting together with the earl of Arundel and Hugh Despenser (the father).[38] According to the *Brut,* it was he who pronounced the charge, accusing Thomas of having 'ridden with banner displayed, against the king's peace, as a traitor' and it was he who refused to allow the earl to answer.[39] Yet Mablethorpe's name does not appear in the official record of the trial.[40] As Thomas's judges this names only his fellow earls: Edmund, earl of Kent, John, earl of Richmond, Aymer de Valence, earl of Pembroke, John de Warenne, earl of Surrey, Edmund earl of Arundel, David earl of Atholl, Robert earl of Angus, as well as other unnamed barons, and other magnates. But that Robert Mablethorpe did play a significant part in the trial is evident from another piece of record evidence: the pardon he obtained in 1327 for having been the justice who pronounced judgement on the earl.[41] Two narrative sources highlight his presence at the trial; by contrast the silence of the record may indicate a certain official embarrassment about the fact that such a man, even though he came from a family rather better off than did most professional lawyers, should sit in judgement on the greatest noble in the land.[42]

---

36. Paul Brand, 'The Serjeants of the Common Bench in the Reign of Edward I: An Emerging Professional Elite', *Thirteenth Century England,* VII (1997, 99), 81-102, 93-5.
37. *Select Cases in the Court of King's Bench,* 4 vols. ed. G. O. Sayles (Selden Society, 55, 58,74, 1939-1957), vol. 1, cxxxiv, vol. 4, xiii; Brand, 'The Serjeants of the Common Bench', 88 n. 51.
38. *Chronicles of Edward I and Edward II*, i. 302.
39. *The Brut*, 222.
40. Printed from the chancery rolls in Harcourt, *His Grace the Steward,* 327-9.
41. According to the pardon, he was fearfully obeying orders, *judicium praedictum per preceptum domini E. nuper regis Anglie, patris nostri, cui resistere non audebat, et pro periculo corporis sui evitando, reddidit,* printed in *Foedera, conventions, litterae,* ed. T. Rymer et al., vols. 1-3 (London 1816-30), Vol. 2 pt 2, 696.
42. His father was prosperous but not a knight, Brand, 'The Serjeants of the Common Bench', 93, 95. 'Socially, the standing of even the most eminent lawyers was not high', E. L. G. Stones, 'Sir Geoffrey le Scrope (c. 1285-1340), chief justice of the king's bench', EHR 69 (1954), 8.

But a few fragments of evidence suggest to me that another professional lawyer played an even more important part in the crisis of 1322. This was Geoffrey Scrope, a Yorkshireman who was to distinguish himself in international diplomacy, in tournaments and in real warfare as well as being Chief Justice of the King's Bench from 1324 until 1338. He became a Common Bench serjeant in 1309 and in 1315 was appointed one of the king's serjeants-at-law (of whom there were four). From 1317 until his death in 1340 he was regularly summoned to councils and parliaments.[43] In September 1323 he was appointed a justice of Common Pleas. When the king appointed as judge a man who had been a king's serjeant, he was appointing a lawyer who had given, as Brand put it, 'proof not just of his professional competence but also of assiduity in the promotion and protection of the king's interests'.[44] This Geoffrey Scrope had certainly shown in his aggressive challenges to the traditional liberties of the City of London during the eyre of 1321.[45] Since he successfully transferred his allegiance in 1326 from Edward II and the Despensers to Isabella and Mortimer, and then from them to the young Edward III in 1330, he was clearly an immensely supple politician. He spent most of the last two years of his life in the Low Countries both on military campaign and as a member of Edward III's diplomatic team. It was he who, according to Geoffrey Baker, made a French cardinal faint by taking him one dark night in September 1339 to the top of a high tower so that he could see just how far the fires started by Edward III's incendiaries stretched over the countryside, saying to him: 'Your eminence, does it not seem that the silken thread which girdles France is broken?'[46] His hostility caused Archbishop John Stratford of Canterbury so much grief that the archbishop's biographer looked upon his death as an act of divine grace. Stones summed him up as 'a shrewd and ruthless lawyer' who was not just 'chief legal adviser to the Government', but also 'a powerful figure from first to last'.[47]

Yet despite being arguably the most famous English lawyer of the first half of the fourteenth century, his role in 1322-23 has been overlooked.[48] Although there is no evidence that he was directly involved in the most

---

43. Stones, 'Sir Geoffrey le Scrope', 1-17.
44. Brand, 'Edward I and the Transformation', 165-6
45. On this see Fryde, *Tyranny and Fall,* 169-71. At this eyre Scrope acted for 42 clients as well as for the king, and won most of his cases, Brigette Vale, article on Geoffrey Scrope in the Oxford Dictionary of National Biography. Her PhD dissertation, 'The Scropes of Bolton and Masham, c. 1300-c. 1450' (York, 1987) is, as its subtitle indicates, principally a study of a northern noble family.
46. *Chronicon Gaufridi le Baker de Swynebroke,* ed. E. Maunde Thompson (Oxford, 1889), 65.
47. Stones, 'Sir Geoffrey le Scrope', 6, 14.
48. With the partial exception of a few tantalising phrases in D. J. M. Higgins, *Judges in government and society under Edward II* (unpublished Oxford D. Phil. Thesis, 1986), 135-7.

high-profile of the trials of 1322, the trial of Earl Thomas on 22 March, and indeed in the fact that he, unlike Mablethorpe, did not seek a pardon in 1327, some evidence that he was not, what he did do in March 1322 is in some ways even more remarkable. On 10 March Thomas of Lancaster had suffered a decisive military blow when he failed to prevent Edward II's army from crossing the Trent, and was forced to retreat northwards.[49] In the fighting for control of the bridge at Burton on Trent one of his principal allies, Roger Damory, had been seriously wounded, and taken to the nearby Tutbury Castle. There, together with the castle, he fell into the king's hands on 11 March. Two days later he was put on trial before a military court headed by the constable and marshal of the army, Fulk FitzWarin and John Weston.[50] According to the official record of the trial, Damory had 'falsely and traitorously' and in the company of attainted traitors made war 'with banner displayed' against the king:

> Roger [...] since your treasons are notorious to all as our lord the king by his royal power awards and records, so this court awards that for the treason you should be drawn, and for the homicides, arsons and robberies you should be hanged. But Roger, because at one time the king loved you, and you were of his privy household and married to his niece, our lord king of his grace and of his regality, puts the execution of this sentence into respite at his discretion.[51]

In the event the sentence was never carried out. On 13 March Roger Damory was a dying man; indeed he seems to have died either on the same day or on the next.[52] Evidently speed was essential if he were to be tried and convicted of treason during his lifetime. Presumably someone advised that the army's military court could do the trick. Given that there is no other evidence for such a court dealing with cases of treason at so early a date, it may not have been an obvious piece of advice.[53] Since the official record reveals that there was a third person on the tribunal, Geoffrey Scrope, a lawyer with known martial interests, it is tempting to suggest that his was

49. *Vita Edwardi secundi*, 122-3.
50. On the status of these two men see Maurice Keen, 'The Jurisdiction and Origins of the Constable's Court', in Keen, *Nobles, Knights and Men-at-arms,* 135-48, 143.
51. 'Placita exercitus domini Regis apud Tuttebiri', printed by Harcourt, *His Grace the Steward,* 400.
52. *Complete Peerage*, iv. 43 note f. According to the *Vita Edwardi*, 'it turned out well and honourably for him that, unlike his comrades, he did not survive until the bitter end', *Vita Edwardi,* 123.
53. Keen, 'Treason Trials', 161-2. If this was indeed a constable's court operating as later, i.e. under civil law, it could levy execution only on the body and chattels (not the lands) of a convicted traitor. In 1379 the Commons in parliament protested against appeals of treason being brought before the constable and marshal as 'contrary to the law of the land and against Magna Carta', Keen, 'Jurisdiction of the Constable's Court', 135-6.

the legal advice which led to this summary court martial of a dying man.[54] Indeed the record of this court survives only because it was called into King's Bench on 19 August 1324, a few months after Geoffrey Scrope's appointment as Chief Justice of that court.[55] Fulk FitzWarin, John Weston and Geoffrey Scrope, still only one of the king's serjeants, were men of remarkably low status to be sitting in judgement on the husband of the king's niece.

There is other evidence that highly important legal decisions were taken at Tutbury. It was from here on 11 March that Edward II sent the orders to all the sheriffs of England to pursue, arrest and imprison Thomas of Lancaster and his associates

> as the king has pronounced them traitors after taking counsel with Edmund, earl of Kent, John de Warenna, earl of Richmond, Aymer de Valencia, earl of Pembroke, Edmund earl of Arundel, John de Warenne, earl of Surrey, and David de Strabolgi, earl of Atholl, and with other barons and magnates, the king having…sent his men and servants before him to Burton-upon-Trent to take lodging for him, whereupon the aforesaid traitors and other rebels adhering to them kept the bridge of the town with armed force […] having made at the end thereof near the town bretasches in manner of war […] conducting war against the king with banners displayed.[56]

These were the letters which meant that when Earl Thomas was tried at Pontefract later that month, he had already been condemned on the king's record as a traitor for 'levying war against the king with banners displayed'. It is certainly possible that Sir Robert Mablethorpe was at Tutbury that day; very probable, given the record of his presence there two days later, that Geoffrey Scrope was.[57]

In July 1322 Edward II appointed a commission of gaol delivery to deal with those rebels who were still in prison, instructing them to make the terms on which the men in gaol could be released. Richard le Waleys, for example, had to agree to pay 2,000 marks if he were to recover the estates he forfeited for rebellion. In terms of legal learning this was an unusually high-powered commission, consisting of the chancellor, John bishop of

54. Curiously Scrope's presence is not mentioned in the account of Damory's trial in Bellamy, *Law of Treason,* 50.
55. Harcourt, *His Grace the Steward,* 399.
56. *Calendar of Close Rolls, 1318-23*, 522.
57. In 1327 when the trials of Thomas of Lancaster, Roger Mortimer and Bartholomew of Badlesmere were declared illegal, part of the case was that the law courts, including both benches, had remained open *per totum tempus,* Harcourt, *His Grace the Steward,* 327-34. None the less the whereabouts of the justices between February (end of Hilary Term 1322) when King's Bench was at Gloucester, and Easter, when it was at York, are unknown (to me at least), *Select Cases*, ed. Sayles, vo. 4, xli, cii. See also Musson, 'The Public and Private Faces', 146-8.

Norwich, the keeper of the rolls of chancery, William Airmyn, the Chief Justice of King's Bench, Henry Scrope (Geoffrey's elder brother), the Chief Justice of the Common Bench, William of Bereford, and finally one king's serjeant, Geoffrey Scrope.[58] Next year when Andrew Harclay, earl of Carlisle, was condemned to death at Carlisle in March 'on the king's record', and in accordance with Edward II's written instructions, the one professional lawyer among the judges was the king's serjeant, Geoffrey Scrope.[59] That the serjeant pleased his political masters in the crisis of 1322-23 is suggested by the fact that he was appointed a justice of common pleas in September 1323, and then promoted to Chief Justice of the King's Bench in March 1324.[60] As Stones pointed out, to go from being a serjeant of Common Bench to Chief Justice of the King's Bench in six months was a remarkably rapid promotion.[61] Another indication that he was seen as a key figure in the events of 1322-23 is the fact that his name appears in a short list of those whom Roger Mortimer was alleged to be planning to murder. The others were the two Despensers, the earl of Arundel and the chancellor, Robert Baldock.[62] Of these five, four were killed in the coup of 1326. Geoffrey Scrope not only escaped; as Chief Justice of the King's Bench he formally accepted Edward's abdication in January 1327 and continued to prosper under both Mortimer and the young Edward III.[63] If we judge a man by the company he keeps, then to find Scrope's name in the record of the trial of Roger Damory, of the July 1322 commission of gaol delivery, and on the list of those whom Mortimer wanted to murder is extraordinarily suggestive.

58. *Calendar of Fine Rolls, 1319-27*, 152-3. Both Henry Scope and Bereford had been serjeants of the Bench, Brand,'The Serjeants of the Common Bench', 88-9.
59. *Parliamentary Writs and Writs of Military Summons, Edward I and Edward II,* ed. Francis Palgrave (Record Commission, London 1827-34), ii, pt. 2, 262-3. The other judges, Sir Ralph Basset, Sir John Pecche, and Sir John de Wysham were soldier-administrators not professional lawyers. Scrope was not yet a high court judge, let alone *pace* Bellamy, *Law of Treason,* 52, a chief justice.
60. He was also knighted in October 1323, but that was the customary advancement for high court judges. On the other hand his elder brother, Henry, chief justice of the King's Bench since 1318, lost that office at about the same time, *Select Cases,* ed. Sayles, vol. 4, xix-xx, lix-lx.
61. Stones,'Sir Geoffrey le Scrope', 6. He did very well in other ways too. In March 1324 he was granted possession of the estates of Richard le Waleys, to be held until he received the 2,000 marks. *Calendar of Patent Rolls,* 395. From 1324 to 1329 he and Maplethorpe were King's Bench colleagues.
62. Confession of Richard de Fernhale, made in Nov 1323, recorded in the *Coram rege* roll for Hilary Term, 1324 (i.e. shortly before Scrope became Chief Justice), printed in *Parliamentary Writs*, II, ii, Appendix, 244ff.
63. 'The most striking aspect of his career is the stability of his position during the two revolutions of 1326 and 1330. The adroitness with which he passed from one allegiance to another seems very remarkable', Stones, 'Sir Geoffrey le Scrope', 4.

In 1322-23 earls and barons were tried and executed, but they were not put on trial in parliament, instead a variety of other courts specially constituted for this purpose were used, including a military court. The role played by professional lawyers such as Scrope and Mablethorpe in 1322 and 1323 suggests that it might be worth going back to earlier 'state' trials to see if there are earlier indications of this new group of professionals being prominently involved. When David of Wales was tried in the 1283 parliament at Shrewsbury, the presiding judge, John des Vaux, was emphatically not a professional, but rather one of the king's longest-serving followers, sheriff of Norfolk and Suffolk and a captain in the Welsh war.[64] The trial of Rhys ap Maredudd in 1292 provides an example of what might be called the routine machinery of justice being employed against rebels.[65] None of the four men appointed to the commission of gaol delivery, however, could be described as a specialist judge.[66] Similarly Thomas Turberville's trial in 1295 (though this was on a charge of betraying secrets to Philip IV of France, not of taking up arms against the king), was presided over by Sir Roger Brabazon, the newly appointed Chief Justice of the King's Bench who was probably not professional in the full sense employed here.[67] In the light of the chronology of the emergence of the professional judiciary established by Paul Brand, there is of course nothing surprising about this. There is, however, significance in the fact that it was one of the most prominent of the king's sergeants of Edward I's reign, Nicholas of Warwick, who prosecuted Nicholas Segrave in parliament in 1305 on a charge of *laesio coronae*.[68]

---

64. Michael Prestwich, *Edward I* (London, 1988), 23, 27, 242. Although he was clearly regarded as a reliable judge and may well have had a considerable interest in the law (Paul Brand, 'Quo Warranto Law in the Reign of Edward I', in Brand, *The Making of the Common Law,* 393-443, 395) See also D. Crook, Eyre Records, 144-7), he was not a jurist, *pace* J. P. Trabut-Cussac, *L'Administration anglaise en Gascogne sous Henri III et Edouard I* (Geneva, 1972), 143-4.
65. A brief official record of his trial survives in the close rolls. Cited *in extenso* in J. G. Edwards, 'The Treason of Thomas Turberville, 1295', in *Studies in Medieval History Presented to Frederick Maurice Powicke*, ed. R. W. Hunt, W. A. Pantin, R. W. Southern (Oxford, 1948), 296 n 2.
66. Peter de Champagne, was a household knight; John de Lythegreynes was primarily a sheriff (1274-8 of Northumberland; 1280-5 of Yorkshire) John of Meaux and William de St Quintin, were administrators/judges. I owe this information to the kindness of Paul Brand.
67. Brand, 'Edward I and the Transformation', 160. Brabazon had been appointed a justice of King's Bench in 1290 and Chief Justice in 1295, a post he held until 1315, 'a record period of unbroken service' within a single court. When age and infirmities led to his retirement, he was accorded the then unique honour of being made a life member of the king's councils, *Select Cases,* ed. Sayles, vol. 4, xii-xiii.
68. Brand, 'The Serjeants of the Common Bench', 98-9. Segrave confessed and Edward asked the peers what punishment should be made. They recommended a death sentence but because he submitted, Edward preferred to spare his life. This

Later in that same year William Wallace was escorted to London, and tried at a special commission of gaol delivery, held on 23 August. The commission included two very prominent members of the king's council of baronial rank, John Segrave and Ralph of Sandwich, as well as the mayor of London, but what struck the anonymous author of the *Annales Londonienses* was the prominent role played in the trial by Peter Malory.[69] He had been a justice of Common Pleas since 1292 and Paul Brand has noted some evidence that before then he might have practised as a serjeant in the Common Bench.[70] In any event by 1305 he was clearly a highly experienced judge. In the record of the sentence in which the charge against William Wallace was set out at length, we have what has been called 'the first example of a lawyer's definition of the crime' of waging war against the king, including the phrase *vexillum contra dominum suum ligium in bello mortali deferendo*. Further legal expertise was demonstrated by the care with which Wallace's status as an outlaw was delineated and hence his liability to summary execution.[71]

Peter Malory was employed again in 1306 as head of a commission of gaol delivery at Newcastle instructed to dispatch rebels captured after the battle of Methven (19 June, 1306). Fifteen Scots and one Englishman (John Seton) were drawn and hanged on 4 August as being guilty of treasons and felonies 'en tesmoigne de quele chose le Rey ad fet fert ces lettres ouvertes sealez de sun privie seal'. This appears to be the earliest example of conviction on the king's record, whereby indictment and verdict were fused into one, and has been described as 'of the utmost importance in the development of the law of treason'.[72] Three months later Malory acted as a

---

was presumably all negotiated in advance of the public declarations. Cf. the analysis of the negotiations and rituals of submission by the defenders of Stirling Castle in 1304 in Matthew Strickland, 'A Law of Arms or a Law of Treason?', 71-75. Cf. Theo Broekmann, *Rigor Iustitiae. Herrschaft, Recht und Terror im normannisch-staufischen Süden, 1050-1250* (Darmstadt, 2005), 152-57.

69. The official record of both the appointment of the commission and the sentence survive only because the author of *Annales Londonienses* copied them into his chronicle, *Chronicles of Edward I and Edward II*, 139-42.

70. Brand, 'Edward I and the Transformation', 162.

71. Bellamy, *Law of Treason in England,* 37; 'idem Willelmus [...] paci predicti domini regis se submittere et ad eam evenire contempsit; et sic in curia ipsius domini regis ut seductor, praedo et felo, secundum leges et consuetudines Anglie et Scotie, publice fuit utlagatus; et injustum et legibus Anglicanis dissonum existat, et creditur, aliquem sic utlagatum et extra leges positum, nec postea ad pacem ipsius restitutum, ad defensionem status sui seu responsionem admitti; Et quia utlagatus fuit, nec postea ad pacem domini regis restitutus, decolletur et decapitetur ', *Chronicles of Edward I and Edward II,* i. 141-2.

72. 'The conviction on the king's record and by notoriety of John Seton, Bernard Mowat and the fourteen Scots [...] had results beyond the Scottish war and the reign of Edward I. It set a fashion for dealing with traitors taken in arms which was to figure prominently in the civil wars of the two succeeding centuries', Bellamy,

judge, together with Sir Roger Brabazon, in the Westminster trial of the earl of Atholl.[73] This trial attracted the attention of chroniclers partly because the earl was a kinsman of the king and partly because his execution, like that of Fraser's a few weeks earlier, was a 'major act of political theatre'. According to an enthusiastic supporter of Edward I's Scottish policy, an anonymous author from Westminster abbey (now in possession of the stone of Scone), the king was a paragon of justice.[74] When some *palatini* questioned the appropriateness of treating his kinsman just like other Scottish rebels, Edward's reply was that the higher the birth the higher a malefactor should be hanged. Atholl was to be taken to London and there he should be *justissime judicetur*. For the king, wrote this author, paid attention not to high lineage but to the judgement of justice (*non sanguinis lineam sed justiciae judicium attendens*).[75] In 1305-06 in Peter Malory the king found a professional justice willing to do his bidding.[76]

In 1318 Gilbert de Middleton, a knight of the royal household, was executed for treason. His offence was the scandal caused by an attack on and robbery of two papal envoys (both cardinals) to England and their imprisonment of the bishop-elect of Durham. Although this flagrant act of brigandage shamed the king of England, it was evidently very different from a rebellion against him. None the less the record of Gilbert's trial before the king (*coram ipso domino rege)* at Westminster is indicative of the way in which terminology and procedures devised to punish Scots were beginning to be more widely applied. 'The king records that [...] Gilbert feloniously as a felon, traitorously as a traitor (*seductive ut seductor)* drew to himself a host of men, not only Scots, the king's enemies, but also other felons, *equitando ad modum gwerre cum vexillo suo displicato*'.[77]

Law of Treason, 41-5. Edward had already, on 28 June 1306 (i.e. 9 days after Bruce's defeat at the battle of Methven) ordered Aymer de Valence to put to death all enemies already taken or to be captured. On the significance of this unprecedented ruthlessness see Strickland, 'Treason, Feud and the Growth of State Violence'.

73. *Chronicles of Edward I and Edward II,* i. 149-50.
74. On this author see Antonia Gransden, *Historical Writing in England c. 550 to c. 1307* (London, 1974), 453-6.
75. The author emphasised the calculated cruelty with which the earl was executed, as well as the treatment of his dead. *Flores Historiarum*, ed. Luard, iii, 134-5. Walter of Guisborough told a similar story, adding the queen to those who pleaded for the earl, *The Chronicle of Walter of Guisborough*, ed. Harry Rothwell, Camden Society, vol. 89 (1957), 369.
76. This was especially important in 1306 when, as Matthew Strickland has emphasised, Edward I's policy towards the Scots took on an unprecedented degree of brutality following Robert Bruce's murder of Comyn and his inauguration as king of Scotland
77. *Select Cases 4, p. 78.* Whether or not Middleton actually had Scots in his following at the time of the attack, the mention of Scots in the indictment is telling. Natalie Fryde suggested that Edward II's condemnation of Thomas of Lancaster as

4. The new instrument of power

It is not possible here to look so closely at the evidence for early fourteenth-century France – nor, indeed, am I remotely competent to do so. Hence I shall limit myself to a number of generalisations culled from well-known secondary works. As the *parlement* of Paris increased in importance, so the number of royal counsellors who were trained in the law increased rapidly. Some of these men came from a relatively humble social background.[78] Influenced by Roman law, the royal judges and officers were often more royalist than the king. They pressed for the Roman law expedient of torture to elicit confessions or even testimony and experimented with the inquisitorial process of trial. In the words of a recent English summary of this work:

> The king's central judicial machinery increased in scope and scale in the period 1270 to 1328. The *parlement*, fixed in Paris from 1303, was becoming more exclusively a legal body with a permanent professional staff, composed in the main of lay and clerical judges in almost equal numbers. Many were [...] from quite humble backgrounds, well versed in the different branches of the law – Roman, canon and customary [...] these developments reflect a move towards an increased professionalization in government and administration. The nobility and higher clergy still performed many of their traditional functions, but they were gradually becoming less influential in affairs of state.[79]

In treason trials those accused such as Bernard Saisset in 1301 and Enguerran de Marigny in 1315 were denied the right to defend themselves. Ways of undermining a noble's right to trial by his peers were increasingly found.[80] As Susan Reynolds has emphasized, 'the dominance of professional lawyers and judges in the courts of late medieval Europe

---

a traitor was probably pronounced when the alleged evidence of his alliance with the Scots was found at Tutbury, Fryde, *Tyranny and Fall*, 60. For a sceptical discussion of Middleton's links with the Scots see Michael Prestwich, 'Gilbert de Middleton and the Attack on the Cardinals, 1317', in *Warriors and Churchmen in the High Middle Ages.Essays presented to Karl Leyser,* ed. Timothy Reuter (London, 1992), 179-94, 183-5.

78. See, for example, the discussion of the social and geographic origins of the king's officers in J. R. Strayer, *The Reign of Philip the Fair* (Princeton, 1980), 36-55, and, less systematically, in F. J. Pegues, *The Lawyers of the Last Capetians* (Princeton, 1962). See also *Histoire des institutions françaises au moyen âge,* ed. Ferdinand Lot and Robert Fawtier, tome II, *Institutions royales* (Paris, 1958), 77-8, 356-8; *Confessions et jugements de criminels au Parlement de Paris (1319-1350),* ed. M. Langlois and Y. Lanhers (Paris, 1971), 14-23.
79. Elizabeth M Hallam and Judith Everard, *Capetian France 987-1328* (Harlow, 2001), 376
80. Cuttler, *The Law of Treason*, 92-3, 95-99.

eliminated the collective judgement that had earlier been traditional and with which judgement by one's equals had originally been connected'.[81] Jourdain de l'Isle-Jourdain's trial in 1323 was the first important treason trial to have taken place in the 'professionalised' *parlement.* The charge against him brought by the king's advocate, Pierre de Maucreux, a man of humble birth and the learned author of a treatise on pleading in court.[82] All that even that small élite group known as the peers of France managed to obtain was the right to be judged only in the king's court, 'a hollow victory, for the king's court was inevitably the court in France that was bound to most dominated by professional lawyers.'[83]

In England, as in France, the emergence of a professional judiciary offered kings a new and convenient instrument of power.[84] It is clear that in practice when men of high-status were brought to trial on a charge of treason, their guilt had already been decided upon – and in the case of armed rebellion was virtually impossible to deny.[85] What remained was to find procedures that enabled rebels to be legally convicted and then to decide upon the penalty. If a king wanted to press for a death penalty then it may well be that in the professional judges he found accomplices who would make little resistance. Richard II recognised as much in 1387 when he asked the judges a series of questions about the royal prerogative and about the appropriate punishment for those who opposed it. In their replies they not only offered him a very authoritarian interpretation of the prerogative, but also stated that those who opposed it should be punished 'as traitors'. It is arguable that the judges managed to stay within the letter of the law by avoiding saying that those who opposed were traitors (which under the terms of the Statute of Treasons of 1352 they appeared not to be), only – only! – that they should be punished 'as traitors'.[86] But this merely demonstrates how determined the judges were to find legal ways of doing the king's bidding. Not surprisingly they later claimed to have given their opinions under duress. Had the king's lawyers in 1322 behaved in much the same way as the judges of 1387? According to the author of the prose *Brut,* when the Despensers looked for ways by which Thomas could be killed 'without the judgement of his peers', the king's justices advised having him convicted for treason on the king's record.[87] The procedure adopted against

81. Susan Reynolds, *Fiefs and Vassals* (Oxford, 1994), 4
82. Cuttler, *The Law of Treason*, 144-5. On Maucreux see Pegues, *The Lawyers of the Last Capetians*, 200-203.
83. Reynolds, *Fiefs and Vassals*, 305-6.
84. Though in fourteenth-century England after the trial of Roger Mortimer in 1330 it was accepted that parliament was the only appropriate setting for major state trials, Nigel Saul, *Richard II* (New Haven, 1997), 192.
85. In contrast four men accused of spying for the Scots in 1296 put themselves on a jury and were acquitted, Bellamy, *Law of Treason,* 32.
86. Nigel Saul, *Richard II* (New Haven, 1997), 173-5
87. *The Brut,* 221-2.

Scots in 1305-6 and against Middleton in 1318 had now been turned against the greatest nobleman in the land and his associates.

Edward II, it is said, recruited a remarkably able judiciary whose intelligence, wit and learning is amply attested in the earliest surviving law reports, the Year Books.[88] Among the opinions attributed to them in this source are views such as that 'against the king who is above the law you cannot rely on legal principles' and that for them to not to obey a direct command from him would be 'tantamount to challenging and disputing the king's authority', which they could not do.[89] One of the reporters of the Kent eyre stated that in one case the judges had acted for the king's advantage and out of fear (*id magis fecerunt ad comodum regis quam ad legem manutenendum & quia fecerunt ad terrorem*).[90] If this happened in relatively minor cases, then it was surely all the more likely in political crises such as 1322. Mablethorpe's claim that he had given the judgement required at Thomas of Lancaster's trial out of fear was evidently regarded as at least plausible in 1327.[91] Moreover although judges' salaries were relatively low, the opportunities for profit were immense – as none demonstrated more impressively than Geoffrey Scrope.[92] It was not a position that someone from a relatively humble background would readily risk losing. Yet judges were the king's creatures, as Edward I very dramatically proved in 1289 when he removed seven of the eight judges in the two higher courts.[93] These, it may be, could not yet have been expected to live up to professional standards.[94] But 'professionally' trained senior judges remained liable to be dismissed as and when the king chose, as happened to Chief Justice William Inge in 1317 and Chief Justice Henry Scrope in 1324. Composed of men of relatively obscure birth, the judiciary was a more malleable instrument than a baronial assembly.

It is, of course, also possible that men who had spent a lifetime in the law, and who were dedicated to justice, were less likely to take account of the political consequences of executing men of high status than were the latter's peers. Some fourteenth-century justices may have sympathised with

---

88. Fryde, *Tyranny and Fall,* 149
89. Musson, 'Public and Private Faces', 155.
90. *Year Books of Edward II: The Eyre of Kent 6 & 7 Edward II, A.D. 1313-14,* ed. F. W. Maitland, L. W. V. Harcourt and W. C. Bolland, vol. 1, Selden Society 24 (London, 1910), 104.
91. See above n. 41.
92. When he went to Flanders in 1340, six ships were needed to carry his horses and retinue, Vale, 'Geoffrey Scrope', Oxford DNB.
93. As well as one of the two justices of northern eyre, and all 4 of the southern eyre, twelve judges in all. Paul Brand, 'Edward I and the judges: the "state trials" trials of 1289-93, *Thirteenth-Century England,* I (1986), 31-40, reprinted in Brand, *Making of the Common Law,* 103-112 .
94. On this subject see the sections on judicial ethics and the enforcement of standards in Brand, 'Edward I and the Transformation', 148-56.

the values of their contemporary, the Westminster monk who praised Edward I for caring more about justice than about blue blood.[95] Conceivably some of these professional lawyers shared the opinion of a much later lawyer, Frederick Maitland. Although he saw that in the new punishments pronounced by Edward I's and Edward II's judges there appeared to be *prima facie* evidence that men had become more cruel, he had another value judgement to add:

> We ought to see that there has been a real progress, the development of a new political idea. Treason has been becoming a crime against the state; the supreme crime against the state is the levying of war against it. A right, or duty, of rising against the king and compelling him to do justice can no longer be preached in the name of law; and this is well.[96]

It also marked the beginning of a long period in both England and France in which for the leading politicians of the age, 'die Spielregeln der Politik' were a lot bloodier than they had been.

---

95. Above n. 74.
96. Pollock and Maitland, *English Law*, ii. 506. Some of the assumptions behind this passage were shared by those nineteenth-century French historians who believed that the jurisconsults and legists in royal service from the later thirteenth century onwards fought for 'law and reason' against 'feudal custom', contributing massively if sometimes tyrannically to the historical destiny of the French people, the construction of a one-class society and the modern state. See Pegues, *Lawyers of the Last Capetians,* 6-23 for a summary of the views held by AugustinThierry, Jules Michelet, Henri Martin and François Guizot.

FRUSTRA LEGIS AUXILIUM INVOCAT

RECEPTION OF A MEDIEVAL LEGAL MAXIM IN EARLY MODERN ENGLAND AND AMERICA

Bruce C. Brasington

1. Introduction[1]

Maxims intrigued medieval and early-modern lawyers.[2] Ideas and arguments unimaginable to the originators of the phrases themselves could be drawn like so many iron filings by their magnetism. *Frustra legis auxilium invocat* (henceforth *FLA*) and its varying formulations is one of the most attractive of all. From medieval commentaries on civil and canon law to the legal quarrels of the American Civil War, this maxim exerted a wide influence on lawyers, political theorists, and even revolutionaries.

2. Origins and medieval reception

The maxim comes from Tryphonius (D 4.4.37.1.)[3] Located in the title concerning minors, it treats *Restitutio in integrum*,[4] specifically minors who,

1. I thank the Inter-Library Loan department of the WTAMU Cornette Library for obtaining many of the works used in this paper. I also thank the director of the Handschriftenabteilung of the Sächische Landes- und Universitätsbibliothek, Dresden, for permitting me to work in this collection.

2. Peter Stein, *Regulae Iuris. From Juristic Rules to Legal Maxims* (Edinburgh: University Press 1966).

3. 'Auxilium in integrum restitutionis exsecutionibus poenarum paragum non est: ideoquoe iniuriarum iudicium semel paratum non est...et non sit aetatis excusatio adversus praecepta legum ei, qui dum leges invocat, contra eas committit.' On Tryphonius, a jurisconsult and under Septimus Severus in the early third century,

still under *tutela*, might be easily defrauded and deprived of property.[5] While their rights were to be defended, with the *praetor* given considerable discretion on their behalf, there were also limitations. If a transaction had been made in good faith and appeared justified, the minor could not subsequently claim – if the deal proved unsuccessful – that it should be voided by reason of his youth.[6] This was the point of Tryphonius' comment concerning a married minor who waited too long to accuse his wife of adultery and, accordingly, divorce her without calumny (*sine calumnia*). He could not excuse himself on the basis of his minor status. In short, whoever violated the law could not appeal to it for any sort of protection.[7]

With the renewed study of civil law in the twelfth century came glosses on the passage. In his *Ordinary Gloss*, Accursius succinctly noted: 'through his own delict, he loses the benefit',[8] a choice of terms rich in meaning both for civil and feudal law. He offers as well a variety of allegations to illustrate how violating the law voided the possibility of its use in defense.[9]

Canonists also commented, for example Ralph Diss, Archdeacon of Middlesex, later Dean of St. Paul's, London.[10] In 1166, Ralph wrote to his

---

see H.F. Jolowicz, *Historical Introduction to the Study of Roman Law* (Cambridge: Cambridge University Press 1932), 397.

4. Jolowicz, Historical Introduction, 234: 'In some cases the praetor's way of dealing with the possibility that general rules of law may have inequitable results is to annul the result which he considers inequitable by restoring the party injured to his original position (in integrum.).' Among many studies see also Thomas John Feeney, *Restitutio in Integrum: An Historical Synopsis and Commentary* (Washington, D.C.: Catholic University of America 1941).
5. Barry Nichols, *An Introduction to Roman Law* (Oxford: University Press 1965) 94-95.
6. Ibid., 94, for example the ability to decide that even if there had been no clear evidence of fraud, the minor could have full restitution if, as Nichols puts it, the minor 'had through experience made a bad bargain.' See also O.F. Robinson, *The Criminal Law of Ancient Rome* (Trowbridge: Duckworth 1995), 17, 65.
7. Compare *Ex dolo malo non oritur actio* and *nemo ex proprio dolo consequitur actionem*.
8. *Accursii Glossa in Digestum Vetus*, ed. Baptista de Tortis (Venice 1489, rp. Corpus glossatorum juris civilis vii, Turin 1969), 169: *Comittit. Notandum quod quis amittit beneficium propter suum delictum.*
9. For example concerning violations of marriage law: D 23.2.42: *§ Si senatoris filia; D 23.2.48: §Si ignominiosam.* As the latter notes: 'Si ignominiosam libertam suam patronus uxorem duxerit, placet, quia contra legem maritus sit, non habere eum hoc legis beneficium.' Men who married illegally did not enjoy legal protection should they wish to divorce. See Thomas A.J. McGinn, *Prostitution, Sexuality, and the Law in Ancient Rome* (New York: OUP 2003), 93.
10. Bruce C. Brasington, 'A Lawyer of Sorts: Ralph Diss' Knowledge of Canon and Civil Law,' in *Law and Learning in the Middle Ages. Proceedings of the Second Carlsberg Academy Conference on Medieval Legal History*, 2005, ed. Helle Vogt and Mia Münster-Swendsen (Copenhagen: DJØF Publishing 2005), 147-66 at 151.

fellow archdeacon, Richard of Ilchester, who had been excommunicated by Becket. The maxim appears as the capstone of Ralph's advice: regardless of what legal position Richard might take, he must submit to the sentence.

Some applied the maxim to *Restitutio in integrum.*[11] In a letter from 1205 to the Bishop of Modena (X 5.19.14), Innocent III considered the case of a usurer complaining about usury committed against him![12] Invoking the maxim, the pope declared that he first must right his own wrongs, restoring what he has "extorted" from others. Only then could the Church come to his aid. The decretalists found this position sensible and had little more to say on the matter.[13]

The maxim also censured clerics who had acted contrary to their ordination. Another letter from Innocent III (X 5.39.45) concerns a cleric who has begun to live as a layman.[14] After three warnings he loses the *privilegium fori*. In addition to *frustra leges invocat*, Innocent adds a well-known maxim from St. Ambrose to strengthen the sanction: *quia pivilegium meretur amittere qui permissa sibi abutitur potestate*.[15] The cleric's abuse of his privilege means he can no longer appeal to canon law for protection.

A related use of the maxim was its application to clerics having taken up arms. A decretal of Clement III (X 5.39.25) rules that once priests have become soldiers they cannot demand the "help of the church." They no longer enjoy benefit of clergy.[16] At least one early thirteenth-century

---

11. R.H. Helmholz, *The Spirit of Classical Canon Law* (Athens: University of Georgia Press 1996), chapter 4, without reference to our text. *FLA* remained a topic of discussion for centuries, as demonstrated by Jakob Carmon, *Positiones inauguraels ad regulam Frustra leges invocat qui contra leges commitit* (Diss jur. Rostock 1731). I thank the Sächsiche Landes- und Universitätsbibliothek for permitting me to examine their copy of this dissertation, which covers the original form of the maxim and its analogues and also commentary from Carmon's own day. Carmon confined his comments to the civil law.
12. 'Non auditur usuarius repetens usurus, nisi prius restituat extortas. Idem. Quia [igitur] frustra legis auxilium invocat qui committit in legem: statuimus, ut si quis usurarius a nobis literas impetraverit super restituendis usuris, vel fructibus computandis in sortem, nisi prius restituerit usuras, quas ab aliis noscitur recipisse, auctoritate literarum ipsarum nullatenus audiatur.'
13. For example, Hostiensis, *Summa aurea* (Venice 1574, rp. Turin 1963) 1634 summarizes the decretal and repeats the maxim.
14. *Corpus iuris canonici*. Pars. Secunda. Decretalium Collectiones. Decretales Gregorii. IX, ed. Emil Friedberg and Emil Ludwig Richter (Leipzig 1881), accessed at http://www.fh-augsburg.de/~Harsch/Chronologia/Lspost13/GregoriusIX/gre_5t19.html on 31 October 2007: 'Per dimissionem habitus et tonsurae non perdit clericus ante trinam monitionem privilegium clericale.' All subsequent citations of the *Liber Extra* come from this online edition.
15. 'Verum quia privilegium meretur amittere qui permissa sibi abutitur potestate, ac frustra legis auxilium invocat, qui committit in legem.' See the *Decretum* of Ivo of Chartres (5.140 and 325) and C 25 q. 2 dpc 21.
16. 'In audientia nostra talis fuit ex parte tua proposita consultation, utrum clerici, qui arma militaria (relicto habitu clericali) gestare nullatenus erubescunt: si eis fuerit

canonist even used the maxim to argue that a bishop could not fight even when his dioceses had been invaded. He could not claim the immunity afforded by canon law when he himself had fought.[17]

With Gregory IX we encounter the application of the maxim to violation of sanctuary. This will become common in later canon and secular law. In a letter of 1235 to the archbishops of Toledo and Compostella (X 3.49.10), Gregory advises that those who violate the immunity granted them by the sacred spaces of churches and cemeteries cannot claim protection from the law.[18] The later gloss by Johannes Andrea refers to Hostiensis, who agreed that no one committing theft in a church could be defended. Johannes notes, however, that Hostiensis did not consider that the thief's intent might mitigate in his favor. He cited the ancient penitential of Theodore, preserved at X 5.18.3, allowing a lesser penance for those stealing because of hunger or lack of clothes.[19]

At the same time that Gregory IX was denying the ability of those seeking sanctuary to abuse its privilege, Bracton referred to *frustra legis* concerning a point of procedural defect. This usage in the case of *disseisin* was closer to the original spirit of the maxim.[20] If the owner fails to pursue proper form in recovering his property, the possessor must be protected. Negligence obviates his former right, an understanding of the maxim's force congruent with Tryphonius' formulation.

There is at least one instance where the maxim was applied to judicial discretion. The question concerned whether torture ought to be used to

---

iniuria corporalis illata...Ad haec tibi breviter respondemus, quod cum frustra ecclesiae implorat auxilium, qui committit in ipsam...'

17. James A. Brundage, 'The Crusade of Richard I: Two Canonical Questions,' *Speculum* 38.3 (1963), 443-452 at 450, lines 55-60, in his edition of a *quaestio* of Nicholas de l'Aigle in the *Quaestiones Londinenses*, London, BL Royal 9 E vii, fol. 191r-198v.
18. 'Nonulli impunitatem suorum excessuum per defensionem ecclesiae obtinere sperantes, homicidia et mutilations membrorum in ipsis ecclesiis vel earum coemeteriis committere non verentur: qui, nisi per ecclesiam, ad quam fugerint, crederent se defendi, nullatenus fuerant commissuri: Cum autem in eo, in quo delinquit, puniri quis debeat: et frustra legis auxilium invocat, qui committit in legem, mandamus, quatenus publice nuncietis, tales non debere gaudere immunitatis privilegio, quo faciunt se indignos.' On this decretal, see R.H. Helmholz, *The Ius Commune in England. Four Studies* (Oxford: University Press 2001), 35, referring to the precedent set by Becket's murder at Canterbury cathedral. In n. 86, Helmholz points the reader to the later commentary by Antonius de Butrio, which unfortunately I have not been able to examine.
19. 'Si quis propter necessitatem famis, aut nuditatis furatus fuerit cibaria, vestem, vel pecus, poeniteat hebdomadas tres: et si reddiderit, non cogatur ieiunare.'
20. Bracton, *De legibus et consuetudinibus angliae*, cited by F.W. Maitland, 'The Beatitude of Seisin,'... available at http://oll.libertyfund.org/Texts/LFBooks/Maitland0161/CollectedPapers/Vol1/HTMLs/0242-01_Pt06_Essays4.html, accessed on 7 May 2007.

establish proof when the accused already bore *fama*. Citing *frustra leges invocat*, the thirteenth-century Italian jurist Gandinus noted that such a man could not claim protection from the very laws of the city which he had broken in the past.[21] As Richard Fraher notes, citizens – provided they possessed the necessary social and political status – had some protection from torture. But *fama* could not be ignored. To preserve peace and the social order, the judge had to use his discretion when trying notorious citizens.[22]

The principal reception appears, however, to be in regard to those either seeking – or having obtained – sanctuary in a church. Sanctuary was one of the most cherished – and violated – ecclesiastical privileges.[23] The maxim often treats, however, those who had either committed a crime on ecclesiastical property or had obtained asylum only to commit a crime.

Various examples come from the later Middle Ages. One particularly interesting example from the fifteenth century appears in the *Diplomatarium Danicum*, where a certain Tymmo had murdered a religious in his monastery's cemetery. Bishop John of Schleswig condemned such a crime that had polluted and profaned sacred ground. Tymmo was denied sanctuary.[24]

The maxim also appears in cases recorded in the English *Year Books*. These fascinating cases demonstrate the variety of ways *frustra leges invocat* could be used in judgment. [25] Some are similar to the violations of

21. Gandinus, *Tractatus de maleficiis* (Laon 1555): 'A quo vel a quibus posit fama incipere ex quo tempore: Ergo ut denotatus et male meritus hic, de quo queritur, non poterit ipsius civitatis…contra cuius mores commisit, pro se aliquod auxilium invocare, quia frustra iuris civitatis implorat auxilium, qui contra illud commisit', cited by Richard Fraher, 'Conviction According to Conscience: The Medieval Jurists' Debate Concerning Judicial Discretion and the Law of Proof', *Law and History Review* 7.1 (1989), 23-88 at 46-47 and n. 195.
22. Fraher, 'Conviction According to Conscience', 47-48.
23. See C 17 q. 4 c. 8. The fate of Becket obviously demonstrated the limitations of canonical protection. In France, royal pressure had also begun to undermine sanctuary during the twelfth century. Canonists were themselves aware that sanctuary could be abused and, by the thirteenth century, had begun to make exceptions, for example in the case of blasphemers and escaped slaves. On these, see Helmholz, *The Spirit of Classical Canon Law*, 68, 282 and, on asylum-seeking, Kathryn L. Reyerson, 'Flight from Persecution: The Search for Religious Asylum in Medieval Montpellier', *French Historical Studies* 17.3 (1992), 603-626.
24. Reg. 4.9 n. 70, 2 April 1403, available at http://dd.dsl.dk/ accessed on 6 March 2007: 'Et quod lamentabilius refer[imus dictu]s Tymmo post tantum scelus [com]missum morte quam dupliciter meruerat preuentus in sacrata terra quam tam uiliter et execratissime polluerat et prophanarat ex[titit] tumulatus. Qui nec. Cum furibus et latronibus famulo illius qu[I uia] uita et ueritas erat uitam furatus meruit sepliri. Frustra enim legis auxilium in[uocat] quid com[mittit in legem…'
25. For example Y.B 9 Edw. IV. F. 28, pl 41, cited by Helmholz, *The Ius commune* 76 and n. 238 referring also to the later commentary on the case by Ferdinand Pulton, *De pace Regis et regni* (London 1609, rp. 1978) Tit. *Sanctuarie and Abjuration*,

clerical orders noted above in the decretals of Innocent and Clement. In 1353, a certain Marmeduke was delivered to the prison of the Abbot of Westminster.[26] He had "broken the abbot's prison"; in defense, he claimed benefit of clergy. Invoking the maxim, Shareshull, the chief judge of the King's Bench, rejected his plea and, as the ordinary also did not defend him, he was hanged.[27]

Other cases of the maxim's use in the *Year Books* relate to breach of sanctuary. In 1321 a woman was accused of having committed murder while under sanctuary in a church.[28] The case had apparently had a complicated history:

> The sheriffs and coroners put the question to the Justices in Eyre, and they put it first to the Bishop, then to the Archbishop and the King's Council. It is answered in the negative; and she is removed and indicted, and at first stands mute. When she later speaks she is not instantly hanged, as a man would have been, but is allowed to plead. She says it happened in self-defense, is told to plead Not Guilty, and is convicted and hanged...In a case of homicide by a woman, reporter notes that 'because she was a woman, the court was willing to take an inquest, and if it had been a man who had spoken thus he would have been hanged without a jury.

An unspecified decretal (likely X 3. 49. 10) is also mentioned, which also suggests that the judges were wondering whether what had specifically been applied to man's breach of sanctuary could also be applied to a woman.[29]

The maxim could also assert the exclusive authority of royal law. Just as the cleric who violated canon law could, through *frustra legis invocat,* lose the *privilegium fori*, so too could a Baron who attempted to resist or coerce a royal judge or bailiff find himself beyond the help of the law. For

no. 5., available in translation by William Hawkins, *A Treatise of the Please of the Crown* (London 1224-26, rp. New York, Arno Press 1972), 336.

26. Y.B. 9 Edw. III F. 30, accessed at http://www.bu.edu/phpbin/lawyearbooks/display.php?=34412 on 27 January 2007. (All subsequent citations of the Yearbooks refer to this site.) Compare also a case from 1313 from the Eyre of Kent concerning presentment of homicide: Y.B. 6 Edw. II. F. 24. Again, the maxim was invoked to deny benefit of clergy.
27. Compare the complicated case recorded in 9 Edw. IV F. 28 where a man accused of homicide first had abjured the realm, only to have this denied. He then pleaded for benefit of clergy, but could not read the assigned verse, though he had apparently made out a few words. At first, there was conflict between the ordinary and royal court over what to do with the defendant; then the ordinary refused to take him. It then came to light that the defendant had originally been in sanctuary. The royal justices ruled that his abjuration had voided his claim to a church court in the first place and also that, being attainted, he also could not claim sanctuary. *FLA* was invoked. He was hanged.
28. Y.B. 14 Edw. II F. 85.
29. Ibid.

this was challenging the king himself. When the Eyre of Kent during the reign of Edward I cited the maxim, the barons, no doubt, had no trouble understanding what the consequences of their defiance might be.[30]

3. Reception in Early Modern England[31]

The *Journal of the House of Commons* for March 1593 records the case of Thomas Fitzherbert of Staffordshire:[32]

> ...being outlawed upon a *capias utlagatum* after judgment,[33] is elected Burgess of this Parliament. Two hours after his Election, before the Indenture returned,[34] The Sheriff arrested him upon this *capias*

30. *Eyre of Kent* (Selden Society) 1.lxxv, cited by James Conway Davies, *The Baronial Opposition to Edward II. Its Character and Policy. A Study in Administrative History* (New York 1918, rp. 1967), 44 and n. 3. Compare also the *Libri feudorum* 2.53.8 (*Institutiones divi caesaris iustiniani*, Venice 1574, 85), and its ordinary gloss, noting the penalties awaiting anyone who formed a conspiracy against the state. As a violator of the law, his property would be confiscated: 'Qui pace iurare et tenere noluerit, beneficio et lege pacis non furatur: Non fruatur cum in eam committat nolendo iurare pacem nec eam tenere frustra enim legis auxilium invocat, qui in eam committit, ut ff. de mi. l. auxilium in fin. Mario Montorzi, Diritto feudale nel basso medioevo. Materiali di lavoro e strumenti critici per l'esegesi della glossa ordinaria ai Libri feudorum, con la ristampa anastatica dei Libri feudorum e della loro glossa ordinaria' (Turin 1991), 271, also *Strumenti per la ricerca scientifica in diritto commune*, accessed at http://www.idr.unipi.it/iura-communia/Strumenti.htm, accessed on 3 January 2007.
31. There was interest in the maxim in Scotland, which comes as no surprise given the reception of civil law there. See Sir Thomas Craig's reference in a lengthy treatment of exceptions to inheritance. Whoever violates natural law, which must include parental affection, cannot expect inheritance. *Equitis....Jus feudale, tribus libris comprehensum* (Edinburgh 1732), 376, available at the *Eighteenth Century Collections Online database*, http://galenet.galegroup.com/servlet/ECC), (hereafter ECC) accessed on 7 October 2005. For comparison, Capel Lofft, *Principia cum juris universalis tum praecipue anglicani*, 2nd ed. (London: Owen and Dilly 1779), 211, available at ECC.
32. 'Journal of the House of Commons: March 1593,' *The Journals of all the Parliaments during the reign of Queen Elizabeth (1682)*, 479-513, accessed at http://www.british-history.ac.uk on 17 January 2007.
33. On the writ, see the entry in The 'Lectric Law Library', at http://www.lectlaw.com/def/c188.htm, accessed on 17 January 2007. As the writ was apparently exercised only against Fitzherbert himself, and not his lands and goods as well, this was the general form which required the sheriff to take the defendant before the king.
34. The indenture was a report by the local government to Crown and Parliament that the election had followed proper form, with candidates and voters suitable and eligible to participate. On indenture, see 'The Men Behind the Masque. Office-

> *utlagatum*. The party is in Execution. Now he sendeth this Supplication to this House to have a Writ from the same to be enlarged to have the Privilege in this Case to be grantable.

There was good reason why Fitzherbert had been outlawed and arrested: he was a notorious Catholic sympathizer. Sergeant Yelverton, one of the committee members in charge of examining the election and return of MPs, argued against Fitzherbert's petition to be allowed to take his seat.

Another, contemporary example of how the maxim had entered wider usage is found in a tract from Francis Bacon dating to 1594.[35] He uses it against Rodrigo Lopez, a Spanish Jew purportedly in the service of Phillip II. Lopez had supposedly attempted to poison Queen Elizabeth.[36] The plot had been exposed by Essex, the Queen's counselor. Newly elected MP for Middlesex, Bacon seized the opportunity to gain fame and patronage from Essex. Echoing earlier usages, the maxim denies sanctuary, construed here as Lopez's claim of diplomatic privilege. Bacon delights in using a phrase from the civil law against the King of Spain.

FLA appears in the literature generated by the political conflicts of early seventeenth century England. In his defense of the Court of Star Chamber, William Hudson employs the maxim to deny the right of one summoned before the Court to sue in another.[37] He also notes that the Court cannot permit an appeal from someone convicted elsewhere of conspiracy, an admission of the Court's highly political nature.

The second example comes from the eve of the war itself, August 1641. It concludes a terse reply from the Lords to a request from the Commons.[38] The Lords declare that Commons has no right to make such a presumptuous request concerning a meeting with the King. The Lords have already seen to the matter; Commons should not 'ask for the law' when it has gone against it. *Frustra legis* speaks the voice of tradition and authority;

Holding in East Anglian Boroughs, 1272-1460', accessed at http://www.trytel.com/~tristan/towns/ mc1_pt5.html , on 17 January 2007.

35. Francis Bacon, 'A Report of Lopez's Treason,' in *The Works of Francis Bacon*, 4 vols. (London: A. Millar 1740), 4.385, accessed from ECC on 7 October 2005. On Bacon's legal knowledge and use of maxims, see Stein, *Regulae iuris*, 170-176.
36. Robert Cecyll and Arthur Dimrock, 'The Conspiracy of Dr. Lopez,' *The English Historical Review* 9.35 (1894), 440-472.
37. William Hutson, 'Treatise of the Court of Star Chamber', in *Collectanea juridica. Consisting of Tracts Relative to the Law and Constitution of England*, 2 vols. (London: E. and R. Brooke 1791-92), 2.133, accessed from ECC on 7 October 2005. See also the discussion in the British National Archives website: http://www.catalogue. nationalarchives.gov.uk/displaycataloguedetails.asp, accessed on 9 October 2005.
38. 'House of Commons Journal Volume 2: 08 August 1641', *Journal of the House of Commons* 2 (1640-1643) (1802), 245-46, available at http://www.british-history.ac.uk/report.asp?compid=7739, accessed on 19 August 2005.

it is a political declaration of the status quo.[39] As we shall soon see, the argument could be used in reverse.

An even more famous usage occurred in the trial of Thomas Wentworth, Earl of Strafford, which had taken place earlier that year. A Bill of Attainder had been brought against the Earl, whom his opponents had accused of fomenting rebellion against Parliament. Countering the Earl's defense that he was being unjustly tried, St. John, the prosecutor, echoed the maxim—along with the Golden Rule of the New Testament: 'He that would not have had others to have a law, why should he have any himself. Why should not that be done to him that himself would have done to others?'[40]

Like books, however, maxims have their fates. They could end up in entirely new contexts.[41] In the case of our maxim, it could be turned against the authority whose power they had originally supported. Like Bacon two centuries earlier, Thomas Spence was a polemicist and political opportunist. But there the similarity ends. I doubt the others listed in this paper would have been comfortable in his presence. Spence was a revolutionary, a defender of the French Revolution. No learned Latin title for his tract: *Pig's Meat; or Lessons for the Swinish Multitude. Collected by the Poor Man's Advocate (An Old Veteran in the Cause of Freedom) In the Course of his Reading for More than Twenty Years*. To Spence, any representative of state power – here represented by the press gangs – could be lawfully resisted. These have no benefit of the law for they have themselves gone against it through their violent oppression of the people. We have come a long way indeed from earlier usages of the maxim, for example in the Eyre of Kent, where *FLA* proclaimed royal law and hinted at the dire consequences awaiting anyone who defied the king and his justices. Now the people judge the authorities and find them wanting. The maxim is turned against the state.

Our final example brings the maxim into the American Civil War. During the rebellion, civil rights that had been guaranteed by the Bill of Rights came under pressure from a federal government intent on prosecuting the war. Freedom of speech and the press were limited; Congress authorized the president – after considerable debate – to suspend

39. Compare the later citation by Sir George Mackenzie's *Observations on the acts of Parliament* (1686) concerning the first parliament of Charles I, accessed at *Early English Books Online*, http://eebo.chadwyck.com on 27 May 2007.

40. *State Trials*, vol. 3.159. See also John Rushworth, *The Tryal of Thomas, Earl of Strafford, Lord Lieutenant of Ireland* (Lincolnes-Inn 1680), 702-03, accessed at *Early English Books Online*, http://eebo.chadwyck.com on 27 May 2007. On the trial, William R. Stacy, 'Matter of Fact, Matter of Law, and the Attainder of the Earl of Strafford', *The American Journal of Legal History* 29.4 (1985), 241-270. On the influence of this case in American law, see below.

41. It is interesting to note that Coke, the most important English jurisprudent of the seventeenth century, did not use the maxim.

habeas corpus.[42] With the suspension of *habeas corpus* for defendants deemed a threat to the United States also came executive orders compelling them to be tried before military tribunals. This unprecedented expansion of presidential power resulted in the so-called Indianapolis treason trials of 1864, which eventually reached the Supreme Court two years later, after the end of the War, as *Ex parte Milligan*.[43] In this charged legal and political atmosphere, the maxim *frustra legis* would stand on the side of the defense.

Charged with treason, several Indiana Democrats, including Lambdin Milligan and William Bowles, were imprisoned without recourse to *habeas corpus*. In September of 1864, they were tried before a military court in Indianapolis. The evidence against the conspirators was, in the main, neither compelling nor sound – having largely been based on hearsay. Only the case against Bowles would have likely stood up in a civil court.[44] But such considerations mattered little to the military judges. Three men, including Milligan and Bowles, were convicted and sentenced to hang.

While the men languished in prison, political and military events changed. The war ended the following spring; Lincoln died a martyr. The president himself had heard appeals from the defendants' lawyers, and was believed, at least by some, to have been persuaded towards mercy. While Andrew Johnson originally took a harder line, the end of the war enabled a writ of *habeas corpus* to be sued. This led to *Ex parte Milligan*, and the defendants' pardon. It was also this moment in the 1865 when Bowles, in collaboration with the attorney Jonathan Gordon, presented their case. In this ringing defense of the rights of citizens to due process, our maxim is invoked—then refuted—in order to challenge a government that ignores the very laws it claims to defend. The relevant passage is worth quoting at some length:[45]

---

42. For detailed discussion, see David P. Currie, 'The Civil War Congress', 73 *University of Chicago Law Review* (2006), 1131-1226, accessed via *Lexis-Nexis* on 11 April 2007.
43. See the comments by Supreme Court Justice Rehnquist, 'Civil Liberty and the Civil War: The Indianapolis Treason Trials', *Indiana Law Journal* 72 (1997), available at http://www.law.indiana.edu/ilj/volumes/v72/no4/rehnquis.html, accessed on 7 May 2007. On *Ex parte Milligan* (71 U.S. 2), see *The Encyclopedia of the U.S. Supreme Court*, ed. Thomas T. Lewis and Richard L. Wilson (Pasadena and Hackensack 2001), 2.611-12. The trials, which were as much about Democratic-Republican rivalry in the state as any intent of treason on the part of Milligan, Bowles, and the other defendants, are discussed in detail by Kenneth Stampp, 'The Milligan Case and the Election of 1864 in Indiana', *The Mississippi Valley Historical Review* 31.1 (1944), 41-58.
44. Rhenquist, 'Civil Liberty and the Civil War'.
45. Jonathan Gordon and William A. Bowles, *An Argument Against the Jurisdiction of the Military Commissions to Try Citizens of the United States*, 5 available at http://books.google.com/books, accessed on 24 March 2007. A slightly later formulation echoing this position is by Francis Lieber, *Manual of Political Ethics*, 2 vols. (London 1875), 1.202-203.

> The State never ceases to protect; even the blackest criminal, the moment before his head falls, is protected. It was a most fallacious argument that, *frustra legis auxilium invocat qui legem committit*, from the *lex talionis*, or as St. John said before the Lords, when he brought in the bill of attainder against the earl of Srafford (sic), (April 29, 1641), "He would not have others have a law, why should he have any himself. Why should not that be done to him, that he himself would have done to others?" Even modern writers have endeavored to derive the punitory power of the State, from the fact that the offender, by doing wrong, declares himself out of the jural society. Nothing can be more untenable in all its bearings. On the contrary, the State being especially a jural society, can not possibly act except by law, and upon jural relations, and as far as the right of an individual is the condition of his union with other rational individuals, punishment is the right of the offender, however paradoxical this may sound at first...State punishment is likewise the protection of the offender, who without it would be exposed to all, even the most extravagant, modes of private redress.

While Bowles won his case, his argument presented in this brief was a decidedly minority opinion. American judges continued to cite *frustra legis auxilium* as their predecessors, from Rome to London, had done for so many centuries: a criminal could not invoke in his own defense a law he had broken.[46] Yet, in their reading of the maxim, Gordon and Bowles not only added a distinct voice to the body of commentary but also a powerful defense of individual rights against the state. To deny a criminal legal recourse was not only to undermine the legal foundations of society, it was the most grotesque hypocrisy. For the state, be it president, judge, or jury member, would become no less criminal than the accused. We have come a long way indeed from Tryphonius.

---

46. *Supreme Court of Nebraska v. Ransom et al (1891)*, in Charles S. Lobinger, *The American Law Register (1852-1891)*, (ALR) 39.4 (First Series. Volume 30; Second Series. Volume 4, April 1891), 265-279, where a father murdered his daughter because, by the provisions of a will, he could inherit property deeded to her. The complicated case is summarized on p. 273: 'The holding that a person cannot take by inheritance the estate of a person whom he murders, for the purpose of removing the life that stands between him and the estate, is sustained by many maxims of the law and considerations of sound policy, and is not in violation of the provisions of the Constitution of the United States, or of this state, against bills of attainder, and that no person shall be deprived of property without due process of law.' See pp. 275ff. for an extended discussion of the case in light of both civil and common law precedents, including citation of *frustra legis*. See also Alexander Dean and his Wife v. Daniel Negley and Sterley Cuthbert, a case heard by the Supreme Court of Pennsylvania in 1862, described in *ALR* vol. 10, no. 5, New Series Vol. 1 (March 1862), 293-289, a case involving a contested will, adultery, and opiates.

4. Conclusion

> On the whole, however, since the seventeenth century, the *regulae* of the Digest have been the victims of extravagant claims made on their behalf and have found little favour with the leaders of juristic thought. Yet the learning about the nature of legal rules, which they stimulated, has passed into the general currency of jurisprudence.[47]

From the specialist's view, Peter Stein could not be more right. The high priests of jurisprudence must be particularly wary of maxims: they are the hardest part of legal science to control. They are prone to fly from court and classroom behind in order to end up in all sorts of places – pulpits, printer's shops, even jail cells in Indiana. Yet it is this volatility that makes them such fascinating and powerful aspects of the law. If the ultimate measure of their success is the duration and scope of reception, then *Frustra legis auxilium* must rank among the most notable maxims passed down from the *Digest*. In exploring that reception, we trace not only the rich and complex legal and constitutional evolution of the Western state but also, and most importantly, the protection of individuals against those magistrates and judges that would deny the help of the law they claim to defend.

47. Stein, *Regulae iuris*, 179.

ANSELM OF CANTERBURY'S VIEW OF GOD'S LAW IN ENGLAND: DEFINITIONS, POLITICAL APPLICATIONS, AND PHILOSOPHICAL IMPLICATIONS

Sally N. Vaughn

1. Introduction

In 1097 Anselm archbishop of Canterbury left England for his first exile, after a five-year power struggle with King William Rufus (1089-1100). In another power struggle with Rufus' brother King Henry I (1100-1135), Anselm entered exile a second time, from 1103 to 1105. During these two exiles, Anselm expressed some of his ideas about the nature of power relationships between king and archbishop, and especially about their foundations in law, in particular expressing a concept of God's Law. In 1097, in his first letter written during his first exile, Anselm explained to Pope Urban II the conditions under which he had left England:

> I saw many evils in that country which I ought not to have tolerated but which I was unable to correct by my episcopal liberty [*episcopale libertate*]. ...[King William Rufus] demanded from me burdensome services which had not been customary to my predecessors [*antecessoribus meis inusitata*]....I saw the law of God [*legem dei*] and the canonical and Apostolic authorities [*canonicas et apostolicas auctoritates*] overrun by arbitrary usages [*voluntariis consuetudinibus*] ...I knew that if I tolerated these

> things to the end I would confirm [*confirmarem*] such evil usages [*tam pravem consuetudinem*] for my successors to the damnation of my soul.[1]

In this passage, Anselm expressed a number of legal concepts. As one of the few letters from the reign of William Rufus preserved in the Canterbury manuscript of Anselm's letters, Lambeth 59, L (excluding its addition La)[2], and as a formal report to Pope Urban of his affairs in England, this epistle would have been very carefully crafted. In it, first Anselm regarded episcopal customs as binding law. Second, he expressed an idea that such episcopal customs, the Law of God, and the canonical and apostolic authorities, represented three separate sets of laws, or kinds of laws. Thus he distinguished between four different types of laws: 1. customs, or customary law, as established by the acts of his predecessors; 2. laws originating from the papal court, or papal decrees, as apostolic authority; 3. the canons, or collections of written law, which he lumped together equally with apostolic authority; and 4, less precisely, the Law of God. Finally, he expressed the concept that if he tolerated any arbitrary usages – that is, not deriving from these four sets of law, his allowance of their continuation would 'confirm such usages' as laws for his successors in perpetuity, simply because the events had occurred. Thus, in Anselm's view, the historical actions of the

---

1. Anselm, *Sancti Anselmi Cantuariensis archiepiscopi opera omni,* ed. F. S. Schmitt (6 vols., Stuttgart-Bad Canstatt, 1963-68). Cited by epistle number. Ep. 206. Fröhlich translates *episcopale libertate* as 'episcopal authority' in his translation. *The Letters of Anselm of Canterbury*, tr. Walter Fröhlich, 3 vols. (Kalamazoo, 1990, 1993, 1994), 2:147. 'Notum est multis...qua violentia et quam invitus et quam contradicens captus sim et detentus ad episcopatum in Anglia,...Videbam enim multa mala in terra illa, quae nec tolerare debebam nec episcopali libertate corrigere poteram. Ipse quoque rex faciebat quaedam quae facienda non videbantur de ecclesiiis,...militibus suis dederat, mihi, sicut eas idem archiepiscopus tenuerat, non reddebat, sed insuper alias secundum libitum suum me nolente dabat. Servitia gravia et antecessoribus meis inusitata, ultra quam ferre possem aut pati deberem, a me exigebat. Legem autem dei et canonicas et apostolicas auctoritates voluntariis consuetudinibus obrui videbam. De his omnibus, cum loquebar, nihil efficiebam, et non tam simplex rectitudo quam voluntariae consuetudines obtendebantur. Sciens igitur quia, si haec ita usque in finem tolerarem, in damnationem animae meae successoribus meis tam pravam consuetudinem confirmarem...'
2. Of the 63 letters surviving during William Rufus' reign in the authoritative modern Schmitt collection, more than half were omitted from L. For a chart of the 'Rufus Collection' and the recipients of Anselm's letters during Rufus' reign,, see S. Vaughn, *St. Anselm and the Handmaidens of God* (Turnhout: 2002), 51-52. For comparison, see the chart of the 'Henry Collection', 54-57. See Appendix I to this paper for a complete list of letters included and letters omitted from the 'Rufus Collection.'

archbishops of Canterbury who were his predecessors constituted law by establishing customs, and his own historical actions would likewise establish such laws for his own successors. Historical deeds as well as words thus constituted law. Such deeds have status equal to canon law and apostolic law. This view is somewhat extraordinary in itself. But what could he have meant by God's Law?

2. Anselm and the law

The answer lies in first elaborating Anselm's interesting assertion that historical deeds constituted law. Mark Philpott argued persuasively that Anselm, far from ignorance of canon law, seemed aware of 'a broader range of canonical opinions' than even his fellow Bec student Ivo of Chartres, for Anselm correctly identified a text which Ivo misattributed; thus Anselm's 'sources and methods were very close to those of "the greatest authority on Canon Law in northern Europe"'.[3] Nowhere did Anselm disparage the authority of the canons in his correspondence. Rather, an infringement of them would cause him to 'call down God's wrath on the malefactor...Similar notions of the importance of canon law and the idea of a consonant "divinarum litterarum corpus" which included the Bible, the Fathers, decretals and canons informed the theology of Lanfranc.'[4] Philpott sees Anselm implying 'an identity of the law with the will of God.' In this, Philpott writes, Anselm 'was not merely following Lanfranc's precedents, but was using the same intellectual tools and resources in a similar context....Anselm was, in the terms of his own day, a perfectly competent canon lawyer.'[5] Thus Philpott's persuasive article establishes Anselm's expertise at canon law, following the example of his teacher Lanfranc.

But in the letter to Urban quoted above, Anselm seems to have asserted the equality of custom, canon law, apostolic law and God's Law. Indeed, Philpott argues correctly that custom and precedent are so prominent in Anselm's letters that there appears to be no room for canon law at all. He accounts for Lanfranc's and Anselm's appeals to the Anglo-Saxon past by identifying their views with the pseudo-Isidorian maxim, *'Ne transgrediaris terminos antiquos, quos posuerunt patres tui. Terminos indubitater transgreditur; qui statuta patrum post ponit atque confundit.'*[6]

3. Mark Philpott, '"In primis...omnis humanae prudentiae inscius et expers putaretur": St. Anelm's Knowledge of Canon Law,' in *Anselm: Aosta, Bec and Canterbury: Papers in Commemoration of the Nine-Hundredth Anniversary of Anselm's Enthronement as Archbishop, 25 September 1093,* D. E. Luscombe and G. R. Evans, eds. (Sheffield: Sheffield Academic Press, 1996), 94-105, at 99.
4. Philpott, '"In primis..."', 103.
5. Philpott, '"In primis..."', 104-105.
6. Philpott, '"In primis..."', 104-105.

Again, Philpott's argument is persuasive within the context of law and its interpretation. This paper will seek to extend the argument further, beyond Anselm's competence at law, to see that competence affecting Anselm's view of God, God's law, history, and the functioning of reality itself.

In the narrower view in which Anselm made his assertion that historical deeds constituted law in his letter to Pope Urban, the specific deeds of successive archbishops of Canterbury would then constitute law for their successors. This would include the founding of the see of Canterbury by St. Augustine of Canterbury, and each of the deeds of his successors up to Anselm's time. Anselm and his teacher and predecessor as archbishop Lanfranc would have had the account of Bede easily at hand to outline these deeds in detail, and indeed Lanfranc used Bede's account of the first archbishops of Canterbury as a legal text in asserting his primacy over the see of York in 1070, as he demanded an oath of obedience from York's archbishop Thomas I at the royal court.[7] 'So we brought in *The Ecclesiastical History of the English People,* a work of Bede...passages were read out which proved....that my predecessors exercised primacy over the church of York and the whole island which men call Britain and over Ireland as well. They extended pastoral care to all; they ordained bishops and held councils where they thought fit...'[8] Later, in 1072 at the Trial at Penendon Heath, Lanfranc began recovering Christ Church Canterbury lands lost to Earl Godwin during Edward's reign from Odo of Bayeux earl of Kent. George Garnett, who sees Lanfranc as a superb canon lawyer, remarks that this conflict between earl and archbishop was 'to a large extent a reprise of that between [Archbishop] Robert of Jumièges and Godwine in 1051-2.'[9] Whether or not Lanfranc had this 1051-52 legal dispute in mind in 1072, the Trial of Penenden Heath clearly replicated it. Anselm later strove with all his might likewise to recover Canterbury lands from other usurpers such as King William Rufus.[10]

In Anselm's letter to Pope Paschal outlining to him on Paschal's accession the reasons for Anselm's first exile, Anselm reiterated these very principles:

> The king demanded ...that I should give my consent to his intentions which were against the law and the will of God [*contra legem et voluntatem dei*]. For [the king] was unwilling that the Pope should be acknowledged or appealed to in England without his command....he has not permitted a council to be held...since he became king thirteen

7. See Lanfranc's account of this trial in his letters: Lanfranc, *The Letters of Lanfranc, Archbishop of Canterbury,* ed. Margaret Gibson and Helen Clover (Oxford: 1979), cited by epistle number. Epp. 3, 4.
8. Lanfranc, Ep. 4.
9. George Garnett, *Conquered England: Kingship, succession, and Tenure 1066-1166* (Oxford: Oxford University Press, 2007), 14.
10. Eadmer, *Historia Novorum in Anglia* (RS, London: 1884), ed. Martin Rule, 26.

> years ago...he gave church lands to his own men...even my own suffragan bishops refused to give me any counsel except that which agreed with the king's will....these and many other things [are] against the will and law of God [*contra voluntatem et legem dei*].[11]

In this letter to Paschal, surely as carefully written a report as had been his earlier letter to Urban, Anselm makes clear that, like his predecessor Gregory I, who had sent St. Augustine to Canterbury and directed his foundation of England's church in successive letters to him and his successors quoted in Bede, and especially in Pope Gregory's letter to King Ethelbert of Kent,[12] the Roman pope's word should be heeded by England's king, the archbishop should hold councils for the reform of the church, and England's bishops owed obedience to its archbishop, not its king. These principles, then, of historical determination of England's laws, are subsumed under the will and law of God. Thus in the limited circumstances surrounding England's kingdom and archbishop, the historical record constituted part of the Law of God.

But Anselm habitually thought more broadly than just about specific circumstances, often enlarging a specific example into a wider principle, or applying a wider principle to a specific example. He had advised his student Guibert of Nogent to interpret texts in the manner of Pope Gregory I, on four levels: literally, allegorically, morally, and anagogically.[13] Just so Anselm thought of his own actions in a multifaceted way. On his election to Canterbury, he wrote to explain to the Bec monks why he must leave his abbacy of Bec to accept the archbishopric of Canterbury.

---

11. Anselm Ep. 210 : 'Videbam in Anglia multa mala, quorum ad me pertinebat correctio, quae nec corrigere nec sine peccato meo tolerare poteram. Exigebat enim a me rex, ut voluntatibus suis, quae contra legem et voluntatem dei erant, sub nomine rectitudinis assensum praeberem. Nam sine sua iussione apostolicum nolebat recipi aut appellari in Anglia, nec ut epistolam ei mitterem aut ab eo missam reciperem vel decretis eius oboedirem. Co ncilium non permisit celebrari in regno suo, ex quo rex factus est, iam per tredecim annos. Terras ecclesiae hominibus suis dabat. In omnibus his et similibus si consilium petebam, omnes de regno eius, etiam suffraganei mei episcopi, negabant se mihi consilium daturos, nisi secundum voluntatem regis. Haec et multa ailia, quae contra voluntatem et legem dei sunt, videns pertii licentiam ab eo sedem adeaundi apostolicam, ut inde consilium de anima mea et de officio mihi iniuncto acciperem.'
12. Bede, *Ecclesiastical History of the English People,* eds Bertram Colgrave and R. A. B. Mynors (Oxford: Oxford Medieval Texts, 1969, reprinted 1979), I:32, 110-115.
13. Guibert of Nogent, *A Monk's Confession: The Memoirs of Guibert of Nogent*, tr. Paul J. Archambault (University Park, Penn., 1996), 60. See also Jay Rubenstein, 'St. Anselm's Influence on Guibert of Nogent', in *Anselm: Aosta, Bec and Canterbury: Papers in Commemoration of the Nine-Hundredth Anniversary of Anselm's Enthronement as Archbishop, 25 September 1093,* ed. D. E. Luscombe and G. R. Evans (Sheffield: Sheffield Academic Press, 1996), 296-309.

> Some say that I was given to you [as abbot] by the will of God, and cannot lawfully or rightly [*recte*] be taken from those over whom I was lawfully or rightly [*recte*] made superior and that they should not give me up. St. Martin was an abbot according to the will of God, yet he was taken from his monks and put over clerics, monks and lay men and women [as bishop of Tours]. I believe that the Apostle Peter held the episcopal chair in Antioch according to the will of God, yet no one said that he sinned when he deserted it and went to Rome to seek a greater harvest [as bishop of Rome]...brothers, I do not compare myself to their greatness, but for this reason I should not be condemned if God does to me the same as he did to them.[14]

So just as Lanfranc and Anselm saw in the circumstances of Canterbury's foundation a kind of template for legal actions that Augustine's successors were bound to emulate, so Anselm saw in the circumstances of his election to Canterbury, forcing him to leave his abbatiate at Bec, a repetition of previous historical circumstances and events in God's selection of bishops St. Martin and St. Peter, an action of God that Anselm's selection as archbishop emulated. Thus Anselm was interpreting God's selection of him as archbishop on both the literal and the allegorical levels. Like St. Martin and St. Peter, Anselm was God's choice for an archbishopric.

I have argued elsewhere that Anselm exerted great effort to bring about his own election as archbishop of Canterbury,[15] and in doing so believed that he was fulfilling God's will. When Canterbury had been vacant for four long years, during which King William Rufus had been exploiting Canterbury revenues and confiscating its lands, Anselm went to England to urge Rufus to choose a new archbishop, preached sermons all over England urging that Canterbury be filled, and sought the help of key magnates and clerics in this endeavor, all in the midst of a great public outcry for his own election. Clearly Anselm felt God wanted him for Canterbury. On his first visit to Canterbury in 1082, he had found a gold

---

14. Anselm, Ep. 156. 'Dicant etiam quidam quia et vobis secundum deum datus eram, et quibus recte praelatus eram, non recte me posse auferri ab illis nec me debere condedere. Beatus Martinus secundum deum abbas erat, et tamen mon achis est ablatus, et clericis et monacis et laicis viris et mulieribus est paelatus. Petrus apostolus puto quia secundum deum Antiochiae cathedram episcopalem tenebat; nec tamen dicit alizuis quia peccavit, cum eam deserendo studio maioris fructus Roman migravit. An ideo dicendum est quia non dililgebant priores discipulos suos, aut quia postea minus eos dilexerunt, aut quia deus contempsit et deservit eos, quia isti eos comporaliter deseruerunt? Utique non est dicendum. Fratres, non me comparo magnitudini eorum; sed tamen non ideo sum damnandus, si de me facit deus aliquid ad similitudinem eorum.'
15. Sally N. Vaughn, *Anselm of Bec and Robert of Meulan: The Innocence of the Dove and the Wisdom of the Serpent,* (Berkeley: 1987), 116-136 for this analysis and that below.

ring which Eadmer interpreted as foretelling such a future for him.[16] Yet on his election, publicly and dramatically he resisted the English bishops who tried to consecrate him, clenching his fists so the episcopal staff could not be forced into them, and finally being dragged into the church.[17] I explained these events by asserting that Anselm saw himself as reenacting a topos of refusing high office, also enacted by such historical figures as St. Cyprian, St. Martin of Tours, St. Augustine of Hippo, St. Ambrose, and Pope Gregory the Great, who hid in a water pot in the forest to avoid his election as pope, only to be seized by the people of Rome and forced into office. Angelo Paredi wrote that 'flight to escape an ecclesiastical dignity is almost traditional' [18] as early as the time of St. Ambrose.

Later, in writing to explain that he was forced to move from Bec to Canterbury by the will and choice of God, Anselm asserted, 'I am compelled to confess that God's decisions increasingly defy my efforts'[19] to avoid promotion to the rich and powerful office of archbishop. He likened himself to Christ's example, pleading that 'this cup pass him by.'[20] Thus on a moral and anagogical level, God's selection of Anselm as archbishop emulated on the highest level Christ's mission as sacrifice for the sins of humankind. Anselm's election as archbishop of Canterbury, and his reluctant acceptance of God's will, emulated countless examples of those who came before him, chosen by God to serve despite or because of their humble protestations of unworthiness and unwillingness. Christ was the ultimate model for such circumstances.

This interpretation of history – and we also might mention of reality, the essence of existence – is quite startling to modern eyes. It is a Platonic vision of history as a cyclical, repeated reenactment of archetypical events, but by definition, then, each repetition would be a flawed version of its archetype. Anselm's student and friend Gilbert Crispin showed this same understanding of history as he described Bec's first abbot Herluin as 'that Hebrew' – a New Moses – leading his people to the Promised Land.[21] Thus Biblical events could, like Christ, serve as archetypes, and we must see the Bible as without doubt a text for God's Law. And the Bible is a history, after all.

---

16. Eadmer, *Vita Anselmi*, tr. Richard W. Southern (Oxford: 1996), 41.
17. Vaughn, *Anselm of Bec,* pp. 116-136, Eadmer, *Historia Novorum in Anglia*, 32-36.
18. Angelo Paredi, *Saint Ambrose: His Life and Times,* tr. Joseph Costelloe (Notre Dame, 1964), 122. Vaughn, *Anselm of Bec,* 117.
19. Anselm, Ep. 156.
20. Anselm, Ep. 148.
21. Gilbert Crispin, *Vita Herluini*, in *Thr Works of Gilbert Crispin,* ed. Anna Sapir Abulafia and G. R. Evans, 188.

Mark Philpott, in his careful analysis of Eadmer's account of the Council of Rockingham,[22] indeed shows Anselm prosecuting a case at law using these very principles. As Anselm's secretary and companion until at least 1100, Eadmer was in a position to follow Anselm's teaching and learn from him. Indeed, Anselm himself called Eadmer a 'monk of Bec.'[23] Philpott's background to the Rockingham trial shows Eadmer carefully and judiciously weaving together conflicting accounts such as Bede and Eddius Stefanus in Eadmer's *Life of Wilfrid*,[24] and in his other *vitae*, to suggest that although Eadmer engaged in some historical interpretation, he had the habits and traits of a good historian, and certainly revered Bede, as Lanfranc and Anselm did. George Garnett believes that Eadmer possessed a sharp and clear critical judgment, seeing clearly the legal issues arising from Lanfranc's and King William's rewriting of history to create the legal fiction that William inherited England from his antecessor King William, and writing with exceptional legal precision.[25]

The crucial episode presented by the Rockingham trial is fundamental to many modern arguments concerning the state in the Anglo-Norman world. 'This is no simple eyewitness description,' Philpott states, 'but an accomplished literary composition. Eadmer presents Anselm as Job, a righteous man struck down by unmerited misfortune, surrounded by false friends and with Scripture as his only support.'[26] And Anselm argues a canonical case, Philpott asserts, citing Christ appointing Peter, the rock on which he would build his church, giving him the power to bind and loose; that whoever hears any of the apostles hears Christ himself, so that all the words spoken to Peter apply to his successors; and finally, render unto Caesar what is Caesars, and to God what is God's.[27] Eadmer states that no one could refute Anselm's arguments because they all rested on the word of God and the authority of St. Peter. His argument was unassailable. Then Eadmer reports a poor knight comparing Anselm to Job, as a popular voice, and the text 'the voice of the people is the voice of God.'[28]

Clearly Eadmer could conceive of Anselm's trials as reenacting Job's trials, a recapitulation of a Biblical, historical template. Michael Staunton points out that Eadmer's description of the trial at Rockingham, where no one dared to speak for Anselm out of fear of the tyrant Rufus, threats,

---

22. Mark Philpott, 'Eadmer, his Archbishops, and the English State,' in *The Medieval State: Essays Presented to James Campbell,* J. R. Maddicott and D. M. Polliser, eds. (London: Hambledon Press, 2000), 93-107.
23. Anselm, Ep. 209.
24. Philpott, 'Eadmer,' 100-103.
25. Garnett, *Conquered England,* 42-105. See 64-65 for the legal precision of Eadmer's wording.
26. Philpott, 'Eadmer,' 103-104.
27. Philpott, 'Eadmer,' 105, Eadmer, *Historia Novorum in Anglia*, 57-58.
28. Eadmer, *Historia Novorum in Anglia*, 61, 62

reproaches and insults thrown at Anselm echoed Christ's condemnation by the high priest. Anselm's silence also echoes Christ's trial.[29] 'Traditionally, one who confessed the faith in circumstances of persecution was regarded as akin to the prophet as a recipient of revelation and a proclaimer of God's word.' The Holy Spirit chose such confessors as vessels through which to speak, and 'in acting as such vessels, they follow in the footsteps of the disciples and martyrs.'[30]

Moreover, the texts Anselm himself cites suggest that as each apostle recapitulates and takes on the mantle of Peter, so each successor to each apostle likewise takes on his mantle, his powers, and his authority. We have a vision here of a cyclical reenactment of history. Eadmer also presented Anselm as reenacting Canterbury's past in just this way. As George Garnett describes it, 'Eadmer records Anselm acting in 1093 in the same way as any new bishop- (with the exception of Rochester) or many abbots-elect after the Conquest, and specifically as Lanfranc himself had done on his elevation to the see of Canterbury in 1070.'[31] He might have added that Eadmer showed both Lanfranc and Anselm as recapitulating the example of St. Dunstan.[32] Likewise, both Anselm's students Osbern and Eadmer portray Lanfranc as directly inspired by his predecessor St. Dunstan in a vision to demolish the arguments of his opponents in a court trial to recover Canterbury lands. This story 'follows a long established tradition in hagiography dating back to the acts of the early Christian martyrs,' and foreshadows the treatment of similar events in the *Lives* of Anselm and Becket.[33]

Anselm's student Guibert of Nogent, in his *Deeds of God through the Franks,* elucidates this vision of history through his account of the First Crusade as a reenactment of scripture, according to Jay Rubenstein:

> The Crusade as an event and the *Dei gesta per Francos* brought together the literal, the tropological, and even the anagogical meanings of Scripture in a way that surpassed all allegory and in a way that Guibert obviously found exhilarating... The Crusaders had not only begun to live out Scripture at a variety of levels—the literal, in their fulfillment of Old Testament prophecies; the moral though their virtue, and the anagogical, in the sense that they prepared the way for Antichrist and the Last Days—but they had also usurped the place of

29. Michael Staunton, 'Trial and Inspiration in the *Lives* of Anselm and Thomas Becket,' in *Anselm: Aosta, Bec and Canterbury: Papers in Commemoration of the Nine-Hundredth Anniversary of Anselm's Enthronement as Archbishop, 25 September 1093,* ed. D. E. Luscombe and G. R. Evans (Sheffield: Sheffield Academic Press, 1996), 310-322, at 314, 319-20.
30. Staunton, 'Trial and Inspiration,' 321.
31. Garnett, *Conquered England,* 49.
32. Eadmer, *Historia Novorum in Anglia,* 3-4, 10-25, and *passim* for Anselm.
33. Staunton, 'Trial and Inspiration,' 313-314.

> Judah....the Franks, his people, are the Chosen People...the Old Testament foretold new events in salvation history...which concerned *moderni* and which Guibert could see himself, in his lifetime. Moreover, the First Crusaders, in Guibert's view, were fulfilling the Divine Plan the Old Testament foretold.[34]

The anagogical level is a spiral – each time the event is repeated, it comes closer to perfection. The Bible – itself a history – is the ultimate historical law, and all subsequent events – or history – are recapitulations of such Biblical archetypes.

This view of History and Reality, extraordinary to our eyes, is also Anselm's view of history and reality. But Anselm goes beyond Guibert in seeing this cyclical, repetitive reenacting of Biblical events as the essence of history. Anselm, it appears, sees these multiple reenactments as the essence of the formation of God's Law. As the events described by Bede in the foundation of the English Church set the laws of the English Church, which Augustine's successors were bound by God's Law to reenact, so the events of the reluctance of episcopal candidates and their forced consecration set the laws whereby bishops should be chosen and consecrated, deriving their ultimate source from the example of Christ himself. Moreover, as Anselm's student Guibert elaborated on this theory, Old Testament events, well known to foretell New Testament events, also foretold subsequent and future historical events, each reenactment a more perfect version of its predecessor. Thus history is headed toward perfection. It is this kind of thinking, which Anselm may have derived from Lanfranc, which may well underlie what George Garnett sees as Lanfranc's and the Conqueror's rewriting of pre-Conquest history and the creation of the legal fiction that King Edward the Confessor was the *antecessor* of King William, and that in reality Harold had never been England's king. Just as William of Poitiers, in an official and legal account of the Conquest, posited William as Edward's heir and successor, Domesday Book rewrote history by applying this concept to all Normans by giving them Anglo-Saxon *antecessores.* Garnett sees this argument as Lanfranc's construction based on his interpretation of canon law.[35] Anselm clearly shared this view of history, and extended it further as God's Law.

Anselm's view of history as God's law may well have been substantially reinforced by the events of his second exile, and the way in which it unfolded. On King William Rufus's death in 1100, his brother Henry galloped to Winchester, seized the treasury, and was crowned king. He immediately wrote to Anselm:

---

34. Jay Rubenstein, *Guibert of Nogent: Portrait of a Medieval Mind,* (New York: Routledge, 2002), 100-101
35. Garnett, *Conquered England*, Chapter One: The Justification of the Conquest, 1-44.

> I, by God's command, although unwilling because of your absence, have been elected and consecrated by the clergy and people of England....I entrust myself and the people of the whole kingdom of England to your counsel and the counsel of those who ought to advise me with you.[36]

King Henry too emulated the archetype of reluctance to accept high office. He was prepared to yield to Anselm on every issue on which Anselm had been at odds with Rufus. Henry and Anselm together held a reform council in 1102 to correct the church. But Anselm, earlier in Rome, had heard with his own ears Pope Urban's ban of clerical homage to laymen, and lay investiture of clerics.[37] When Henry requested Anselm's homage—which Anselm had rendered to Rufus – Anselm refused. Thus, as apostolic decrees were made, they took on the quality of God's Law – they became history. Canterbury's customs were not frozen in stone because of their occurrence in the past, but could be modified by successive historical events – and the reverse as well. One clear example is Anselm's hearing in Pope Urban's presence the ban on homage and investiture, which apostolic ruling became a canon, and overrode England's customs. A reverse situation is Pope Gregory I's apostolic letter proclaiming two archbishoprics in England, London and York, which was overridden by historical events which maintained Canterbury rather than London as the archiepiscopal seat. It is here that Gregory VII's pronouncement that God did not say 'I am custom' but 'I am Truth' may be explained.

We seem to be dealing here with a fluid interaction between the four aspects Anselm envisioned as comprising God's Law: custom, canon law, apostolic law, and God's Law, which may well have been seen as revealed in historical events—which could alter the previous three aspects of law. This situation is not unlike that faced by King Henry II, whom George Garnett describes as writing King Stephen out of England's history in the same way that Lanfranc and the Conqueror had written out King Harold, yet having to recognize the reality of Stephen's land grants to various laymen and churches. Henry II dealt with this often by just granting the land exactly as Stephen had granted it, but as if Stephen had never granted it. The theory behind this practice is reflected in the major historical records of Bec monk Robert of Torigni, and the Chronicles of Battle Abbey and St. Alban's Abbey[38] – both chronicles consisting of original accounts from the time of

36. Anselm, Ep. 212.
37. Anselm, Ep. 214.
38. Garnett, *Conquered England*, Chapter Four: The Problem Solved, 262-352.

their first post-Conquest abbots, who were in fact monks of Bec[39] who may well have shared their teachers Lanfranc's and Anselm's view of history.

3. The second exile

Thus Anselm entered his second exile, a repetition of the first—but not exactly. Upon his close reading of Bede, Anselm would have seen that under Archbishop Augustine's successor Archbishop Lawrence, the first bishop in the kingdom of Essex, Mellitus, became bishop of London. Mellitus converted the king of Essex, but this king's pagan successor expelled Mellitus from Essex.[40] He fled to Archbishop Lawrence and his suffragan Justin bishop of Rochester in Kent, where 'it was decided by common consent that they (Mellitus and his companions) should return to their own country (Kent) and serve God with a free conscience rather than remain fruitlessly (in Essex) among barbarians who had rebelled against the faith.'[41] Indeed, Lawrence himself contemplated exile under a bad king. Here would have been a clear archetype for Anselm's first exile in the Canterbury historical record. Indeed, Eadmer begins *Historia Novorum* with an account of alternating good and bad kings of England, and the consequent suffering of England's archbishops, mirroring Bede's account;[42] and these accounts may well explain Anselm's student Eadmer's vilification of King William Rufus as a homosexual, Jew-loving atheist – a clear barbarian--in his account of Anselm's first exile.[43] Eadmer reported that in William Rufus'reign, Anselm viewed himself as an old sheep yoked to a wild bull, rather than the ideal royal/archiepiscopal archetype of two (necessarily equal) oxen yoked to the plow of the Church, drawing it through the land of England.[44]

Anselm's second exile was quite a different matter. It was marked by a propagandistic dance of royal and papal letters in a power struggle for public approval between king and archbishop very much as equals.[45] Henry and some of the bishops quoted to Anselm Augustine of Hippo's doctrines

39. Three successive Bec monks ruled Battle Abbey: Henry, 1096-1102; Ralph, 1107-1124; and Warner, 1125-1138. Bec monk Richard d'Aubigny ruled St. Albans from 1097-1119.
40. Bede, *ecclesiastical History* II:3, 5, 142-145, 149-155.
41. Bede, *Ecclesiastical History* II:5, 149-155.
42. Eadmer, *Historia Novorum in Anglia,* 3-8.
43. See Eadmer, *Historia Novorum in Anglia,* 48 for homosexuality; 99-102 on Jews; 101-103,106-107 for atheism, building to a crescendo of insanity.
44. Eadmer, *Historia Novorum in Anglia,* 36.
45. For a very full discussion of this duel by letters, which took place in the context of Henry's effort to conquer Normandy from his brother Robert Curthose, see S. Vaughn, *Anselm of Bec and Robert of Meulan,* 243-264 for events leading to Anselm's exile, 274.

forbidding a bishop to leave his sheep under any circumstances.[46] Henry, perhaps not fully understanding Anselm's view of God's Law, also used Anselm's own doctrines against him by accusing him of refusing to be with Henry as Archbishop Lanfranc had been with his father King William I.[47] For, as we have seen, Anselm himself, during his struggles with Rufus, had likened England's king and primate to two oxen yoked together as equals, pulling the plow of the church through England. The king ruled by his *potestas* – power – and the archbishop by his *magisterium* – teaching.[48] This paradigm of England's power structure visualized England's king and primate as equals, and Anselm would have found a historical source for it in Pope Gregory I's letter to king Ethelbert, included in Bede, counselling the king to listen to his archbishop as his first counsellor, for he spoke for God.[49] Anselm's secretary Eadmer portrayed three successive English kings and archbishops as such co-rulers: Dunstan and Edgar (the Peaceable),[50] Lanfranc and William I,[51] and ultimately Anselm and Henry. For in one passage Eadmer portrayed Anselm explicitly as speaking for God.[52]

But History was spiralling towards perfection, and Anselm would have viewed his relationship with Henry, without homage, as more perfect than that of Lanfranc and the Conqueror, for in Anselm's time more of God's Law had been revealed by Pope Urban's decrees against homage that Anselm had heard with his own ears. And indeed Anselm's second exile ended with a great public ceremony of reconciliation between king and archbishop at Bec in 1105,[53] an event from which Henry proceeded to the battle of Tinchebrai to conquer Normandy from his brother Robert Curthose. Anselm rejoiced, Eadmer reported, quoting his letter to Henry,

46. Anselm, Epp. 310, absent from Lambeth 59, Anselm's edition of his own letters, but transcribed in Eadmer's *Historia Novorum in Anglia*, 160-162; 318, 327, 346.
47. Anselm, Ep. 318. For Anselm's reply that he had never promised to be with Henry as Lanfranc had been with William I, see Ep. 319.
48. Eadmer, *Historia Novorum in Anglia,* 36.
49. Bede, *Ecclesiastical History,* I:32, 110-115.
50. Eadmer, *Historia Novorum in Anglia,* 3: 'In the reign of that most glorious king Edgar, while he governed diligently the whole realm of England with righteous laws, Dunstan, prelate of Canterbury, a man of unblemished goodness, ordered the whole of Britain by the administratiohn of Christian law; Under his influence and counsel King Edgar showed himself a devoted servant of God.'
51. Eadmer, *Historia Novorum in Anglia,* 10-12: 'Lanfranc had the ear of King William, not merely as one of his advisers but rather as his principal advisor...he always took great pains both to make the king a faithful servant of God and to renew religion and right living among all classes throughout the kingdom.'
52. Eadmer, *Historia Novorum in Anglia*, 78: '...there arose at the mere whim of the king's malice...a quarrel...without any basis in fact but wilfully fabricated to preclude Anselm from having any opportunity of approaching the king to speak for God – *pro Deo loquendi.*'
53. For a complete reconstruction of this settlement at Bec, see Vaughn, *Anselm of Bec and Robert of Meulan,* 301-307.

that the king attributed his victory not to any action of his own, but solely to God.[54] In 1106, King Henry and Archbishop Anselm jointly presided over a great reforming council, the Council of Westminster of 1106, in which the king filled all the vacant sees of England and some in Normandy too, with the archbishop's advice.[55] Anselm's second exile had ended in a more perfect conclusion.

This vision of England's power structure would seem conclusive were it not for the prominent involvement of Henry's queen Edith-Matilda in the struggles of Anselm's second exile. Anselm wrote as frequently to the queen as he did to the king from 1103-1106,[56] and Edith-Matilda wrote a letter to Pope Paschal herself, arguing Henry's case to him, to which he replied personally to her.[57] This correspondence and Anselm's views on marriage reveal that the queen must also play a powerful role in Anselm's vision of the power structure of England. In a sermon Anselm delivered on his first visit to England, Eadmer reports:

> To married persons he taught how great was the fidelity, love, and companionship with which they should be bound together both in matters pertaining to God and to the things of this world; that the man on his side should love his wife as himself, knowing none other but her, having regard for the welfare of her body as of his own and entertaining no evil suspicions. That the woman likewise should submit to her husband with all loving obedience, that she should diligently encourage him in well-doing, and calm his spirit with her mildness if he were perchance unjustly stirred up against anyone.[58]

Here we have a vision of marriage as almost a reciprocal agreement between equals, much like Anselm's view of the relationship between king and archbishop.

Anselm wrote to a number of actual married couples stressing this loving and equal relationship between husband and wife. To his sister Richeza and her husband Burgundius, he counsels that they talk together

---

54. Eadmer, *Historia Novorum in Anglia,* 182-4; Anselm Ep., 402 for Anselm's letter congratulating Henry, and William of Malmesbury, *Gesta Pontificum, The Deeds of the Bishops of England,* tr. David Preest (Woodbridge, Suffolk: 2002), 76, for Henry's letter reporting his victory to Anselm (not in Lambeth 59).
55. Vaughn, *Anselm of Bec and Robert of Meulan,* 308-310: Eadmer, *Historia Novorum in Anglia,* 184-187; and Malmesbury *Gesta Pontificum* tr. Preest 77-79.
56. Anselm's correspondence contains 30 letters to or from King Henry, 17 to or from Queen Edith Matilda. See S. Vaughn, *St. Anselm and the Handmaidens of God* (Turnhout: 2002), 54, and 220-250 for an analysis of this correspondence with the queen.
57. Anselm, Epp. 323, from Edith-Matilda to Paschal, 352 from Paschal to Edith-Matilda.
58. Eadmer, *Vita Anselmi,* 55-56.

about their joint eternal life.[59] On Burgundius' departure for Crusade, he is to 'see that you have no sin in respect of your wife, whose goodness you know better than I; she shall so remain behind that she may not be without support and counsel, whatever God may do with you, nor be driven from your house and estate against her will as long as she lives.'[60] Husband and wife are equals caring for each other. To Clemence countess of Flanders, he wrote that he knew her husband did not invest abbots in Flanders. 'As this was not done without his prudent clemency, so ... it was not done without your clement prudence. The more I rejoice about your good deed, the more truly do I love you both in God...It is your duty... to mention this and other similar things frequently to your husband and advise him to prove that he is not lord of the Church but her advocate....Admonish him never to oppose God's law...I beg Countess Clemence to admonish and counsel her husband so that Divine Clemency may raise both him and her to the kingdom of heaven.'[61]

Anselm wrote similarly to Queen Edith-Matilda, to counsel her husband to follow the counsel of God and not men, 'privately and publicly, and repeat them often, and ...undertake them (yourself) with zeal.'[62] King and queen share a partnership of rule. The queen's duty is to correct the king's 'barbarous' tendencies, to keep him on the right path and reinforce his commitment to God's plan. As an ideal wife writ large, she was to tame her husband's wildness, leading him by her prudent counsel toward Christian behaviour and good conduct, in a partnership of responsible rule.[63] Edith-Matilda is to soften King Henry's heart toward Anselm, which is both fitting to her, useful to the king, and pleasing to God.[64] Moreover, she is to rule the churches of England herself in Anselm's absence, taking them under her wings like an angelic mother hen.[65] Anselm had used this metaphor for himself as abbot of Bec, who, like a mother hen, cared for his chicks, his monks.[66] These images of rulers as mother hens refer to the archetype of Christ's lament for Jerusalem: 'O Jerusalem, Jerusalem, which killest the prophets, and stonest them that are sent unto thee; how often would I have gathered thy children together, as a hen doth gather her brood under her wings, and ye would not!'[67] Christ characterized himself as a mother hen over the children of Jerusalem; likewise, Anselm saw himself as

59. Anselm, Ep. 258.
60. Anselm, Ep. 264.
61. Anselm, Ep. 249.
62. Anselm, Ep .296.
63. See S. Vaughn, *St. Anselm and the Handmaidens of God,* 222 and note 80.
64. Anselm, Ep. 246.
65. Anselm, Ep. 288. For a fuller discussion of Anselm's view of Edith-Matilda as co-ruler of England, see Vaughn, *St Anselm and the Handmaidens of God* 225-236.
66. Anselm, Ep. 205.
67. Luke 13:34, Matthew 23:37

a mother hen over the monks of Bec; and likewise, he saw Queen Edith Matilda as a mother hen over the churches of England. As he said to her later, 'I beg you to cause the churches of God, which are in your power, to know you as a mother, a nurse, a kind mistress and queen—*vos cognoscant ut matrem, ut nutricem, ut benignam dominam et reginam.*'[68] Like Archbishop Anselm, the queen ruled England's churches. Interestingly, as we saw above, Anselm visualized king and queen as equal partners in rule, and king and archbishop also as equal partners in rule. The power relationship Anselm articulated during his archiepiscopacy, with its power struggles between king and archbishop, thus makes king, queen and archbishop three equal partners, a kind of trinity, in the rule of England.[69] Thus Anselm saw God's Law, made manifest through History, unfolding.

4. Conclusion

As archbishop of Canterbury from 1093-1109, St. Anselm engaged in a major power struggle with two successive English kings: William Rufus, 1093-1100, and Henry I, 1100 to Anselm's death in 1109. In the course of these Church-State struggles, Anselm expressed in his concurrent letters numerous comments on God's law, the nature of law as custom, the application of such customary law, and the actual, philosophical and theoretical consequences of such applications. He saw God's Law as consisting of four interactive parts: custom, canon law, apostolic law, and historical deeds. As always, he was operating on four levels at once: literal, allegorical, moral and anagogical. When gathered up and taken together these scattered comments in Anselm's correspondence, combined with Eadmer's accounts and those of some of Anselm's other students, constitute a coherent theory of God's law not only as 'custom', but also as history, and the historical record as a kind of legal document constituting customary law, canon law and apostolic authority interacting together in repetitions of archetypal historical events in an upward spiral toward perfection. As applied specifically to England, this theory allocates to the archbishop of Canterbury equal ruling power with the king and queen. It is no accident that Becket's archiepiscopal career mirrors Anselm, in its disputes, issues and exiles; that Becket sought Anselm's canonization; and that his good friend and colleague John of Salisbury wrote Anselm's *vita.* Indeed, the Council of Northhampton mirrors the Trial of Rockingham in a number of ways, as Michael Staunton has shown. He concludes that Anselm's and

68. Anselm Ep. 346.
69. S. Vaughn, *St. Anselm and the Handmaidens of God,* 222-241, 247-250, on Anselm's full correspondence with Edith-Matilda; 259-262 on ideal aristocratic marriages; and 258-265 for Anselm's concept of troika or trinity.

Thomas's disputes 'are seen to operate both on a contemporary worldly level and on an eternal heavenly level..."a spectacle for men and for angels"' in the words of Herbert of Bosham. 'It is impossible to remove the events of these archiepiscopates from the context of an ongoing defence of Christ and the church'.[70] Such was Anselm's extraordinary view of God's Law as history carried on and writ large in the time of his own successor and fervent emulator, Thomas Becket.

70. Staunton, "Trial and Inspiration," 321.

APPENDIX

1. Anselm's Letters in L (Lambeth 59) during the reign of William Rufus:

149 to Osbern of Canterbury
153 to Robert duke of Normandy
154 to William bona anima archbishop of Rouen
156 to Prior Baudry and the Bec monks
157 to Prior Baudry and the Bec monks
158 to Roger abbot of St. Evroul
160 to Fulk bishop of Beauvais
161 to Gosfrid bishop of Paris
162 to Waleran cantor of Paris
167 to Ida countess of Boulogne
170 to Wulfstan bishop of Worcester
171 to Wulfstan bishop of Worcester
180 to Robert prince of Flanders
182 to Henry prior of Canterbury
185 to Matilda abbess of Wilton
186 to Lanfrid abbot of St. Ulmar
187 to Gervinus bishop of Amiens (?)
188 to Richard monk of Bec
189 to William monk of Chester
191 to Walter cardinal legate
192 to Walter cardinal legate
194 to Walter cardinal legate
196 to Richard monk of Bec
197 to Lambert, abbot
198 to the Bishops of Ireland
199 to Monks of Bec collectively
201 to the Clerics and People of Waterford
203 to the prior and monks of St. Albans
206 to Pope Urban II
210 to Pope Paschal II
211 to Anselm's sister Richeza and her husband Burgundius

2. Letters omitted from L (Lambeth 59) during reign of William Rufus:

148 to the monks of Bec collectively
150 to Gundulf bishop of Rochester and the monks of Bec
151 to the monks of Bec collectively
152 to Osbern bishop of Canterbury
155 to the monks of Bec collectively
159 to Gilbert bishop of Evreux
163 to Eudo dapifer of the king
164 to Prior Baudry and the monks of Bec
165 to the monks of Bec collectively
166 to Abbot William and the monks of Bec
168 to Gunhilda of Wilton
169 to Gunhilda of Wilton
172 to Osbern bishop of Exeter
173 to Abbot William and the monks of Bec
174 to Boso monk of Bec
175 to Ralph abbot of Sees
176 to Hugh bishop of Lyons
177 to Osmund bishop of Salisbury
178 to Abbot William and the monks of Bec
179 to Prior Baudry and the monks of Bec
181 to Ivo bishop of Chartres
183 to Abbess Eulalia and the nuns of St. Edwards Shaftesbury
184 to 'M' (daughter of Richard of Clare?)
190 to Osmund bishop of Salisbury
193 to Pope Urban II
195 to Osmund bishop of Salisbury
200 to Maurice bishop of London
202 to Walchelin bishop of Worcester
204 to the prior and monks of St. Albans
205 to Abbot William and the monks of Bec
207 to Malchus bishop of Waterford
208 to Hugh archdeacon of Canterbury
209 to Boso and the monks of Bec

Reflections on the Insertion of Bureaucratic Structures in Medieval Clientelic Societies

Michael H. Gelting

1. Introduction

It is told that one day, during a hunt, Count Geoffrey the Fair (or Plantagenêt) of Anjou got separated from his companions and lost his way in the forest. He was saved by coming upon a charcoal-burner who guided him back to his castle of Loches. The sooty fellow was evidently ignorant of his companion's identity, so Geoffrey the Fair profited from the occasion to ask his rescuer what people were saying about the count of Anjou. The beginning of the charcoal-burner's answer dutifully painted the picture of the ideal prince: 'As far as he himself is concerned, or that which is carried out in his presence, we neither say nor think anything bad: for he is a friend of justice, a guardian of the peace, fighting off enemies, and, what is particularly splendid in a prince, he is the kind helper of the oppressed.' However, the pleasure which this description may be assumed to have given Geoffrey was quickly dispelled as his guide went on: 'But woe to us, Mylord, who without his knowledge suffer from numerous enemies who are the more oppressive as they are concealed!' – and he gave the count an appalling picture of the county being plundered and abused by brutal and greedy officials. As he said, 'It is a wonder, Mylord, in what way they manage to conceal from our lord the count what is carried out in the presence of all, unless it is so that the masters are the last to know the evils of their own houses.' When they reached Loches, the count rewarded the charcoal-burner richly and then called upon all of his subjects to submit their complaints against his officials. Having thus humiliated his officials into confessing their crimes, he forced them to make restitution to all of his subjects who had been despoiled by them, and to hand over for pious purposes all of their illicit gains. Thereupon the count laid down the rule that henceforth all officials would have to clear all of their expenses before leaving office, and if the office's revenues were insufficient for this, they were to cover the deficit from their own purse, even if that meant taking usurious loans.[1]

2. Bureaucracy and society

In this way Jean de Marmoutier, writing c.1170, described the origins of accountability in the county of Anjou in the second quarter of the twelfth century. However, the structures of society made the repression of administrative abuse a far more complex and difficult matter than Jean de Marmoutier implied.

This essay is intended to deal with these complexities and difficulties in the age when centralized mechanisms of accountability and of control of local agents were introduced and developed in almost every part of Latin Christendom. This means, roughly, the time from the second half, or even the last quarter, of the twelfth century onwards. The end of the Middle Ages (whenever that is supposed to be) did not mark any break in continuity in this respect; fundamental changes did not occur until the eighteenth century. In this essay, however, I will limit myself to the conventional medieval period.

Leaving out the centuries before c.1175 also means leaving out the debate about the appropriateness of the term 'feudal' for characterizing medieval societies. The main point of the Anglo-American critics of the 'tyranny' of the 'construct' of 'feudalism' is that historians have been unduly interpreting the scattered evidence of 'feudal' terminology in earlier centuries in the light of the written feudal law and customs that were elaborated during the later Middle Ages and beyond, beginning with the first compilation of the *Libri Feudorum* in Lombardy in the mid-twelfth century.[2] That point is well taken; but it also means that feudal law developed alongside the administrative mechanisms that are the subject of this essay. In the Francophone area (which tends to be the focus of discussions on 'feudalism'), the spread of feudal tenure was explosive from the last quarter of the twelfth century onwards. It was possibly a little faster than the spread of accountability, but both phenomena should be seen as

1. *Chroniques des comtes d'Anjou et des seigneurs d'Amboise*, ed. Louis Halphen & René Poupardin (Paris: Picard, 1913), 183-191.
2. E. A. R. Brown, 'The Tyranny of a Construct: Feudalism and Historians of Medieval Europe', *American Historical Review*, 79 (1974), 1063-1088; Susan Reynolds, *Fiefs and Vassals: The Medieval Evidence Reinterpreted* (Oxford: Oxford University Press, 1994).

part and parcel of the same development: the growth of administrative monarchy.

Having set aside these debates on 'feudalism', it should be pointed out emphatically that they do not in any way affect the concept of feudalism as a term for a type of social formation. In choosing the term 'feudalism' for this type of social formation, Karl Marx was undoubtedly harking back to the revolutionary rhetoric of 1789, and the appropriateness of the *term* may certainly be questioned; but such quibbles do not detract from the relevance of his observation that in this type of social formation, primary producers controlled the means of production, while the extraction of surplus was carried out through extra-economic means. In their most basic form, such extra-economic means might take the shape of brute force: looting and plundering. However, no stable and viable system of exploitation could be established by such means. Instead, the threat of brute force was used to legitimize extensive payments for protection; it was the internalization of this legitimation that the charcoal-burner expressed at the beginning of the speech which Jean de Marmoutier placed in his mouth. It is irrelevant whether the conversation between the charcoal-burner and the count ever happened. There is no doubt that this internalization of the legitimation of 'feudal' society actually took place.

Nevertheless, the charcoal-burner's tale points to an essential problem: the notion of the lord as protector of his subjects did not admit any role for intermediary agents. Yet it was at the level of such intermediary agents that power was exercised in practice. It is to the exercise of power at their level that we will now turn.

If we are to look for a common denominator for those features of medieval European societies that are most relevant to the subject of this essay, the term 'clientelic societies' might seem to be appropriate. The neologism 'clientelic' has been chosen in order to make clear that it is not my intention to confuse the issue by introducing another –ism alongside 'feudalism'. Clientelic relationships were highly important, but they are insufficient by themselves to characterize the structure of any society;[3] they have to be understood in their connection to other mechanisms of power and solidarity, such as kinship, communities and, in the case of medieval Europe, public power. Hence the study of clientelism, which had its heyday among sociologists and anthropologists from the 1960s to the 1980s,[4] appears more recently to have been subsumed under broader approaches, whether these are called 'network analysis' in the Anglo-American

3. See Christopher Clapham, 'Clientelism and the State', in *Private Patronage and Public Power: Political Clientelism in the Modern State*, ed. Christopher Clapham (New York: St. Martin's Press, 1982), 1-35, at 32-33.
4. A good synthesis of this research is S. N. Eisenstadt & L. Roniger, *Patrons, clients and friends: Interpersonal relations and the structure of trust in society* (Cambridge etc.: Cambridge University Press, 1984).

tradition[5] or 'studies of sociability' in the Continental European tradition.[6] Nevertheless, within the limited scope of the present essay it may be permissible to single out clientelic relationships for particular study.

Clientelic relationships involve, by definition, a patron and a client. Usually the patron is superior in power and status to the client. Such relationships are characterized by asymmetrical exchanges of gifts, favours, and services. Such exchanges are dependent upon the dissimilarity of the two parties: each has something to offer which the other party wants – e.g. protection on the part of the patron as against labour services on the part of the client. The relationship is open-ended: it is not terminated by one exchange; rather, the initial exchange involves an understanding of an indefinite obligation to continue the reciprocation. Hence, clientelic relationships are dependent upon being constantly reaffirmed and renegotiated by new exchanges between patron and client. A clientelic relationship that is not maintained by such regular exchanges will tend to lapse. Thus, while the clientelic structuring of a given society as a whole may be fairly stable, individual positions within the clientelic structures tend to be fragile and subject to sudden change. From such a perspective, feudal institutions strictly speaking – the fief and homage – might be interpreted as an attempt to stabilize clientelic relationships by institutionalizing them (thereby, however, fundamentally altering the nature of the relationship).

Another important aspect of clientelic relationships is their predominantly dyadic character: they link one client to one patron (although the patron may have numerous clients, and a client may have different patrons for different purposes). A special relation between patron and client is created, frequently implying a moral obligation of solidarity going beyond the actual exchanges of goods and services. Since clients tend to use their patrons, if possible, for getting advantages over their own peers in situations of competition for scarce resources, the dyadic nature of the clientelic relationship tends to inhibit the organization of larger interest groups along class lines.

In complex societies – and later medieval societies were fairly complex – few patrons are able to appear solely in the role of patrons. They may have access to some resources which they can distribute freely, as patrons; but for procuring other, and perhaps more important, advantages for their clients they may have to address themselves, as clients, to more powerful or more distant patrons. In this role, such intermediary patrons are

5. E.g. Paul D. McLean, *The Art of the Network: Strategic Interaction and Patronage in Renaissance Florence* (Durham/London: Duke University Press, 2007).

6. E.g. Simon Teuscher, *Bekannte – Klienten – Verwandte: Soziabilität und Politik in der Stadt Bern um 1500*, Norm und Struktur: Studien zum sozialen Wandel in Mittelalter und früher Neuzeit, 9 (Cologne/Weimar/Vienna: Böhlau, 1998).

termed brokers.[7] For obvious reasons, the concept of brokerage is of particular interest when reflecting upon the role in a clientelic society of officials who were accountable to a higher authority.

The insertion of accountable officials in a clientelic society did not immediately change the rules of the game. Such appointments should still be interpreted within the framework of clientelism, in a twofold way:

First, the official was the natural patron of the people subject to his authority towards third parties. In those respects where he was able to exert arbitrary power over 'his' subjects the relationship would tend to be mediated through inferior power brokers with clientelic networks of their own. On the other hand, in order to consolidate his authority, the official would have to develop useful 'friendships' (a crucial concept in clientelic societies) with autonomous patrons within his field of authority. And he might have to cope with lords who wielded such power locally, and perhaps also such influence at court, that the official would have to act with great circumspection in cases involving the interests of those lords. Sometimes these realities of the exercise of power shine through in legal texts such as the Danish law book called Eric's Law for Sjaelland (c. 1247?):[8] according to one article of that law, the king's local official was not allowed to exact a personal gift from the taxpayers when collecting the king's taxes; but if a taxpayer had not voluntarily given the official a present, the latter would not be obliged to help that taxpayer if he were to get into trouble at court.[9]

7. For an important discussion of the role of the broker, see Robert Paine, 'A Theory of Patronage and Brokerage', in *Patrons and Brokers in the East Arctic*, ed. Robert Paine, Memorial University of Newfoundland, Institute of Social and Economic Research, Newfoundland Social and Economic Papers, 2 (1971), 8-21, esp. 19-21.

8. For the date of this law, see Helle Vogt, *Slægtens funktion i nordisk højmiddelalderret – kanonisk retsideologi og fredskabende lovgivning* (Copenhagen: Jurist- og Økonomforbundets Forlag, 2005), 96-97.

9. Bk. 3, art. 63: 'Æn bethæs nokær bryti sic giæf stuth til handæ. tha hauær han thes [ey] æfnæ at thrænge han til giæf stuthin. um han hauær lagh stuthin før ræt. for thy at thær gar ængin socn æftær. Giuær bondæn konungs bryti æcki. tha tharf han swa mykli minnæ hanum wetæ um hanum fallær a hændær.' ('But if any reeve should ask for a gift-subsidy to his own hand, he has no power to force him [i.e. the householder, cf. the following] to (pay) gift-subsidy, if he has paid his lawful subsidy, because there is no suit for this. If the householder does not give anything to the king's reeve, then he [i.e. the reeve] is so much less obliged to assist him if 'his hands are felled' [i.e. if the householder fails to prove his case by oath with co-jurors]').*Danmarks gamle landskabslove med kirkelovene [DGL]*, ed. Johs. Brøndum-Nielsen & Poul Johs. Jørgensen, vol. 5, *Eriks sjællandske lov: Text 1-2*, ed. Peter Skautrup (Copenhagen: Gyldendal, 1936), 357 Cf. the Danish translation in *Danmarks gamle Love paa Nutidsdansk [DGLN]*, trans. Erik Kroman & Stig Iuul, vol. 2, *Eriks sjællandske Lov – Jyske Lov – Skaanske og Sjællandske Kirkelov* (Copenhagen: Gad, 1945), 128. The wording of this passage does not allow the hypothesis suggested by Kroman and Iuul in *DGLN*, vol. 3, *Retshistorisk Indledning – Kommentar – Sagregister* (Copenhagen: Gad, 1948), 131, (following

Another article in the same law foresaw the situation when a man had obtained a sentence against another who was the tenant of a man so powerful that the king's official did not want to take action against him; in that case the winner of the lawsuit was entitled to deprive his adversary of his peace, and ultimately to take physical revenge.[10] In practice there was hardly much likelihood of such private sanctions being applied against a man with a lord so powerful that the king's officer did not dare to take action against him; what is interesting is rather the law's explicit admission of the limits to the power of a royal officer in a setting where the king was far away, and the local magnate was very present.

Second, appointment to office was itself part of a clientelic system at a higher level. For the lord, appointing one of his men to an office was not just a matter of entrusting a servant with the duty to exercise his office to the best of his lord's interests. It was at the same time bestowing an important favour upon the lord's man, enabling him to expand his own clientelic network and to enrich himself. As long as this did not happen to the detriment of his lord, the official remained within the terms of the agreement. Even his extortionate behaviour would be acceptable as long as the lord partook of its profits. In a charter of Count Thomas of Savoy, in 1189, the count granted some land, abandoning to the grantee 'all the rights and injustices, and all the practices of exaction and oppression that my father had there hitherto, or which might henceforth be thought out by my officials.'[11]

Poul Johs. Jørgensen, *Dansk Retshistorie: Retskildernes og Forfatningsrettens Historie indtil sidste Halvdel af det 17. Aarhundrede*, 2nd ed. (Copenhagen: Gad, 1947), 286) that the 'gift-subsidy' might be intended for the king; cf. Johannes C. H. R. Steenstrup, *Studier over Kong Valdemars Jordebog: Efter trykte og utrykte Kilder* (Copenhagen: Rudolph Klein, 1874), 167.

10. Bk. 2, art. 52: 'Æn cumær thet swa at then ær hans fæ ær af dømd. at anti han hauær ey fæ til. ællær tho at han | bór undær thæn man ær umbutsman | wil ey gøræ gen. ællær umbutzman | gør swa illæ at han takær wæghsæl foræ…' ('But if its happens so that the man who has been sentenced to lose his chattels, either does not have any chattels, or he is living under such a man against whom the [king's] officer does not want to act, or the officer acts so badly that he takes bribes...'). *DGL*, vol. 5, p. 173 Cf. *DGLN*, vol. 2, 58-59. The word *wæghsæl* appears to be a *hapax legomenon* (G. F. V. Lund, *Det ældste danske skriftsprogs ordforråd: Ordbog til de gamle danske landskabslove, de sønderjyske stadsretter samt øvrige samtidige sprogmindesmærker (fra omtr. 1200 til 1300)*, (Copenhagen: 1877 [repr. Copenhagen, Københavns universitets fond til tilvejebringelse af læremidler, 1967], 168), but the meaning seems obvious.

11. 'Et ut prefatum munus jam dictis canonicis libere liceat obtinere. omni jure et injuria. et omni usu exactionis vel oppressionis. que ibidem pater meus hactenus habuit. vel deinceps ab officialibus meis excogitari posset. me et posteritatem meam penitus exuo'. *Chartes du diocèse de Maurienne: Documents recueillis* par Mgr Alexis Billiet, Archevêque de Chambéry et M. l'abbé Albrieux, Chanoine à

The clientelic nature of the exercise of power explains why, on the part of the people subject to the authority of the officials, a premium was placed on limiting the duration of tenure of the offices to the shortest time-span that was practically possible. This would prevent the officials from getting too involved with local factions and clientelic networks, favouring some against others. The most well-known instance of this policy is the judicial offices of the Italian city-republics, where the chief officers of justice were usually limited to a tenure of six months. But the principle was applied in other settings too. In the Savoyard castellany of Maurienne, the privileges conceded to the inhabitants in the second half of the fourteenth century limited the tenure of the castellan's subalterns, the *métraux*, first to three years, later to one year, barring the official from taking up the same office for the next ten years. While the office of castellan itself was too important politically for the similar concessions concerning that office ever to be observed, it was actually respected in the case of the subaltern offices.[12]

Clientelism being the inevitable condition of the exercise of power, the boundaries between extortion, embezzlement, abuse of power, and legitimate patronage were blurred. Hence the punishment of officials for irregular behaviour occurred in a highly arbitrary fashion, probably connected more often to shifts of influence and favour at the prince's court than to the intrinsic seriousness of the offences; or punishment might arrive after the official's death, when his widow and children might be easy prey for the fiscality of the prince.

Yet all of this did not mean that there was no criticism of administrative practices that we would nowadays characterize as corrupt. The literate men who devised the practices of accountable bureaucracy had their education from schools that taught the Ciceronian ideals of virtuous, disinterested service of the public good. The centuries that witnessed the growth of accountable bureaucracy also witnessed a rich flowering of literary genres castigating corruption at all levels of society and extolling the ideal figure of the practically non-existent honest official.[13]

Saint-Jean de Maurienne, Académie Impériale de Savoie, Documents, 2, no. 22 (Chambéry: Puthod, 1861) 39.

12. Michael H. Gelting, 'Les mutations du pouvoir comtal en Maurienne (XIVe-XVe siècle)', in *Amédée VIII – Félix V: Premier duc de Savoie et pape (1383-1451). Colloque international, Ripaille-Lausanne, 23-26 octobre 1990*, ed. Bernard Andenmatten, Agostino Paravicini Bagliani & Nadia Pollini, Bibliothèque historique vaudoise, 103 (Lausanne: 1992) ,215-228, at 224-227; cf. the list of *métraux* of Modane in Maurienne from 1315 to 1407 in Christiane Girard & Marc Bernard, *Modane: Des origines à 1860*, La Ravoire (2002), 276-277.

13. John A. Yunck, *The Lineage of Lady Meed: The Development of Mediaeval Venality Satire*, Publications in Mediaeval Studies, 17, (Notre Dame: University of Notre Dame Press, 1963).

The principal reason why this widespread criticism did not have much effect in practice was that in clientelic societies the exercise of power remained an intensely personal matter. When St Louis in 1247 called upon all of his subjects to submit complaints against the royal administration in France, there were several instances of people complaining that they had not won their lawsuit even though they had given presents to the royal official:[14] what offended them was not the venality of the official, but his failure to keep his part of the deal. The tacit rules of the relationship between patron and client had been flouted. Conversely, the state did not have the power to prosecute officials for abuses against individual subjects; that right pertained to the victim alone. In 1321 the *maire* of Crouy near Soissons had been imprisoned by his superior the *bailli* on suspicion of having killed one woman, raped two others, and robbed their houses. The case must have been rather flagrant for the *bailli* to take such a step, but in the end he had to let the man go because nobody lodged a complaint against him.[15] Because of this, official inquests into the practices of the prince's officials were limited to those aspects that concerned their loyal service to their master: cases of embezzlement and corruption that involved a diminution of the prince's revenues. And at this level too, the mechanisms of clientelism came into play. Even if the misdemeanours of an official were so serious that he was removed from office, which happened not infrequently, he would have a fair chance of being pardoned and given office anew if he had otherwise shown himself to be a loyal servant of the prince.

The personal nature of the exercise of power was neatly expressed by the monks of Déols in 1354, when the royal *bailli* of Bourges came to arrest a murderer who had sought sanctuary within the abbey's liberty: 'We do not know who you are,' the monks told the *bailli*, 'you are nothing but an English knave; we will not obey you in any way, we will not give a turd for you or your commandment.' Even if the king were present in person they would not hand over the murderer; they did not hold their immunity from the king, nor would they allow the king to take it away. Of course this affront was punished, but the monks' words were characteristic of a widespread attitude.[16]

14. Romain Telliez, *Les officiers devant la justice dans le royaume de France au XIVe siècle* (Lille: Atelier National de Reproduction des Thèses, 2002), vol. 1, 149.
15. Telliez, *Les officers devant la justice*, vol. 1, 623.
16. Telliez, *Les officiers devant la justice*, vol. 1, 678-679.

3. Conclusion

Hence there was a permanent chasm between ideals and realities of the exercise of bureaucratic power. Since favouritism, clientelism, and corruption were entrenched in the structures of power, the only way to bridge this chasm was to dissociate the prince from the actions of his officials. The story of the count of Anjou and the charcoal-burner with which I began my paper was retold in countless variants all over Europe. Apocryphal though it was, it contained a grain of truth: in an administrative system where it was impossible to control the actions of the individual officials, and where corruption and clientelism were unavoidable facts of life, frequently the only means of redress was to get the prince's ear. In the later Middle Ages this was to some extent institutionalised; in many places, most notably in England, the prince's archives were no longer seen solely as a treasury of muniments for the defence of his own interests, but also to some extent as a public resource to which the subjects might appeal in order to find confirmation of their rights over and against overbearing and extortionate officials.[17]

The chasm between ideals and realities of bureaucratic power, and the ensuing fiction of the dissociation between the just prince and his corrupt officials, were not phenomena that were limited to the Middle Ages. They remained an essential part of the structures of power in Europe as long as the *Ancien Régime* lasted. In a way, they epitomized the *Ancien Régime*, and the *Ancien Régime* fell when the crucial ideological fiction of the dissociation between the just prince and his evil servants could no longer be upheld. And when, due to complex changes in society and mentality, the impersonal exercise of public power became a viable proposition. But until then, the practices associated with clientelism should not be seen as a dysfunction[18] or a perversion of bureaucratic structures. They were an integral part of the workings of such structures.

17. V. H. Galbraith, *Studies in the Public Records* (London etc.: Thomas Nelson and Sons, 1948), 84-85; Michael H. Gelting, 'Les hommes, le pouvoir et les archives: autour des reconnaissances du Mas Diderens à Hermillon (1356-1529)', *Etudes Savoisiennes*, 3 (1994), 5-45, at 24-25.
18. Cf. the discussion of the 'dysfunctional' aspects of the patron-client relationship in Howard F. Stein, 'A Note on Patron-Client Theory', *Ethos*, 12 (1984), 30-36. Stein's criticism of the functionalist approach to the study of such relationships is apposite, but his own argument undercuts his characterization of the patron-client relationship as being dysfunctional. It could only be seen as dysfunctional if social exchange were intended to produce social harmony. As a mechanism for establishing and consolidating power, the patron-client relationship is highly functional.

Contributors

GERD ALTHOFF is professor in medieval history at the Westfälische Wilhelms-Universität Münster. His main research topics are the culture of writing, symbolic communication and conflict handling in medieval society.

PER ANDERSEN is associate professor at the Department of Law, University of Aarhus. His main research topics are legal change in Denmark and Europe in the twelfth and thirteenth century, especially concerning legal procedure, and the interaction between learned law and local lawmaking.

DOMINIQUE BAUER is senior lecturer at the Hogeschool voor Wetenschap en Kunst, Ghent/Brussels, teaching history of art, cultural history, philosophy, and psychology. Her main research topics are the history of the individual in its public-private context and cultural history of the twelfth and thirteenth centuries, focussed upon legal and canon law doctrine.

BRUCE C. BRASINGTON is professor of history at the Department of History, Political Science, and Criminal Justice, West Texas A&M University. His main research topics are canon law down to 1200, comparative legal history, and perceptions of the Middle Ages since the Enlightenment.

CHARLOTTE CHRISTENSEN-NUGUES is lecturer in the history of ideas and sciences at Lund University. Her main research topics are the interaction between sacramental theology and Canon Law in the formation of the consensualist doctrine of marriage, specifically in disputed legal domains and marriage cases.

MICHAEL H. GELTING is senior research archivist at the Danish National Archives (Rigsarkivet) and external professor of Early Scandinavian Studies at the University of Aberdeen. His main research topics are legal and social change in Denmark in the twelfth and thirteenth centuries, and the effects of the Black Death on fourteenth-century society, in Europe in general and more particularly in Maurienne (Savoy).

JOHN GILLINGHAM is emeritus professor of history at the London School of Economics and a Fellow of the British Academy. His principal research interest is in narrative sources, primarily those composed in north-western Europe, as evidence for the perceptions and values which shaped the conduct of war and politics.

ELDBJØRG HAUG is associate professor at the Department for Archaeology, Culture, History, and Religion, at the University of Bergen. Her main research interests are medieval political history, particularly the relationship between church and state, legal history, and ecclesiastical history.

JOHN HUDSON is professor of legal history in the Department of Mediaeval History, University of St Andrews. His main research topics are legal history, particularly of England, c. 900-1250; historical writing; and the history of political thinking in twelfth-century Europe. His volume of the Oxford History of the Laws of England is published in 2012.

BRIGITTE MEIJNS is professor at the Department of Medieval History at the Katholieke Universiteit Leuven. Her main research topics are religious and political history of the County of Flanders and especially the history of the canonical order, the functions of the collegiate churches in society and their relations with the ecclesiastical and secular rulers during the central Middle Ages and especially during the 'Gregorian' Church Reform.

MIA MÜNSTER-SWENDSEN is associate professor at the Saxo Institute, Department of History, University of Copenhagen. Her main publications deal with socio-cultural aspects of medieval education and her present research concerns the production of legal knowledge within European learned milieus.

HANS JACOB ORNING is professor in history at the University College of Volda, Norway. His main research topics are medieval literacy in Scandinavia, the relationship between conflict and power, and theoretical discussions concerning the use of multi-disciplinary and anthropological methods on Scandinavian medieval history.

ANNE IRENE RIISØY has been post.doc at the Department of Archaeology, Conservation and History at the Faculty of Humanities, University of Oslo. Her main research interests are the relationship between state and church concerning the administration of justice, outlawry and sexuality, law and legal practice in a Norwegian and comparative perspective.

MATTHEW STRICKLAND is professor of medieval history in the Department of History at the University of Glasgow. His principal areas of research focus on chivalric culture and conduct in warfare, as well as on the political and military history of the Anglo-Norman and Angevin period. He also works on the nature of aristocratic rebellion in England and Normandy from the Norman Conquest to the later thirteenth century.

JO RUNE UGULEN is senior archivist at Riksarkivet, Oslo. His main research topics are medieval aristocracy and nobility, social, agrarian, and legal history.

SALLY N. VAUGHN is professor of history at the University of Houston. Her main research topics are teaching and learning in Northern Europe in the period c. 1000- c. 1200, especially the abbey and Anselm of Bec, Robert of Meulan and St Anselm. She is currently at work on a book on the teachers and students of the Norman abbey of Bec titled 'Prudent Pilots and Spiritual Charioteers'.

HELLE VOGT is associate professor in legal history at the Faculty of Law at University of Copenhagen. Her main research topics are Nordic legal history and the interaction between local law and learned Christian legal ideology.